Beyond the Promised Land

JEWS AND ARABS ON THE HARD ROAD TO A NEW ISRAEL

Glenn Frankel

A TOUCHSTONE BOOK

Published by Simon & Schuster

TOUCHSTONE
Rockefeller Center
1230 Avenue of the Americas
New York, New York 10020

Designed by Irving Perkins Associates
Manufactured in the United States of America

1 2 3 4 5 6 7 8 9 10

Library of Congress Cataloging-in-Publication Data

Frankel, Glenn.
Beyond the promised land : Jews and Arabs
on the hard road to a new Israel / Glenn Frankel.
p.   cm.
"A Touchstone book."
Previously published: New York: Simon & Schuster, © 1994. With revised epilogue.
Includes bibliographical references and index.
1. Israel—Politics and government.
2. Jewish-Arab relations—1973– 3. Intifada, 1987–
4. National characteristics, Israeli. I. Title.
DS126.5.F716   1996
320.95694—dc20   96-10604
CIP

ISBN 0-671-79649-6
ISBN 0-684-82347-0 (pbk)

Grateful acknowledgment is made to The Free Press, Macmillan Publishing, for permission
to reprint *With Friends Like You: What Israelis Really Think About American Jews* by Matti
Golan. Copyright © 1992 by Matti Golan.

To Betsyellen Yeager

Contents

Resisting fate is not enough. *We must master our fate; we must take our destiny into our own hands!*

—David Ben-Gurion

Once I sat on the steps by a gate at David's Tower. I placed my two heavy baskets at my side. A group of tourists was standing around their guide and I became their target marker. "You see that man with the baskets? Just right of his head there's an arch from the Roman period. Just right of his head." "But he's moving, he's moving!" I said to myself: redemption will come only if their guide tells them, "You see that arch from the Roman period? It's not important: but next to it, left and down a bit, there sits a man who's bought fruit and vegetables for his family."

—Yehuda Amichai, "Tourists"

Prologue: Another Country

NATIONS, like people, face moments of truth. They travel through periods of history that challenge their survival, redefine their values, make them stronger or do them lasting damage, and propel them into the future. Sometimes they move in new, uncharted and unknown directions, other times down very clear and predictable paths. And if the nations involved are important to us, if their history and identity and power are linked somehow to our own, then we too play a role in their crisis. We become an actor on the stage, yet simultaneously a critic in the front row.

Israel is undergoing such a crisis. Quietly, hesitantly, painfully, it is making the transition from a small, collectivist, mobilized garrison-state under siege to a more open, pluralistic, bourgeois and democratic country. The old Zionist state, for better and worse, is dying; a new post-Zionist Israel is being born. Driven by sweeping changes from both within and without its borders, it is struggling to emerge from the shell of the past to become . . . another country.

Change is often an elusive creature—it darts from hole to hole, seldom pausing long enough to allow a clear sighting, its presence and impact often concealed beneath the familiar surface of the old. When Prime Minister Yitzhak Rabin shook hands with Palestine Liberation Organization Chairman Yasser Arafat on the White House lawn in September 1993, many people who have followed Israel's fortunes over the four-and-one-half decades of its existence were stunned. Little that we had seen or read in recent years had prepared us for the shock of seeing two of the world's bitterest enemies come together in a moment of supreme hope and desperation. For years we had been conditioned and numbed by the sameness of headlines and incidents into concluding that what was taking place in Israel and the occupied territories was not curable by ordinary means of politics and diplomacy, that it was an extension of a hundred-year-old intractable conflict between Arab and Jew with nothing new except a different set of names and causes of death on history's remorseless police blotter. Some of the best books about Israel in recent years—Amos Oz's *In the Land of Israel,* Conor Cruise O'Brien's *The Siege,* David K. Shipler's *Arab and Jew,* Thomas L. Friedman's *From Beirut to Jerusalem*—tend to reinforce the fatalistic image of a promised land locked into an unbreakable cycle of violence and retribution, of kill and be killed.

But while we were fixated on the familiar country we thought we knew, a new Israel was taking shape. Suddenly a country whose Arab neighbors had hidden for four decades behind the implacable formula of no talks, no recognition and no compromise found itself at a peace table with virtually all of them. A country that had been isolated and demonized internationally was courted by East and West, African and Asian alike, establishing diplomatic relations with more than thirty other states within a three-year period. A country that had sacrificed much of its economic potential in the name of security found itself spending vast sums in shopping malls, new-car lots and American-style pizza parlors. And a country that had prided itself on a strategic doctrine of massive retaliation and military self-reliance found itself hunched over anxiously in sealed rooms while Scuds fell, waiting for the United States and its Gulf War allies to put an end to its ordeal.

The process of change began long before 1987 and will continue long after 1996 is consigned to history. Nonetheless, even by Israel's hyperactive standards, this decade constitutes a momentous period of civil unrest, political upheaval and diplomatic crisis in which many of the long-standing assumptions, beliefs and practices that lay at the very heart of this society were shaken, challenged and ultimately remade or swept aside. Throughout this period, what was at stake wasn't Israel's survival, but its future.

The change began with the Palestinian intifada, a wholly unexpected explosion of popular rage and great expectations in the Israeli-occupied West Bank and Gaza Strip that shattered the low-cost, low-pain status quo in which Israel and its Palestinian subjects had been frozen for twenty years. But the intifada was only the opening step in a process. The rise inside Israel of new political forces, the fall of the Soviet Empire and the arrival of nearly a half million Jewish immigrants, the death of socialism, the eclipse of Arab military power and the ascendancy of the United States—all had an enormous impact on the Jewish state.

It takes two sides to end a siege—those within the fortress walls and those without. At the same time Israelis were undergoing political and economic transformation, Palestinians were changing as well. The old arrangements were shattered under which Arabs in the occupied territories had been consigned to a life of sullen tranquility and political passivity. Palestinians for the first time took their fate in their own hands. Through riots, acts of terrorism and a coherent political assault, they raised the psychological price of military occupation above the limits of Israel's willingness to pay. And with much hesitation and little finesse, they gradually came to offer Israelis an alternative prospect—a partition of the land into two independent states. What the Arab states in 1948 had rejected, many Palestinians forty-six years later seemed prepared at last to embrace.

The transition was a bloodstained and unhappy one. Even as Israeli and Palestinian leaders sat down to hammer out a peaceful resolution to their Hundred Years War, extremists in both communities sought to reassert their power with guns and bombs and smother the new arrangement before it took hold. The mass murder of Palestinian worshippers in Hebron in February 1994 and the subsequent suicide bomb attacks on passenger buses that killed dozens of Israelis were all too familiar, as were the pitiless photographs of hapless victims and grieving relatives. But the dynamic had changed. Whereas before, every killing was another justification for the status quo, now every act of violence became a reason for leaders to press on more urgently and finish the work of partition that they had begun. The militants might yet be able to kill the new peace, topple Arafat and defeat Rabin, but they could never return to the conditions that had existed the day before the White House lawn signing. The past was dead, even if the future remained uncertain.

"Imagine coming to the Land of Israel without savoring its fever!" David Ben-Gurion once wrote. I have had no such misfortune—from the moment I first set foot in Israel in 1970, I have savored fully its fevers, obsessions, dilemmas and possibilities. I spent my first summer in Israel as a volunteer worker at Gonen, the Upper Galilee kibbutz I describe in Chapter 11. Israel was still in the first flush of success and optimism after its stunning triumph in the 1967 Six-Day War. By my next visit in 1978, much of that enthusiasm had been drained following the traumatic Yom Kippur War and the rise of Menachem Begin. I returned again in 1984 to write about the aftermath of Israel's most indecisive election result for the *Washington Post,* and in 1986 I came with my wife and two young daughters for a three-year stint as Jerusalem correspondent for the *Post.*

The Israel I encountered then was the stagnant, fearful, unhappy country I have portrayed in the opening chapter of this book, a nation that seemed trapped between a tragic, exhausting past and an uncertain future. Both the politicians and the public had forged a sort of devil's bargain: Israel's leaders would avoid making hard, unpleasant choices and its voters would not push them to do so. Things were too fragile, people were too divided to take such risks. Seldom had there been a country so robust and self-confident on its surface, yet so shaky and vulnerable at its core.

I had come to Jerusalem from South Africa, where I had witnessed and written about the tense, violent state of emergency that a faltering white-minority government had sought to impose on an increasingly rebellious black majority. Israeli friends would smile and declare with a note of relief, "At least you've come from the one place where things are worse than they are here." At first I would nod in agreement, but eventually as I began to take the measure of my new assignment, I offered a more pessimistic rejoinder. Don't be so sure, I told them. South Africa, for all its problems, was a big, robust country with many natural resources and a shared Christian faith and sense of values between the white rulers and their restless black subjects. Israel, by contrast, was far too small and poor a land to be divided between two sides that were each determined to hold it all. All it really had to offer were symbols and holy sites—intangible visions that by their very nature are incapable of being divided or shared. Winners have always taken it all; losers get nothing but a one-way ticket to exile. And I began to suspect that Israelis and Palestinians would still be conducting their low-grade war of populations long after blacks and whites in South Africa had made a separate peace.

I spent much of my three-year stint writing about the conflict between Arabs and Jews, yet much of the time I saw another Israel struggling to assert itself. This was the Israel I wanted to explore and occasionally wrote about, the Israel that constantly found itself outshouted and overshadowed by the old. And indeed, when I left in July 1989 to become the *Post*'s London correspondent, the country seemed locked more than ever into a straitjacket of its own devise. A few days before my departure, Prime Minister Yitzhak Shamir had undercut his own tepid peace plan by surrendering to demands for revisions by the hard-liners in his own party. Contrary to the conventional wisdom at the time, I had been impressed by Shamir's political acumen—and convinced he would stall, maneuver and dissemble to avoid making any substantive concessions to the Arab states or the Palestinians. But events gradually forced even this most implacable of men to move forward. A man who had predicated his policies and strategies on the presumption that nothing in life ever really changed found the world around him and his own people shifting in ways he had never anticipated. I returned to Israel five times between 1989 and 1992, and each time the country seemed more open, more eager and more prepared to enter the world. And slowly the theme of this book began taking shape.

When I moved back to Jerusalem in August 1992 to begin work on the book, Shamir and fifteen years of right-wing Likud domination had just given way to Yitzhak Rabin and a return to the more pragmatic, less ideological rule of the left-of-center Labor Party. I watched as Rabin groped with and resisted the meaning of his own victory; he seemed very much a man determined to tie up the loose ends of the past rather than leap into the future. His triumph led inevitably to the scene on the White House lawn; nonetheless it was a moment too fantastic for any novelist to have devised. It could only have come from reality. In a sense it was too good to be quite true. Yes, Israel had changed but perhaps not that much, or at least not that quickly. Rabin, perhaps for the first time in his political life, was out in front of his people, leading by oratory and painful example. Yet the Israeli people were not so very far behind. Like Rabin, although drenched in skepticism and second thoughts, they too had changed. And like him, they saw no other realistic choice.

This book, then, is a portrait of dramatic change and the people and events who were swept up by it. Some of these people, like Prime Ministers Shamir and Rabin and Russian Jewish activist Natan Sharansky, are major actors whose names and faces are well known both in Israel and abroad. Others, like religious party leader Arye Deri, army general Amram Mitzna and Likud politician Dan Meridor, are known to most Israelis but far less familiar to the outside world. And still others, like former kibbutznik Haim Goren and Palestinian academic Jad Isaac, are barely known outside their own small communities.

These are tales of truth and betrayal, of people who made decisions or refused to do so and of the consequences that ensued. The story as I have chosen to tell it possesses little sense of physical or geographical decorum; it roams freely between Israel's highest offices and its bleakest alleyways. It portrays a wide range of people who themselves have never sat down and talked with one another and probably never will. Each place it goes, it asks two related questions: what drove a particular person to do what he or she did; and how did these actions fit into the larger picture of a country caught in a process of rapid, often traumatic change? Some of the people I write about grew or even blossomed under the stress of the new, developing situation, and some just coped; others were crushed. But no one walked away untouched and unshaken by the dramatic events of the past decade.

It is no accident that many of these people have in some way or other been scarred. Mitzna, the Israeli general in charge of suppressing the Palestinian uprising, still bears the marks from shrapnel that buried itself into his back and legs during the 1967 Six-Day War. Others carry scars that are less visible, but no less real. Yitzhak Shamir's wounds from his years as an underground warrior and from the murder of his entire family in Poland are visible in his every public utterance and private maneuver. Natan Sharansky still suffers periodic bouts of ill health from his nine years in KGB security cells. Haim Goren was shaken by combat shock during the Yom Kippur War, Jad Isaac by the ordeal of five months' imprisonment without formal charge. Gaza journalist Taher Shriteh's hands still quivered when he recounted to me his eleven days of psychological torture and physical pressure in an Israeli interrogation cell. Cabinet minister Deri, an immigrant from Morocco, carried the burden of being an outsider in two worlds—the Ashkenazi-dominated yeshiva society and the brutal, freewheeling world of secular Israeli politics. Russian émigrés Emma and Boris Weinberg were traumatized by their difficulty in adjusting to their new country. Jewish settler Yisrael Zeev came close to tears as he recounted the day he shot dead a fellow shepherd on a West Bank hillside. There were times when entrepreneur Yair Mendels felt frozen by the awesome burden of his own restless intellect and ambition.

I must confess to a great fondness for all of these people. They made mistakes, sometimes fatal ones. They misled others and, all too often, themselves. Sometimes they refused to face reality, falling back on folk myths and shopworn formulations that they knew were unsustainable. Yet they all seemed determined to pursue their dreams to the fullest, take risks and make commitments. In this book I describe them, analyze their qualities and their mistakes, and show where their decisions and reactions led themselves and their country. But I cannot pass moral judgment on them. How does one judge Amram Mitzna, who sought to steer his soldiers through the ethical maze of suppressing a civilian uprising while maintaining their own dignity and that of their Palestinian subjects? Or Haim Goren, who finally turned his back on his socialist dream after twenty-five years of personal sacrifice? Or Yitzhak Shamir, who deeply believed that Israel was too small and vulnerable to take the risks the world demanded of it? Or Yitzhak Rabin, who after a political career of missed opportunities returned to the top and took the biggest risk of all?

The main character, of course, is Israel itself. Despite its legendary verve, chutzpah and iron nerve, this is at heart a very conservative country. It abhors rapid change, perhaps because it has undergone so much in its brief, turbulent history. Like its people, Israel is scarred in many ways by the tangled and tragic history of the Jewish people and by five full-blown wars and nearly five decades of constant tension with the Arab states outside its borders and the Palestinians within. It struggles with an outmoded and chaotic political system, an economy still striving to throw off the dead weight of collectivism, and a deeply divided and fearful population that knows it can no longer live in the past yet understandably resists taking an existential leap into an uncertain future.

The book marches more or less chronologically. It begins with a portrait of Shamir, prime minister for most of the time I write about, and examines why this cautious champion of the status quo came to be the appropriate custodian of Israel's sense of inertia and anxiety in the fateful year of 1987. It describes the shattering of the status quo with the Palestinian intifada and the Israeli army's harsh response—and how the army's disaffection with its role in the occupied territories gradually seeped into Israeli society and forced the Shamir-led government into a halfhearted peace proposal that almost caused his downfall. It charts the rise of a new ultrareligious and populistic political party that helped destroy the hegemony of the Israeli right and the country's religious establishment. It also depicts the dramatic arrival of Jews from the former Soviet Union who made new demands on the society and sped changes in politics and the economy. It examines the pivotal impact of the Gulf War on these changes.

Nothing in Israel happens in a vacuum. With every move they make, Israelis and Palestinians glance furtively over their shoulders to see if we in the United States and the West are watching and to catch a glimpse of acceptance, disapproval or astonished disbelief in our faces. When we look at Israel, we hold up a cracked mirror to ourselves as well. Israel's survival is of deep concern to us. Its dilemmas and evasions, its dreams, even its crimes and misdemeanors, are in some undeniable way ours as well. It makes righteous demands on our checkbooks and our sympathy. Israel's fate matters not only to its own people, but to us as well. And so this book includes chapters on the troubled relationship of American Jews and their Israeli brethren and on the historic confrontation between the Shamir government and the Bush administration that helped bring to an end fifteen years of Likud political domination and propel Israel forward into a new, uncertain era of political change. The book concludes with the trials and tribulations of the Rabin government as it reluctantly steered Israel into the future.

Israel is one of the easiest places in the world for a foreign correspondent to work. Israelis generally are open, friendly and eager to persuade you about the justness of their cause, and they love talking about themselves, their motives and their fears. Palestinians, after years of trial and tribulation, must be counted as the most candid and open people in the Arab world. While Palestinians and Israelis seldom talk to each other, they have for a generation conducted a sort of long-distance dialogue through the press. Israel still functions under military censorship, a long-discredited, archaic and unworkable institution. I lost my government press card for twenty-four days in April 1988 for defying censorship to write in the *Washington Post* about the Israeli army's assassination of Khalil Wazir, the number-two leader of the PLO. Yet even then, although denied official cooperation, I was allowed to work and found most Israelis no less willing to honor me with their views.

With such a large, lively marketplace, the writer's job becomes one of selection: how to separate truth from distortions, self-interest from objectivity. I have too much affection and admiration for the people I have written about and, for that matter, too much anger over the terrible deeds that have happened, to qualify as an objective or uninvolved observer. Instead, I have striven to be passionately fair: to get as many perspectives as possible and to accurately capture the reasoning and motivations of the people I have sought to portray. This is an untidy and inexact method. Some readers will recognize truth within these pages; others no doubt will consider this book a compendium of lies, distortions and slander. But if every reader is compelled to think anew about what Israel has become and where it is going, then I will have succeeded in some small way.

This book is a narrative: it has a story to tell, and in doing so it often leaves important subjects aside. There is little here about the impact of the Holocaust on Israel or about Israeli Arabs, subjects that have been sensitively explored in recent books by Tom Segev (*The Seventh Million*) and David Grossman (*Sleeping on a Wire*). There is also little about broader strategic issues or Israel's relations with neighboring Arab states, even though these issues are of great significance. And my chapters on Palestinians in the occupied territories are designed largely to explain and illustrate my larger point about Israel and provide no more than a cursory look at the forces and movements among Palestinians. I have instead told the story that most interested me, the one I was best equipped to tackle and the one I had not heard told before. I have tried to portray an Israel that only recently has made its appearance in our newspapers and our public consciousness, an Israel that is still struggling to be born.

The changes are not always an unmitigated blessing. Some of the things that made Israel special—its sense of community and collective responsibility, its willingness for self-sacrifice, its egalitarianism and idealism—stemmed from the country's isolation and sense of siege. Israelis lived on the edge; it made them impossible yet also irresistible. Their distinctive language and culture thrived behind the high walls they built for self-preservation. With the lifting of the siege, they will struggle to decide what it is they truly value about their society and how to maintain it in the face of a new onslaught of American and European money and media. They will also be forced to redefine their relationship to each other. Issues of church and state, of democracy versus theocracy, of majority rule versus minority rights, of the obligations people owe to their government and the government owes to them—questions that Israelis have postponed confronting for the first five decades of statehood—will now demand to be addressed. So will the relationship between Israelis and outsiders, especially American Jews. With the lifting of the siege, we will all need to find a new basis for our feelings and ties to a country that in its own way should command our loyalty and affection and respect as much as or more than the one we thought we knew.

It may be painfully unfamiliar to us now, but this is the country Israel was always meant to be. The earliest Zionists sought to liberate the Jewish people from the role of international victim and free it from the ghetto. Theodor Herzl had envisaged the Jewish state not as a nation constantly on its guard, but as a normal, open and secure state. "We shall live at last as free men on our own soil, and die peacefully in our own homes," he predicted in his landmark Zionist tract *The Jewish State*. "The world will be freed by our liberty, enriched by our wealth, magnified by our greatness." Yet for much of its existence, survival rather than normality was by necessity the guiding principle of Israeli national life. Much of what happened over the past decade that I write about was bloody, wrenching, desperate and at times tragic; it may be even more so in the immediate future. Yet the end result has inevitably moved the country much closer to the benign fate that Herzl and others originally predicted for it. This book is about how and why that happened.

1. The Guardian

*Men make their own history, but they do not make
it just as they please; they do not make it under
circumstances chosen by themselves, but under
those directly encountered, given and transmitted
from the past. The traditions of dead generations
weigh like a nightmare on the minds of the living.*

—KARL MARX, *The Eighteenth
Brumaire of Louis Bonaparte*

IN the spring of 1987 Israel marked the twentieth anniversary of the Six-
Day War. It was one of the most momentous events in the country's short
history, yet the celebration was curiously dispirited. Israelis could not commemorate the war without taking stock of its legacy—the occupied West
Bank and Gaza Strip and the 1.5 million Palestinians who lived there. Like
uninvited guests, their presence spoiled the party.

For twenty years Israel had held the territories in a state of suspended
animation. Governments rose and fell, two wars were fought, peace
processes started and stopped, the president of Egypt journeyed to
Jerusalem one incredible night. But the occupied territories remained as
they had been—half gift, half burden, both a treasure and a time bomb.
Right-wing governments since 1977 had encouraged piecemeal Jewish colonization, but even they did not take the irreversible step of annexing the
land or evicting its Arab inhabitants.

Two memorable events occurred during the commemoration, one of the
body and one of the mind. The first was a tightrope walk by the French
high-wire artist Philippe Petit three hundred feet above the Hinnom Valley

on a cable linking West Jerusalem to Mount Zion and the Old City walls. Petit's breathtaking performance was meant to reaffirm the unity of the once-divided city. Yet divisions between the city's neighborhoods were actually growing. Israelis did not feel safe in the Arab parts of town and Palestinians seldom ventured into Israeli neighborhoods, while ultra-Orthodox Jews increasingly separated themselves from both. The physical border had been erased in 1967, but the psychological one remained firmly in place.

The other event was the publication of novelist David Grossman's book-length essay on the territories in the crusading weekly *Koteret Rashit*. Israelis read Grossman's compelling account of life in the West Bank as if they were reading about another continent. Few had ever been there; fewer still could imagine what that life was like. At the end of the essay, published in English later that year as *The Yellow Wind,* Grossman said he feared that the current situation could continue exactly as it was for another ten to twenty years. "We have lived for 20 years in a false and artificial situation," he writes, "based on illusions, on a teetering center of gravity between hate and fear, in a desert void of emotion and consciousness." Someday, he warned, "it will exact a deadly price."

Grossman sought to kindle a sense of urgency about the territories. But most Israelis felt no real burden and therefore no real pressure to make changes. Palestinians remained sullen but supine. Despite occasional flare-ups of civil unrest Israel was able to maintain order in the territories with less than a thousand constantly rotating troops, supplemented by the ubiquitous informer network of the Shin Bet internal security service. Everyone knew the occupation was a problem, but in the congealed political climate of 1987 many considered it the least onerous of a bad set of options.

The same sense of stalemate, of dreams and dilemmas deferred, pervaded Israeli society as a whole. Israel in 1987 was a curious mixture of pugnacious success and resigned failure. There were monumental achievements: Israel had absorbed double its original population in immigrants, turned vast amounts of desert into productive farmland and factories, pioneered technological breakthroughs in industry and agriculture. It boasted one of the world's highest rates of literacy and book publishing and a ravenous appetite for music and theater.

Yet nearly forty years after its birth all of the basic questions of Israel's existence remained unresolved, and its very survival seemed somehow tenuous. Israelis had yet to decide on the size, shape and character of the state they lived in. They had not reconciled the innate contradiction between living in a Western-style democracy and in a Jewish state. They could not even agree on who should qualify to be a Jew. They had not determined how they felt about the Jews who lived outside their state, nor about the Arabs who lived within. They fiercely cherished their independence yet had come increasingly to rely on the largesse and support of a foreign power in Washington whose interests too often did not coincide with their own.

Most of all, they had not yet answered the fundamental question of what it meant to have a state in the first place. Was Israel a fortified haven for Jews to hide from a relentlessly hostile world behind high walls and loaded weapons? Or was it a nation among nations, with embassies and alliances, friends and enemies, a homeland where the Jewish people could take their place in the community of nations?

In effect, Israel was two very different countries inside one tightly stretched border. One was a small, heroic, ideologically pure garrison-nation waving its defiant flag before implacable enemies in a treacherous part of the world. Its unifying historical myths were the twin traumas of Masada and the Holocaust. Its heroes were military men, its operating political model was the zero-sum game—"for me to win, my enemy must lose"— and its defining moment was the Six-Day War. It was an existential state with a well-honed sense of paranoia and a nuclear arsenal large enough to blow Damascus, Tehran, Baghdad, Beirut and Tripoli to oblivion. It functioned as an American strategic asset in the static, bipolar world of the Cold War. It was, finally, a nation in a state of siege.

The capital of this Israel was Jerusalem, the austere, forbidding fortress in the hills, reunited and redeemed by the 1967 war. Cold, beautiful, intense, Jerusalem's mottled stones evoked mortality and eternity in the same breathless moment. "Elsewhere you die and disintegrate," Saul Bellow writes. "Here you die and mingle." It was a city of ideology, nationalism and fundamentalism, of passion and fanaticism, a city that radicals of various religious and political cults had carved into narrow strips of turf as if they were the Sharks and the Jets. Jerusalem brooked no compromise and took no prisoners. Even the public trash cans served as soldiers—Palestinians planted bombs in litter baskets in the Israeli sector, while ultra-Orthodox Jews set fire to their bins and used them as burning barricades to do battle with the police.

In the basement meeting hall of Jerusalem's largest auditorium, an auto worker from Cleveland named John Demjanjuk stood trial that year for his alleged role in slaughtering thousands of Jews at the Treblinka death camp during World War II. Day after day the hall was packed with Israelis who listened to searing eyewitness testimony about the genocidal crimes the Nazis and their accomplices had committed. Many in the audience came away believing that Jews could never come to terms with the outside world. The risks were too high, the wounds too deep. A few blocks away ultra-Orthodox Jews staged riots for several weekends that summer to protest violations of the Sabbath, further proof that Jews had yet to come to terms with fellow Jews as well.

Traditional politicians, Israeli and Palestinian alike, struggled to maintain their monopoly of political and economic power in the old Israel. Both Likud and Labor defined themselves by their approach to the siege and had a strong stake in its continuation. It helped them mobilize their constituencies and preserve their own power. A nation under siege was too focused on survival to worry about official corruption or public accountability. Alternative institutions and causes—environmentalism, feminism, gay rights, consumer protection—could not plant roots in the cold, stony ground. The Palestine Liberation Organization, exiled in faraway Tunis, also benefited from the deadlock. Stalemate kept local Palestinians victimized, passive and vulnerable, and helped the hierarchy abroad maintain its web of control.

Israel in 1987 spent nearly twice as much of its gross domestic product on defense as did the United States. It still operated one of the most centralized, state-run economies this side of North Korea. *Bitahon,* the Hebrew word for "military security," dominated people's lives and dreams. Israeli men spent three years after high school in compulsory military service and at least a month in reserve duty every year after that. They paid more than half their incomes in taxes, much of it to support one of the world's most sophisticated defense establishments. There was one television station and it was state-owned. Each night more than 75 percent of the adult population sat before their screens at 9 P.M. to watch *Mabat,* the daily newscast that produced a steady stream of nightmarish, bloodstained reports on Arab attacks against Jews. Every year on Memorial Day Israel dispatched to its elementary schools the parents of slain soldiers to tell the story of their children's sacrifice and plant the seed of fear, pride and determination in a new generation. When pollsters Hanoch and Rafi Smith asked the Israeli public if the Arabs would still drive Israel into the sea if they could, nearly 70 percent replied yes.

The old Israel made most of the headlines. But there was another, younger Israel, an increasingly bourgeois, pluralistic, self-confident, consumer-oriented society struggling to emerge from the shell of the old. The turning point in economic terms came in 1985 when the new coalition government agreed to begin dismantling the huge public sector empire, cut state subsidies, slash defense spending and liberalize Israel's capital markets—moves that began a shift to a more open, entrepreneurial economy. It was a painfully slow, at times halfhearted process, but an irreversible one.

Economic growth had been sluggish for nearly a decade. Yet at the same time consumption had shot up—2.1 percent per capita each year between

1979 and 1988, higher rates than in either the United States or West Germany. Wages climbed 24 percent during that time, the number of private cars and telephones doubled, and the average size of new houses increased by nearly one-third.

This was American-style consumerism and it washed over Israel like a tidal wave. American films, music and social attitudes swept through a society that seemed frantic to embrace them. Supermarkets and gaudy shopping malls sprouted on the edge of Israel's cities. Coca-Cola and rock 'n' roll arrived, as did American-style bowling alleys, pizza parlors and multiplex cinemas. A country that in 1967 had been a sedate enclave of socialist realism with a thin veneer of European culture increasingly came to think of itself as a distant outpost of New York–style glitz.

Tel Aviv was the heart of this new country—a loose, sprawling, steamy, improvised Mediterranean capital with a beach, prostitution, illegal drugs, pornographic movies, nightclubs and the funky aroma of money and action and youth culture. The air was bad, as was the humidity, and the entire city needed a fresh coat of paint. It was brazen, ugly and wide open, equal parts high culture and low sleaze. One page of *Yediot Ahronot,* the country's biggest-selling daily newspaper, boasted ads for "personal services" establishments offering "beautiful models beyond compare" and prostitutes in army uniforms, while the page opposite featured ads for the Israeli Philharmonic. The whores in olive drab were a delicious mingling of the sacred and the profane—Israel's most revered institution servicing its crassest form of commercialism.

Tel Aviv beckoned, but Israel remained at heart a nation on edge and on its guard. The self-confidence of its enormous military might and growing economic power collided with a deep-seated institutionalized pessimism when it came to issues of war and peace, and Israelis remained haunted by fears of their own vulnerability. "We will have to fight again," said a twenty-year-old inductee named Shlomi, serving in a special infantry unit. "Everyone here talks about it. We all expect it. We just don't know when."

Israelis in 1987 were a bruised, tired and skeptical people trapped in a sluggish political interregnum. They remained deeply divided over what risks, if any, they should take for peace. Polls suggested that between 50 and 60 percent of Israeli Jews opposed territorial concessions and 30 to 40 percent favored outright annexation of the occupied territories followed by steps to encourage Arab residents to leave. With the public polarized, both Labor and Likud tended to keep their own positions blurred and their agendas partially concealed so as not to offend their left- and right-wing flanks of supporters. The parties and the people made a collective decision to put off all the intractable historical, political and moral questions that had sat on the table since the Six-Day War. "The big problem in Israel is we're between visions," said political scientist Daniel Elazar. "We've said goodbye and good riddance to the supercharged idealism of the founders of the state, but we have yet to replace it."

A dynamic, visionary leader might have lifted the country from its moral and political fatigue and inspired it to face the challenge. But the man who presided over Israel in 1987 was a guardian, not a visionary. To many Israelis, Yitzhak Shamir seemed like a relic, the last of a dying breed; he annoyed and embarrassed them. But it was no accident that he was prime minister. While many did not share his hard-line ideology, there was something about his innate caution, his restraint and his toughness that spoke to the deepest fears of Israelis. Frozen by suspicion, and perhaps by self-doubt as well, Shamir was the appropriate custodian for a suspicious, self-doubting nation.

Yitzhak Shamir often opened his front door as if he were expecting the enemy. By standing behind the open door to his official residence on Smolenskin Street in Jerusalem, he could see his visitors through the crack before they could see him. It was an old habit, left over from his days in the Jewish underground when an unexpected guest might well have been a British policeman with a gun. And like so many of Shamir's habits, it was designed to give him a psychological edge. Beware, it said, this is an unusual man—unusually suspicious, unusually well prepared and very much alone.

He was a barrel-chested man, with wavy gray hair and bushy eyebrows hovering above a rubbery, asymmetrical face and a trim, almost indiscernible mustache, as if he had forgotten to shave his upper lip two mornings in a row. Although he was barely five feet four, he did not appear frail or easily intimidated. Ariel Sharon, the former general and defense minister and a keen connoisseur of human weakness, recounts in his memoirs taking Shamir along on one of his clandestine trips to Lebanon to meet with the Christian warlords who in those days were allied with Israel. The two men found themselves in the middle of a sudden flare-up between rival gunmen. There was much shouting and guns were drawn. "While I was used to this kind of thing, having been to Beirut so many times, Shamir was not," writes Sharon. "Always interested in seeing how people react to pressure, I glanced at him and saw his face showed absolutely no trace of emotion, let alone fear. The man had complete self-control."

Shamir's routine seldom varied. He awoke at five-thirty, ate a light breakfast, glanced at the morning newspapers and then worked in the study downstairs. By eight he would be sitting in his office behind the large gray desk, ready to receive his aides. One by one, never in a group, they would meet with him: the secretary of the government, the director general of his office, the military aide, the press spokesman. Like the underground commander he once was, he would issue orders and assign tasks. Duties were compartmentalized so that one aide never quite knew what another was doing. Everything was on a need-to-know basis.

By 2 P.M. he would go home for lunch, prepared by Shulamit, his wife of more than forty years. It was always a full meal—sandwiches were "uncivilized," he said. Then he would nap for half an hour. By four he would be back in the office, where he would put in another four hours. Some of his advisers made secret fun of his zeal for routine, but others understood that he was in essence a man of the Old World who clung to routine as his anchor in the new one. He never learned to drive a car, struggled with the buttons on his new telephone, could not read a speech from a TelePrompTer. Not once, he confessed, had he even tried to use a computer. And in an age of self-scrutiny and public confession, he kept his feelings to himself. Talk could be harmful, for enemies were constantly listening, probing for weakness. Emotion showed vulnerability; it, too, was a dangerous luxury.

There were many scheduled meetings, of course, with local politicians, visiting foreign dignitaries and American Jewish leaders, for whom a private session with the prime minister of Israel was both a rite of passage and a credential. But there were also huge gaps in the official diary, hours at a stretch with no appointments. These were the times when Shamir was happiest, when he would sit behind his desk, alone in the room, and pore over diplomatic cables and intelligence reports from the Mossad espionage agency, the Shin Bet internal security service and Military Intelligence. He hated digests; he preferred the raw data from the person best placed to provide it—the man in the field, the man he himself had been during his own years with the Mossad. The papers would always be returned unmarked in exactly the same order he had received them. No one could tell by examining them what had caught the prime minister's eye, what he had taken in and what he had missed.

Shamir seldom let down his guard. But there were moments when the mask would drop and a careful observer could steal a glimpse of the open wounds beneath. At a public gathering commemorating victims of the Holocaust, his voice trembled and his hands shook slightly as he described how his father, Shlomo Yezernitsky, had escaped from the Nazis in Poland only to be killed by fellow Poles. "While seeking shelter among friends in the village where he grew up," Shamir recited in the emphatic monotone he used on all public occasions, "they, his friends from childhood, killed him."

And he read out a list of names: his father; his mother, Pearl; his sisters, Miriam and Rivka; their husbands, Mordechai and Yaacov, and their children. He was the sole survivor of his family.

Their memory still governed Shamir's life: his belief that the world was a dangerous place for Jews, that it was important to have friends, but that in the end you could trust only yourself because friends might betray you, that in such a world Jews must rely on themselves.

Shamir's heroes were men like Lenin and Mao—decisive, ruthless leaders who believed in themselves and in the power of ideology. Like them, he harbored the expectation of betrayal. He searched for enemies in his political party, in his cabinet, and among Jews in Israel and abroad. Advocates of territorial compromise were "defeatists" and "collaborators"; American Jews who met with PLO leaders were "traitors." He set agents even among his own closest aides and advisers. No one was pure enough; no one could be trusted. Moshe Arens, his presumptive successor, was too weak, Sharon too ambitious; even Dan Meridor, the young cabinet minister who was his favorite son among the inner circle, was suspect. "He heard every whisper, every small movement," recalled Yossi Achimeir, a former aide. "His antennae were working all the time." Ultimately, "Shamir believed only in Shamir."

Despite the tough-guy image, Shamir constantly agonized over the dangers Israel faced. It was a mere Lilliput of a country, he told visitors, small, fragile and surrounded by powerful enemies. In such an environment it was madness to take risks. This was why it could never afford to yield any part of *Eretz Yisrael Hashlema* ("the Integral Land of Israel"), which included all of Israel proper and the territories it occupied in 1967. While outsiders saw the Arab leaders as chronically demoralized, weak and divided, to Shamir they posed a terrible threat. "When one of them does put on a smiling face," he warned, "he is only trying to cheat us. He wants, in return, that we should close our eyes and enter a trap."

That such a man could be prime minister of Israel in 1987 said much about the man but even more about the country. Israelis, wrote *Haaretz* newspaper columnist Gideon Samet, were "a conservative, hesitant people pursued by fears. They prefer preserving the present situation not because they feel it is good but because they are overcome with anxiety about the prospect of change. To a public such as this, it is better to present someone who does not offer change . . . a man like Shamir. He is the anti-leader. He is the old uncle who sits at home in slippers in an easy chair in front of the TV telling the family . . . that only bad will come from trusting the goyim."

But Shamir was not just a crotchety old uncle. As a young man he had been an underground warrior who had fought and killed for the sake of

Jewish independence. This gave him a certain mystique with many Israelis, who respected a man with blood on his hands. Shamir was a classic extremist; he believed Jews could accomplish anything through strength of will. After all, his own long career was living proof.

Yitzhak Yezernitsky came to British-ruled Palestine from Poland at age nineteen, four years before World War II began. An ardent Zionist, he arrived on a student visa and registered for law school at the new Hebrew University in Jerusalem. He had not come to study the legal order, however, but to overthrow it. He quickly dropped out of school and made his way into the Irgun, the smaller of the two armed Zionist movements seeking to establish a state for the 400,000 or so Jews living in the territory (there were about a million Arabs). When the Irgun split in 1938, Shamir sided with the smaller, more violent faction, rising quickly to second-in-command of its Tel Aviv group.

Palestine was locked those days in a brutal three-way conflict between Arab and Jewish nationalists and their British rulers. The Arab Revolt, a three-year campaign to oust British rule, quickly deteriorated into a series of bloody attacks on innocent Jews. The Irgun retaliated with operations that inevitably killed far more Arab civilians than combatants. Shamir has acknowledged that he took part in some of these attacks, but beyond that he has never been specific.

History is less discreet. Newspapers from the time recount the August 26, 1938, reprisal bombing, carried out by Shamir's unit, of an Arab vegetable market in Jaffa in which twenty-four people were killed and thirty-five wounded. In his memoirs, Yaacov Eliav, a top Irgun operative in Jerusalem, recalls bombings of Arab markets, cafés, bus stations and a movie theater, all designed to "make the Arabs aware of the severity of their actions."

The outbreak of World War II caused another split in the Irgun. The larger faction chose to suspend attacks against Britain, while the smaller one, led by a dashing, fanatical classics scholar and poet named Avraham Stern, vowed to keep fighting the British Empire even if it meant aiding Hitler's Germany. Shamir joined with Stern, even though his movement was scorned by the Zionist establishment, which helped the British hunt down its members. The splinter of a splinter, Stern's organization called itself Lehi, a Hebrew acronym for Fighters for Israel's Freedom. But those who considered its killings, abductions and bank heists the acts of deranged criminals called it the Stern Gang.

The Polish-born Stern, code-named Yair, was a melodramatic dreamer with a hand grenade. At one point before World War II, he attempted to organize an Army of Palestinian Liberation consisting of 40,000 Jews whom he planned to train and arm in Poland, then ship to Palestine for an invasion that would drive out the British. At another, he sent emissaries to the Nazis and the Italian Fascists to negotiate a joint offensive with Jewish gunmen against the British. But the basic strategy behind his operations in Palestine was assassination. "The more British officials, soldiers and policemen were eliminated, the sooner the foreign occupier would have to leave Israel," wrote Eliav.

While the British fought the Nazis, Stern fought the British. He attracted to his side a ragtag collection of misfits and fanatics, described by author J. Bowyer Bell as: "A tiny group of strange men and women, desperate beyond measure, on the far edge of history, despised by their opponents, abhorred by the orthodox, denied by their own, hunted and shot down in the streets; they lived briefly, during those dark years of despair, on nerve rather than hope." Lehi became "a haven for those dedicated to the absolutes, those without restraint, for those who could feel in each other the dream at work."

Stern himself described them best in a poem that presaged his own death:

> *We are the men without names, without kin*
> *Who forever face terror and death.*
> *We serve our cause for the length of our lives*
> *A service which ends with our breath.*
> *We will wrestle with God and death.*
> *. . . Let our blood*
> *Be a red carpet in the streets,*
> *And on this carpet our brains*
> *Will be like white lilies.*

The stolid, taciturn Yezernitsky was no poet and no dreamer. But he was drawn to Stern's dedication and ruthless absolutism, and to the cold fact that in 1940 no other Jewish leader was still willing to wave a gun in Britain's imperial face. Stern, he wrote, "was the one man who connected our daily dealings, our fears, our self-doubts and our often failed plans to the mainstream of Jewish history, bidding us to see ourselves as part of a larger scheme of things, not as chosen but as having chosen." When Stern was hunted down and summarily executed by British police in 1942, it was Yezernitsky who painstakingly put Lehi back together after escaping from a British detention camp.

Despite the difficulties Yezernitsky's years underground were the happiest of his life. He was ideally suited for the discipline of a secret life in windowless rooms. He adopted a series of aliases and took one of them, Shamir—the Hebrew word for "thorn"—as his own. He met and married one of his agents, Sarah Levy, code-named Shulamit, a Bulgarian émigré. Their first child, a boy they named Yair, was born while they were both in the underground. When Shulamit entered the hospital to give birth, Shamir arranged for a fictitious husband to accompany her so that the authorities would not become suspicious.

Under Shamir's authority, the wild, spontaneous and scattershot violence of the early Stern Gang was replaced by rigorous, disciplined, cautious operations. When one of Shamir's closest comrades, Eliahu Giladi, became violently erratic, threatening other members of the organization and plotting to kill David Ben-Gurion and other Jewish leaders who opposed Lehi, Shamir did not flinch at ordering his execution. Giladi was tricked into a meeting on the beach south of Tel Aviv, where someone shot him in the back of the head. The identity of his killer was not revealed, but some retired members of Lehi believe Shamir himself pulled the trigger. Shamir was all of twenty-eight, yet his followers began referring to him as "the old man."

He was the architect of Lehi's most daring attack, the 1944 assassination in Cairo of Lord Moyne, Britain's top Middle East official. It was a classic Shamir operation—planned for more than a year and executed with precision. Shamir monitored every step; he chose the target and the two young men assigned to carry out the deed. At first British investigators were mystified, assuming the two assassins must have been Nazi operatives. Only later did they realize that the killing was the work of Jews.

In the summer of 1946 Shamir was arrested and shipped to a prison camp in Eritrea. Five months later he and four comrades escaped, fleeing to Addis Ababa stashed inside an empty water tanker. By the time he returned to Tel Aviv in 1948, the war against the British was over. Mandatory Palestine was about to be partitioned between Arabs and Jews according to a United Nations General Assembly resolution. Opposed to partition, Shamir and Lehi fought on, both in the Independence War against the Arabs and in their own private campaign against those they perceived as enemies of the new state. Shamir was one of the triumvirate of leaders who approved the gang's most controversial killing, the assassination of United Nations mediator Folke Bernadotte, who was working on a plan to end the war on terms that Shamir deemed dangerous. The deed, which Ben-Gurion abhorred, further marked Shamir as an outcast in his own community.

Shamir never publicly discussed Lehi's assassinations, shooing away questions with a dismissive wave of his hand. But he once told author Gerold Frank, "A man who goes forth to take the life of another whom he does not know must believe one thing only—that by his act he will change the course of history." It is a succinct summation of the terrorist's creed, and it captures the cruel pragmatism at the core of Shamir's own being.

Looking back many years later, he marveled over what the small Jewish community had achieved in the face of British, Arab and international opposition. "When you look at the circumstances, you can never understand why Zionism succeeded," he said. "We were such a small minority and all the conditions were against us. So why were we the winners? Because we did what the others didn't dare to do."

The first years after Israel's independence were hard ones for Shamir. Lehi's intoxicating mixture of rabid nationalism, anti-imperialism and Bolshevism caused it to quickly self-destruct in the fresh air of the new state. Like other former members he was treated as a pariah by the Labor-dominated government. When Shamir sought a low-level job in the new Interior Ministry, Ben-Gurion, who had become Israel's first prime minister, vetoed it with a brisk note to the minister: "I have learned that you are about to hire that terrorist, Yezernitsky. I am against it." After an attempt to run Lehi alumni as candidates in the 1949 Knesset elections failed badly, Shamir bounced through a dismal series of dead-end jobs, including directing an association of movie theater owners.

Then in 1955 the establishment opened its doors. The head of the Mossad, Isser Harel, recruited Shamir and other former Irgun and Lehi members into the spy agency, where their operational experience was put to use. In nearly a decade with the Mossad, Shamir left few fingerprints. It is known that he was a middle-level manager handling agents working in the organization's European operations and that he and his family lived a spartan, clandestine existence in Paris under a false name. It is also known that he helped organize Operation Damocles, the 1962–63 Mossad campaign to terrorize the German scientists building rockets for Nasser's Egypt. Threatening letters were sent, followed by at least two letter bombs, and a half dozen people were killed.

When Harel lost a power struggle and was forced to resign from the Mossad, Shamir left, too. By 1966 he was back in the cold, an outcast yet again, struggling to make a living. But within a year a historical event in which he played no role would change the face of Israel and offer the former gunman the opportunity not only to participate in public life but to govern it.

The warplanes left in waves on that crystal blue Mediterranean morning in June 1967, headed due west over the sea, then hooked back to enter Egypt from behind, flying less than a thousand feet above the ground to elude radar. It took them thirty-five minutes to get there and forty more to accomplish their mission. By 10 A.M. it was over. Israel had destroyed more than three hundred Egyptian combat planes, three-fourths of the Middle East's largest air force, most of them on the ground. Six hours later an anonymous officer finally worked up the courage to bring an incredulous Gamal Abdel Nasser the bad news: "I have come to tell you that we no longer have an air force."

The Six-Day War re-created the Middle East. For Israelis it was a time of joy and redemption, a harrowing, narrow escape from the jaws of destruction for a nation that saw itself as small, lonely and beleaguered. Suddenly a country whose territory had previously been confined to a narrow strip between a series of armistice lines controlled the entire Sinai Peninsula, the Gaza Strip, the Golan Heights and the West Bank, a vast stretch of land three times its original size and a crucial margin of security against future invasion. And it won the most symbolic prize of all—Jerusalem, the cradle and capital of world Jewry, now reunited under Jewish rule for the first time in more than two thousand years.

But the war bestowed a poisoned gift: one million stunned, frightened and potentially hostile Palestinians in the West Bank and Gaza whose presence posed a permanent security threat and whose frustrated aspirations challenged the Jewish state and the democratic ideals upon which it was founded. They confronted Israel with a three-sided dilemma: to give back the territories and risk another Arab invasion; to retain the territories and give Arab residents full rights, which would inevitably erode the Jewish character of the state; or to keep the land and the Arabs in a state of animated suspension pending further developments. Given the dangers of the first two options, Israelis saw little choice but the third.

The war changed everything about Israel—its borders, its economy, even its dreams. It helped speed the collapse of the ruling Labor Party aristocracy, which was confronted with a prize of occupied territory that the Israeli left could neither fully embrace nor abandon. It unleashed new forces within Israel that were more nationalistic and extremist. Some on the right saw the hand of God in Israel's military triumph and believed a messianic era had begun. For them, the territories were Israel's biblical heartland, Judea and Samaria, and they felt a religious duty to settle there. Others on the right saw the territories as a basic security requirement. Together these two groups formed an alliance that combined hawkish, populist politics with religious zeal. With the left in disarray, Israel's political mainstream shifted to the right.

The main beneficiary of this trend was Menachem Begin, Shamir's old counterpart from the Irgun, a man who had spent the two decades since Israeli independence toiling in the political wilderness as leader of the small, ineffectual Herut Party. As power began to shift his way Begin sought to expand his organization, searching for loyalists who could carry out orders without calling attention to themselves. In 1970 he turned to Shamir, rescuing his former rival from obscurity and appointing him director of the immigration department of Herut, which in 1973 merged with smaller factions to become the Likud. By all accounts, Shamir repaid Begin with unimaginative but doggedly faithful service, first as a party bureaucrat and Knesset member and then, after Begin's stunning electoral triumph in 1977, as Knesset speaker and, finally, as foreign minister.

Begin believed that problems had solutions, that somehow, with enough good intentions and painstaking negotiations, a formula could be derived that would satisfy all reasonable men. That was the principle behind the Camp David accords, the 1978 peace agreement that Begin concluded with Egypt's President Anwar Sadat.

Shamir did not believe in legalistic solutions. He saw life as a constant power struggle. Victory went to the strong, the cunning and the patient, those with the strength to outwait and overcome their enemies. He had no use for dramatic events or sweeping breakthroughs, only for the slow, steady accumulation of power and advantage. Had Shamir been prime minister instead of Begin, many of Shamir's closest aides believed, there would have been no peace accord with Egypt, no bombing raid on the Iraqi nuclear reactor in 1981 and no Operation Peace for Galilee, the ill-fated 1982 invasion of Lebanon. No wins, no losses. History would not have been made, merely preserved.

Shamir was under no illusions as to where he stood with Begin. He was a useful tool, nothing more. After serving as Likud campaign chairman in 1977, Shamir expected to receive a cabinet post but was forced to settle for the empty titular role of Knesset speaker. In 1979, after Moshe Dayan's resignation as foreign minister, Begin offered the post to two other politicians, both of whom turned him down, then held it himself for six months before succumbing to internal party pressure and appointing Shamir. The new foreign minister showed up the next day at the office alone, with no aides or cronies. He quickly drafted a team of bureaucrats and diplomats who stuck with him for more than a decade. Yossi Ben-Aharon, his first hire, recalls him plowing through Henry Kissinger's memoirs in the early days at the ministry, a tattered Hebrew-English dictionary close at hand. After such giants as Abba Eban, Yigal Allon and Moshe Dayan, Israel now had a foreign minister whose anonymity was exceeded only by his inexperience.

Despite the occasional humiliations only once did he openly defy Begin. That was over Camp David, which Shamir adamantly opposed and on which he abstained in the final Knesset vote. He argued that Begin had given away too much in agreeing to dismantle all Jewish settlements in the Sinai Peninsula and return the entire region to Egyptian sovereignty. Still, ten years later when Shamir needed to forge a peace initiative of his own, he wrapped himself in the cloak of Camp David and used it as a device to blunt Arab demands for the return of the occupied territories.

Otherwise, he was Begin's silent subordinate, a foreign minister who was, in the words of critics Zeev Schiff and Ehud Yaari, "a zealous nationalist in striped pants. . . . Shamir always aligned himself with the most ardent of the extremists, supported every proposal for radical military moves and never brought diplomatic alternatives before the cabinet or presented the political risks and consequences involved." When Sharon seduced Begin in 1982 into the invasion of Lebanon, the foreign minister kept his misgivings to himself.

He was silent as well later that year when Sharon's Lebanon adventure led to the slaughter of hapless Palestinian civilians by Israel's Lebanese Christian allies at the Sabra and Shatila refugee camps. Schiff, defense correspondent for the newspaper *Haaretz,* was one of the first to learn about the massacre. He took his information to Communications Minister Mordechai Zipori, the cabinet's most ardent critic of Sharon. Zipori then phoned Shamir, informed him that a slaughter was reportedly taking place at the Beirut camps and pleaded with him to take up the matter with senior military officials at a staff meeting later that day. Shamir, by his own account, never said a word, and the killing continued for another day.

The Kahan Commission, which assessed responsibility for the massacre, concluded that Shamir may have misunderstood Zipori's words and in any event ignored them because he dismissed Zipori as a constant, whining critic of the government's Lebanon policy. "It is difficult to find a justification for such disdain for information that came from a member of the cabinet," the panel's report said, but it confined itself to the judgment that Shamir had "erred" in not passing on the information. Critics put it more bluntly: Shamir had kept silent, they said, because he believed Palestinian lives were simply not worth worrying about. Arabs simply did not figure in his moral calculus. And indeed, in political terms his calculation proved correct: Zipori soon was dumped from his job; Shamir, although publicly embarrassed, kept his.

Shamir was not chastened. What he remembered best about Sabra and Shatila was that the massacre had been bumped from the headlines in the United States after a few days by a national scare over the contamination of Tylenol. "We were saved by a bottle of aspirin," Shamir told colleagues, amazed and gratified by the short attention span of the American media.

And then the underground man became prime minister of Israel. This was not according to anyone's plan, not even his own. When Begin's chariot of fire burned itself out in 1983 and the great man resigned and fled into self-imposed exile, Shamir, who was already sixty-eight, was chosen to serve as a caretaker prime minister until younger, stronger and more politically adept men could sort out the succession. He became the Likud establishment's candidate against David Levy, a young, iconoclastic outsider from the Moroccan Sephardi community. Levy appeared to have a majority in the party's central committee until Sharon, sizing up which man might be easier to unseat at a later date, threw his support behind Shamir. Israel's inflation rate was galloping into triple figures, its army ensnared in the quagmire of Lebanon, its relations shaky with its chief ally, the United States. A new election, one that Likud was projected to lose, was only a year away. Better to let the diminutive new caretaker, the accidental prime minister, take the blame. Later, others could pick up the pieces and begin anew.

It did not turn out that way. Despite a lackluster campaign Likud managed to dodge the massive electoral defeat that the opinion polls had predicted for it in 1984 and finished a close second to the opposition Labor Party. Voters were fed up with the Likud, but they did not trust Labor enough to allow it unfettered control. Shamir downplayed his ideology, portraying himself as a trustworthy, low-key pragmatist. Neither party won enough seats to form a government, so after weeks of jockeying the two formed an improbable hybrid coalition government in which the premiership rotated between Labor Party leader Shimon Peres and Shamir.

Both men had been born in Poland, but that was their only similarity. Shimon Peres had come to Palestine while still a child and had been raised and educated in the heart of the Zionist establishment. While still in his early twenties, he had become a favorite of David Ben-Gurion and Levi Eshkol, two of Israel's founding fathers, and had risen rapidly in the hierarchy. Before he reached thirty he was running the country's fledgling Defense Ministry, and he deserves much of the credit for building Israel's modern military-industrial establishment, air force and nuclear weapons program. But Peres also gained a reputation as a tireless hatchetman for both Ben-Gurion and Moshe Dayan, his comrade and idol. And after Ben-Gurion faded from the scene, many of the cantankerous leader's rivals within Labor rose up and settled their scores with Peres. He finally became leader of the divided, embittered party in 1977 on the eve of its watershed defeat by Menachem Begin, and he lost again to Begin in 1981 by the narrowest of margins. When he at last won the premiership in 1984, it was as head of a curious hybrid concoction known as the "national unity government."

Somewhere along the way Peres made the transition from pragmatic security hawk to fervent dove. He came to believe in economic development as the great cure for the Arab-Israeli conflict and preached it unceasingly. His model was Europe—if the slaughterhouses of Germany and France could be turned into economic powerhouses less than a generation after World War II, surely the Middle East could also be transformed. Peres conjured grand visions. He quoted poets and philosophers and spoke in aphorisms. Sophisticated and cultured in appearance, he saw himself as no ordinary politician, and he won the respect and admiration of political leaders abroad. The only problem was that Israelis did not trust him. They saw the seams in his carefully constructed persona—the machinations and the years of backroom dealing. And they passed a harsh judgment on his character by chaining him to Shamir, a man whose politics and obsessive caution he mocked and despised.

Ruling by consensus, the new coalition government tamed Israel's triple-digit inflation, brought home most Israeli troops from Lebanon and, perhaps equally important, cooled some of the overheated, demagogic rhetoric of the Begin era and reestablished a modest level of civility in Israeli public life. Most of these achievements were accomplished by the creative, hyperactive Peres during his two years as prime minister. By the time Shamir took over the reins in the fall of 1986, the coalition was out of gas and bereft of ideas, drifting through a season of stalemate in the cautious hands of a leader for whom stalemate had become a way of life.

That spring Shamir demonstrated his devotion to the status quo when he was confronted with an opportunity to attend an international peace conference with Israel's Arab enemies. The conference proposal was the outcome of a seven-hour secret meeting in London between Foreign Minister Shimon Peres and Jordan's King Hussein. Much of it was pie-in-the-sky. The conference would be hosted by the five permanent members of the U.N. Security Council, but only if the Soviet Union and China dropped their long-standing policy and granted diplomatic recognition to Israel. Yasser Arafat's Palestine Liberation Organization would have to renounce terrorism and recognize Israel's right to secure borders or else it, too, would be excluded. Nonetheless Peres considered the agreement with Hussein a breakthrough.

Shamir saw it as treachery. Peres had refused to take Shamir to London or even inform him in advance of what he was doing. When the foreign minister returned to Jerusalem he did not show the prime minister the document he had obtained. Instead, Shamir was first read the agreement by U.S. Ambassador Thomas Pickering, who served as a key messenger between Peres and Hussein. Shamir believed he understood all too well what the agreement was about: it was the Americans, the Jordanians and Peres conspiring behind his back to force Israel to a conference at which all the other participants would gang up to compel him to make territorial concessions. If Shamir refused to go along, then Peres had the perfect excuse for breaking up the government and forcing an early election. It was a trap.

Shamir launched a campaign in Jerusalem to undermine the agreement, branding it "an insane and monstrous idea" that "only someone wishing the loss and destruction of his country would favor." But the real battlefield was in Washington. Peres dispatched aides who pleaded with U.S. Secretary of State George P. Shultz to undertake a diplomatic mission to nail down agreement to the conference proposal from other Arab states and force Shamir to accede. Burned by his last Middle East effort—the disastrous U.S. attempt to mediate a peaceful conclusion to the Israeli invasion of Lebanon—Shultz was skeptical. But he succumbed to Peres's and Hussein's entreaties. He had President Ronald Reagan write a "Dear Yitzhak" letter to Shamir, urging the prime minister to reconsider. "I believe that we may now have an historic opportunity to make progress toward our shared goal," Reagan told Shamir.

The prime minister was unconvinced. He sent Arens, a cabinet minister without portfolio and his most senior political ally, to Washington to tell Shultz that Likud was firmly opposed to the proposal and urge Shultz not to get involved. A trip to the region now would amount to direct interference in domestic Israeli politics, Arens warned. Shultz backed off, leaving Peres on his own.

The foreign minister then decided to force a vote. But Peres, who was so adept at the complex whirl of international diplomacy, proved incompetent at the harsh, simple math of winning a majority in the Knesset. When Peres counted noses, he found he was two short of the sixty-one he needed to bring down the government. The game was over before it had really begun.

For Shamir it was an easy victory—perhaps too easy. It confirmed his own cynical view of the Americans, the Arabs and Israel's domestic political deadlock. He saw the Americans as impatient and ultimately uninterested when it came to the Middle East. He knew he could stall and manipulate them because they cared less about the outcome than he did. They did not have his nerves, his patience and his sense of historical inevitability. Just as the sea would always be the same sea, he told his aides, the Arabs would always be the same Arabs. They would always resist, yet they would slowly give way to the reality of Israel's existence and its evertightening grip on the occupied territories. And with the Arabs unwilling to yield, Israeli politics would remain paralyzed between hawks and doves, and Peres would never be able to mobilize a majority for his schemes.

The great phony game of the Middle East peace process would go on. All of this was fine with Yitzhak Shamir, who wanted to prolong the process until hundreds of thousands of Jews had settled in the West Bank and the question of returning the territories to Arab control became moot. Time, he believed, was on his side. Israel, Shamir occasionally confessed, had more important goals than peace. "For me it's not burning," he told one interviewer. "I can wait, because for me it's more important to achieve our national aspirations."

Shamir was certain that the status quo would endure. He and his generals and his intelligence chiefs, men of talent and caution, saw nothing on the horizon that could disrupt it. But his refusal to even consider compromise or take incremental steps to ease the occupation caused a buildup of tension and pressure in the territories that led inevitably to an explosion.

Forces were bubbling under the surface in the occupied territories that would smash the status quo and scatter its jagged pieces across the political landscape. Young Palestinians in the West Bank and Gaza Strip were becoming increasingly radicalized. They were angry at their parents who for twenty years had lived with the personal humiliation and indignity of occupation. They were angry at their exiled leaders who had grown comfortable and corrupt abroad and evinced no strong desire to upset long-standing arrangements. They were enraged by their own dead-end economic prospects, by the increasing rates of crime and drug abuse in their cities, and by their own apparent powerlessness to do anything about it. But most of all, they were enraged by the Israelis, the keepers of their prison and, as far as they were concerned, the ultimate source of their agony.

No longer was the Israeli army fighting professional terrorists infiltrating from outside the occupied territories. By 1987, according to the army's own analysis, about 80 percent of violent incidents were initiated locally, most of them by young, politically unaffiliated Palestinians who felt they had nothing to lose and were intent on inflicting pain and misery on their jailers. "We have felt insecure ever since we were born," said Samaa, a twenty-three-year-old university student from the Calandia refugee camp. "Violence is the only way the whole world will see us and hear us. They may see us as terrorists, but this way is the only way."

The new Palestinian generation had few heroes. It paid lip service to aging figures such as Yasser Arafat and George Habash, but many felt abandoned by both the PLO and the Arab world in general. A few spoke glowingly about Abu Nidal; the nihilism of his terrorist group struck a chord in a desperate generation.

Their real role models were homegrown fanatics, angry, frustrated young men who were ready to kill and be killed. They thrilled vicariously in May 1987 when six young Palestinians escaped from the Gaza Central Prison, which Gazans considered an Israeli torture center. When four of the escapees were killed in a shootout in October in which an Israeli Shin Bet agent was also killed, they earned a place in the melancholy ranks of Gaza martyrs. The following month a young, anonymous commando from Ahmed Jibril's Palestinian splinter group flew a hang glider from Lebanon into northern Israel, landed outside an army camp, and mowed down six Israeli soldiers and wounded thirteen others before he himself was killed. Together, these separate incidents helped puncture Israel's image of invincibility among young Palestinians. For the first time they felt a sense of their own power.

Older Palestinians who had sought to come to terms with the occupation also found themselves increasingly at odds with the Israeli authorities. In the fall of 1987 Jad Isaac, a middle-aged Palestinian academic from the Christian Arab town of Beit Sahur in the West Bank, wrote a paper that he entitled "The New Palestinianism." Palestinians could never hope to end the occupation until they ended their own economic dependence on Israel, Isaac argued. His call for self-sufficiency and political pragmatism became a blueprint for the uprising known as the intifada.

Palestinians directed much of their anger and violence not only at the army but at the 65,000 Jews who had settled in the territories. The success of the settlement program stimulated Palestinian reaction. Sitting in their villages and cities, Palestinians could see that the status quo was far from static—each year brought an influx of thousands of settlers. New settlements with their familiar boxlike structures and red-tile roofs sprouted from the hilltops. They were a symbol and an affront. They forced Palestinians to a new level of realization and desperation: the land was not being held in trust pending the end of Israeli occupation; it was instead being eroded from under Arab feet.

Many of the newer settlers were not messianic ideologues but rather middle-class suburbanites who had moved to the West Bank to take advantage of clean air and cheap, government-subsidized mortgages. But gradually they, too, were being sucked into conflict with their Arab neighbors. In April 1987 after a Palestinian near the West Bank settlement of Alfei Menashe tossed a gasoline bomb through the open window of an Israeli car, killing Ofra and Tal Moses, a Jewish woman and her five-year-old son, settlers rampaged through the streets of nearby Kalkilya, breaking windows, overturning cars and shooting at houses. A few weeks later another band of Jewish vigilantes, fed up with having their cars stoned by Arab youngsters, stampeded through the Dehaishe refugee camp, firing shots and smashing windows and beating up residents and even soldiers.

The army increasingly found itself caught in the middle between these two warring forces. In the past soldiers usually stood by idly during settler retaliations. But a new commander had recently taken charge of the West Bank, one who insisted that both settlers and Palestinians obey the law. Major General Amram Mitzna ordered the arrest of thirteen settlers and called their attack on Dehaishe "an abomination," serving notice that the army would no longer tolerate vigilante tactics by Jews in the territories. Mitzna and his troops quickly found themselves trapped between the Palestinians and the settlers. The confrontation at Dehaishe proved to be just a dress rehearsal for larger conflicts to come.

Social scientist Meron Benvenisti, the former deputy mayor of Jerusalem and a prophet without honor in his own land, monitored the rise in violence among Palestinians and Israelis in the territories in 1987. He characterized it as "a twilight war, an intercommunal strife that has nothing to do with diplomatic initiatives and that renders them totally superfluous." He saw the Arab-Israeli conflict reverting from the modern pattern of state against state, Israel versus Jordan, Syria and Egypt, and returning to its original contours of Arab against Jew, two warring nationalisms in a deadly struggle for control of the land west of the Jordan. While Israeli leaders bickered over acceptable terms for an international peace conference they believed would never take place and American diplomats shuttled between Middle East capitals searching for common ground between the immovable and the merely implacable, two national movements that had grappled with each other in various forms for a hundred years were returning to what Benvenisti called their "primordial brawl."

Palestinians, soldiers and settlers were locked in a deadly embrace. Together they would change dramatically the face of the territories—and, inevitably, of Israel as well.

2. Jad Isaac's Shed

I don't think Israel is holding Gaza anymore.
I think Gaza is holding Israel.

—MERON BENVENISTI

THE uprising began outside Baraket Abu Rashid, a pool of slick brown water trapped in a garbage-strewn gulley below a strip of sand dunes and withered trees that bisect Jabaliya, the Gaza Strip's largest, poorest and mostly densely populated refugee camp. Up from the stagnant pool, across a pockmarked road and an open sewer, sits a one-story shack with concrete walls and a thin, corrugated asbestos roof. The corner house on a street with no pavement and no name, the shack has been designated as T-117 by the United Nations planners who oversee the camp. For many years the empty expanse of sand between the gulley and the house also had no name, but now it is known as Martyr's Square. There are no plaques here—Israeli soldiers quickly dismantled the few attempts to leave some flowers—but every Gazan knows this spot. It is the birthplace of the Palestinian intifada.

At eight-thirty on the morning of December 9, 1987, Mahmoud Muhaisen, age fourteen, was finishing history class in the seventh grade of Jabaliya Preparatory School B. As he began shifting his books a handful of boys from a nearby high school crashed the classroom, frantically summoning everyone to a demonstration taking shape at nearby Baraket Abu Rashid. Nothing about this was unusual—stone-throwing protests were a common form of recreation in Gaza for the disaffected, the reckless and the bored, and the youth of Jabaliya fitted easily into all three categories. For weeks they had spent more time on the streets playing cat and mouse with soldiers than attending school. It was a ritual with well-established rules: the kids would throw rocks and bottles at passing jeeps, then melt into the alleyways as the soldiers gave chase, using clubs, tear gas and rubber bullets. Occasionally rioters were caught and beaten, and sometimes bones were broken. Once in a while someone got shot. And, perhaps ten or twelve times a year, someone died.

Lately, however, the ritual had become more lethal. Things had gotten especially turbulent after October 6, when the army arrested Sheikh Abd Aziz Odeh, a popular local cleric who was considered the spiritual leader of Islamic Jihad. The Jihad was a small underground group of fighters who had fired local imaginations with a series of killings of soldiers and Israeli civilians, and the spectacular jailbreak from a Gaza City holding cell and subsequent shootout with Israeli soldiers. Muslim fundamentalism was on the rise in places like Jabaliya, where politics and economics were equally desperate, and the shootout, followed by Odeh's arrest, had set off two months of increasingly bitter protests.

On the afternoon of December 8, an Israeli semitrailer carelessly plowed into a car filled with Jabaliyans returning from work in Israel, killing four people. The driver claimed it was an accident, but Palestinians insisted it was a revenge attack for the stabbing death of an Israeli in the Gaza City market a few days earlier. The funerals took place that same evening, giving a new focus to an old rage. "Jabaliya was like a barrel full of dynamite," recalled Hawad Mabhouh, a local journalist and bookshop owner. "The road accident was the match."

Mahmoud Muhaisen could hear the distant rumble of the crowd before he could see it. When he turned the corner he was stunned. There, under a flat gray sky hundreds, no thousands, of Jabaliyans had poured into the square to protest the deaths. They were chanting Palestinian slogans and clapping their hands rhythmically.

Periodically a small convoy of Israeli military vehicles sought to penetrate the swelling mob, drawing stones and bottles as it went. When the convoy halted and soldiers leaped from the back of the vehicles pointing their automatic rifles, the crowd would recede, seeking refuge in the maze of backyards and side streets. But the minute the soldiers climbed back aboard, the stone throwers would reassemble, hurling abuse—often in Hebrew, a language many had learned from working in Israel—as well as rocks and occasional bottles filled with gasoline. Mahmoud, who at fourteen was already a veteran of this kind of combat with two previous arrests, joined in.

Sometime near 10 A.M. he and some friends took aim at an Israeli command car that had made the mistake of navigating through the mob alone.

The driver halted the vehicle and the youths dashed for the corner house with three soldiers in hot pursuit. Mahmoud made it through an open window and climbed onto the roof, where he and other youths rained rocks on the Israelis. The soldiers fled inside the house while a gasoline bomb set the command car on fire. The driver and a fellow soldier scrambled to put out the blaze, while a third tried to hold off the mob and a fourth kept hold of a young captive inside the house. Loudspeakers from the nearby Ibrahim mosque entreated residents: "Come to the aid of your brothers!" As the crowd surged forward the soldiers opened fire. Mahmoud was hit in the sole of his left foot by a shot fired blindly through the asbestos roof of the house. But he was the lucky one. Three other youths were hit. One of them, seventeen-year-old Hatem Asisi, died instantly from a bullet through the heart. He was the first Palestinian to be killed in the intifada.

By noon Hatem Asisi's body was being carried through the streets of Jabaliya toward Makhbarat Cemetery, a forlorn garden of rock and sand near the army base. The army declared a curfew and ordered everyone to return to their houses, but it was far too late for that. Billowing pillars of thick smoke rose from burning tires and garbage dumpsters at virtually every street corner. The air was saturated with the acrid smell of black smoke mixed with tear gas. Young men barricaded the streets with boulders, broken furniture, concrete blocks and huge stainless-steel sewage pipes meant to improve Jabaliya's chronic sanitation problems. The soldiers who sought to penetrate these defenses found themselves confronted by men, women and children, some of whom opened their arms and bared their chests, cursing at the soldiers and pleading to be shot.

By next morning the rioting had spread to Gaza City, Khan Yunis, Rafah, Bureij, Nusseirat, Maghazi and elsewhere—three cities and eight refugee camps, 650,000 people in all, mobilized, enraged and defiant. Bob Simon, the veteran CBS bureau chief in Tel Aviv, raced with his crew from town to town, filming as they went. Simon had seen many riots over the years, but this one seemed different. Why? "Because of the looks in their eyes, because of the generality of it," Simon later recalled. "It wasn't just Jabaliya or Gaza City or Khan Yunis, it was the whole fucking place, everywhere at once.

"You could see it in the faces of the soldiers. They didn't know what was going on. They didn't understand it and they didn't know how to deal with it. They couldn't round up the usual suspects. I saw Israelis behaving in a way I'd never seen before. At one point I was looking the other way and saw this command car with a Palestinian kid tied on top. They were using him as a human shield. I physically turned the cameraman around to get the shot. The soldiers were just completely overwhelmed. It surprised everyone. They weren't prepared for it and they didn't know how to react."

Gaza's Palestinians did not know quite how to react either. What was happening was a chaotic, leaderless, undefined outburst, a cry of despair from people with no previous voice, no power, no name and no strategy beyond the politics of rage. The organized Palestinian movements—Yasser Arafat's mainstream Fatah, the smaller, more radical PLO splinter groups, the Muslim Brotherhood with its growing number of adherents to Islamic fundamentalism—were as stunned as the army. No one had anticipated the extent of the anger, nor the power of the spontaneous combustion that was taking place. And no one knew quite what to do with it. "People felt if they went on for one or two weeks then the army would withdraw from Gaza," said Hawad Mabhouh. "We had no way of knowing how long this would last and how hard it would be."

Still, the early days of the intifada set a pattern that continued with variations for many months: the spontaneous rage of young Palestinians, aided and abetted by their parents and their neighbors; the harsh, improvised response of Israeli soldiers, caught up in a struggle they could neither understand nor cope with; and the watchful eye of the media, fascinated and repelled by what it was seeing. The rage and the violence quickly spilled over into the West Bank, where it took on new patterns and new adherents.

Mahmoud Muhaisen spent a month in bed recovering from his wound. Later he would be shot again, this time in the left calf, and spend months hobbling around the camp on a metal crutch. He would be arrested and beaten and serve four months in an Israeli prison. He would lose two years of schooling and the chance to go on to a university. And he would watch as the intifada was gradually seized by Palestinian organizations, became institutionalized and turned inward on itself, with Arabs killing hundreds of other Arabs accused of "collaboration" with the Israeli enemy. Much of this he would regret, but none of it would dull his pride in what he had helped begin. "It doesn't matter what happened to me or to anyone else," he would say later. "The intifada was a glass that everybody must drink from. There was no choice."

The real surprise was not that the Gaza Strip blew up in December 1987 but that it had not happened years earlier. Abandoned by its Arab brethren, neglected by its Israeli rulers and exploited by both, Gaza was the most wretched by-product of forty years of Arab-Israeli conflict. Everyone condemned its poverty and underdevelopment, yet no one accepted responsibility for it. Gaza had many parents; it was, nonetheless, an orphan.

Egypt, which had seized Gaza during Israel's Independence War in 1948 and ruled it for nineteen years, had established its refugee camps, filled them with Palestinians fleeing their homes in what had become Israel, and left them in the camps as an open wound to fester before the new Jewish state. When Israel conquered the Strip during the 1967 Six-Day War, it inherited, in effect, a giant prison, a thin, enclosed coastal strip twenty-eight miles long and five miles wide jammed with some 390,000 Palestinians, 150,000 of whom were refugees. By 1987 the population had swelled to 650,000 according to Israeli figures, or 800,000 by some Palestinian estimates.

Israel established control of the camps following a harsh counterinsurgency campaign led by General Ariel Sharon but achieved little else. An effort to move some of the people by building modern housing outside the camps foundered over objections from the Arab states, international indifference to the Gazans' plight and lack of funding. Israel provided a minimal standard of living for many. Some 60,000 Gazans traveled to Israel daily for work, most of it the manual labor and menial employment that Israelis themselves shunned. The Gazans built Israel's houses, picked its crops, cleaned its toilets, took out its garbage, dug its ditches. This was a major source of Gaza's livelihood—Israeli economists estimated that perhaps one-third of the Strip's income flowed from Israel—but it came at a high price. Israeli employers provided minimal benefits and frequently dealt out abuse, while soldiers manning the Erez checkpoint, the main entryway into Israel proper, searched for contraband and sometimes made their own demands for goods and money. Virtually everything Israel did only increased the sense of despair. It blocked industrial development, confiscated local land for Jewish settlement and collected taxes but provided no accounting for how they were used. It improved health care, but that meant increases in the birthrate to more than four children per hundred per year, one of the world's highest.

By the late 1970s, Israel embarked on a policy of counteracting support for the secularized PLO by tacitly encouraging the growth of the Islamic movement, which at the time seemed conservative and apolitical. The West Bank, with its heterogeneous population and relative prosperity, remained secular. But Gaza, isolated, impoverished and overwhelmingly Muslim, was fertile ground for the Islamic message. By 1987 traditional Muslim groups with their emphasis on family values, charity and prayer were being pushed aside. A new, more militant brand of Islam that combined religious fervor with a strong sense of nationalism and a hatred for all things Israeli and Jewish had become the most dynamic force in the Strip. Some neighborhoods looked like Ayatollah Khomeini's Iran. Their streets were filled with women wearing long dark robes and traditional scarves, and some who defied this dress code had acid thrown at them or were knifed. Restaurant owners eliminated wine lists and retailers moved liquor supplies behind the counter. The last cinema houses closed as the number of mosques in the Strip doubled.

Islamic Jihad first appeared in this charged atmosphere in February 1986 when someone tossed a grenade at a group of soldiers and Jewish settlers in the main Gaza market, wounding eight people. There were several more attacks that year, including the stabbing deaths of three Israeli civilians and a hand grenade assault on an elite Israeli infantry unit outside the Old City of Jerusalem. The young men involved often came from prominent Gaza families, and some were students at the Islamic University in Gaza City. Their common denominator was religious absolutism.

"We are members of the Islamic Jihad," Khalid Jaida told an Israeli military court in the summer of 1987 after he and two colleagues were given life sentences in the three stabbing deaths. "We appreciate death more than life. We either achieve victory and liberate our land, or die. We have not forgotten the massacres committed against us every day. I will gladly accept the court's sentence, for I have no remorse over what we have done." His words set the tone for the brazen élan with which many young Palestinians confronted Israeli troops in the Strip when the intifada began.

By the time the Israeli intelligence cracked the Jihad's embryonic cell structure, other groups were rising to take its place, most notably an underground offshoot of the Muslim Brotherhood that called itself the Islamic Resistance Movement—its Arabic acronym is Hamas, which means "zeal." Although they, too, were caught off-guard by the intifada, the Islamists recovered quickly and got a head start over their secular Palestinian rivals. In Gaza they issued the first political leaflets, organized the first clandestine cells and self-help committees, enforced the first strikes and conducted the first attacks on purported collaborators. It was an advantage they never relinquished.

While Israel was creating Palestinian heroes, its prison system was fostering a class of authentic militants, such as Diya Hanawi, a slim, baby-faced, fifteen-year-old athlete. In other circumstances Diya might have been perfecting his jump shot or studying mathematics, but in Gaza he was working on stone throwing instead, and he was typical of the young men who ignited the intifada.

Diya's career as a radical began with a small student demonstration in March 1987 at the Palestine Secondary School in Gaza City. The students marked the thirtieth anniversary of Israel's withdrawal from Gaza after the Suez crisis the same way they celebrated all of the anniversaries on the crowded calendar of Palestinian nationalism—by pelting Israeli soldiers with rocks and bottles. The soldiers responded with clubs and rubber bullets, and a dozen youths were rounded up, including Diya. His first night in a drafty holding pen was also the first time he had ever been away from home.

Diya, whose father worked as a clerk for the Israeli administration, was sentenced by a military court to two months' imprisonment for inciting a riot. He was taken to a makeshift detention center next to the Mediterranean seaside. There he was crammed into a damp, chilly cell with about thirty other Palestinians, ranging in age from twelve to twenty-four. The food was bad, the mattresses filthy, and the treatment by Israeli guards ranged from indifferent to casually brutal. Diya was terrified of what would happen to him.

He learned many lessons in jail. After a few weeks together the prisoners staged a four-day hunger strike for more blankets and better food, and he got to know the others in the intense way that people do in difficult circumstances. He also developed a burning contempt for Israelis, none of whom he had ever met before. When he came out in May, Diya found he was considered a hero by his classmates and neighbors.

By the fall of 1987 there were hundreds and thousands of young Palestinians like Diya Hanawi walking the streets of Gaza. Known in Arabic as the *shabab* (the "guys"), they had been through a process of radicalization that began in the alleyways, in the schools and in their own homes. But it was the crucial first run-in with Israeli troops and military prison that turned many angry young men into fighters. In court they often appeared trembling, demoralized and close to tears. But gradually they learned to be tough. By their second trip to court, Diya recalled, he and his fellow inmates defiantly sang Palestinian songs in the prison van. "The first two days I was so scared, but the other boys supported me. But by the time we got out, we were much more nationalistic than when we went in."

Even the *shabab* were surprised by what they unleashed in December 1987. Civil unrest was commonplace in Gaza, but it usually burned itself out after one or two days, especially in the winter rainy season. This time, however, the fire would not die.

Over the course of four short weeks the *shabab* turned Gaza into a combat zone. They had help from the Israeli army, which was panicked by a new kind of war for which it had no training and little stomach. It reacted in many instances by firing on stone throwers with live ammunition, killing twenty-nine Arabs and wounding more than two hundred. Parts of the Strip looked like Beirut. Khan Yunis, Rafah and Gaza City had been turned into urban wastelands: the shops were shuttered, the streets littered with rocks, makeshift barricades and burning tires.

A general strike brought commerce to a standstill. When they arrived early in the morning, the merchants of Omar el Mukhtar Street, Gaza City's main shopping street, were greeted by masked young men who ordered them to remain closed. A few hours later Israeli soldiers in purple berets and armed with automatic rifles ordered them to reopen the stores. When the soldiers left the *shabab* returned and ordered them to close again. Most of the Gazans who traveled daily to jobs in Israel were cut off from their only source of livelihood.

Eventually the conflict altered even the face of Gaza's squalor. The army sealed off the main entrances to the refugee camps with rocks and concrete-filled steel drums tied with ribbons of razor wire. Alleyways were closed off with ten-foot-tall concrete slabs held in place by mounds of sand. No one could slip through the cracks to throw a rock and disappear into the maze. The army camp in Jabaliya, nicknamed Fort Apache by the wary reservists stationed there, became an isolated fortress. Army bulldozers cleared a fifty-yard swath of no-man's-land around the base, while engineers built a new lookout tower twice as high as its predecessor and doubled the height of the chain-link and barbed wire fences surrounding the compound. It was hard to know who were the captives—the Israeli reservists huddled deep inside the base or the Palestinians entrapped in the teeming refugee camp without.

"I don't think Israel is holding Gaza anymore," Israeli social scientist Meron Benvenisti declared. "I think Gaza is holding Israel."

The intifada began as a street war between Palestinian young men and Israeli soldiers, but as it spilled over from Gaza into the more affluent, more secular and more politically sophisticated West Bank it took on a different color and dynamic. The West Bank had its share of street warfare, but this was overshadowed by another kind of intifada, one of organization and initiative, one that sought to decouple the territories from its Israeli rulers. The heart that unleashed and powered the uprising was the angry young men of Jabaliya. But the brain that attempted to channel their rage into an authentic Palestinian independence movement was located in the West Bank. One of the best places to chart how it grew was a small Christian town called Beit Sahur, where a mild-mannered university professor and some of his friends were about to become improbable revolutionaries.

Jad Isaac had come back to Beit Sahur in the winter of 1968, spurning a breezy, uncomplicated life as a postgraduate at Cairo University for an uneasy future under Israeli military occupation in the West Bank village of his ancestors. He had commemorated his return by planting 250 saplings on the family acre in the legendary field where shepherds first heard word of the birth of Christ. They were mostly fruit trees—apples, pears, peaches, olives, almonds, apricots, pomegranates, hazelnuts, lemons—for Isaac was a practical man, a biologist who believed his first duty was to feed himself, his family and his neighbors.

There was nothing dramatic about Isaac. He was a slightly built man with a rhythmic voice and a sly, sardonic smile. By 1987 what remained of his hair was slowly graying above his scholarly, wire-framed glasses. He was soft-spoken and slow to anger, at times laconic. But he had a deep sense of pride and of personal autonomy. He wore a freshly ironed shirt and pants and shaved each day, leaving a neatly trimmed goatee. Even under military occupation Isaac believed he was entitled to certain rights. He expected to be treated with respect. He knew he had no right to free expression or to organize politically, but he believed that as long as he did not encourage violence he would be allowed to participate in local politics and to speak his mind. Isaac knew the Israelis had unwritten rules that divided what was politically acceptable from what would land a man in prison. He worked assiduously to stay on the acceptable side of those rules. But he failed to understand that once the intifada began, the rules disappeared.

Beit Sahur was a tidy cluster of church towers, shops and houses on a ridge that gracefully sloped east from Bethlehem, its larger and more famous neighbor. Most of its residents were fierce nationalists, yet many had prospered financially during the years of Israeli occupation. There was little of the raw hatred for Israel and Israelis that was conspicuous in the bleak slums of Gaza. Instead, many Beit Sahuris had come slowly, albeit reluctantly, to accept that Israel was an ineradicable reality, perhaps even a potential asset. Long before the PLO announced it as policy, they spoke openly about a two-state solution—a Palestinian state in the West Bank and Gaza that would coexist alongside Israel, not supersede it—and many embraced the idea of free commerce and open, permeable borders between the two states. They were, in sum, exactly the kind of moderate yet authentic nationalists whom Israel should have been talking to and negotiating with.

About 12,000 people lived in Beit Sahur, three-quarters of them Christian, most Greek Orthodox like Isaac, making the town the most predominately Christian community in the largely Muslim West Bank. Most came from eight large clans, some of which had lived in the area for fifteen centuries. Beit Sahur boasted the highest proportion of college-bound youngsters (17 percent) and the lowest illiteracy rate (7 percent) in the region. Isaac's own survey counted fifty-three engineers, twenty-five physicians, twenty university professors, eight pharmacists and six dentists. While there were several large manufacturing companies, the local economy was dominated by more than a hundred small-scale businesses, including forty-three olive wood and mother-of-pearl factories catering to the tourist trade.

Jad Isaac's ancestors had arrived in Beit Sahur in 1635. Most of the family had remained there ever since. Jad was born in Lydda,* a town in central Palestine where his father worked as a mechanic for the British army. A year after Jad's birth in 1947, the Isaacs were driven out of Lydda on foot when a brigade of the fledgling Israeli army, led by a young commander named Yitzhak Rabin, swept through the area during the Independence War, carrying out what Rabin later described as a forced evacuation of the Arab civilian population. They returned to Beit Sahur, which was on the Arab side of the armistice line separating the new state of Israel from the Jordanian-controlled West Bank. Forty years later Jad Isaac still held a refugee's identity card.

When Isaac left Beit Sahur for Cairo University to study agriculture in 1964, the town was still part of Jordan. When he returned four years later on a visitor's permit, it had become part of Israeli-occupied territory, conquered during the Israeli army's lightning sweep through the West Bank in the Six-Day War of June 1967. Rabin, now chief of staff of the Israel Defense Forces, had found Jad Isaac again.

The fruit trees that Isaac planted that winter became his hobby, then his passion. The orchard settled him down, made him more patient and persistent. He started seeing a young woman named Ghada Andoni Ibrahim from one of the village's most prominent clans. When they married in June 1974 they decided to build their house in the middle of the garden. But before they started, Isaac decided to pursue his Ph.D. at the University of East Anglia in Norwich, England, choosing plant physiology as his subject. He came back in 1978 to a teaching position at Bethlehem University, eventually becoming dean of science.

The new house was finally completed in August 1982. Ghada designed most of it herself after taking a correspondence course in architecture. It had five different levels and two long porches. In the sitting room where the family entertained guests, there was a personal computer and an English-language *Encyclopaedia Britannica*. Outside on the front wall was a metallic Star of Bethlehem with a meteor tail pointing toward the city of Jesus' birth.

But the most unusual feature was the garden. Isaac and his father had expanded it, adding chickens, goats and a wide variety of crops, including tomatoes, zucchini, okra, eggplant, squash, green peppers, grapes, string beans, strawberries, potatoes and lettuce. Almost everything the family ate

* Now the Israeli town of Lod.

was homegrown. The garden was a little island of the kind of self-sufficiency that Isaac believed Palestinians would have to strive for if they were
ever to break free of Israel.

Like many Beit Sahuris, Isaac got on Israel's security list early. He was
involved in an abortive attempt to organize a teacher's union in the West
Bank and Gaza. He also helped establish a political think tank, the Arab
Thought Forum, that sought to analyze growing Palestinian economic dependence on Israel and find ways out of it. When faced with a political
problem, Isaac took to his desk, not to the streets.

He considered himself a technocrat and boasted he had no allegiance to
any particular Palestinian faction. After the humiliation in Lebanon in
1982, when Israeli forces had sought to destroy the PLO and no Arab state
had lifted a finger to oppose them, Isaac began to reevaluate PLO dogma,
which called for Israel's destruction and replacement with a secular Palestinian state. He knew enough Israelis by then to know they would never
accept such a country, and he had come to recognize that Israel could not
be defeated militarily. And he knew better than to expect deliverance from
the Arab world. Palestinians, Isaac came to believe, would have to make it
on their own. That meant, among other things, coming to terms with their
enemy.

For the Beit Sahuris, the intifada began as distant thunder from Gaza a few
weeks before Christmas. But by January 1988 it had swept into town like an
angry winter storm. Masked teenagers pelted the vehicles of Israeli soldiers
and Jewish settlers with rocks and bottles, barricaded roadways with
makeshift collections of garbage, old furniture, boulders and construction
materials, and coerced local shopkeepers into honoring the commercial
strike that gripped the territories. The army declared nightly curfews. Many
people found themselves caught between their own children and the soldiers, fearful of what the former provoked in the latter. The disruptions also
caused practical problems: the few fruits, vegetables, fresh eggs and meat
on the market shelves grew expensive and scarce.

Isaac, ever the practical man, quickly saw a connection between politics
and food. One Sunday that month, he and civil engineer Issa Tawil, a childhood friend, drove to Jericho, a West Bank agricultural center, and came
back with seeds and 500 seedlings to distribute to neighbors and relatives.
Word spread quickly, and by the next day the seedlings were gone. Isaac
went back for 2,000 more, and eventually distributed 40,000 along with
bags of seeds, fertilizer, pesticides, rubber hoses and secondhand chicken
cages. A friend across the street donated a shed and some land for a small

gardening shop. Fourteen people invested a total of about $18,000 to outfit the store. By early March, Isaac, Tawil and Gerasmus Kharroub, a fellow biologist, were doing serious business. They hired three people to work in the shop and even bought a small tractor to rent out for plowing.

In the process they became an essential part of the uprising. While Israelis and most of the world focused on the strikes, the rock-throwing riots and the death toll that averaged one Palestinian per day, a quieter but equally important feature was the attempt to break the political and economic link between Israel's military rule and its Palestinian subjects. Some 60,000 West Bankers traveled into Israel daily for work that, even though menial, had helped create a new Palestinian middle class, independent of the old clans and social structures. This new class had some money and education but no formal political power. It was totally dependent on Israel for its wealth and influence.

By declaring war on the civil administration, the emerging leadership of the uprising demanded that Palestinians seize control over their own affairs, whether it was education, commerce, health or policing. Semiweekly leaflets distributed by a clandestine committee of activists exhorted residents to form popular committees for these purposes. Beit Sahur's victory gardens fitted snugly into the theme of self-sufficiency. They also won Isaac fame well beyond the village. Soon residents from across the West Bank were pulling up in rusted station wagons and wheezing pickup trucks for gardening supplies and free advice.

The shed, a squat, cinder-block bunker with one door and no windows, quickly became the nerve center for Beit Sahur's intifada. It was a place where people would gather each morning to talk about things that had happened and to lay plans. Practical problems were tackled: when the village's Arab policemen resigned following a demand in a leaflet by the underground leadership, people from the shed organized a committee to patrol the streets for traffic violators and to provide an early-warning system when soldiers or armed settlers entered the town. Another committee established home-tutoring classes to mitigate the effects of school closures. Eventually there was a committee to organize first-aid training, one to monitor prices at local shops, another to clean streets, and another to donate money and food to residents who had lost their jobs. A committee of local merchants decided to stop paying the value-added tax, the equivalent of a sales tax. Gradually this network of popular committees became a source of power within the village, challenging the authority of the Israeli-appointed municipal officials. When the army ordered the mayor to hold a meeting at which he pleaded with some twenty prominent businessmen to pay their taxes, two masked young men broke up the session by their mere appearance in the room. The committees, backed by the ominous power of the street, had taken control.

Beit Sahur's quiet revolt spread gradually to neighboring towns and villages. It resonated throughout the underground leaflets issued from East Jerusalem and Ramallah. "It was eerie," Isaac recalled. "Things we discussed at our meetings would end up in the next leaflet. The Israelis began to believe we were the nerve center for the entire intifada. It's incredible, but they thought it was all Beit Sahur."

Caught off-balance, the authorities took several months to focus on Beit Sahur. But in May the pressure began. Isaac, Tawil and Kharroub were summoned four times to the military headquarters building in Bethlehem, interrogated and released. They insisted that their project was the product of their old friendship and mutual love of gardening, not intifada politics, but the authorities were not convinced. Two weeks later an army raiding party stormed Isaac's house and hauled him away. He was held until after midnight and warned he was under surveillance.

After that the gardeners were regularly summoned to headquarters for questioning. At first they took it as something of a joke; each took turns spending the day at headquarters, bringing sandwiches, coffee and newspapers and sitting as if in a doctor's waiting room. But then a new interrogator who called himself Captain Yuval took over. He banished the newspapers and food and made clear to the men just where they stood. "You are for me no more than stones," he told them. "If you disobey me I will break your heads."

When Isaac reached home that afternoon he found an army checkpost had been set up next to the house and his phone had been cut off. That same day Isaac posted a "Closed" sign on the shed. He did not want to be a hero or go to prison.

Something had started in the shed, however. By summer tax collections in the West Bank had fallen nearly 50 percent. The self-sustaining machine of the occupation was beginning to run down. Fearful of the consequences for the beleaguered civil administration, the authorities decided to make an example of Beit Sahur. One hot July morning soldiers swept into town and imposed a curfew. Then they went house-to-house seizing private cars and ordering people to report to the local boys' secondary school. There the tax authorities checked off names against a long list of alleged nonpayers. All outstanding bills had to be paid immediately or else the cars were to be auctioned off. In some cases soldiers returned to houses to confiscate appliances, furniture and valuables.

On the second day of the curfew townspeople gathered at the municipality and turned in their Israeli-issued identity cards, symbols of the hated occupation. Isaac, who had been out of town that morning, arrived to find hundreds of ID cards piled on a desk. At four o'clock the army arrived to confront the protesters. The local captain, using a bullhorn, ordered everyone to disperse immediately or face arrest. The townspeople stood their ground. Soldiers waded into the crowd with clubs. Isaac was among dozens of people who were seized and released later that night.

The next day, however, the authorities returned with a detention order. Isaac was handcuffed and blindfolded in front of his wife and four children and hauled off. He was taken along with seven other prisoners to a steamy, mosquito-infested cell in the Bethlehem military center. At eight-thirty that night a guard opened the grate and threw in three pieces of stale bread and a plastic plate of cooked tomatoes. Jad Isaac, the intifada's most prolific eater, took a quick look and decided to go on a hunger strike. He did not know it then, but his odyssey through the depths of the Israeli military prison system was just beginning.

By the time of Isaac's arrest in the summer of 1988, the Palestinian uprising had turned a corner. What began as a confrontation between stone-throwing Arab teenagers and youthful Israeli conscripts had blossomed into a full-scale intercommunal struggle between Arabs and Jews—"a war of populations," in the words of Israeli journalist Joel Greenberg. All over the West Bank and Gaza ordinary Palestinians like Jad Isaac, people who had never been arrested or spent a day in jail, found themselves sucked into a bitter protracted struggle. Students could not attend classes because the Israeli authorities had ordered West Bank schools closed. Shop owners were caught in the cat-and-mouse game of enforced openings and closings between the army and the *shabab.* Arab policemen who had stood on the sidelines for twenty years, working for the Israeli administration yet shunning security cases, were forced to resign after receiving a threatening directive from Palestinian activists. Farmers and merchants who sold their produce and wares in the markets that dotted the West Bank and Gaza were cut off from their livelihoods and confined to their homes by soldiers determined to raise the price of rebellion. Workers, too, found they were prevented from traveling to their jobs during curfew periods.

The intifada destroyed the system that had bound Palestinians to Israel for twenty years and, in the process, shattered the psychological bonds of the occupation. In response, the army set about to puncture the sense of euphoria and triumph that had marked the early days of the uprising by demolishing new intifada-inspired structures wherever they arose, and by cajoling, threatening and collectively punishing the population into returning to its pre-intifada state of grudging submission. But the impact of what both sides were doing was exactly the same—they were tearing down the status quo wherever they found it and, in the process, shattering many of their own assumptions about each other and themselves. Together they did immense damage both to the quality of life and to the personal autonomy of the average Palestinian. No one got off lightly. Everyone, eager warrior and reluctant spectator, was conscripted into the struggle for control. "You may not be interested in war," writes Leon Trotsky, "but war is interested in you." The intifada touched everyone.

Each side appeared determined to inflict the maximum pain on the other. Palestinians burned an Israeli school bus, so the army bulldozed trees. Arabs stoned cars of Jewish settlers and settlers vandalized Arab cars. Someone threw a Molotov cocktail at an Israeli fuel tanker and the army cut off gasoline supplies for a week. Arab police resigned, so the army restricted car travel, closed markets and cut off international phone lines. Palestinians retaliated by spreading an epidemic of arson through Israel's arid forests and farmland. Defense Minister Rabin compared the contest to the 1969–70 War of Attrition that Israel fought with Egypt across the Suez Canal. Each side was seeking to wear down the other, he told the cabinet. "I can assure you, the army will not be the first to tire."

But the Palestinians did not tire either. Collective punishment was a blunt, unwieldy instrument that by its nature hurt the bystander as well as the instigator, the neutral as well as the committed, and then bound them closer together in shared chains of misery and communal identification. "Who are the ones who make international phone calls and need gasoline for their private cars?" asked Mubarak Awad, an activist whose advocacy of nonviolent civil disobedience had won him a small but loyal following. "These are the wealthier people, and the pain they are now feeling brings them closer to the common Palestinian. It's actually a beautiful thing the Israelis are doing."

In late March the army inadvertently handed the intifada an enormous psychological victory when it sealed off the territories for three days and confined 1.5 million Arab residents to their homes or villages in anticipation of disturbances. Suddenly with eight terse sentences in a press statement, Rabin and his commanders had effectively reestablished the Green Line, the old 1967 border between Israel proper and the territories. Roads on which traffic had moved freely in and out of Israel were blocked off by soldiers checking identity cards and license plates, turning back Israelis on one side and Palestinians on the other. Motorists whose Israeli-made maps had not shown a border for the past decade wandered in confusion, uncertain about where Israel proper ended and the West Bank began. It was a harbinger of things to come: more repression, more barbed wire and increased separation of Arabs and Jews—both physical and mental. And it was a de facto admission by Israel's most venerated institution, its citizen army, that it could no longer live with the territories.

These were impersonal forces, yet they played out in the most personal of ways. The most affected were the Palestinian children who had begun the intifada and who sustained it with their blood and their naïveté. Once the uprising started, these youngsters lived inside the harrowing chaos it created. More so than anyone else's, their psyches were altered by it—their world, their thoughts, even their dreams permanently changed in ways large and small. They also died in it. Despite orders prohibiting troops from opening fire on children, B'Tselem, an Israeli human rights monitoring group, estimated that ninety Palestinian youths under age seventeen were killed in the first eighteen months of the intifada, twenty of them twelve years old and under.

The institutions that had once framed and ruled their lives were largely shattered. Their schools were closed, their towns and villages turned into battlefields. Their parents, who were supposed to supervise and protect them, had lost control. Jad Isaac's four children were among the luckier ones. Even when their father was locked away in an Israeli prison, their mother and grandparents made certain there was always enough food to eat and a steady level of discipline and parental expectations. They missed their father, but their world remained intact.

Others were not so fortunate. For many, the intifada cut mercilessly through the web of traditional family ties. Children defied their parents, and parents could no longer control or protect their children. "It's a very powerful image to see your father or mother, your two strongest protectors, be humiliated," said Cairo Arafat, an Arab-American clinical psychologist who interviewed dozens of Palestinian children during the first year of the uprising. When Israeli soldiers entered a house, "they take from children their only sanctuary. Nothing's safe anymore. No one is protected."

To replace those damaged authority figures the youngest Palestinian children often found new ones in their older brothers and sisters, the true leaders of the uprising. Sometimes they constructed fairy tales and myths around their new heroes. Such was the case with Mohammed Abu Aker, a thin, curly-haired seventeen-year-old who became a legend and a living martyr to the children of the Dehaishe refugee camp, located just south of Bethlehem.

Dehaishe, one of the rawest, most impoverished camps in the West Bank, straddled the main highway south from Jerusalem. Each morning youths would dart out from alleys to rain stones on the passing Israeli cars and on the red-and-white passenger buses that plied the route. Motorists seldom got a good look at the stone throwers, but those who did often expressed surprise. Children as young as seven or eight were playing the stone-throwing game. Soldiers insisted that the children were simply doing it for the thrill, but even the youngest among them knew whom they were aiming at. "It is the Jews," announced Said, a barefoot six-year-old with a permanently runny nose, frayed trousers and a smudged face.

Abu Aker was one of their leaders. He assigned kids to pile stones at strategic corners, ferry buckets of water to help ward off the effects of tear gas or serve as scouts watching out for soldiers. For eight months he was on the army's most-wanted list until one day during a stone-throwing confrontation a soldier fired a high-velocity bullet that exploded inside his abdomen. By the time he was brought to Makassed Hospital in East Jerusalem, Abu Aker was dying. Doctors removed most of his large and small intestine during three operations. They told his family to prepare funeral arrangements. But Abu Aker would not die. His friends attributed this to his strength of will and to the hand of Allah. Children began making pilgrimages to his hospital room, which was decked out like a shrine with Palestinian posters, miniature flags and other memorabilia scattered among the thicket of tubes and machines that kept him alive.

Gradually the legend was born. According to the stories passed around by the youths, Abu Aker had been arrested and tortured but had refused to talk, winning the grudging respect of his brutal interrogators. He was always on the front line during demonstrations, it was said, and had even been hit by a ricocheting bullet yet showed no pain. Tape recorders were brought to his hospital bed to preserve his whispered words "as if they were seeking the advice of an oracle," Israeli journalist Ori Nir wrote.

After two months the military authorities allowed Abu Aker, his father and his doctor to fly to Boston for treatment. He stayed three months at the New England Deaconess Hospital, where his father learned how to operate a catheter that was surgically implanted in his chest and to attach it to a bag of liquid nutrients that had to be pumped directly into his bloodstream each day. The $100,000 hospital bill was paid by the Naim Foundation, an Arab-American charitable organization.

On the day of Abu Aker's triumphant return to Dehaishe, a mob of small children greeted him. They choked the entranceway to his family's modest stone house for a glimpse of their hero and waited solemnly on a winding reception line for a chance to touch him and kiss both his cheeks. "All the children of Dehaishe know Mohammed's story," said Yusuf Milhem, a family friend. "When you see them playing in the alleyways, they all want to be him. This celebration is like a big wedding because we have not had much to be happy about this past year."

Other self-myths were all too easily shattered by the living nightmare of the intifada. Mimouna Shukarna, who was nine years old in 1989, was a self-proclaimed little warrior who lived in the West Bank village of Na-halin. She sang the intifada's songs, recited its slogans and basked in its fragile glory. When Israeli troops invaded her village she pelted them with stones. Above all, she declared proudly, she was not afraid. But at night the warrior vanished and a little girl returned. After Israeli Border Police shot dead five villagers in a clash that spring, Mimouna cried in her sleep and wet her bed, an anxious child living in constant fear that the soldiers would come back and shoot her as well.

The intifada had a dual impact on children like Mimouna: it built a strong sense of Palestinian identity at the same time it created a heritage of fear and hostility toward Israelis. After the shootings in Nahalin a group of Israeli peace activists came to the village to express their regrets and voice support for a Palestinian state alongside Israel. They handed out buttons to the children showing the Israeli and Palestinian flags side by side. Two months later Mimouna was still wearing the button, but had scratched out the Israeli flag after soldiers came back and detained her two oldest brothers. She made clear she had no use for any Israelis, peacenik or otherwise.

"I hate them," she said. "All of them."

Four days after he began his hunger strike at the Bethlehem holding pen, Jad Isaac was awakened early, blindfolded, handcuffed and placed aboard a prison bus with fifteen or so Palestinians bound for Dahariya, an old British army camp twenty minutes south of Hebron. The ordeal began on the three-hour bus ride with a young Israeli soldier who went up and down the aisle punching and kicking the captives. At the prison Isaac spent eighteen days confined in a small cell with twenty-four other Palestinians. Many ate standing up because there was not enough space for everyone to sit on the floor. "Dahariya was misery," he recalled. "There was one small window. One stinking bucket in the corner for a toilet. The food was miserable. I had only two showers in eighteen days. We all wore the same stinking clothing. We were allowed out of the room only three times in the entire period. There were no papers, no books. No interrogation either. For eighteen days I just sat there."

The worst day was when his wife, Ghada, came to visit along with the children. "I know it sounds hard, but I wished she hadn't come. You are a different person in prison—not shaved, dirty, in a size-50 blue denim outfit that's way too big. You stink. The kids couldn't even recognize me. Firas, my oldest son, was filled with tears but turning his eyes so I wouldn't see him crying. My little boy stared at me speechless. Deema was clinging to her mother. I tried to joke with them but it was so terrible. I couldn't wait for them to leave."

Soon Isaac was on his way again. Blindfolded and handcuffed, he rode all day on a bus to nowhere. He could see nothing, hear nothing beyond the metallic jangle of the bus. Then just before dusk, it came to a halt. The men were pushed and pulled out of the bus and across flat open ground to a tent where their blindfolds were removed. Isaac and the others were given a sheet of paper announcing they were being administratively detained—to be held for six months without charge or trial. Each prisoner was issued a denim shirt and pants, a folded wooden cot, five blankets, a toothbrush, a blue plastic dish and a prison number. To his Israeli guards Isaac was now Prisoner 5012. As he stepped outside and looked into the darkness, he began to sense the enormity of where he was and what he had become.

Ketziot is Hebrew for "dried figs," an appropriate nickname for a vast, open-air desert prison in the northwest corner of the Negev that the Israelis had created in the hopes of drying out and withering the intifada. It was a monotonous rectangular thicket of chain-link fences and razor wire, broken by dikes of fresh-moved earth and deep ditches, all overseen by awkward guard towers. Inside the fenced rectangles were large, standard-issue military tents with side flaps that were kept open during the day and closed at night. Each tent contained twenty to thirty narrow foam mattresses laid end to end on wooden slats with a one-foot-wide aisle between each row. There were no tables or chairs. In July and August daytime temperatures regularly soared past one hundred degrees; even with the flaps open, the tents were like ovens. After 10 A.M. it was impossible to read or even move in the oppressive heat.

Ketziot was supposed to be a temporary emergency measure. Before the intifada Israel's civilian prison service had run most of the detention centers, with the army operating only three small holding facilities. But the intifada produced a huge influx of prisoners. Eventually, the army estimated that at least 50,000 Palestinians would spend time in Israeli cells—between one-third and one-fourth of the male population between the ages of sixteen and forty. Human rights groups put the figure as high as 150,000, and Middle East Watch, the New York–based rights organization, estimated that Palestinians in the occupied territories had the highest imprisonment rate in the world.

Ketziot was the most notorious of the prisons. Opened in March 1988 at a base about forty miles southwest of Beersheba, its capacity of more than

7,000 prisoners was four times larger than that of any other facility. The administrative detention sections where Jad Isaac was placed "hold as many intellectuals and professionals as can be found in a small West Bank city," noted Middle East Watch. Ketziot's very location was a violation of Article 76 of the Fourth Geneva Convention, which stipulated that residents of an occupied territory could not be imprisoned outside the territory itself. But the Israeli Supreme Court ruled in November 1988 that the convention did not apply because it had never been incorporated into Israeli law.

The military justice system was harsh and often arbitrary, but there was a certain routine even to its cruelest rituals. Beatings and physical abuse almost always took place during arrest and interrogation. Once the questioning ended and a Palestinian entered a prison facility, the beatings generally stopped. Only at Ketziot did prisoners speak of routine beatings in the isolation cells where rebellious detainees were held. Isaac was never beaten—his age and his stature made him a forbidden target. But he suffered the punishments meted out collectively by an undermanned prison staff that often felt like a small cork plugging a large and turbulent bottle. On the August day when the prison commander shot and killed two unarmed Palestinians during rioting within the open-air cell blocks, Isaac's tent was teargassed. The smell and the nausea lasted for days.

That month he received his first and only legal hearing. The prosecutor alleged that he was a supporter of George Habash's Popular Front for the Liberation of Palestine, a banned organization, and a member of a popular committee for agriculture. He was also accused of being "active" in the intifada, of encouraging other residents not to pay taxes and of instigating the returning of the identity cards. There were other accusations, the prosecutor said, but these were "privileged." The judge could see the file, but not Isaac or his lawyers.

Isaac's two lawyers—one of them Palestinian, the other Israeli—insisted he was a political moderate who had closed his shed when ordered to do so by the authorities. But the military judge, a Tel Aviv lawyer serving as a reservist, rejected his appeal. "The purpose of administrative detention is preventive and not punitive," the judge wrote. The fact that Isaac's membership in a popular committee was not illegal did not matter. "A danger to security can result from any sort of activity, and not necessarily a terrorist or violent one." The judge said he had examined Isaac's secret file "meticulously" and concluded that Isaac was an "active and leading activist encouraging the uprising against the authorities of the district."

For weeks Isaac had waited for Israeli justice to assert itself. Now he knew it would not. "For the first month or more I couldn't really believe this was happening to me. I knew I didn't deserve administrative detention, and I just couldn't accept that it would happen anyway. But after the hearing, when I read what the judge had written, I finally realized there was no way out."

There were no heating units in the tent, and that first fall the prisoners had no coats or sweaters. By October the five blankets each prisoner had been issued were not enough to keep warm. As soon as night fell, the prisoners would huddle in their cots. "I've been to many places where it's cold, but the desert cold was totally different," Isaac recalled. "The pain is as if somebody is driving a nail deep inside your bones and moving it around all the time. You'd use a blanket for a pillow, and you'd put another one under you to try to ward off the cold from the ground below. That left three to cover your body, and it was never enough. You're cold all the time, and you just lie and wait for the sun to come. You feel like a reptile in a freezer."

After two months at Ketziot, Isaac had his first look in a mirror. "I couldn't believe it was me."

Isaac's five months in Ketziot were like a cram course in Palestinian nationalism. He taught English and studied applied politics from men who had spent their lives at war with Israel. The prisoners were highly organized and disciplined. They fashioned little booklets out of spare notebook paper and wrote out and studied the history of the Palestinian movement. Isaac kept a diary. He conducted a socioeconomic survey of the 194 detainees in his section, detailing their ages, place of residence and work, and the ostensible reasons for their imprisonment.

One prisoner was selected as leader of each tent, usually a political man with a reputation from his hometown and knowledge of Hebrew so that he could communicate demands to the camp authorities. Once when a prisoner admitted he had cursed an Israeli soldier, he was punished by his fellow inmates, who required him to clean all of the tent's utensils for a week. "Cursing was degrading," Isaac said. "We considered ourselves national freedom fighters, not gangsters. We wanted to gain the respect—of ourselves and of our enemy."

While Jad Isaac was confined to Ketziot the intifada was running out of steam. The Israeli army screwed the lid back on top of the occupied territories in part by launching a concerted attack on civilian life. The army closed the West Bank's primary and secondary schools, cutting short an academic year already halved by a previous four-month closure. Universities remained closed all year. Elsewhere in the region factories worked at 50 percent of capacity, shops were open only three hours a day for five days a week by decree of the activists. Major development projects funded by foreign donors were frozen.

Living standards plummeted. Commerce, agriculture, industry, trade, education, health, travel—the various pieces that together constitute that intangible known as the quality of life—fell under the siege. Social scientist Meron Benvenisti calculated that the gross domestic product of Gaza and the West Bank fell 25 percent in just eight months. "All the incremental improvements of the past twenty-one years have been swept away almost overnight," he said.

Some of the economic wounds were self-inflicted. Palestinians sought to build a sense of unity, self-sufficiency and defiance by a prolonged commercial strike that did more harm to their own prosperity than to Israel's. Following Beit Sahur's example, many towns and villages also pressed a tax boycott that at one point sliced Israeli revenues by half, leading to harsh reductions in services such as health, welfare payments and education. The number of Arab patients granted specialized care in Israeli hospitals was cut by two-thirds, and those who went had to be prepared to pay $150 a day unless they were insured.

Other wounds were part of a coordinated military effort to reassert Israel's control. The myth of the benign occupation was unceremoniously dumped; there was no pretense that what the army was doing was for the good of the local population. The idea was to punish everyone long and hard enough so that the silent, moderate, miserable majority would apply the necessary pressure on its own children to quiet the situation. Tax raids, telephone and electricity cutoffs, restrictions on travel and food supplies, limits on the flow of capital, plus the creation of countless new bottlenecks through which Palestinians were forced to pass to obtain new identity cards, car licenses and business permits—all this was designed to inflict pain not just on violent offenders but on the entire community.

Isaac was released from prison at the end of November 1988 and came home to find Beit Sahur on the edge of economic ruin. The intifada was still alive but had drastically changed character and shape. The popular committees, formally outlawed in August, had begun to shrivel. So had the victory gardens. The organized political factions, which had taken a backseat in the early days of the uprising, were filling the vacuum and reasserting control. Gone was the cohesiveness of the early days when Beit Sahuris cooperated across political and ideological lines. "I could see the rivalry and competition returning between factions," Isaac recalled. "At the beginning the kids would come round and say today's a demonstration day and everyone would participate. But later when one faction would come by, the others would sit on the sideline and count numbers. Money went for boots, trousers, training suits for rival groups. We were killing the grassrootedness of the intifada by this attitude."

The one grassroots activity still flourishing was the tax boycott, fueled partly by defiance but also by the fact that people simply did not have enough money to live, eat and pay taxes. The guiding spirit was pharmacist Elias Rishmawi, a stubborn local businessman. A few days before Isaac's release the authorities had arrested Rishmawi and three other local pharmacists, charging them with refusing to pay taxes. After ten days they were released on bail, but they refused Israeli demands that they submit. Then in June 1989 a large truck, a dozen tax collectors and an army commander pulled up outside Rishmawi's pharmacy in the center of town and went to work dismantling it. "They confiscated everything, even the dust," he said.

It was a dress rehearsal for a bigger assault three months later when hundreds of soldiers sealed off the entire town, then escorted dozens of tax collectors in a house-to-house search. It was the largest tax raid ever carried out in the West Bank. "We are going to teach them a lesson there," Defense Minister Rabin told a Knesset committee. "We will not allow this kind of civil disobedience, and we have to pass through this test. We should tell them, forget it, even if the curfew on Beit Sahur lasts two months."

The siege lasted forty-two days. The authorities seized more than $1.5 million in cars, televisions, appliances, furniture and commercial goods, sometimes smashing what they did not feel like removing. At least 350 houses were raided. Nearly fifty people, including Rishmawi, were arrested and charged with tax evasion. Most were released after eighteen days, following a public outcry by prominent Israelis. The press was barred, as were diplomats from various consulates who tried to enter the town. With no independent witnesses to monitor them, the army and the tax authorities had a free hand to conduct what locals described as a reign of terror. At the home of the Kokaly family, headed by a sixty-three-year-old retiree, a dozen soldiers and tax collectors dumped books, clothes and chests of drawers on the floor, rifled Mrs. Kokaly's purse and even tipped food out of cupboards and the refrigerator, according to an affidavit filed by the family with Al Haq, the Palestinian human rights group. They arrested Issam Kokaly, a teenaged son. Al Haq said the entire operation fitted *Black's Law Dictionary*'s definition of "plunder": "The forcible taking of private property by an invading or conquering army from the enemy's subjects."

"If I were to try to apply a portion of the measures I have used to step up the collection of taxes in the territories within the boundaries of the Green Line, they would hang me in Zion Square [in downtown Jerusalem]," confessed Mordechai Barekat, deputy head of the department of customs and excise.

The Beit Sahuris fought back with their only remaining weapon: world opinion. They issued a ringing public statement citing the principle of no taxation without representation: "Why do we not pay our taxes? First, the military authority does not represent us, and we did not invite them to come to our land. . . . Second, the collected taxes are used to increase the harsh measures against our people. Must we pay for the bullets that kill our children? Or for the growing number of prisons? Or for the expenses of the occupying army?"

The Arab states introduced a resolution in the United Nations Security Council condemning the siege of Beit Sahur. It was vetoed by the United States. Later, after the siege was lifted, South African Archbishop Desmond Tutu and other celebrities would come to call and pay tribute. But world opinion was not about to rescue little Beit Sahur.

When the Israelis finally pulled out they left a ghost town of empty stores and deserted businesses. Even worse was the fact that the campaign of civil disobedience failed to spread to the rest of the West Bank. "For us September 1989 was the turning point," recalled Rishmawi. "The local strategy was supposed to be part of a general structure. Then we discovered all of a sudden that nothing was happening. It was like opening your eyes and discovering you are in the middle of the sea. You thought you had a big ship underneath you and all of a sudden you didn't have anything.

"The first year of the intifada, the Israelis were in chaos. We were designing tactics, changing tactics. We were accumulating knowledge, experience, preparing ourselves for the great moment of civil disobedience. But something happened. We moved from action to reaction. Neighborhood organizations lost direction. The strategy of confrontation shifted from the masses to a limited confrontation with the young people. There was a lack of collective will."

Some blamed the Israelis, contending that the military's harsh strategy had worked in weakening the cohesion and leadership of the intifada. Others said the Beit Sahuris were naïve to expect other West Bank communities, none of which enjoyed their town's combination of social cohesiveness, affluence and commitment to nonviolence, to follow their lead and commit economic suicide. Still others saw something more sinister in the failure of the PLO to deliver on its promises of support. With the collapse of Beit Sahur the PLO reasserted its authority. Perhaps it had never really wanted an independent, authentic grassroots revolt.

As for the army, its crackdown was all short-term tactics, with no regard for the long-term price. It damaged most the middle-class, politically moderate Palestinians who were Israel's potential interlocutors, those with something at stake, not the kids and not the activists. But the army was like a home owner whose roof was on fire, lurching from tactic to tactic, desperately seeking to put out the spreading blaze before it consumed the entire house. No one thought much about long-term strategy, only about buckets of water. Beit Sahur was a threat not because of the money involved but because of the possibility that the tax strike could spread, that the intifada would gain momentum as a nonviolent resistance movement. So while Israel publicly bemoaned the perceived lack of a nonviolent, politically coherent, locally based leadership with which it could negotiate, it sought to punish those like Jad Isaac and Elias Rishmawi who fit the criteria.

The army could smother Jad Isaac but it could not crush him. Prison validated his credentials as an authentic local leader. After his time in Ketziot no one could accuse him of selling out to the Israelis even when he spoke of compromise and a two-state solution. And in a funny way prison helped moderate his own views. His activities brought him in contact with Israelis on the left whose views he respected. Some became his friends. Even his contacts with the army did not embitter him. He saw the soldiers for what they were—a mixed group of confused men, some sensitive and decent, others ruthless and crude. Above all, he saw their vulnerability. Even though he could not accept their fears, he began to understand them. The intifada had toughened yet also humanized him. He quit his tenured faculty post at Bethlehem University and opened his own think tank. "The intifada changed my whole life. It exposed me to a new world away from the ivory tower of the university. I think I'm more aware, more committed to my community. I tried not to surrender to the bitterness I felt in prison. But I learned a lot."

It was scant consolation for a town that saw not only its wealth destroyed but also its spirit disfigured. The intifada had captured Beit Sahur's imagination, demanded the town's participation, raised its expectations, then dashed them against the stone wall of the occupation. It had made promises it could not keep. But it had accomplished one thing. Although it could not deliver the future, it had permanently shattered the past. Nothing about the Palestinians of the territories—their work, their children, their relations with Israel and with each other, even their dreams—would ever be the same.

3. Buried Alive in the West Bank

The question is not: Who are the Palestinians?
The question is: Who are we?

—AMOS OZ, *The Slopes of Lebanon*

A few weeks before the intifada began Major General Amram Mitzna, one of Israel's most highly decorated combat veterans, got a premonition of the upheaval to come. It happened in Balata, a swollen Palestinian refugee camp on the outskirts of the West Bank city of Nablus that had been slipping out of the army's control for several months. A new generation of hardened young activists, many of whom had spent time in Israeli prisons, had deposed the camp's *mukhtar,* the traditional elder who had served as the Israeli-appointed arbiter of camp life. They formed roving bands of street fighters, ambushed Israeli patrols with stones, extracted tribute from local merchants and enforced their own brand of law and order. Balata had become, in effect, "liberated" Palestinian territory.

For months the army did nothing. But by November 1987, the Shin Bet internal security service was warning that what was happening in Balata could spread elsewhere. Mitzna, who was in charge of the West Bank, decided it was time to go in. He imposed a curfew on the entire camp of 14,000 Palestinians, confining everyone to their ramshackle shanties, then sent soldiers from house to house to round up hundreds of men and haul them to a local schoolyard. There they were ordered to sit and await interrogation.

Caught by surprise, Balata's residents at first were silent and submissive. But gradually they began to stir. Women ignored the curfew order, slipping out of their homes to search for their husbands and sons. When soldiers sought to block their path, they began to shriek wildly and resist. Some of the soldiers handled them roughly and a few even shot in the air. The men inside the yard heard the gunfire and feared their women were under attack.

Slowly, suddenly, spontaneously, as if they were rising from a long enforced slumber, several hundred men rose to their feet. They pressed against the young soldiers holding automatic weapons who surrounded them. "Let us go! Let us go!" some screamed. "Fuck you and fuck your mother's cunt! You're fucking cowards!" Some stripped off their shirts and thrust their bare chests against the soldiers' rifles. The soldiers, many of them experienced Druze Border Police who spoke the same colloquial Arabic as their prisoners, screamed back obscenities. Volumes and temperatures swiftly climbed; the smell of massacre was in the air. Shaken by what he was seeing, Mitzna was unsure whether he could control his own men for much longer, let alone the prisoners. He was not prepared to find out. He declared the operation over and ordered the captives released.

It was a sobering moment. After twenty years of military occupation, for the first time in anyone's memory the Israeli army had been confronted and had its will thwarted by a collective act of defiance by unarmed Palestinian civilians. It was a small retreat for an army not accustomed to backing down.

For Amram Mitzna, the incident at Balata raised difficult questions. The choice had been to shoot or run. He believed that he had made the right decision; a soldier who believed in ethical values could make no other. But he saw that the thin line demarcating tough, effective military conduct from immoral behavior was hard to find in the dark turbulence of a Balata riot. A commander in the midst of restoring order could easily miss it and inflict needless harm on Palestinian civilians, damaging the fragile relationship between Arabs and Jews and damaging his own soldiers as well.

Amram Mitzna's army was Israel's most cherished and esteemed institution, a citizen army that founding father David Ben-Gurion considered his young country's most notable achievement. The Israel Defense Forces had not only preserved the Jewish state from a multitude of enemies in a very dangerous part of the world, it had compelled both friend and foe to redefine what it meant to be a Jew. The pathetic, defenseless, easily slaughtered Jew of Eastern Europe's ghettos had disappeared from history; the Hebraic warrior, last seen in the days of the Maccabees, had returned.

It was a true people's army. Every Israeli Jewish male followed his three years of compulsory service with thirty or so years of annual reserve duty. Those who became officers did an extra year of active service and many stayed on in the permanent officer corps. "In a state where almost one out of every seven citizens is a soldier (either full-time or part-time), it is al-most impossible to distinguish between society and the military," wrote Reuven Gal, the army's former chief psychologist. "This is its greatest source of strength, but this is also its vulnerability."

Like many of Israel's key institutions—the giant Histadrut labor federa-tion and its network of public companies, the school system, the political parties, the kibbutz farm collectives—the army had predated the state. It began life in 1920 as the Haganah, the security force of the Histadrut. Dur-ing the 1936–39 Arab Revolt the Haganah's slogan was "Move out beyond the fence"—take the initiative and attack. No motto better summed up the military ethic that distinguished Zionism's New Jew. The Jews of the ghetto had never ever moved beyond the barrier that separated themselves from a hostile world; Ben-Gurion's Israelis knew no barriers and few limits be-yond those they chose to create for themselves.

The Haganah became the nucleus of the modern Israel Defense Forces, which was born officially twelve days after Israel declared its independence on May 14, 1948. The IDF gained its military reputation as one of the world's most dynamic armies by a series of successful wars beginning with the 1948 Independence War. But its political reputation was at least as im-portant. In a young and difficult society the army managed to develop and sustain an image as a true meritocracy and training ground, a melting pot where Israel's wildly varied cultures mixed and merged. Military service remained an essential rite of passage into the noisy, spirited national family. Those with proper discharge papers got cheaper mortgages and better jobs; those without them—including Israel's Arab minority—were suspect and stigmatized.

Image sometimes exceeded reality. The IDF was no better and no worse than the society it sprang from. It was dominated for years by the same Eastern European, Labor-oriented elite that ran the rest of Israel, and like that elite, it was chronically bureaucratic, arrogant, inefficient and disorga-nized. Western Ashkenazim dominated the special fighting units, while Eastern Sephardim, who were treated as second-class citizens and soldiers, often served as cooks, janitors and suppliers. But while other institutions came to symbolize the society's shortcomings, the army somehow always managed to embody the best that Israel had to offer—its creativity, re-sourcefulness, impulsiveness and intuitive optimism. It wielded an enor-mous influence over Israel's inner life. *Bitahon,* the Hebrew word for "military security," was not just a strategic concept but a national obses-sion. The army was Israel's backbone and its heart as well, the keeper of the keys to both the past and the future.

The Six-Day War was the high-water mark of the IDF's power and prestige. Yet no Israeli institution was more vexed by the vast changes that followed. An army that prided itself on embodying the national consensus and that saw itself as romantically standing astride Israel's borders was assigned the uncomfortable role of enforcing the occupation. The territories became a black hole for IDF officers: rising young stars on their way to generalships did their best to avoid serving there; those who could not duck the duty often ended up mired there for the rest of their careers. Accountability was minimal and corruption endemic in a world where Israelis were the masters and Palestinians the supplicants. Flare-ups of civil unrest were frequent, but they seldom posed a serious security challenge and rarely resonated across the Green Line into pre-1967 Israel.

Fearful that the IDF could deteriorate into an army of professional occupiers and lose sight of its real mission to defend the country from attack, Israel's commanders opted to shuttle regular and reserve units in and out of the territories rather than assign a permanent force there. Soldiers were not trained for occupation duty because they were not supposed to be occupiers. There was a presumption of temporariness about the occupation that dominated IDF doctrine even after two decades. And when the explosion finally came it caught most soldiers ill-equipped and unprepared.

There were only fifty-five men in the military reserve unit assigned to oversee Jabaliya, the refugee camp of more than 50,000 Palestinians that was the focal point of the opening riots. They lacked adequate supplies of shields, helmets and clubs, spare tires for their vehicles and tear-gas canister tubes. They were not trained in how to disperse a crowd or control a riot or enter someone's house to make an arrest. When they pleaded for reinforcements Yitzhak Mordechai, the military commander responsible for the Gaza Strip, told them to tough it out. Chief of Staff Dan Shomron was also slow to react. Afterward a reservist said he and his fellow soldiers felt like the last bluecoats at Fort Apache when the Indians went on the warpath.

Four days after the troubles began Defense Minister Yitzhak Rabin confirmed the government's ignorance and indifference by embarking on a week-long diplomatic mission to the United States. He went to Washington to work out the price for seventy F-16 fighter planes that Israel wanted to purchase, sign a memorandum of understanding on sales of Israeli-manufactured equipment to the U.S. Department of Defense and rub elbows with Washington's security elite. He was dealing with the world in which he and the IDF's senior commanders felt most at home—a tidy, reassuring world of geopolitical strategy and sophisticated weaponry in which Israel took its proper place at the right hand of a superpower.

But in Gaza and the West Bank, a very different world—darker, dirtier, primal and outraged—was bursting into the IDF's dreams.

Amram Mitzna embodied much of the IDF's brilliance, arrogance and élan. A veteran of three wars, he had been wounded four times in combat. He was a wiry man of medium height with a full head of black hair, slightly curling at the ends, a bushy Old Testament beard, crinkly eyes and a bright, infectious smile. He was the most photogenic of the IDF's senior commanders and certainly the easiest to pick out of a crowd. He was intelligent, logical, serious and analytical—a gifted, multidimensional warrior nearing the apex of a brilliant career.

To those who worked for him Mitzna was cold, remote and demanding. In the informal world of the IDF elite most generals were called by their first names; Mitzna was known only by his last. He gave out few favors and expected none. Yet his obvious efficiency and dedication inspired many of those who worked for him. "He had no friends in the army, but he had many followers," said a former staff member.

Mitzna was born in 1945 on Kibbutz Dovrat, a collective farm in the northern Galilee region that his German Jewish parents had helped to found. When he was a small child his parents left the kibbutz and eventually settled in the port city of Haifa. Mitzna was a problem student—a little too smart, a little too bored, far too restless. Looking for a disciplined environment to channel his energies, his parents sent him off to the Reali school, whose military boarding college produced many of Israel's finest officers. At age eighteen he followed his classmates into the army and into the tank corps. He rose through the ranks as a platoon commander, brigade commander, division commander and chief of operations.

On June 5, 1967, the first day of the Six-Day War, Mitzna was wounded three times while helping lead his tank battalion through the Sinai Desert. The first blow was a bullet that ripped cleanly through his left shoulder as he stood exposed in a tank turret. The second was a direct hit that riddled Mitzna's back with shrapnel and killed the battalion commander riding next to him in the turret. Bleeding, Mitzna led the tanks into an assembly area before his men pulled him from the turret. While awaiting treatment he was wounded again in an attack by Egyptian commandos.

Six years later during the Yom Kippur War, Mitzna's battalion led Israeli tanks across the Suez Canal in a daring midnight counterattack. There was a dense fog, and when it lifted slightly around 4 A.M. Mitzna and his men found themselves in the middle of an Egyptian army division headquarters. Suddenly three enemy tanks loomed in front of the column just twenty-five yards away. Mitzna's gunners beat two of the tanks to the draw and they burst into flames. But the third tank squeezed off a round that killed Mitzna's gunner and loader and threw him out of the turret. He could not move. After two weeks in the hospital and several operations Mitzna made a full recovery, except for a missing right kneecap and a road map of small scars on his back and legs.

Mitzna was not an overly modest man, but he saw no particular heroism in his wartime deeds. He judged himself by the same demanding criteria he used to judge his men. "To be a hero is to take a decision between options," he would say. "In these situations I had no real choice to make. And when there's no option there's no hero."

Despite his achievements and his decorations Mitzna never really considered himself a career soldier. The army demanded total loyalty and total immersion—it wanted body and soul. But Mitzna fought to keep his inner self private and independent. He infuriated some of his commanders and colleagues, who saw his aloofness as a statement of personal superiority. Mitzna, whose political antenna was discerning, would sometimes try to assuage these feelings, but he never really succeeded. He needed personal autonomy and he was willing to pay a certain price in unpopularity.

In 1982 he almost threw away his shiny military career to protest Ariel Sharon's conduct during the Lebanon war. Like many fellow commanders, Mitzna believed Sharon had been reckless and deceitful, and had misled the Israeli cabinet into approving a purportedly limited incursion into southern Lebanon in June that had turned into a full-fledged invasion. Sharon, he believed, had tarnished and abused the IDF. But Mitzna kept his mouth shut until the Sabra and Shatila massacres in September. He was listening to a Knesset debate on his car radio as Sharon sought to defend the army's lack of response during the massacres, which were carried out by Israel's Christian Lebanese allies. Sharon suggested that this was nothing new, that the IDF had sat by idly once before during the slaughter of Palestinians at the Tel Zatar refugee camp in Beirut seven years earlier.

This was too much for Mitzna, who wrote a letter that night asking to be relieved as commander of the Staff and Command College until Sharon was no longer defense minister. At the time Mitzna believed he would be forced to resign from the army. But after a private meeting with Menachem Begin in which the prime minister told him it was his duty to continue in his post, Mitzna withdrew his request. Some saw the resignation as a heroic moment—an act of moral bravery in the face of powerful evil. Others saw the recantation and wondered just how brave Amram Mitzna really was.

In May 1987 Mitzna, at the age of forty-two, became head of Israel's central command, one of the army's top ten posts. He was in charge of protecting Israel's heartland, including Tel Aviv and Jerusalem, but his troops also guarded the border with Jordan and oversaw the West Bank. Sharon, who had been forced out of the Defense Ministry after Sabra and Shatila but remained a cabinet minister, had sought unsuccessfully to block the appointment. Mitzna had a permanent foe in the cabinet, one who bided his time.

Gaza may have been a powder keg, but it was geographically compact and easy to seal off and it contained fewer than 2,000 Jewish settlers, all of them tucked into readily defendable enclaves. But the West Bank was a long, heterogeneous landmass with dozens of roads connecting it to central Israel. There were by 1987 at least 850,000 Palestinians of varying religious and political persuasions—Muslim fundamentalists in the south, Christians in Jerusalem and the Bethlehem area, rabid nationalists in Nablus and Jenin to the north—along with some 65,000 Jewish settlers. It was a volatile mix, hard to contain, harder to control.

Mitzna was not contemptuous of the Palestinians he ruled over. He understood that he was an occupier and he knew the Palestinians despised the occupation. He spoke no Arabic and met infrequently with Palestinian leaders. Yet he could understand their anger and their humiliation, and he believed it was important not to exacerbate either. Although circumstances might dictate harsh measures, he believed that those he governed should be allowed to maintain a modicum of dignity. He even upbraided his driver for rudely cutting off Arab motorists.

Mitzna was able to separate his analytical insights from what he perceived as practical necessity, and he felt compelled to do many things that he knew would cause harm. Once the intifada started, his first goal was to restore order. Sometimes that meant forcing merchants to open their shops in defiance of strike days, or closing schools and confining thousands of Palestinian schoolchildren to their homes. Sometimes Mitzna's men harassed and beat teachers who were caught "illegally" providing home-study lessons to their pupils in defiance of his order that all education cease. He was aware that such measures helped unite the Palestinian middle class behind the intifada, creating solidarity out of misery. Yet he was locked in a chess game of expectations and demands. He could not do nothing. He could neither surrender nor quit the battlefield. Action was required, even when it was counterproductive and self-defeating.

Along the way he had to adjust his freewheeling style. In the early days of the intifada he startled foreign journalists by admitting how little he cared for his assignment. While he issued the standard public denial that his men were engaged in widespread abuses, he was more candid when it came to assessing the damage and difficulties his soldiers faced. A soldier is combat-trained "not to ask too many questions but to open fire when he sees the enemy," Mitzna explained. "But here the situation is different. It is not conquer the hill and use all the means. You have to use your brain, you have to use your head on the one hand, and of course you have to use your hand on the other. You have to deal with civilians . . . not to see each of them as an enemy but only those who are acting against you." Such differentiations were "very very difficult," he acknowledged.

There were many times, Mitzna confessed, when "I don't feel so well when I wake up in the morning." The mission he and his soldiers had been given was "confusing from every point that you will look at it."

The days were long: Mitzna started work at 6 A.M. with the overnight reports of activity in the territories and often finished up after midnight. Weeks would pass when he was unable to return home to Kibbutz Ein Gev in northern Israel to visit with his wife, a school principal, and their three children. Instead they watched his image almost nightly on the 9 P.M. television news as he described the latest incident, gave the latest explanation of what the army had or had not done, offered the latest justification or expressed the latest regret. He became a small-scale media star in the West as well, appearing on CBS, NBC, BBC and Ted Koppel's *Nightline*. His voice became the voice of Israel—intelligent, tough yet humane—but it was curiously detached from the man himself. His own feelings were concealed beneath the public ritual.

He was prepared to use collective punishments: to impose curfews, sanction mass roundups, cut off electricity, prevent workers from going to their jobs and children from attending school. Yet there was a limit beyond which he would not go. He did not want to punish so severely that Palestinians would feel they had nothing more to lose. And he did not want to violate his own complex moral code.

Although many of his men worshiped Mitzna, some distrusted him. For them he was too slick, too media-conscious and too quick to find scapegoats among his own subordinates when the going got tough. Everyone thought they knew him and, this being Israel, everyone had a view. "Israelis placed on Mitzna's shoulders a burden of expectations too heavy to bear," wrote columnist Nachum Barnea. "A mythos was created around him and labels were coined: Mitzna the Leftist, Mitzna the Hesitant, Mitzna the Just, Mitzna the Hypocrite, Mitzna the Brute. The man became a symbol and the symbol served as a comfortable answer for hard questions, scary ones. . . ."

But Mitzna persuaded his men that time was on their side, that if the army kept up the pressure the Palestinians would run out of steam. "Look, you come here for three weeks or a month, then you leave," he told impatient reservists outside the Dehaishe refugee camp one day. "Think about the people who live here in the camp all the time. They can't go away. The people of Dehaishe cannot go on and on and on. They can go one month, a year, two years. But they must have some outcome, some benefits, concrete results."

That was the view from the top of the army command. From the bottom, however, things often looked different—more painful and more humiliating. In the early weeks of the intifada soldiers felt trapped when confronted by stone-throwing youths. They had no training in riot control and no feel for the streets of the cities and villages they patrolled or for the people who confronted them. At first they had but two choices—they could stand and take it, or they could open fire, claiming later that their lives had been in danger. But then another option appeared, one that seemed far more satisfying than doing nothing and less lethal than shooting, yet one that in the end would prove more searing and destructive to both sides.

The Arab village of Hawara, just south of Nablus, was wrapped in a chilly darkness on the evening of January 21, 1988, as a busload of Israeli soldiers accompanied by two jeeps pulled into town. The major in charge handed a list of twelve young male suspects to the village *mukhtar,* who quickly gathered them together. Soldiers tied the young men's hands behind their backs and steered them onto the bus. They were driven to a small olive tree orchard at the edge of the village where the soldiers hauled them out in groups of three. The soldiers laid them facedown on the ground, shackled their legs and stuffed flannel cloths into their mouths. While the bus driver revved his engine to drown out the noise, the soldiers carried out their orders.

One by one they whacked away with wooden clubs at the arms and legs of the young men. It was systematic and tedious work. Many of the clubs splintered. Some of the bones did not break right away. The soldiers carefully avoided hitting the men on the head or chest. When they got to the twelfth man the soldiers broke his arms but not his legs so that he could stumble back to the village and fetch help for the others moaning helplessly on the orchard's cold floor. "Most of them stopped screaming after fifteen to twenty seconds," one of the soldiers, Lieutenant Omri Kochva, testified later. "Their legs didn't jerk any longer. . . ."

The scene on the edge of Hawara was replayed with many variations throughout the occupied territories during the first weeks of 1988. Under orders from Defense Minister Rabin, Chief of Staff Lieutenant General Dan Shomron and Mitzna himself, the IDF embarked on a widescale campaign to inflict physical punishment on Palestinians purported to be involved in the intifada. The written orders specified that the beatings should be used only to subdue those engaged in acts of rioting. But the resulting actions, as in Hawara, were often very different.

Like almost everything the army did during those early months of the uprising, the policy backfired—it inflamed rather than subdued the Arab population, it blackened Israel's public image, and it caused an enormous crisis of confidence and conscience within the soldiers themselves, who were neither equipped nor trained to carry out such extraordinary orders. Some reacted with horror, refusing to participate or, in a few cases, even preventing their comrades from doing so. But there were others who seemed to relish the chance to settle scores with Palestinians and whose enthusiasm for the new orders frightened and disturbed their own commanders, Mitzna included.

The beatings were not an isolated tactic but part of a broad policy of attrition designed to get tough with the civilian population and smother the uprising. In the first eighteen months of the intifada—the period in which Mitzna served as overall commander in charge of the West Bank—the army shot dead more than 400 people and wounded by gunfire more than 5,000 others in the West Bank and Gaza. It arrested more than 30,000 people, holding 12,000 of them without charge or trial; it expelled 50 people, demolished 150 houses and imposed 1,600 curfews. It harassed people randomly, forced shopkeepers to open their stores during strike days and close them down on non-strike days. It cut off telephones and electricity and prevented farmers from harvesting their crops or sending produce to market. All of this was designed to convince Palestinians that there was a high price to pay for their revolt and to persuade them to return to the sullen but relatively tranquil status quo of the days before December 9, 1987.

The beatings policy was born of desperation. The prisons were full, the military justice system was in a state of collapse, and scenes of heavily armed Israeli troops opening fire on young stone throwers were playing throughout the world like a videotaped nightmare. Rabin and the top commanders, including Mitzna, saw it was not working. Rabin, the old general, was especially angered to hear from soldiers that they felt frustrated and vulnerable when confronted with the young, mobile stone throwers who played an endless game of cat and mouse. The general staff decided to deploy larger numbers of troops, put trouble spots under curfew and distribute "cold weapons"—wood and fiberglass clubs—to soldiers to disperse rioters and inflict an immediate penalty of pain on those they caught up with.

Rabin, as usual, was the front man who articulated the reasons for the policy with a brutal candor he would come to regret. In a number of appearances in Gaza and the West Bank he told soldiers to use "force, power and blows" against demonstrators. To the commanders he briefed in the field, he spoke of the need to inflict pain. Later he would insist that he had never

used the term "break their bones" and that he had always meant that force
should be used only to subdue rioters while they were being pursued or
were resisting arrest, that it should never be used as punishment or used after a suspect had stopped resisting.

But many commanders understandably did not hear it that way, and neither did their men. They understood that, with the prisons full and young
Palestinians running amok, it was up to them to mete out punishment, that
a stone thrower with a broken hand or arm or leg would be out of action for
at least four weeks. The policy became an oral order, and the order was simple: "Break their bones."

"What did you imagine would happen?" a soldier asked Rabin and
Shomron on a visit to Nablus after a number of men in his unit were ar-
rested for beating someone already in custody. "You gave us the clubs.
What did you think we'd do with them?"

In meetings with his commanders and in the written orders he distributed, Mitzna tried to make clear that physical force could be used only during an active riot, not as summary punishment afterward. Still, some of his
public utterances were as provocative as Rabin's. Palestinians "will have to
understand that they can't get up at 9 or 10 A.M. and make stone throwing
and tire burning their national sport and expect no consequences," Mitzna
told reporters.

For a time Mitzna insisted that cases of abuse were exceptional. But evidence to the contrary accumulated until it was impossible to deny. In the
West Bank city of Ramallah, Mitzna's soldiers beat merchants who did not
open their shops fast enough when ordered to do so. They dragged some
Palestinians to a vacant lot behind a pastry shop off the main square and
clubbed them with lead pipes and wooden sticks. They took others to a bus
parked nearby, beat them in the narrow aisles and carried them out on
stretchers. In Nablus young Palestinians were taken to the third floor of an
observation post near the casbah and given what the local commander,
Colonel Yehuda Meir, called "a short treatment." Two dovish members of
the Knesset counted 197 people with broken bones one day in Gaza City,
including men in their sixties and seventies.

A team of American medical experts representing Physicians for Human
Rights, three from Harvard Medical School and one from the City University of New York, who had roamed the territories for a week in February
1988 described "an unrestrained epidemic of violence by the army and police." Their conservative estimate was that 7,000 Palestinians had been
beaten. Many suffered midshaft hand and arm fractures that appeared premeditated, systematic and assembly-line in style—not the kinds of blows
inflicted during confrontations. "The word 'beatings' simply doesn't con-

vey the medical magnitude of what's been happening," said group leader H. Jack Geiger, professor of community medicine at CUNY. By the end of that first year, estimates for the number of beating injuries ran as high as 20,000.

Eventually Israel's legal establishment intervened. Even Attorney General Yosef Harish, who had a well-deserved reputation for official subservience, issued a letter in February ordering Rabin to prohibit explicitly the use of physical force for any purpose except dispersing riots or making arrests. Citing "numerous complaints of cruel treatment to the inhabitants," Harish wrote that the number of cases of abuse was so high that Rabin's claim that such acts were "irregular deeds no longer properly reflects reality." He warned that property damage was also "strictly forbidden."

But the gap between formal orders and day-to-day reality remained vast. Yoki Amir, a philosophy professor at Hebrew University and a reserve army captain, said that before entering Gaza for a month of duty his unit got lectures from the army's legal department about how to conduct themselves. Officers gathered for a therapy session on how to cope with the dilemmas of policing Gaza. These sessions were designed to ensure that the unit behaved according to the rules. But once they arrived in Gaza, Amir recalled, different rules applied. "From the local officers you got the clear impression you were expected to beat people. It was never written down. But we as officers got a very very clear message, and our soldiers knew it from reading the newspapers, from talking to friends. We all knew what was happening."

What was happening to the army was an explosion of rage. Soldiers were angry at Palestinians for defying and humiliating them and flaunting the intifada in their faces. They were not just soldiers; after all, they were Israeli citizens, and they saw the uprising as a direct challenge to their own society. They were also angry at their own commanders for putting them in the untenable position of doing riot police duty in a bleak, surreal wasteland for which they had no training and no preparation. Like the young Palestinians themselves, the soldiers were lashing out. And when the two groups of young people clashed, it was like rival street gangs fighting over primordial national turf. The fact that one side was an army, that it wore uniforms and was supposedly well-disciplined, made little difference. The ragtag gangs of Palestinian teenagers in effect won a major victory—they had brought Israel's most hallowed institution down to street level.

"It was as though all the traditional roles had been switched," wrote analysts Zeev Schiff and Ehud Yaari. "An army that prided itself on taking the initiative, dictating the moves, and besting the enemy through flexibility and speed was reduced to reacting to such petty provocations as bottles, stones, and the taunts of children. Having lost control of the territories, it was beginning to lose its own composure."

This was not what Mitzna and his commanders had bargained for, and it deeply troubled some of them—less because of the damage inflicted upon wounded Palestinians than because of the psychological injuries to their own men. Many of the best soldiers, the ones known for their initiative and creative thinking in training exercises and actual combat, tended to shy away from involvement in the beatings, while others came to the fore. "You had the feeling that the weakest, most negative elements within the army were taking the initiative," said Yoki Amir. "The people who tended to do the most beating were the cooks, the drivers and the worst officers."

The damage spread from individual soldiers to entire units. The unit was the stable, sacred heart of the IDF's combat structure. Those who went through basic training together as teenagers often stayed together for their entire military careers. They knew one another intimately—personal interests, talents and political views. Relationships often extended into civilian life—a reservist who needed a hard-to-come-by new phone line would approach his buddy from the unit whose brother-in-law worked for the phone company. And every unit had a hierarchy. Some members excelled while others were deemed unskilled or unreliable.

But the intifada overturned the old order. The most effective members of a unit were often those who spoke Arabic or those most prepared to be brutal to civilians. They became the new leaders—and the cause of much friction within the units. Confrontations arose between soldiers who seemed to enjoy intimidating Arabs and those who did not. When the unit was returned to combat duty, the hierarchy was supposed to flip again. But sometimes it was not that simple. Doubts and bad feelings lingered. The commanders could remove a unit from the West Bank, but they could not always remove the West Bank from the unit.

The Yom Kippur and Lebanon wars had hurt the army, but the damage had been mostly external—a conflict between the army and the civilian leadership. The intifada caused a different kind of internal damage because the orders were vague, the mission was complex and ill-defined, and the commanders often were perceived to have abandoned their men. The tension between the orders and reality led many in the lower ranks to shave the truth, to tell the commanders what they wanted to hear and skip the messy or illegal parts. It was a bad habit, especially for an army in a combat situation where those who do the planning and strategizing must have precise, accurate information about what is happening in the field.

The intifada was like gangrene, eating away at the IDF's moral core.

When Hani Elshami, a forty-two-year-old Palestinian resident of Jabaliya, died from a severe beating, a military court-martial could not determine whether the fatal blows had been struck by the four soldiers accused of beating him inside his house or by the fifteen to twenty others who had punched and kicked him after he was taken to a detention center. The four soldiers had beaten Elshami, who purportedly was protecting his teenaged son from arrest, with rifle butts and a broomstick and admitted jumping on his chest from a bed after they wrestled him to the floor. After Elshami's limp body was dumped at the prison camp, Sergeant Ayal Yehudah testified that he and several officers watched other soldiers beat Elshami but made no attempt to stop it. "I didn't care if they play with Arabs," Yehudah told the court-martial. "I kept peeling potatoes, I won't cry about it—it seemed natural that Jews will have a good time with Arabs. The Arabs brought for holding must have done something."

Mitzna wanted to believe that the stories he read in the press about excessive beatings were distortions. At first he spent little time checking them out. His first priority, after all, was to suppress the intifada. He knew very well that an aggressive internal investigation of military behavior would only further damage the already shaky morale of his troubled troops and make his mission even harder. But eventually he found he had no choice.

In mid-February he received a report that three soldiers had used an army bulldozer to bury alive four young Palestinians accused of stone throwing outside the West Bank village of Salem. An army sergeant had forced the four at gunpoint to clear rocks from the main road leading into the village, then ordered them to lie down while the bulldozer dumped a full load of earth on top of them. Arab witnesses said the sergeant then ordered the bulldozer to run over the mound, but the driver refused. After the soldiers left, the four were pulled out alive by friends.

Mitzna was certain the story was a lie. He ordered a quick investigation—and was stunned when military police reported back that the incident had indeed occurred. "Even in my worst dreams I would never imagine such a thing," he confessed, as he announced the arrest of two of the soldiers. "I warn the commanders all the time to expect the worst possible things when soldiers in certain places find themselves in control deciding about the lives of civilians. It's difficult to think of such a thing, but we should have thought."

The incident became a metaphor for the army itself. The soldiers had buried Palestinians, but it was the IDF's reputation that was truly buried alive in the West Bank.

There were more shocks to come. Two weeks later CBS News broadcast several minutes of footage of four soldiers on a hillside in Nablus battering two supine Palestinian young men. The men had been part of a group that had thrown rocks at the soldiers, who then charged up the hill and ran down the two. While CBS cameraman Moshe Alpert filmed from the road below using a telescopic lens, the soldiers hit, kicked, beat and hacked away with rocks at the heads, arms and legs of the two young men. It was the most graphic footage of the entire intifada and CBS bureau chief Bob Simon phoned Mitzna to get his response. Mitzna was shocked by what he saw— these men were paratroopers and kibbutzniks, members of the IDF's combat elite; they were pure-bred Israelis like himself. Mitzna phoned back almost immediately to offer Simon a seat on his helicopter. Together they flew up to Nablus, where Mitzna released the two Palestinians from jail and ordered the arrest of the four soldiers. Three were arrested immediately; the fourth, Saguy Harpaz, who had gone home to Kibbutz Gesher for the weekend, was hauled out of the public dining room by military police during the Shabbat evening meal in front of his family and neighbors.

That same evening Mitzna appeared live on the Friday night news program to condemn the beating and warn soldiers that anyone who engaged in such actions would be punished. He knew he would be criticized for taking to the airwaves—some Israeli politicians accused him of kissing the asses of the foreign press; one called him "the champion of blah blah blah"—but he felt it was necessary to let his troops know there was a red line of behavior they would not be allowed to cross. To hammer it home Mitzna summoned all of his officers above the rank of captain the following Sunday and made them watch the entire forty-five-minute tape. "We were shocked and couldn't say a word after we saw this film," he said afterward.

The soldiers themselves were harder to shock. "Okay, so we hurt them a little bit," Harpaz later told an interviewer. "They mouthed off. You're tired. It's not that you're particularly in a frenzy and you want to hit people. You don't want to hit them and you don't want them to hit you. You're helpless. If it'd been up to me I'd have shot him in the leg and that would be it." The forty-five-minute beating he and his comrades administered that day was far from unusual, Harpaz claimed. "It was a norm. That's the way it was. Everyday."

Eventually there was a legal reckoning for a small fraction of what had happened. In the cases of Hani Elshami and Iyad Akal, a teenager beaten to death in Gaza, officers and soldiers of the elite Givati brigade were arrested and court-martialed. In each case the defendants sought to turn their day in court into a trial of the army itself. Colonel Emmanuel Gross, the judge in one case, expressed astonishment to hear from witnesses "expressions of hatred and contempt for the value of another person's life." Such shameful behavior, Gross concluded, was "the outcome of a disregard for norms which was apparently legitimate and even encouraged by commanders and unfortunately senior officers as well." The IDF, he said, "must have the courage to look at itself in the mirror."

The West Bank, too, had its share of legal controversies and, in the end, Mitzna himself did not emerge unscathed. For every incident involving the bulldozer or CBS footage, there were others that took place off-camera and out of sight that Mitzna chose not to pursue. The beatings at Hawara, for example, were one of several incidents that occurred in mid-January that had been ordered and sanctioned by Yehuda Meir, the local Nablus area commander. Rumors and eyewitness accounts appeared in the local press but nothing happened until the International Red Cross made a formal complaint to army headquarters. Even then the army chose not to prosecute; Meir was reprimanded and forced to retire but allowed to keep his officer's rank and pension. He understood that his superiors did not wish to pursue the matter because they knew that he had acted under orders that were purposely ambiguous and because they realized that a trial could be an embarrassment to them as well as him. The matter would have died there, but the Association for Civil Rights in Israel decided to appeal to the Israeli Supreme Court. It ruled that Meir must stand trial. He, too, sought to put the army in the dock beside him.

Testimony revealed that a few days before the incident at Hawara, Rabin had traveled to Nablus accompanied by Shomron and Mitzna. Meir and other officers testified that Rabin told them, "You must catch them and break their arms and legs. . . . Go in and break their bones." When Meir expressed reservations about how such activities would look in the press, he said Rabin had replied, "You do the work, I'll take care of the media."

Meir conceded that he had given his men an illegal order but insisted that it had been approved by his superiors. Other middle-level officers corroborated his testimony. But Mitzna and Meir's other superiors denied it, and produced written orders and documents emphasizing that the use of force must be restricted to pursuit and arrest. The judge believed them, not Meir, who got a suspended sentence and was busted down to private. He was the most senior officer to be found guilty of illegal behavior during the intifada.

After it was over Meir felt betrayed by both Rabin and Mitzna. He still insisted that they had ordered and sanctioned the use of beatings as punishment but had kept a margin of deniability for themselves that the men in the field, the ones who did the dirty work, could not claim. When it came to beatings, Meir said, Mitzna was guilty of moral double bookkeeping. "Mitzna always wanted to stay clean," Meir told Ariela Ringle-Hoffman of the newspaper *Yediot Ahronot*. "When it came time to stand up for his soldiers, he would get cold feet. He sold his soldiers dirt-cheap. He knew exactly what was going on . . . but at the trial he forgot everything."

Looking back after the trial Meir argued that the beatings policy was justifiable and effective. "Everyone knew that we did what had to be done," he said. "I honestly believed that you must punish these people, because this was war, a militant confrontation . . . and we had to defend ourselves and to maintain order. That's what we were there for—to do the dirty work."

Was the IDF exceptionally brutal in putting down the intifada? By the standards of war, the answer must be no. The Israeli army twisted itself in knots to avoid doing what armies do naturally—kill people. It resisted the temptation to follow the advice of right-wing politicians and members within its own ranks to apply a wartime solution—put tanks in the streets of Nablus, raze the city centers, expel thousands and open fire on every stone thrower.

Still, many Palestinians died unnecessarily. By the standards that police use in dealing with civilians, the IDF was unusually violent. For the first eighteen months of the intifada, undertrained, undermanned, underequipped soldiers killed a Palestinian a day. By contrast, the highly trained riot police of South Korea, faced with a steady barrage of firebombs and brutal attacks, killed a total of one person during a year of constant unrest in the mid-1980s. IDF commanders went on an endless search for the perfect weapon. For a while they tried a gravel thrower, then water hoses, then so-called plastic bullets. These were supposedly nonlethal, yet by the IDF's own count they killed forty-seven Palestinians over a five-month period.

Other riot-control weapons also proved lethal in IDF hands. Tear gas was designed to scatter menacing crowds and disperse a threat before it could turn violent. The American-made canisters displayed printed warnings in English against using the gas in enclosed areas. Yet soldiers in hundreds of incidents fired tear-gas shells into houses, courtyards, classrooms, prison cells and even hospitals. Massive quantities of the gas—the IDF never disclosed figures on its use—were dumped into Jabaliya and other refugee camps. Its abuse became so routinized that the American manufacturer of the gas was forced by a publicity campaign in the United States to stop selling to Israel (the army found other suppliers). The impact of tear gas was strongest on the most vulnerable members of the population—small children and the elderly. Reliable figures were impossible to come by; Palestinians claimed every suspicious death or miscarriage was tear-gas-related while the army steadfastly denied that anyone had died from the gas. But there was no question that several dozen of the very young and very old died from exposure to gas improperly fired by soldiers.

The orders for opening fire also grew looser and looser as time went on.

First Rabin ordered that all firebomb throwers should be shot at, then all masked people, then all stone throwers who fled rather than obeyed orders to halt, then all people visibly carrying a weapon. The orders themselves were absurdly complex: soldiers were required to first shout a warning, then shoot in the air and only then fire at the legs. The rules were seldom obeyed—and the soldiers learned to lie about it to one another and to their commanders. It was all right, they told themselves, because any other army, faced with similar provocation, would have indulged in a bloodbath. Yet five years after the intifada began, the army was still killing Palestinians, many of them children, because it steadfastly refused to lower itself by becoming an occupation police force and by training for riot duty.

Reuven Gal, the retired chief army psychologist, said the IDF had tried to cope with the intifada in a "no tea, no coffee" manner: "On the one hand it was not very effective, and on the other hand it was not too brutal or too immoral. But in the end, we came out as both ineffective and immoral at the same time."

The impact on Palestinians of the army's campaign was in many ways counterproductive: it reinforced their growing sense of grievance and solidarity, and helped destroy the status quo that they themselves were rebelling against. But its impact on its own soldiers was in many ways equally devastating.

Throughout its history the IDF's institutional personality has been shaped by the wars it has fought. The 1948 generation of Yitzhak Rabin that dominated the army for two decades was forged in the desperate days of the Independence War. It was succeeded by the 1967 generation of Amram Mitzna that triumphed in the Six-Day War, absorbed a brutal blow at the opening of the Yom Kippur War, then recovered and clawed its way to victory. Each war created its own glory and its own myths of heroism and resourcefulness. The intifada brought forth its own new generation of officers and conscripts who spent more time chasing children through the streets of the West Bank than defending Israel's borders. Some came away embittered, others merely disappointed. But the intifada touched them all, challenging their view of their mission and themselves. And unlike other wars, the intifada produced no myths of heroism, only a reality of painful ambiguity.

Like many young Israelis, Omer Rasner was eager to serve in an elite fighting unit. Rasner was slim, wiry and athletic, with short-cropped brown hair, olive skin and small, jug-shaped ears. He was incurably optimistic; he believed every situation had a handle that could be found and grasped, and he would recall his time in the army serving in the occupied territories less with anger than with a certain grim bemusement. His father, who was a plastic surgeon, had been a paratrooper; his mother was a career army officer. They lived in Herzliya, a comfortable suburb north of Tel Aviv. All of Rasner's friends had sought to join elite combat units. Poor eyesight disqualified him from the air force, but he was accepted by the paratroopers. It was a unit with a glorious combat tradition and Rasner felt at home from the first days of basic training in November 1987. Even the barracks tent where he slept had a familiar scent. But the mission did not.

Rasner's unit was serving in Yehuda Meir's jurisdiction when the beatings order came down. "We were told there was no room for arrested people. So you don't arrest, you just hit, but if someone needs medical care afterward you must take him in. It was like a contest—who could bring in the most broken clubs. Now I'm not a guy who does things like that. I don't hit old women. But there was a woman, sixty or seventy years old. We took her son and she came at us with a concrete block. I shoved her with my club and my hand and someone else hit her with his club because she kept coming. A few weeks earlier an officer had been hit and seriously hurt in the same situation. You have to do it and it bothers you.

"When I caught someone I'd stop beating when they stopped resisting. But if I'd been chasing someone for four hours, when I got up to him, he would turn around and sit and throw up his hands. This guy got a club—one big, good, hopefully dry blow. Just to keep myself sane.

"When I'd come home on leave my parents asked a lot of questions about what we were doing, what they saw on TV. I wanted to make them feel worse. They didn't understand how their little child could become a beast."

Army psychologists insisted that most soldiers came through the intifada little damaged. But Gal, the chief psychologist who retired from the army and opened a research center on army behavior, saw a very different pattern. Most of the men were fine as long as they remained in their own army unit, which provided the bonds of camaraderie, trust and admiring support to protect them from the outside world. But when a soldier left the unit and returned to civilian life, those bonds broke down and some men began to fall apart. "It's when he finishes the army and comes back home without his comrades that you begin to see the problems: psychological breakdowns, depression, melancholia, daydreaming, lack of concentration," said Gal. "And because it happens not when the man is actually serving but later after he leaves the army, the IDF doesn't know about it. There are no statistics, no ways of measuring. But we see it all the time."

A soldier named Danny described his recurring nightmare to Gal after serving in Gaza. He is a Nazi dressed in uniform, yet also a Jew. His unit raids the house of a Jewish family. Danny tries repeatedly to make eye contact with the family, to let them know it is all right, that he is really one of them and they do not have to be afraid. But he does not succeed. He is trapped in a uniform and an identity he despises. Army psychologists confirmed that the dream of breaking into a sleeping family's house was one that most often disturbed soldiers during the intifada.

Faced with the psychic pain of waging war against civilians, many soldiers simply went numb. One of Mitzna's top reserve commanders was a lieutenant colonel in his early thirties named Nimrod. His father had been a brigade commander during the Six-Day War and was the first senior Israeli officer to enter Ramallah. Nimrod spent long stretches of reserve duty in the same city during the intifada, and he feared that twenty years hence his two-year-old son would also be there. Nimrod said he felt trapped in an unreal world of stone throwing and shooting. At one point during his reserve duty he shot in the leg a young Palestinian who was leading a mob. "I felt nothing, nothing at all; it was all a game," Nimrod recalled, amazed at his own indifference.

When you are numb anything becomes possible. An air force colonel, temporarily assigned to Ramallah, described to Abraham Rabinovich of the *Jerusalem Post* how he felt about conducting house-to-house searches. The first night, he recalled, soldiers threw property around and arrested a teenaged boy whose mother burst out crying. "I felt terrible. How could I participate in something like this? The next night we did the same thing. This time I said to myself, 'Well, what do you expect?' . . . The third night it was already routine and when the woman starts to cry you say, 'Oh God, is that wailing beginning again?' The fourth night you're shouting at the woman, '*Uskut!* Shut up!' I felt us hardening from day to day."

Ido Sela's 1993 documentary film, entitled *Testimonies,* presents a series of interviews with soldiers who speak of the pain and the dilemmas of serving in the intifada. Matti Ben Tsur, a deputy tank battalion commander, recalls an incident in the Tulkarm refugee camp when he and his men shot round after round of tear-gas canisters into a house where suspected rioters had fled. A man came out, says Ben Tsur, "with a two-year-old girl dying of suffocation. At that second it stopped being a game of cops and robbers and I understood. I started swearing at the father. 'Why didn't you open up?' I wanted to die."

Sela's interviewer asks Ben Tsur why he had not apologized later to the family. "They have to ask my forgiveness too," Ben Tsur replies. "For the fact that they led me into this situation. They didn't open up."

The IDF was unprepared and unwilling to recognize much of what was happening within its own ranks. It did not want an "intifada generation" of soldiers, so it often did its best to ignore the impact of the uprising internally. "Morale, motivation, all kinds of measures remained high or grew higher," insisted Colonel Moshe Even-Chen, the army's chief mental health officer. "Yes, it took us a year to get ourselves together as an army and define what is allowed and where are the borders. The restrictions we put on ourselves made it difficult to adjust, but in my opinion it demonstrated our strength of character."

Omer Rasner did not want to be in Nablus. But he was young and resilient and determined to see it through. One of his teachers once told him that in every person there was a small switch to turn on in case of war. "When you go out to the territories, don't forget to turn it on," he told Rasner. "And when you come back again, don't forget to turn it off." It was not always so easy. Sometimes when strolling through Tel Aviv Rasner found himself scanning the rooftops, looking for snipers and rock throwers as if he were still in Balata. The intifada was a memory he could not erase and could hardly explain.

"In Nablus there's no name for it. You can't define it. If you haven't been there then you'll never get it. The smells, the look in the eyes, the hatred. There was so much hatred. I felt I'm just a nice guy, so why do they hate me?

"Listen, every time there was a funeral of someone shot by the army, the city would explode. After a while people would come digging up bodies from the cemetery just to hold more funerals. So it was decided that we had to put a stop to this. We ended up lying all night in the cemetery between the stones waiting for these guys. They never came. And that's me lying between tombstones all night long waiting for ghosts. It was truly fucking crazy."

Palestinians were not the only problem that Mitzna and the IDF commanders faced in those first months of the intifada. Israel's right wing—both the Jewish settlers living in the occupied territories and their political allies in the cabinet and the Knesset—was a constant source of friction, pressure and opposition. It demanded that the army produce a military solution to a problem whose roots and essence were political.

Mitzna and his boss, Chief of Staff Shomron, early on had staked out a principled position, telling Shamir in the first days of the rioting that the army would not engage in a "reign of terror" to restore order. Mitzna refused demands that he dispatch tanks to Nablus and level entire neighborhoods. Firearms could be used only in self-defense, he and Shomron told the prime minister, and soldiers would not shoot at stone throwers because the physical risk was not grave enough to justify opening fire. The only viable strategy was to keep the lid on by suppressing large demonstrations and applying economic pressure on the population. "The more violent we get, the more we do not distinguish between the guilty and the innocent, the more the violence on the other side will increase," Mitzna explained. "We'll get into a vicious cycle that we'll never be able to get out of."

This was not what Shamir wanted to hear, but he acceded. His right-wing colleagues, however, did not possess his patience. Within a few months Sharon, with his score to settle with Mitzna, was leading the cabinet hard-liners in attacking the generals, saying they were too soft and "unimaginative" in dealing with the intifada. Yehoshua Saguy, a Likud Knesset member who had once been chief of army intelligence, dressed down Shomron at a committee hearing, claiming that by the army's refusal to use more brutal tactics, "you created the intifada with your own hands."

Shomron was an indecisive, ambivalent figure, but on this point he stood firm. He informed Saguy's committee that "there is no such thing as eradicating the intifada because in its essence it expresses the struggle of nationalism." He told the cabinet: "If anyone wishes to achieve this objective at the expense of issuing a directive to the IDF to violate the country's laws . . . if that's the price, it'll have to be without me."

Shamir, Sharon and the right-wing political establishment they represented were resistant to the army's cries of pain. They had many scapegoats for the intifada: "terrorists," Arabs in general, the press, the commanders, but never themselves. They simply pressed Mitzna to do more and do it more effectively. They wanted results, not angst. This was the mission, so do it. Give us "operational proposals," not lectures, Saguy shouted at Shomron.

Mitzna and the other commanders chafed, but they did not rebel. Before the November 1988 election Mitzna told himself and his men that their job was to keep the lid on until the Israeli electorate could decide at the ballot box what kind of government and what kind of peace plan it wanted. After the election produced a government as internally divided and indecisive as the previous one, he carried on, pleading with Rabin to come up with something to take the army off the hook and make its job easier. Rabin, himself a former army chief of staff, understood and shared Mitzna's frustrations. But by himself he could do little in a cabinet where the prime minister was afraid of taking on or alienating his own powerful right wing. "Everything here is a political minefield," Mitzna privately complained.

Lacking a political channel, the army's anger and humiliation turned inward. The show trials of those accused of illegal beatings aggravated splits inside the ranks and widened the gap between the commanders at the top, whose hands and orders were clean, and the men who did the deeds. But although the politicians would not respond, gradually the army's disenchantment began seeping through to the society at large. Reservists came back with horror stories of their time in the territories. Whole units published letters and protests. Some soldiers turned to the left, while others veered right. But there was broad agreement that the occupied areas—the refugee camps, the cities, the villages—were alien territory. "It wasn't that we decided we should give it back," said Micha Odenheimer, a journalist and rabbinical scholar, recalling his reserve duty in Ramallah. "It's that sitting up there on the roof, watching what was going on, it was clear that it wasn't ours to give back in the first place. It belonged to someone else—they controlled it, not us."

The other broad agreement was that something needed to be done. Some soldiers endorsed the idea of surrendering much of the territory and even allowing an independent Palestinian state. Others embraced "transfer"—a euphemism for the forced eviction of the Palestinian population from the territories, a concept championed by Rabbi Meir Kahane and supported, according to various polls, by somewhere between 25 and 40 percent of Israeli Jews.

Either way the common denominator was change. At first Avraham Burg, who helped run the Labor Party's election campaign in 1988, was puzzled that private polls commissioned by the party showed sizable majorities in favor of Israel's attending an international peace conference and negotiating with the PLO, and similar levels of support for cracking down harder on the intifada and expelling the Arabs. It made no sense for both the far left and far right positions to be gaining popularity. But Burg quickly recognized what the two extremes had in common: "Israelis felt they were in the middle of Catch-22, and anyone who offered a way out, they'll try it."

It was not necessarily a matter of morality. For every Amram Mitzna who agonized over the mission, there was a Yehuda Meir who believed force was the only way and who was prepared to take young men bound and gagged to an open field and break their bones. But it was a question of pragmatic solutions. "Ultimately the intifada made soldiers less tolerant of extremes and fantasies and more interested in practical dispositions," Mitzna insisted. "They've seen that nothing was like you thought it was when you were sitting at home."

As it grew in size, momentum and intensity, the intifada became a test of strength, will and character that Mitzna and his soldiers could neither overcome nor evade. Mitzna himself believed he and his men did the best they could with a mission impossible. In general, his men had behaved better than any army could be expected to. Israel could look at itself in the mirror because the IDF had stood the test.

Mitzna shed much of the introspection he had displayed in the early days of the intifada and many of his illusions as well. He no longer spoke about returning the situation to the relative tranquility of pre-uprising days, but pursued the more realistic goal of holding down the violence and keeping the main roads open. While he once had argued that the majority of Palestinians desired tranquility, he now understood that many, if not most, had been swept up in the spirit of civil revolt. It was the army's task to puncture their elation, to bring them back to reality.

Mitzna's goals were modest, befitting a military commander treading cautiously in a civilian battlefield. But there was another group of Israelis for whom the West Bank was not a field of operations but a home. These Jewish settlers had a much different attitude toward the intifada, and as the violence escalated they, too, began to join in. Their anger and their recklessness presented Mitzna with his most painful dilemma—and eventually helped force him from his post.

4. Souls on Fire

*Once it took hold, there seemed no halting the piti-
less spread of violence. . . . It seemed as if events
had escaped all human control; often, in Algeria,
the essential tragedy was heightened by the feeling
that—with a little more magnanimity, a little more
trust, moderation and compassion—the worst
might have been avoided.*

—ALISTAIR HORNE, *A Savage War of Peace*

Bʏ the spring of 1988 a blood fever was rampaging throughout the occupied territories. While most of Israel proper beyond the Green Line carried
on undisturbed and unperturbed by the intifada, a contagion of apocalyptic
hysteria was spreading next door through the sealed atmosphere of the West
Bank and Gaza Strip. Part of it was created by the Palestinian child-war-
riors, intoxicated and astonished by their own fury and by the power they
had unleashed; part was the angst and anger of Israel's soldier-enforcers.
But by April a third force had come into play, one whose self-righteous-
ness, dedication and fear raised the temperature and the stakes for all sides.

When the uprising began there were some 65,000 Jewish settlers living
in the West Bank and Gaza. Their steady growth and implacable physical
presence had been an important element in the fuel that had caused the explosion of the intifada in the first place. Now their very existence fanned
the flames. For Palestinians they were both a visible cause of grievance and
a ready target. They themselves were determined not to be passive victims
and some were prepared to be aggressors. While many showed restraint

when faced with a steady assault of rocks and Molotov cocktails, a sizable core of hotheads and ideologues exploited the intifada as an excuse to wage vigilante warfare on their Arab neighbors and political war on their own government. When it came time for retribution, any Arab would do: the innocent bystander was inevitably an easier prey than the agile, elusive activist.

The original two-way game between soldiers and youths, brutal as it was, had a certain symmetry and set of rules. But once the settlers were drawn in, the new conflict was more volatile and vicious. A struggle between the occupier and the occupied rapidly disintegrated into something rawer and more atavistic—a blood feud between two entangled communities. Decent men did merciless deeds. The young died on both sides. And both groups, Arabs and Jews, inevitably turned in on themselves, focusing on purported traitors and collaborators within their own fractious ranks, identifying the hideously distorted face of the enemy in their own cracked mirrors. Arabs killed other Arabs in numbers that came to match and then exceed the number killed by Israelis. Jews did not kill other Jews, but an internecine hatred developed that destroyed the long-standing Israeli consensus on security issues.

There were souls on fire in the West Bank. Some of them were reluctant warriors, while others danced joyfully with death. Eventually their rage broke free from its boundaries and crashed through the Green Line into Israel proper, where it became a critical factor in breaking down the old status quo and making Israelis reconsider the Arabs in their midst. But first there came a day in a nondescript Arab village called Beita when all of the passions—the anger, the hatred, the fear and the confusion—came together in a moment so raw and terrible that it scarred them all.

The rocky hills behind Beita have been worked for generations by Arab farmers who coax a modest existence out of unforgiving soil. Villagers have painstakingly carved terraces out of the hard, calloused ground and planted a scattering of olive trees and other hardy crops. A network of narrow paths crisscrosses the fields like veins in the back of an old man's hand, winding in and out of valleys and up steep slopes. This is Bible country where ancient prophets, as intolerant as the harsh desert sun, had stormed through the weathered landscape in search of God and revelation.

Like so many Arab villages, Beita sat haphazardly among the fields on the hillside. There was no visible order or uniformity to its sprawl. Ancient sandstone hovels and modern, multistoried concrete houses sat side by side, broken occasionally by dusty gardens and empty, garbage-strewn sandlots. Donkeys, goats and chickens wandered freely. And there was the inevitable mosque, its minaret towering above the other buildings.

A few miles to the north, perched on a hillside overlooking Nablus, was the Jewish settlement of Elon Moreh. Its planning and orderliness were in marked contrast to Beita: the boxlike houses were uniform in size and design and carefully laid out. A lookout post guarded the main entrance. But the real contrast with Beita was in the sense of power. Sitting atop the highest hill in the area, buffeted by strong winds in winter and harsh sun in summer, Elon Moreh seemed commanding, relentless and defiant.

The Bible says Abraham built an altar to God on the spot, his first way station upon entering Canaan. The settlers, who saw it as the cradle of Judaism, fought a prolonged skirmish with the Rabin-led Labor government of the mid-1970s for the right to settle on the hillside. After Menachem Begin won his landmark electoral victory in 1977, he followed in Abraham's footsteps, making this one of his first stops as prime minister. Holding a Torah scroll aloft, he pledged to build "many more Elon Morehs!"

Born of the messianic euphoria following the Six-Day War, the settlement movement known as Gush Emunim ("Bloc of the Faithful") received an enormous boost from Begin's triumph. The new prime minister appointed Ariel Sharon as minister of agriculture and granted the hawkish war hero sweeping powers to confiscate local Arab land and build Jewish settlements. The vast program that Sharon initiated continued on a small but steady scale during the six years of the national unity government under Shimon Peres and Yitzhak Shamir. Peres's Labor Party had managed to place strict limits on the number of new settlements, but was unable and unwilling to stop population growth in existing ones. Indeed, many Laborites admired the settlers' pioneering spirit—it evoked for them the early days of Zionism—even while they disagreed with the settlers' political goals. Settlers took advantage of the political paralysis between the Israeli left and right and the passivity of a supine and self-pitying Palestinian population to continue an ambitious program of colonization.

The settlers were a more diverse group than their grim, hard-line public image suggested. Some were clearly moved by ideology and messianic zeal, believing that they were preparing the ground for the biblical End of Days. But many others came to live in the West Bank because of its cheap, government-subsidized housing, uncrowded schools and clean air. The majority were more inclined to pack credit cards than pistols. Many thought of their presence here in only the vaguest of political terms and gave little or no thought to the 850,000 West Bank Arabs living around them. No one troubled to ask the Palestinians in the valleys what they thought of having Jewish settlers on the hilltops.

A handful of settlers forged relationships with their Arab neighbors.

Some believed they would inevitably have to come to terms with Palestinian aspirations. But many more believed the land was their sacred heritage, a legacy from God, and their attachment to it was not subject to compromise. The Arabs who had lived on it and farmed it for generations were caretakers, strangers in someone else's Promised Land.

The intifada, with its rocks and bottles and Molotov cocktails, transformed the Arab population into a threatening presence. Confined to their cities and villages by the army, Palestinians could find few Israelis to vent their rage on. The settlers, driving the main roads of the West Bank on their way to work or school or home with their telltale orange Israeli license plates and Jewish skullcaps, were an inviting target. Palestinians had taken pains to describe the uprising as essentially an act of nonviolent resistance to military occupation by an unarmed civilian population. But for the settlers, the stones and Molotov cocktails were just as frightening and, on occasion, proved just as lethal as guns and bombs. Ten Israeli civilians were killed and more than 400 injured during the first year of the intifada and thousands of cars were damaged. About 3,000 Israeli passenger buses were also damaged, including 41 that were gutted by fire.

The figures paled in comparison to the estimated 350 Palestinian deaths and 11,000 wounded that first year. But for the settlers, the numbers and the fear became a dominant fact of daily life. People who had once traveled the roads freely took to driving with loaded guns on their laps and replaced the glass windows in their cars with shatterproof plastic.

As it transformed Palestinians, the intifada transformed the settlers. It made them more frightened, less conciliatory, and forced them to think more about the political implications of why they were living in the West Bank and what it meant to stay. Just as every Palestinian had a friend or relative who had been jailed, shot or beaten by soldiers, so every settler had a neighbor whose car had been hit by rocks or trapped by angry Arab youths. As the settlers' solidarity grew, so did their alienation from mainstream Israel. A small, cohesive population, perceiving itself under siege, embraced a set of imperatives, demands and behavior that was far removed from those of the majority of Israelis. Their fever stopped at the Green Line. The settlers claimed they were establishing the boundaries of the new Jewish state, that they were fighting for the right of all Jews to live west of the Jordan. But many Israelis were beginning to see that claim—and the settlers themselves—in a very different light.

One of the ways that the settlers sought to demonstrate their control of the land was through nature hikes. The walks provided an opportunity to spill sweat on God's soil and claim it for their own. There was never any question of asking Arabs for permission to trample through their fields or villages. The message of the hikes was that such permission was superfluous. We are the inheritors here, said the hikers to the villagers. Our claim is deeper, our love of the land of a different, more profound nature than yours. Even during the height of the intifada, settlers refused to curtail such trips. Some saw it as a duty to hike even more frequently to demonstrate to the Arabs that no so-called uprising could supplant Jewish sovereignty or make a righteous Jew cower in his own homeland.

So when Menachem Ilan, a fifty-five-year-old resident of Elon Moreh, gathered a group of sixteen Jewish teenagers from the settlement on a sunny April morning and set off for the winding trails east of Beita, none of their parents objected. They did not even raise a question when Ilan invited along Romam Aldubi, a bearded, chubby-faced, twenty-six-year-old religious militant who was considered a troublemaker and a fanatic even by the broad standards of the settler community. Aldubi was obsessed with founding a Jewish settlement in the heart of Nablus and had started a yeshiva there at the site of Joseph's Tomb. He had clashed so frequently with the army that Amram Mitzna had taken the unusual step of banning him from Nablus for six months. Ilan himself had been convicted in 1984 of obstructing justice by concealing a gun used by another settler to kill an eleven-year-old Arab girl during a stone-throwing melee.

Ilan took along an M-16, Aldubi an Uzi submachine gun. Ilan did not inform the army of his itinerary, let alone seek advice on the wisdom of marching unarmed youngsters through remote Arab villages during the peak of the intifada. He simply informed the security guard at the settlement and borrowed a walkie-talkie tuned only to an Elon Moreh frequency.

The hikers stopped for breakfast at an old well, where they were seen by Arab farmers preparing their spring crops. Word quickly spread through Beita that settlers with guns were moving through the land. Several dozen farmers and village teenagers gathered near the hikers. Some threw stones. Aldubi walked toward them and fired warning shots from his Uzi. Ilan scolded him and ordered him back. The hikers then set off through the wadi, a narrow, dry riverbed, and more stones followed. One girl was hit in the thigh. Aldubi opened fire again, this time hitting in the back a man named Musa Sallah Daoud who was about fifty yards from him and apparently running away at the time of the shots. He died almost instantly.

The central mosque in Beita broadcast an alarm, calling on villagers to resist a settler invasion. Shocked by the gunfire, Ilan scuffled with Aldubi and forced the younger man to give him the Uzi and take his own slower, bulkier M-16. But Aldubi soon fired the M-16, wounding at close range a villager who he believed was about to try to seize his weapon. Angry villagers surrounded the small band and marched them into Beita.

"When the Arabs saw that one of them had been shot, they descended from all the ridges and hills and completely surrounded us," said Rachel Savitch, one of the teenaged hikers. ". . . They formed a chain, a real tight ring, and there was nothing we could do. They told us, you come with us or else. Either we were going to walk with them or they were going to murder us right there in the valley."

The hikers and the Palestinians entered Upper Beita, a makeshift clutter of stone houses and winding alleyways crammed on a steep, descending hillside. Here, in the narrow streets choked with angry villagers and frightened settlers, each side confronted its nightmare. For the villagers, it was Aldubi, a warm M-16 in his hands, stalking into Beita after killing one of their young men and wounding another. For the Israeli teenagers, it was the sight of hundreds of angry Arabs brandishing knives, pickaxes and clubs, gathering on rooftops and in the alleyways in a growing fury, some of them shouting, "Kill the Jews!"

Aldubi and Ilan had the youngsters form a tight ring around them to prevent villagers from seizing their guns. They hoped to make their way through the village and out to the main Nablus–Jerusalem road nearby, where they could flag down help. But as they crossed through the village, a car arrived carrying the corpse of Musa Daoud. Stones began flying again. Someone punched an Israeli teenager in the face, pulled the camera from his neck and smashed it. Then Munira Daoud, Musa's sister, maneuvered her way behind Aldubi and clubbed him in the back of the head with a rock. As he went down he opened fire blindly, spraying bullets in a low trajectory. One of the bullets hit and killed a villager; another struck the back of the head of fifteen-year-old Tirza Porat, one of the hikers standing in front of him.

Villagers struck several more teenagers with rocks, while Ilan was pummeled into unconsciousness and his Uzi seized. Several Palestinians jumped on Aldubi and battered his head. They took his gun. Both weapons were later found broken into pieces. Most of the mob then fled, leaving the dazed, bloodied teenagers, their two fallen guards and Tirza sprawled on the ground, blood and brains oozing from the back of her skull.

During the attack several villagers had pushed their way into the crowd and sought to pull the youngsters to safety. Afterward a young Beitan named Azzam Bani Shemseh pushed on Tirza's chest to try to restore a heartbeat while Rami Hoffman gave her mouth-to-mouth resuscitation. Other members of the Bani Shemseh family brought water to the teenagers, while another Arab family took three of the girls to their house. Villagers escorted others to the main road, where they flagged down cars.

Israel Television that night showed the scene as the army arrived: the blood-spattered youths, the girl's body with its frozen eyes and gaping mouth being loaded into an ambulance, another girl sobbing wildly. A CBS camera crew that got to the scene some thirty minutes before the first soldiers arrived sought to gather the youngsters and console them.

Amram Mitzna arrived in Beita just before dusk, got a briefing from the local commander and met with reporters on the outskirts of the village. He relayed essentially the account that the youngsters and Ilan had given to military investigators, that Tirza had been killed by stones thrown by the villagers. Within hours the army would discover that this version was false, that Tirza had been shot and that the bullet had come from Aldubi's weapon.

Mitzna ordered his soldiers to surround and seal off the village, and round up all men between ages fifteen and sixty at a local schoolyard, where they were held for questioning. Dozens who had fled to neighboring villages slowly trickled back after Mitzna ordered the word spread that no reprisals would be taken if they returned. In his eyes the cordon was designed to protect the village from settler retaliation as much as to confine the Beitans.

Hundreds of villagers were forced to stand outdoors blindfolded with their hands cuffed behind their backs through the night. Shin Bet interrogators worked their way through the crowd, using their usual methods. Villagers said later they were kicked, beaten and threatened until they gave satisfactory accounts of what had happened and who had been involved. Mitzna feared that if the army was not quick and careful enough, Beita could become a symbol to extremists on both sides.

The army withheld the autopsy results until after the funeral the next day, an emotional affair at which Yitzhak Shamir and other rightist politicians called for harsh retribution and several speakers demanded that Beita be razed and its inhabitants expelled. "Beita must be erased!" Rabbi Haim Druckman, a Knesset member from a small, nationalist religious party, told the crowd. "A place where such a detestable murder is committed cannot remain in existence." There were amens from the crowd.

Elon Moreh leader Benny Katsover, who had allowed his own daughter and the other teenagers to go off with the two dubious guardians, rained abuse on Shamir, who was standing nearby. Standing over the stretcher on which Tirza's corpse was laid under a black canvas shroud, Katsover accused the army and the government of "shameful games." He demanded: "Why do you fear to order Israeli soldiers to fire at anyone who tries to harm us? Why didn't you hit them on the head in time?"

That night after the funeral, the army's revised version blaming Aldubi for Tirza's death was broadcast on Israel Television. The settlers, who believed they had found a martyr for their cause and a rationale for a full-scale crackdown, were furious. They grew angrier still when Lieutenant General Dan Shomron, the army chief of staff, appeared on television and radio and emphasized that a number of villagers had come to the aid of the youngsters. "I want to note that during this event there were locals who tried to protect the children from the others, and even women who hid the girls in some groves and other places to prevent the mob from hurting them," he told reporters. Later on Israel Radio he added: "Do you really think that if hundreds of the villagers intended to kill them, that those opposed would have been able to stop them? I sincerely believe that they didn't want to kill them."

Still, Mitzna was under intense pressure from the government, his own commanders and the Shin Bet security service to take harsh steps against Beita. The day after the incident, while Mitzna remained in Beita, he dispatched his deputy to an emergency meeting at Rabin's office in Jerusalem. The atmosphere was tense and the consensus was that the army had to crack down hard. Mitzna got word that he was expected to demolish at least thirty houses and deport a similar number of villagers. "We have to show them that we know what to do," was the message.

Mitzna, too, felt that tough measures were necessary to prevent an explosive situation from leading to further eruptions. He was especially fearful that Palestinian activists would follow Beita's example and launch attacks on settlers. The red line between the violent, unstable but manageable status quo and a real conflagration, with Arabs and Jews killing each other wantonly, was thin and fragile. Mitzna felt he needed to reinforce that line.

He was prepared to use all the means available to him to restore tranquility. He had no qualms about demolishing houses of suspects or expelling Palestinians without legal hearing. But he balked at setting an arbitrary figure for punishment. Mitzna wanted to be certain that only those who had been involved in the incident were punished. The innocent should not be harmed. Retaliation had to be based on some fundamental notion of justice. Faced with the demand for thirty house demolitions, he told his superiors, "Put it in writing." They never did.

Mitzna spent three days in the village, sifting through interrogation reports and meeting with investigators to nail down as quickly as possible exactly what happened and who was responsible. By the end of the week, he had identified fourteen villagers allegedly involved in the incident. He ordered their houses demolished and six of them deported. Some seven acres of olive trees were uprooted, purportedly to prevent them from sheltering wrongdoers. Soldiers also shot and killed an Arab teenager who they claimed had tried to flee the village and did not stop even after being warned. This killing was never properly explained or investigated; even under the army's rules for opening fire, it seemed totally unjustified.

One of the demolished houses belonged to the family of Azzam Bani Shemseh. He had fled that Wednesday evening with hundreds of other villagers because he feared what the army would do. While he was away, three villagers from a rival clan identified him as one of the assailants. When he came back on Friday he was arrested, beaten and held for a day. When he claimed he had helped the young Israelis, his Israeli interrogator spat in his face. "You think you're a white dove from Mecca?" the officer mockingly asked. Only after some of the Israeli youngsters identified him as one of those who had aided them was he released. The military governor of Nablus issued a public apology and later Bani Shemseh's father received compensation for the demolished house.

As far as the settlers were concerned, the punishments were pathetically insufficient. By Sunday two right-wing Knesset members were calling for Shomron's resignation, complaining the army had been too soft on the villagers. That same day, after huddling with settlement leaders and politicians, the Jewish teenagers appeared at a press conference to present a new account, one that seemed suspiciously well rehearsed. Rami Hoffman now described hearing gunshots and being hit by an explosion. Arik Avivi, fifteen, said he had seen an Arab man standing on a low roof firing a Kalashnikov rifle into the crowd. Both insisted that it was impossible for Aldubi to have shot Tirza.

At the weekly cabinet meeting Likud ministers strongly attacked the army. Ariel Sharon, Mitzna's old enemy, rapped the general for giving interviews and the IDF for leaking the autopsy results. Sharon suggested evacuating and razing the entire village and building a Jewish settlement in its place. "You can't kill all the Arabs all the time," retorted Ezer Weizman, himself a former defense minister. That evening an alarmed Israeli President Chaim Herzog warned that political attacks on the IDF "will bring catastrophe upon us."

Seeking to relieve the political pressure on himself and his men, Mitzna appointed an investigative committee and spent three weeks sifting through the evidence before issuing a report on the incident that he wrote himself. The report placed primary blame on the villagers who had assaulted the hikers, but it also criticized the lack of planning and coordination by the hike's organizers and stated that "negligence in operating the weapon [and] a lack of caution and superfluous hastiness in pulling the trigger" helped escalate a minor incident into a fatal confrontation.

Faced with a Solomonic task of judgment, Mitzna felt he had been fair to both sides, but few critics agreed. On the left, the *Jerusalem Post* editorialized that the report showed "the apparent reluctance of the authors to give offence to the West Bank settlers, and to their political patrons." Nonetheless, it added, the finding that Aldubi had fired the fatal bullet had thwarted settlers' hopes of turning Tirza into "a patron saint of Israel's territorial expansionism."

On the right, the Council of Judea and Samaria, the leading settler group, expressed "astonishment" at the report's finding of negligence by Aldubi in firing his weapon. Elon Moreh leader Katsover claimed falsely in the settler magazine *Nekuda* that the report vindicated the view that "it was the Arab rioters who fell upon our children who are solely responsible for what happened in Beita."

As time passed many Israelis held the settlers themselves responsible for the events at Beita. Never mind the politics, many said, how could they have allowed their children to go out into what one newspaper columnist described as "the local equivalent of Injun country, with the natives on the warpath?" Nimr Murkos, an Israeli Arab, put it simply: "Nobody with any common sense would take his children into a battlefield." The fact that the settlers had done exactly that lessened their credibility and support among mainstream Israelis who might admire their pioneering spirit, and even sympathize with their goals, but were horrified at their callous ideology and their lack of responsibility for their own children. It mirrored the Israeli criticism of Palestinian parents who seemed unable or unwilling to prevent their children from participating in confrontations with the army.

There was also anger over the impossible position the settlers had put the army in. The IDF was being forced into a policing role, editorialized the newspaper *Haaretz,* even while "it is being slandered by Jews intoxicated with messianic fervor whose contribution to security exists only in their imagination."

The army was tarnished as well by its attempts to defuse the situation. Its rush to judgment—first claiming Tirza had been stoned to death, then backtracking once it had autopsy results to the contrary—called its integrity into question. The army's claim of being an impartial arbiter was compromised. Shomron told a Knesset committee that some of the settlers would have to stand trial for not notifying the army in advance and thus denying the teenagers army protection. This never happened. Military justice for the Beitans also proved dubious. Hamad Ben Ishams, whose house had been one of those demolished, spent seven months in prison even though his Israeli employer came to court three times to testify that Ben Ishams had been working in Israel on the day of the incident. Rami Hoffman had identified him as an assailant and that was enough for the military judge, who said of the employer, "Even Jews make mistakes."

Beita took a large toll on Amram Mitzna. His relations with the settlers, always testy, became even more troubled. His profile as a tempting target for right-wing politicians grew larger. And his isolation grew as well. Rabin and Shomron continued to express full confidence in him. But he realized that when difficult decisions had to be taken, he was on his own. His friends and putative allies had stood on the sidelines. Mitzna enjoyed the limelight and had thrived in it. Now he had felt its heat. He wondered how many more Beitas he could withstand.

Beita slowly faded from Israel's memory, replaced by larger, even more bloodstained events. But the incident left a tear in the country's moral and communal fabric. Before Beita, philosopher Yaacov Hasdai told the *Jerusalem Post,* incidents in which Jews, especially children, were killed, had evoked a sense of unity and mutual loss that had bound the society closer together. People of conflicting political beliefs had mourned side by side. Now such tragedies had become another cause for bitter debate and finger-pointing. A rupture had occurred that was fundamental and irrevocable. The settlers were placing themselves outside the consensus. By their fanaticism they were forfeiting their hold on national sympathy.

"Our problem at this stage isn't the Arabs, it's the Jews," Hasdai told reporter Abraham Rabinovich. ". . . If we don't restore our basic values—honor, decent behavior, responsibility—and send the extremists back to their corners, we don't have much time left to us."

Romam Aldubi was not the only settler to shoot the wrong person for the wrong reason. In the hothouse atmosphere of the West Bank, even the most decent of men, confronted by fear, could suddenly open fire. Such a man was Yisrael Zeev.

He was the shepherd of Shiloh, a Jewish settlement of some ninety families set atop the hill where the ancient Israelites had first placed their tabernacle upon entering the Promised Land. American-born, religiously observant, painfully shy and soft-spoken, Zeev had a wife, Nancy, six children and a flock of sheep. Although most of the residents of Shiloh were teachers or businessmen or professionals, Yisrael Zeev worked the land. Of all the people who lived in the settlement, none boasted better relations with neighboring Arab villagers. He shared their calling, their love for the land and their sense of tradition, for he, like them, was doing what he imagined his forefathers had done in centuries past.

Zeev owned a white horse, an impetuous mare that only he could ride. In the afternoons after work they would barnstorm the hills around Shiloh and sometimes ride into the nearby Arab village of Turmus Aya. He would often stop at the house of Jodeh Mohammed Awad, a fellow shepherd. They would drink coffee and talk about the animals. Zeev sold Awad's father a goat and Awad occasionally worked for Zeev. They were not exactly friends, more like colleagues in an ancient livelihood. Friends would describe them in similar terms—moderate, soft-spoken, responsible family men. Awad had three children, and in the spring of 1988 his wife was pregnant with a fourth.

Then came the intifada, and the road to Shiloh became a gauntlet of rocks and bottles. The settlers began to see all Arabs as a potential danger, while the villagers of Turmus Aya no longer opened their doors even to a fellow shepherd. In March the army issued a warning to heads of security at various settlements that terrorists disguised as shepherds might seek to infiltrate and attack a settlement. The fever was rising.

One afternoon in early May a Jewish woman became alarmed when she spotted Palestinian shepherds grazing their sheep a few yards from the children's playground at the outskirts of Shiloh. She called the security chief, who in turn called Yisrael Zeev, a trained soldier who served as part of the volunteer guard at the settlement. He arrived on his motorbike with his M-16 strapped to his back and encountered three young Arab men. They refused his warnings to leave, yelled insults and moved toward him. It was a standoff—one man with a gun, three with their pride, poised defiantly a few yards apart in the hair-trigger afternoon.

"It didn't look good," Zeev recalled later. "They wouldn't leave and the whole thing was menacing. I unshouldered my weapon and shot up in the air to impress them, but they continued. They weren't interested in leaving."

To move them along, Zeev shot at the ground in front of their feet. But the bullets hit higher than he expected. He hit one of the Palestinians in the leg. The man hobbled off with his two panic-stricken friends. Then Zeev saw there was a fourth man lying on the ground. His head was open and there was blood everywhere. "I was stunned. I had had no intention of hurting anyone. I couldn't believe it. I went back a second time to be sure. He was still there. The whole thing was a fluke. I didn't know what had happened, but I knew it was bad. When I got home, I told Nancy, 'I've ruined our lives.' "

Later Yisrael received another shock. He learned that the man he had killed was Jodeh Awad.

Most settlers involved in shootings of Palestinians went free after brief investigations, but Yisrael Zeev's case was singled out and rigorously pursued. He spent five months in jail before trial because bail was not granted by a judge who warned that too many settlers had become "trigger-happy." At first he was charged with murder. There were stories in the Israeli press, based on police leaks, that a land dispute was the real motive for the shooting and that Zeev knew exactly whom he was shooting. The accounts of the Palestinians contributed to this version. They claimed they had waved to Zeev and called out, "Yisrael, don't shoot! It's us!" before he aimed his M-16 and opened fire. Amal Awad believed Yisrael killed her husband as part of a settler attempt to steal Arab land and perhaps because he bore a grudge after some of his sheep came down with an infection acquired from Arab herds.

The charge eventually was reduced to manslaughter, and the Palestinian testimony collapsed in court when an Israeli witness backed up Zeev's story. But Zeev's own account had a few holes. He originally told police the shepherds had thrown rocks at him, but later he conceded that one of the men had merely raised an arm in a threatening manner. The judge sentenced Zeev to three years' imprisonment, of which he served two.

But perhaps the most chilling part of Yisrael Zeev's tale was what followed. During his two years in prison Zeev grew more religious and came to see his life in a much different light. He came to believe that Awad's killing had been part of a trial God had planned for him. "Aside from meeting my wife, it was the most positive experience of my life," he claimed. "I saw many people broken in prison. But it built me, spiritually speaking. It made me closer to God. If you believe God is actively involved in life, that He doesn't just sit back after creating the world, then something like this can't happen without His causing it. I'm sure God looked down one day and said, 'Here's Yisrael Zeev, he needs this experience, he needs two years in jail,' and He created this situation."

When he discovered that he had inadvertently killed an Arab he knew and respected, Zeev was stunned and deeply shaken. He sobbed as he recounted the shooting at an initial court hearing before his trial. But eventually he came to believe that God had singled out Awad for punishment. Awad had "earned" his death, according to Zeev, because two of Awad's brothers were convicted terrorists. He felt regret but no remorse and no guilt, and he made no attempt to communicate any grief or apology to Awad's widow. It all somehow became part of God's plan for Zeev and for Shiloh. In Zeev's personal drama of challenge and redemption, Awad, the victim, became the invisible man.

Yisrael Zeev had nothing against Jodeh Awad. He did not hate him, did not even think about him very much, and certainly meant him no harm. In the grand saga of the Jewish return to the West Bank, there was little time to contemplate, let alone mourn over, such deeds. There was a war to be fought, a land to be won. One Arab's life was irrelevant; so too was his death.

Awad had been a "nice guy," Zeev recalled, but then "all the Arabs seem like nice guys and it doesn't mean a thing. You can't turn your back on them, as we've all found out. Truth be told, I believe God chose him as well as me, maybe because he came from such a 'good' family. His brothers were terrorists. Who knows what he had in his heart as well?"

For the settlers, incidents like Beita and Shiloh were dramatic signposts on the road to their alienation from the Israeli mainstream. Their environment had turned on them. It was no longer their natural home but rather a hostile, alien and dangerous place. Now their protectors in the army had turned on them as well. They were quick to resort to apocalyptic rhetoric, calling for drastic steps and pointing an accusatory finger at "leftists" such as Mitzna in the IDF's high command. They demanded action: they wanted dozens of Arab houses demolished wherever a stoning incident occurred, procedures for opening fire eased, hundreds, even thousands, of "inciters" expelled. Had the army killed a hundred rioters in the first week of the intifada, settler leaders argued, the violence would have stopped immediately. Blame was being transferred. The Arabs were no longer responsible; after all, they were just doing what came naturally to them. It was the army, by refusing to take the necessary steps, that was responsible for the continuation of the intifada.

Their hostility was returned in kind. Defense Minister Rabin openly despised the settlers. He viewed them as fanatics who complicated the already difficult mission of the army to maintain order in the territories, and he met with their leaders as infrequently as possible. Shomron, Mitzna and the other commanders did their best to keep lines of communication open and to listen to the settlers' many complaints, although they too had limits to their patience. And because the IDF was a citizen army, Israelis of all political persuasions were exposed to the territories and could make their own judgments about the behavior of the settlers. In the field, relations were often emotionally charged, especially between radical settlers and veteran reservists from the Israeli left.

In his documentary film *Reflections,* reservist Yishai Shuster portrays the hostility the men in his unit feel for the settlers they were assigned to protect in Hebron. His soldiers call the settlers "terrorists" and "Jewish fascists" who live off the state, which subsidizes the settlers' housing and large families and protects them from the Arab population. One soldier named Eyal describes his disgust at guarding Jews at the Tomb of the Patriarchs. There were ten settler women and twenty children, "all the same height. . . . It was like a cowshed. I felt like vomiting."

The settlers in the film are equally contemptuous of the army and the Arabs. Nachum, a settler spokesman, tells Shuster he is too proud to let the Arabs abuse him the way they abuse the army: "I will not let them piss on me. We shoot to kill, to lift them in the air. They are more scared of us than of you." Rafi, a settler's thirteen-year-old son, tells Shuster that the only solution is to expel all Palestinians from Hebron. He has a question: "How can you identify an Arab? I know him by his stink. All Arabs stink. Arabs stink and will always stink."

The settlers claimed their presence in the territories enhanced Israel's security. In fact they posed an enormous burden for the army, which had to stretch its overburdened forces to protect the many roadways that settlers frequented. Not only did the soldiers have to deal with repeated incidents where settlers opened fire without justification on Palestinians or smashed property; relations deteriorated to the point where angry settlers took out their frustrations on the soldiers themselves. Several soldiers, including a brigade commander, were slapped around or spat upon; others were verbally abused, accused of condoning the "holocaust" that Palestinians were seeking to inflict upon Jews.

In January 1989 outside the West Bank settlement of Yakir, settlers staged a confrontation with the army over the erection of a stone memorial to Shimon Edri, a taxi driver killed by Arab terrorists a week earlier. Under orders from Rabin, soldiers came to dismantle the monument, and the army roadblocked the area and sealed it off. Settlers surrounded them and blocked the roads. There were fistfights between settlers and soldiers. The next day a soldier was slashed in the face with a knife by a settler woman who cried, "Blood will be spilled!" Daniela Weiss, a leader of Gush Emunim, crawled under an army command car and refused to come out. Women soldiers had to drag her out screaming and crying. Shamir, appearing at a memorial service in the area, was heckled and branded a "traitor." Some settlers attempted to attack his car. He called them *meturafim*—"crazies."

Amram Mitzna had been a special target for the settlers ever since his first days as leader of central command. During the intifada he strived to keep the settlers under control, denying their requests for legal authority over security in their areas and prohibiting them from patrolling Arab villages. Such activities, he told aides, would be like allowing "cats to guard the milk." By 1989 he was pleading for help from the Knesset in controlling radicals among the settlers. Describing how settlers had physically assaulted two of his officers, he warned a legislative committee, "We are in an explosive situation because of settler attitudes and actions."

Mitzna would soon be tested again. In early February 1989 a settler named Albert Jerassi was killed when the cab of his pickup truck caught fire near the settlement of Alfei Menashe. Police were uncertain about the cause of the blaze but the settlers, recalling the firebomb killing two years earlier of Ofra and Tal Moses, had no doubt that Palestinians were responsible. Dozens of settlers piled into cars with their Uzis and handguns and headed for Kalkilya, the nearest Arab town, to seek revenge. Most of them never made it. Anticipating the settlers' reaction, Mitzna had stationed dozens of soldiers on the roads leading out of Alfei Menashe and forced the settlers back at gunpoint. Then he went to the settlement and met with the mayor, Shlomo Catan, himself a reserve army officer. "Look, Shlomo, we can do this one of two ways," Mitzna told him. "If I have to, I will bring in two or three battalions just to control the Jews. Or, if you cooperate, I can concentrate the forces to do the investigation and search for the Arabs responsible."

Catan acquiesced, but local residents were less compliant. As Mitzna made his way to the local sports center to meet with them, settlers shouted, "Nazi! Leftist! Liar! Murderer!"

The auditorium was jammed with several hundred sullen, angry people. One man who had been turned back from Kalkilya pointed his finger at Mitzna. "I want to travel at any hour I wish, and I won't tolerate any army officer of any rank preventing a Jewish citizen from coming and going from his settlement as happened tonight," he warned. "There will never be a curfew on a Jewish settlement. Tonight was the last time. Next time I will attack soldiers."

Another man, who said he had attended four funerals of killed settlers in the past two years, told Mitzna he should be fired. "Your security system has gone bankrupt," he said. "The water is up to the top of our heads and we will not tolerate this anymore." There was much applause.

Mitzna waited until they calmed down, then tried to reply. He told them that Jews were a civilized people, that they must let the army deal with security and not take the law into their own hands. "There is only one IDF and no one is willing to take its place," he said. "Therefore you have to trust it. . . . This conflict didn't begin yesterday. It has gone on for a long time. And if we don't have the patience and the perseverance and the ability to cope with the problems in a democratic fashion . . . then we won't be the state that we want to be."

The settlers dispersed quietly that night, and a few weeks later it was determined that the fire in Jerassi's truck had been caused by a freak accident. Nonetheless, Mitzna was shaken by the depth of anger and hatred he had seen that night. After each incident, it seemed, settlers were demanding ever more drastic measures. The politicians were pressing too. Mitzna could see his effectiveness eroding. A few weeks after the Alfei Menashe incident, he told Rabin that he wanted to resign.

The defense minister was furious. How could Mitzna leave now when there was so much work to be done? How could he abandon his men in the middle of the battle? But Mitzna did not see it that way. The intifada was not a conventional war that would end with a military victory. It could go on for years until the politicians came up with a coherent peace plan. He did not intend to wait that long. He had served two years, seen the army through the tough early days of the struggle and helped establish a new West Bank command structure. That was enough.

After much argument Rabin acceded. In July Amram Mitzna took a year's leave of absence to study at the Center for International Affairs at Harvard University. His military career was permanently sidetracked. When he returned from Harvard he was made head of the IDF's planning branch, a respectable high-level staff job but one that took him out of the running for the top position as chief of staff. Mitzna's gold-plated career had been tarnished by a war he knew he could not win yet had struggled to come to grips with. He was a victim of his own moral compass—he had been too harsh to win the sympathy of the Israeli left, yet too fastidious to please the right. He walked away believing he had done the right thing, yet he also knew that some of his actions had damaged the Palestinians, his own men and himself as well.

As the settlers sought scapegoats among fellow Jews, Palestinian grievances turned inward as the intifada ground on. The early sense of euphoria—the notion that a few more days or weeks of suffering would somehow miraculously lead to an end to the occupation and to a Palestinian state—had long been punctured by the army. Much of the core of veteran, middle-aged activists, loyal to the mainstream PLO, had been hauled off to Israeli military prisons. The intifada was now controlled by younger, more radical, more impulsive groups of teenaged street fighters whose loyalties were only to themselves and whose sense of politics was often primitive. They helped turn what had once been a popular and spontaneous rebellion with mass support into a hardened, personalized affair conducted by small roving bands who made war on their own people more ruthlessly and effectively than on the IDF.

If Beit Sahur had represented the dream of self-sufficiency of the lost intifada that could have been, then Nablus, the West Bank's largest Arab city, became the nightmare of the intifada that came to be. The blood fever reigned there. Nablus had the uprising's highest casualty rates: by 1990 more Palestinians had been shot dead by Israelis in Nablus than anywhere else in the West Bank and Gaza; at the same time more Palestinians there had been killed by other Arabs than in any other city. PLO supporters gradually lost control to armed, masked gangs that stalked the city's clogged thicket of alleyways, ambushing Israeli army patrols and hunting for Palestinian "collaborators." By the summer of 1990, collaborator killings had overtaken army shootings as the number-one cause of Palestinian deaths.

The killers were teenaged executioners like Jaber Hawash, a thin seventeen-year-old who had belonged to the Red Eagles, one of Nablus's most notorious street gangs. A few weeks after his capture, Hawash described in a dull monotone on Israel Television how he had killed eight supposed collaborators with axes and knives. One of them was his own cousin, a woman named Umm Barakat. "I took her out in the street to the spot where I intended to kill her," he recalled. "I tied her up. I blindfolded her and smashed her head with an axe." He killed her, he said, because her collaboration "had put a stain on me. We were tied by blood. I had to kill her." He spoke of "purifying" Palestinian society, as if the blood and screams of his victim were some kind of cosmic miracle cleanser.

The IDF struck back with undercover squads whose mission was to search out and kill armed Palestinians. One unit surrounded a barbershop in Nablus and mowed down three alleged leaders of the Black Panthers, another street gang that was loosely connected with the PLO's Fatah wing and had reportedly murdered fifteen people. A fourth man, apparently an innocent bystander, was also killed and three others were wounded. The ambush enhanced IDF morale but did little to stop the killings. Within two weeks the Panthers were back promising a "new campaign of elimination" in the casbah.

At first Palestinian leaders supported attacks against alleged collaborators in the hopes that these would help destroy Israel's elaborate intelligence network in the territories. The first killings had sent a powerful message to informers, and had led several to renounce their roles publicly and turn in their weapons. Palestinians insisted that each "execution" had been preceded by a thorough investigation and was authorized by PLO headquarters in Tunis. But as the violence spun out of control, the leadership began to see and fear the chaos that was overtaking cities like Nablus.

Collaborators were far from the only targets. A Fatah activist in the West Bank village of Yaabad was killed after he had allegedly refused to share funds from Tunis with more militant factions. An Arab worker in Gaza was axed and knifed to death by a mob after he refused to surrender his new identity card, which he needed to continue working in Israel. A drug addict in Nablus was beaten and burned to death by Muslim fundamentalists for alleged immoral behavior. Fundamentalist and secular street gangs in the casbah seemed more eager to brawl with one another for control of the streets than to fight the army. Palestinians were set on fire, hacked to death in front of mobs or hanged from the tower at Clock Square in downtown Nablus. Pregnant women, housewives, teachers, nurses and doctors fell victim to intifada justice.

The old image of the uprising had been David and Goliath—young men with stones braving armed soldiers. The new image was the executioner's snarl of Yasser Abu Samahadna, triumphantly waving his gun after pumping a bullet into the head of Jamil Fada, a fellow Palestinian accused of collaboration, while residents scurried away. A photographer for Agence France Presse captured the scene, which took place in December 1992 in broad daylight on a main street of the Rafah refugee camp in the Gaza Strip. The intifada lay there as well, alongside Fada's crumpled corpse. It, too, was bleeding to death.

The uprising had become "the beast that devours its children," wrote Adnan Damiri, a former security prisoner, in the Arabic newspaper *Al-Fajr*. "The fear relates to everyone. To the writer, the peasant, the farmer, the clerk, the laborer and the academician. We fear for ourselves and from ourselves, from our dream which has become a nightmare. The false god whom we've created, whom we worship and whom we are consuming today, is the intifada. . . ."

Wrapped inside their intimate dramas, Palestinians and Israelis usually viewed each other as the impersonal symbol on the other side of the wall. Israelis saw the masked, blood-crazed Arab stone thrower, Palestinians the armed and arrogant Israeli soldier or the gun-toting, Bible-quoting, fanatical settler. Each impinged on the other's lives only as an aggressor and an agent of disaster. Only rarely did the human being behind the image break through—and even then, the result often only added further to the pain.

Mohammed Nasir Hawwash was a child of the Nablus casbah. He had been born and raised in its alleyways, one of eight children brought up in a run-down, cold-water flat in a makeshift tenement building beside a winding hillside road. Twenty years old, he worked as a sewing machine operator in a local clothing factory. By custom he would have remained in his father's house until he married and, perhaps, if the money was not sufficient, for a long time after that. He was, his father later recalled, a dependable son who faithfully brought home his paycheck and honored his parents. Had he the choice, the family insisted, Nasir would never have placed his father in the terrible position of having to decide the fate of another man.

It was the end of the first year of the intifada and Nablus was a kingdom of disorder governed by the young militants. Israeli soldiers entered the claustrophobic confines of the casbah as if they were invading enemy territory. A few days earlier soldiers had shot dead a fourteen-year-old boy. On an ash-gray Friday morning the new martyr was to be buried. Caches of stones and bottles had been stacked along the route of the funeral procession. Trouble was more than expected; it was inevitable.

There is no reliable way to reconstruct exactly what happened that morning. The official military account said that soldiers opened fire when their lives were endangered by rioters throwing stones. The unofficial Palestinian version asserts that the soldiers provoked the violence by positioning themselves along the procession's route and daring the youths to attack them. Nasir was among the youths. Whether he was a ringleader or a stone thrower or an innocent bystander will never be clear. Israeli sharpshooters shot eight young Palestinians in the head. Five died immediately, but three others lay in a coma, brain-dead but still alive. They were taken to Makassed Hospital in East Jerusalem with bullets in their brains.

Two days later an Israeli businessman named Yehiel Yisrael was wheeled into an operating room at Hadassah Hospital across town for open-heart surgery. He was forty-six, a husband and a father of three. His family lived in a large apartment in the quiet, prosperous, tree-lined Beit Hakarem neighborhood—a long long way from Nablus. The operation should have been a routine valve replacement procedure, but something went badly wrong and Yisrael was soon near death. He needed another heart. Later that day a relative watching Israel Television's nightly news broadcast saw the scene from Makassed, the three young men in a coma, the grieving families. Here, perhaps, was Yehiel Yisrael's chance to live.

The Yisraels' surgeon phoned Makassed and determined that of the three dying men only Nasir Hawwash's heart was appropriate for a transplant. But the hospital could not approve the procedure without his family's permission. The Yisraels did not approach the Hawwashes themselves, but a family friend who spoke broken Arabic placed a call to Makassed. She reached Nasir's older brother Ghassan, twenty-seven, who was appalled that an Israeli could ask such a thing. She told him, "This is how we'll make peace between Arabs and Jews." He was not buying. "How can you make peace when you shoot someone and then you take the heart to give life to another Israeli?" he told her.

Yehiel Yisrael's wife, Yehudit, pleaded. "We are all people and if we cannot help each other, then we have no values, we have no basis to live on."

The Yisrael family enlisted the help of Jerusalem Mayor Teddy Kollek and a handful of left-wing members of the Knesset, and there was talk of a large cash payment to the Hawwashes—more money than they would have seen in a lifetime. Palestinian figures became involved, including several who were prominent supporters of the PLO. The sessions between the two sides began to take on the air of a Middle East peace conference. People argued, they made speeches; there was much talk, a lot of anger, but little communication.

Arab sentiment divided three ways. Those associated with Fatah, the main PLO wing, encouraged the family to donate the heart as a gesture of humanitarianism that might send a positive message to Israelis and shame them as well. There were Islamic fundamentalists who opposed the donation for religious reasons. And there were radicals who warned, as one later put it, "If we give the Israelis this heart, soon they'll be shooting us for our organs."

In the end Nasir's father said no. Within a few days Yehiel Yisrael was dead. "Politics won and life lost," said Dedi Zucker, one of the Israeli lawmakers who had sought to arrange the transplant despite strong opposition from his own wife, who said it was too much to ask from a bereaved Palestinian family. Rumor on the West Bank said the father had bowed to the pressure from fundamentalists, but Jammal Hawwash did not characterize it that way. A few weeks later the pain of his decision still sat visibly on his tired shoulders and he slumped despondently in a dank brown armchair. The mourning period was far from over, and blurry color Polaroids of Nasir's smiling, chunky face lined the walls of the small flat. He had not wanted anyone to die, Jammal Hawwash said, not his own son, not Yehiel Yisrael. But he could not cope with having Nasir's heart removed, even after death, to go to someone whose fellow tribesmen had killed him. He was angry, he was miserable, and he was bewildered all at the same time. He did not know why God had singled him out for such a terrible test. Worse, he could not say if he had passed or failed.

"What did they want from me?" he asked. "This was my son. They took him away, then they wanted his body. This I could not give."

5. The Breakup

On principles I don't make any compromise.

—YITZHAK SHAMIR

JANUARY in Nablus is a bitter month. The despair of the people who live there seems to seep into the dank atmosphere. Icy winds ride the treeless hillsides while rain clouds carelessly dump gray water on the land. Liquid and dirt combine in the city's open sewers to create a dark, viscous substance that clings to the boots and the nostrils. Anyone in too big a hurry can easily slip on the treacherous mire.

Yitzhak Shamir came to Nablus in January 1989 and fell flat on his face. Trailed by a battery of reporters and cameramen, he came to visit with Israeli troops and demonstrate his concern for the men assigned by his government with the onerous burden of smothering the intifada. But the focus quickly shifted from Shamir to the men themselves, reserve officers of an elite paratrooper brigade who had been diverted from their usual duty of training for the next high-tech war with Syria to the ignoble task of chasing riotous young men and small boys through the damp, anonymous alleyways of the casbah. These men were the cream of the army and they were miserable, and they used the occasion to vent their anger and frustration on a hapless Shamir.

While the cameras whirred, the officers told Shamir that he and other politicians had no idea what was going on in places like Nablus. One officer said the written orders for opening fire or subduing suspects bore no resemblance to the reality on the ground. Another spoke eloquently of the pain of serving in the occupied territories and pleaded with Shamir for a way out. "I have a very bad feeling," he told the prime minister. "I feel humiliated in the face of the man I have to beat. These are not the values that I grew up with—the values of honor.

"The situation is catastrophic," the officer concluded. "It is destroying us and strengthening them. We need an urgent political solution."

Shamir looked surprised and embarrassed, but unmoved. He praised the soldiers, saying their feelings reflected "our special character and our special situation," and he blamed the Arabs for the officers' predicament. "We want to live in peace with everyone, but they force us to take guns and do things you don't like to do," he told them. "But you must do this and we all must do this if we want to live." Later he told reporters that the soldiers' remarks were but the "words of a few people." And he made sure never to hold another such public session.

Nonetheless, the increasingly vocal complaints and protests by the army's officer corps had an impact. Combined with pressure from the dovish half of his ruling coalition, from the new Bush administration and from an American Jewish community dismayed by what it was witnessing almost nightly on its television screens, the army's anguished plea finally compelled even Yitzhak Shamir—a leader who believed that once an order was given every Israeli, soldier or civilian, should button his lip and carry it out—to pay heed.

For Shamir the intifada was at first an unforeseen and unwelcome security problem, then a serious diplomatic headache and, finally—thanks largely to the army's disgust and despair—a stubborn and inescapable domestic political issue. From the beginning he believed that the intifada was nothing new, only another expression of the same unrelenting Arab enmity toward Jews that had existed since the first wave of settlers arrived on the shores of Palestine in the 1880s. Therefore it required no new strategy or response. Israel had only to be strong and demonstrate its superiority in the face of a very old and familiar threat.

As Likud and Labor shared the government both had responsibility for dealing with the intifada, so neither was able to score effective political points against the other. While fringe politicians like Ariel Sharon on the right and Ezer Weizman on the left criticized from the sidelines, the basic leadership core of Shamir, Yitzhak Rabin, Shimon Peres and Moshe Arens refrained from open attacks on one another about the intifada even during the 1988 election campaign. Peres sought to relate the conflict to the peace process, arguing at one point that Shamir had become "the murderer of peace" by blocking Peres's strenuous diplomatic efforts. But Peres never publicly advocated a major change in strategy in coping with the intifada.

After all, the main architect of that policy was the number-two man in his own party, Defense Minister Rabin.

After the election, however, Israel received a rude wake-up call from an unlikely source—its old friend, departing U.S. Secretary of State George Shultz. In December 1988, after a long, comical diplomatic ballet, a reluctant Yasser Arafat renounced terrorism and endorsed U.N. Resolution 242, effectively recognizing Israel's existence and its right to secure borders. This was, as far as Shultz was concerned, a major breakthrough, and following a carefully crafted script, he responded by initiating a dialogue between PLO officials and U.S. diplomats in Tunis, where the PLO was headquartered. The long American quarantine of the PLO was ceremoniously laid to rest.

To Shamir and his aides, this was nothing less than betrayal, and it caught them totally off-guard. The prime minister denounced it, arguing incessantly that the PLO remained a terrorist organization dedicated to Israel's destruction. But his arguments were not persuasive. His own refusal to talk directly to the PLO or to any other authentic Palestinian leadership, following his persistent rejection of Shultz's year-long effort to restart some kind of Middle East peace talks, made him appear intransigent and uninterested in peace.

So the pressure began to build on Shamir to do something, come up with some plan that would take the heat off and give the Israeli public and the American administration a sense that Israel was ready, willing and eager for peace. Close colleagues like cabinet ministers Arens, Dan Meridor and Ehud Olmert urged him to make a dramatic public gesture to Palestinian leaders in the territories. But Shamir was not capable of such moves, nor did he believe they would succeed. He wanted something far more cautious that would involve little risk on Israel's part. If it was too cautious for the Palestinians, that was fine too. The idea was not to reach a settlement but rather to take the pressure off Israel's back. Even Yossi Ben-Aharon, Shamir's director general and his most hawkish aide, warned him, "If we don't do something ourselves, we'll face something far less palatable from outside, perhaps from Washington or even from the United Nations."

Deep down, Shamir believed that the Arabs were not reconciled to Israel's existence and did not want peace, and he himself was far more interested in consolidating Israel's hold on the occupied territories than in engaging in a phony peace process. But he also understood that he had to try to initiate something, and that any initiative, no matter how tame, carried with it some degree of risk. In developing a tame but workable proposal, he found an unusual ally—Labor's hawkish defense minister.

• • •

Yitzhak Rabin was just a few years younger than Yitzhak Shamir and he had the same dour demeanor, but he came from a very different background and saw the world through very different eyes. He was a native-born Israeli and the ultimate product of the Israeli military establishment. He and the IDF had come of age together, and like the army, his personality had been molded in the early years of combat and statehood: his keen intellect, his pragmatism, his taciturnity, his skill at improvisation—and his icy disdain for most of mankind.

He was born in Jerusalem in 1922, the son of Russian immigrants. His father was a tailor; his mother, the indomitable Rosa Cohen, an austere, talented woman who became an important political figure in the *yishuv,* the small Jewish community of pre–World War II Palestine. She had an iron will and intellect but a frail heart, and Rabin recalls in his memoirs running to fetch a doctor after each of her heart attacks, always fearing she would be dead when he returned. "Rachel [his younger sister] and I lived under the shadow of this dread throughout our childhood," he writes. When she died in 1937 he was fifteen.

Rabin was serious, intense and disciplined, much like his mother, but painfully shy, with a sense of insecurity that stemmed at least in part from his fears over her illness. Even as a child he was solemn; at the agricultural school he attended as a teenager he was the only student without a nickname. Yet he was clearly bright and physically striking; the early photographs depict a tall, thin, handsome young man with wavy dark hair and piercing eyes. Although he graduated near the top of his class, his Hebrew was coarse and inexpressive, his humor blunt and often vulgar. He had hoped to continue his education—at one point there was even a plan to study engineering in the United States—but the army intervened.

He had received his first military training at age thirteen, and at nineteen he became a full-time soldier in the fledgling Haganah. By twenty-six he was a brigade commander in the Independence War, charged with defending the perilous, ambush-strewn road to Jerusalem. Impatient, prickly and tautly wound, Rabin was no inspired leader of men. But he impressed his elders with his keen analytical mind, his love of detail, his emphasis on training—and his willingness to obey orders. When Ben-Gurion gave the command Rabin did not flinch from firing on the *Altalena,* a Jewish arms ship docked off the Tel Aviv shore by Menachem Begin's rebellious Irgun in June 1948. Jew fought against Jew in a ten-hour battle in which fifteen people were killed, until Begin's forces agreed to surrender their weapons to the new state. Likewise, Rabin felt no compunction about using force to drive out some 50,000 Arab civilians from their homes in the towns of Lod and Ramle because they purportedly threatened Tel Aviv and the main supply route to Jerusalem.

He was in those days an Israeli primitive—chain-smoking, hard-drinking, crude in manner. When he was commanded to represent Israel's forces at the armistice talks on Rhodes in 1949, he had never before worn a tie and did not know how to knot one. The problem was solved by a colleague who knotted the tie before Rabin left for Rhodes and showed him how to take it on and off by pulling it over his head.

By age thirty-two Rabin was a major general, and ten years later he was named chief of staff. He was one of the originators of the IDF's modern methodological approach to combat: First look at the options, then devise a strategy based on what was possible, and then, if it does not work, scrap it and move quickly to another. Most of all, always be prepared to take whatever the enemy and circumstances give you. It was the ultimate pragmatist's approach—ruthless, unsentimental and opportunistic.

Still, although his intelligence was undeniable, the human dimension always seemed to be missing. He tended to look in some other direction when he spoke to guests or subordinates, and often he neglected to say goodbye, terminating sessions abruptly without a word. Time and again throughout his career, he made decisions based on his reading of the strategic situation or balance of forces—and ignored or miscalculated the impact on people. His mobilization of Israeli troops and provocative moves during the weeks before the Six-Day War in 1967 prodded Egyptian President Gamal Abdel Nasser to escalate his own bombastic rhetoric and troop movements, and helped draw both countries toward a war that neither really wanted.

There was one moment when he tried to reach out. Near the eve of the 1967 war, after weeks of late nights, four-cigarette-pack days and unremitting pressure, Rabin felt panic welling up in his gut. He unburdened himself to Ezer Weizman, his top deputy, telling the former air force chief that he feared he was leading Israel to military disaster. He asked Weizman if he should step down as chief of staff. Weizman sought to reassure him, persuading him that he was exhausted and needed sleep. After a day of rest Rabin felt well enough to return to work and two weeks later he led the army to its brilliant triumph.

Seven years later Weizman disclosed the breakdown in an attempt to undermine Rabin's candidacy for prime minister. Rabin survived the attack politically, but he never forgot the lesson. The one time he had confided in someone he had been betrayed.

Great fame and high positions followed the Six-Day War. Although he had no experience as a diplomat and a sandpaper personality, when Rabin retired from the army he asked for and received Israel's most coveted diplomatic post—ambassador to the United States. He arrived in Washington in 1968 during the height of the Vietnam War, and he watched the demise of Lyndon Johnson's administration and attended the fateful Democratic convention in Chicago. Rabin took careful note: even the strongest country in the world could not sustain a war without a popular mandate. Later he learned geostrategy and realpolitik from two of the masters, Richard Nixon and Henry Kissinger.

When the Labor Party's elderly mandarins chose him over Shimon Peres to become prime minister in 1974, he was the first native-born Israeli to achieve the post. As the winner of the Six-Day War he felt a deep obligation to come to arrangements with the Arabs and rid Israel of most of the occupied territories. But he was a political neophyte, constantly undermined and hemmed in by rivals such as Defense Minister Peres and former Prime Minister Golda Meir. Too often, however, Rabin's biggest enemy was himself. He found it impossible to engage in the little things that matter in politics. He made unnecessary enemies, alienated potential allies. When he resigned in disgrace in 1977 after a minor scandal involving a checking account that he and his wife illegally maintained in Washington, even he conceded his premiership had been riddled by mistakes.

Most men would have quit politics, but Yitzhak Rabin was haunted by his errors and by his enemies. He craved restitution and redemption. For seven years he sat on the Knesset backbenches designated for yesterday's men. He maintained a tempestuous feud with Peres that damaged both men and the party as well, and that had little to do with ideology and much to do with personal ambition and pride. Finally, they decided to put their differences aside for the sake of the party and run as a united ticket in the 1984 election.

Rabin emerged that year as Labor's most fervent security hawk and most powerful vote-getter. More than any other politician, he appeared to occupy the middle ground where most Israelis lived. Because of his military background and his pragmatism, he managed to touch the core of their concerns—their obsession with security, their fear of destruction, yet also their desire for peace. His experience, his analytical approach, his unflagging honesty, even his crudeness—all of these impressed Israelis. The man who could not communicate with people spoke instead to a nation.

After the stalemated election in which neither Labor nor Likud won enough votes to form a coalition without the other, Peres ensured that his old rival received the Defense Ministry in the new unity government. Rabin returned to the Kirya—Tel Aviv's equivalent of the Pentagon. The old soldier had come home.

He quickly became the center of gravity in the new cabinet between its two main warring components, Shamir's Likud and Peres's Labor. No one dared challenge Rabin's authority or question his judgment on security affairs. He was tough, demanding and uncompromising, especially when it came to the Palestinians under his authority in the occupied territories. Even though he and his father had been detained without trial by the British in 1946 and he fully understood its impact, he revived administrative detention, expulsion and house demolition without compunction or remorse. "I've kicked out more Arabs than anyone you can name," he snarled at one right-wing heckler. Allegations of mistreatment and torture of Palestinians—abuses that had decreased during the Begin years—began to resurface.

He was equally contemptuous of Jewish settlers. He called the Gush Emunim movement "a cancer in the body of democratic Israel." He detested Jewish fanatics and feared their messianic obsessions would destroy the democratic nature of the state.

What he cared about most was the army. "I regard every IDF soldier as my responsibility—almost as if he were my son," he writes in his memoirs. This was not the usual political hyperbole but, in many ways, Yitzhak Rabin's deepest self-truth.

When the intifada began, the human dimension eluded him once again. He and his intelligence analysts at first blamed it on radical governments in Iran and Syria, a total misreading of the local rage that sparked the uprising. After several harrowing weeks in which soldiers opened fire all too frequently on unarmed Palestinians, he issued the infamous "break their bones" command. The idea was to save lives by substituting clubs for bullets in putting down the intifada; a broken arm seemed a more humanitarian punishment than a bullet in the head. But Rabin never realized how such beatings would look on international television screens, nor did he conceive of the searing, demoralizing impact such close, personal, hand-to-hand combat would have on his own men.

Rabin and Shamir, although far from friends, were both hardened, cynical survivors of long struggles within their political parties and they had a grudging respect for each other. Retired Israeli diplomat Gideon Rafael described them this way: "Shamir's intransigence is convictional, unlike Rabin's obstinacy which is congenital."

But Rabin was far more pragmatic than Shamir. By 1989 he had come to the conclusion that a new strategy was necessary to cope with the pressures the intifada had inflicted. He was especially concerned about the erosion of morale in his cherished army. He was opposed to an independent Palestinian state and believed that opening talks with the PLO would be a step in that direction. But he and his analysts identified the green shoots of a new Palestinian leadership rising from the rich soil of the intifada, and they saw in this leadership a potentially moderate alternative to the PLO. People like Faisal Husseini of East Jerusalem or Jad Isaac of Beit Sahur might be willing to negotiate political autonomy, and finally might settle for territorial compromise in the West Bank and confederation with Jordan, which Rabin saw as the ultimate solution. But first they must be freed from subservience to the PLO hierarchy in Tunis. The first step in helping them gain such independence, Rabin believed, was to hold elections in the territories to choose leaders who would be authorized to negotiate.

It was, in many ways, a flawed strategy. In the name of security Rabin's army was busy locking up such potential interlocutors as fast as they arose and thus producing a new generation of enemies rather than peace partners. There was no chance that these local leaders were prepared to divorce themselves from Tunis. Nonetheless, it was at least a coherent strategy. Shamir was not enthusiastic. He did not share Rabin's vision of what a final settlement should be. Local Palestinians were useful to him only if they were prepared ultimately to settle for a permanent form of autonomy that would leave Israel in control of the land, water and security and effectively give Palestinians only limited powers to run their own schools and hospitals and collect their own garbage. Still, Shamir needed a plan and he needed allies. Despite the differences he authorized his cabinet secretary, Elyakim Rubinstein, and his trusted colleague Meridor to work out a proposal with Rabin.

They devised a plan in early 1989 calling for elections followed by an interim period of autonomy of three to five years during which local Palestinians would run most of their own affairs on a trial basis while negotiators began working on a final settlement. Shamir added provisions banning PLO participation in the talks and declaring in advance that the final negotiations would not result in a Palestinian state. He and Labor agreed to omit mention of several issues that divided them, including whether East Jerusalem's Arabs should be eligible to vote in these elections and what kind of participation, if any, should be granted to exiled Palestinians outside the territories. And the plan was mute on the biggest issue of all: whether Israel was ultimately prepared to exchange occupied territory in return for a peace pact. It was, said one Labor participant, an exercise in "constructive ambiguity," the first time Likud and Labor had ever agreed on a joint peace proposal.

The "Shamir Plan" was not exactly a rousing diplomatic breakthrough. It offered virtually no concessions beyond what Israel had already agreed to

eleven years earlier at Camp David. It did not suspend or restrict the building of new Jewish settlements nor limit the army's tough measures against
the intifada. "Shamir came up with the bare minimum necessary to placate
the United States and world opinion without negating his party principles,"
said Harry Wall, Israel representative of the Anti-Defamation League. "His
dilemma was how to continue the peace process without destroying his
party." But despite its tepid provisions, Shamir's plan inevitably triggered
another round in the permanent power struggle within his own party.

Even in the best of times Israeli politics was a cauldron of grand schemes
and petty ambitions in which the main ingredients were greed, egotism,
willfulness and betrayal. Political parties were odd collections of tribal
identities, personal interests and patchwork coalitions. Separation of church
and state was a non sequitur; clerics who in the United States would have
been confined to their pulpits ran their own political machines, selling their
votes to the highest bidder. Agreements between factions, as Shamir had so
starkly demonstrated in 1988, were often not worth the paper they were
written on. There was a certain logic to the system: in such a young, evolving and diverse society, it was argued, all groups needed some stake in the
political process, and the smaller the party, the more truly representative of
a particular interest group it could be. But by 1990 the oxygen of pure
democracy—a political party needed only 1 percent of the popular vote to
win a Knesset seat—had soured into the stench of chaos.

Knesset members were accountable, but only to their own parties, not to
the voters at large. Each party ran its own list of candidates and the electorate voted for the entire list. If Labor got 25 percent of the vote nation-
ally, the first thirty people on its 120-member list became Knesset
members. Likud had the most democratic structure; its list was chosen by a
central committee of about 3,000 members, whereas until 1988 Labor's was
chosen by four men sitting in a dark room in the party's Tel Aviv headquarters. Thereafter it, too, gave this power to its central committee. The system
rewarded party loyalty above all else, producing more good soldiers than
gifted legislators.

In such a system political wars had no beginning and no end. Israeli governments were based on such thin majorities that rivals both within and
without the ruling party had sound reasons to continue chipping away.
There was no culture of winner takes all; even after election day, winners
could never really feel secure and losers never quite lost.

Lacking a written constitution or a formal system of checks and balances
to provide restraints on governmental power, Israel relied instead on the
vast array of smaller parties to put brakes on the ambitions of the larger

ones. No party had ever ruled Israel alone; even Ben-Gurion, Israel's first and most revered leader, had never won as much as 40 percent of the popular vote. The system coughed and sputtered but continued to function as long as one of the big parties finished well ahead of the others, as Labor did from the birth of the state in 1948 until 1977, and as Likud did until 1984. But then the two major parties became locked in mortal stalemate. For six years they struggled desperately for supremacy by constructing jerry-rigged coalitions of disparate, hostile factions riddled with internal contradictions. The system not only gave the smaller parties enormous leverage; it also encouraged them to cause frequent crises so that they could gain more rewards. Too often it was a sanction for anarchy.

Yitzhak Shamir put together just such a dubious marriage of the far right and the ultra-Orthodox after the 1988 election, when the Likud nosed out Labor by only one Knesset seat—forty to thirty-nine. He cobbled it together only to abandon it when Labor agreed at the last minute to return in a subordinate position in a partnership government in which Shamir himself was prime minister. But this arrangement was doomed from the start. Labor's Peres, relegated to finance minister, made no secret of his ambition to overthrow the new government and return himself to the prime minister's chair. The main force holding him back was Rabin, who once again was named defense minister and enjoyed the power and credibility that serving in such a broad coalition bestowed.

Shamir had even bigger problems within his own camp. The Likud was an uneasy alliance between two distinct movements. First was the traditional right—the heirs of the Jewish militants from Eastern Europe who had formed the heart of Zeev Jabotinsky's Betar youth movement and were later a part of the anti-British underground in the 1930s and 1940s. They were the narrow power base of Menachem Begin's Herut, the small political party that for the first two decades of statehood continually finished a distant second, or worse, to Ben-Gurion's broader-based, left-wing Labor. What transformed the ideologically pure but politically anemic Herut into the modern, powerful Likud was an infusion of a new generation of populist voters, largely Eastern Jews, the Sephardim, who came from Morocco and other Arab countries. They felt permanently relegated to second-class status by the haughty Labor Zionist establishment and craved equal rights and economic opportunity. Begin's charismatic personality welded these disparate forces together into Israel's most powerful political movement, but charisma was an asset that Shamir sorely lacked. Almost as soon as Begin stepped down in 1983, the conflict between these two unnatural allies reemerged.

It was exacerbated in 1988 by the new coalition arrangement with Labor.

Under the deal Israel's major cabinet posts were evenly divided among the parties, leaving fewer slots for Shamir's Likud colleagues. He named Arens, his closest ally and a Betar alumnus, to the Foreign Affairs Ministry, leaving powerful party rivals David Levy and Ariel Sharon with minor cabinet posts. The two men had little in common: Levy was a pragmatic, Moroccan-born, ethnic politician with a silver-gray pompadour and a large grassroots following among working-class Sephardim, whereas Sharon was an Israeli-born war hero and ideological hawk with a bulldog demeanor who had joined Likud in the early 1970s. But they were united by their common resentment at being cast aside and by their supreme disdain for Shamir, the accidental prime minister. They were joined by Yitzhak Modai, a misfit politician of small constituency but vast ego who had briefly been finance minister in the old national unity government.

Together, these three volatile personalities tore into Shamir's bland peace plan like hounds into a newborn lamb, branding it a betrayal of Likud principles and likening it to treason. They harassed Shamir for months, seeking every opportunity to challenge and insult him. Sharon eventually resigned from the cabinet, dropping his bombshell in the middle of a rancorous party conference while outshouting the prime minister. Under Shamir's leadership, he cried, "Palestinian terror is running wild, Jewish lives have been abandoned." Despite their bombast the three ministers lacked the power to overthrow Shamir, but their complaints and shrill warnings were the background noise that he was compelled to overcome each time he tried to make a move.

Upon this internal domestic Israeli game, an outside party was about to intrude.

George Bush's administration arrived in Washington in January 1989 with a limited agenda on the Middle East and no great residual affection for Israel. James Baker, the new secretary of state, was a cold, calculating man who was quick to size up what worked and what did not, a man not inclined to repeat the mistakes of his predecessor, George Shultz. Baker was interested in results, not sentiments. The new administration was willing to exploit the opening it had inherited from its predecessor—the dialogue with the PLO. And it was interested in seeing what the Israelis might have to offer. But Baker approached the issue like a Wall Street lawyer sizing up a takeover target. He wanted to know the bottom line. While Shultz had offered his own plan and no deadline, allowing Shamir and the Arabs to kill it simply by never saying yes, Baker offered no blueprint but insisted that both sides propose their own.

"We begin with a sense that there are strict limits to what we can accomplish by ourselves," a senior National Security Council aide explained in the spring of 1989. "We could have twenty special envoys and an entire fleet of shuttles—but we can't make decisions for the parties involved or impose peace. We can play a helpful role at critical junctures, but the bulk of the work must be done by the local players."

To the Americans, Shamir's proposal represented the first break in the Likud-led government's intransigence and an opportunity to chisel their way to a breakthrough. Just as Jimmy Carter's diplomats had battered and cajoled Menachem Begin into recognizing the legitimacy of Palestinian aspirations at Camp David, so did they hope to drag Begin's heir into a diplomatic process he could neither dictate nor escape.

But there was a fundamental contradiction between Washington and Jerusalem that made the task next to impossible. After initiating its dialogue with the PLO, Washington saw the organization as an indispensable partner in the negotiating process. Without the PLO's blessing, the Americans believed that Palestinians in the territories would never agree to participate in negotiations for local elections and self-rule, so the administration set out to win PLO acceptance of the peace process without forcing the Israelis into a direct dialogue with the movement. By contrast, Shamir saw the PLO as a mortal enemy. The main purpose of the entire process for him was to create a more moderate alternative Palestinian leadership that would undermine the movement. If there was no alternative to the PLO, then Shamir was content that there be no process.

Washington wanted Arafat in; Shamir wanted him dead. Between those two positions there was no room for compromise. "Our logic is completely opposite to yours," Yossi Ben-Aharon told U.S. Ambassador Thomas Pickering.

Arens was the first to feel the new chill out of Washington. As a former ambassador to the United States, a man who had been raised in Chicago and whose accent and manners were quintessentially American, Arens believed in the U.S. connection, which he saw as his particular franchise. His relationship with Shultz had been intimate. He saw no reason it should not continue with another Republican administration. But on his first trip to Washington as foreign minister in March 1989, Arens found out how much things had changed. He had a brisk, no-nonsense private meeting with Baker, then was surprised when the secretary of state went before a congressional committee the following day to say that Israel had better come up with something useful or it might one day have to talk directly with the PLO. This was very different from what he had heard from Baker in private and he immediately sought a second meeting. He did not get one. Arens came back to Jerusalem shaken and upset.

Shamir was next. Two days before he arrived in Washington in April 1989, President Bush met with Egypt's President Hosni Mubarak. Speaking to reporters afterward, Bush called on Israel to end its occupation of Arab territory. It was the kind of blunt statement that Ronald Reagan never would have made, and coming just before Shamir's own scheduled visit it sent an unmistakable message.

Three days later Shamir stepped into the Oval Office. It was a chilly, jangled meeting. He arrived with his "plan"—it had yet to be introduced to the fractious cabinet, let alone approved—and he outlined to Bush the ideas it contained, including the call for local Palestinian elections. Bush told Shamir that the United States would try to help get the plan off the ground by talking to the Arab states.

Then Bush raised the issue of Jewish settlements. He told Shamir they would be an obstacle to getting negotiations going and argued passionately that if Shamir really wanted peace he must suspend new construction, just as Menachem Begin had done during the Camp David talks a decade earlier. Shamir, a little surprised by the president's vehemence, gave a typically enigmatic response. "It will not be a problem," he told Bush. What he meant was that, in his view, settlements were a phony issue; if the Arab states really wanted to negotiate peace with Israel they would not allow settlements to be a stumbling block. But Bush heard Shamir's words differently. To him, "it will not be a problem" meant that Shamir was prepared to suspend or at least retard building new settlements in order to give the administration a chance to get negotiations under way.

George Bush believed he had a commitment. Yet a few days after Shamir returned to Jerusalem, Israel announced plans to establish a half dozen new settlements. The president felt he had been played for a fool. "He sat in that chair right there and told me no more settlements," an irate Bush complained to American Jewish leaders when they visited the White House.

For his part, Shamir had left Washington convinced that Bush was no friend of Israel, was tilted toward the Arab side and was obsessed with obtaining a freeze on settlements.

Shamir and Bush had laid the groundwork for four years of mistrust and miscommunication. Both would remember that opening session and those six little words, each one certain that the other was to blame for the misunderstanding.

A few weeks later Baker laid out the parameters of the administration's disagreement with Israel. In his first major address on Middle East policy at the annual meeting of the American Israel Public Affairs Committee in May, Baker warned that Israel would have to relinquish occupied territory and suspend settlements if it ever hoped to make progress toward peace.

"For Israel, now is the time to lay aside once and for all the unrealistic vision of a Greater Israel," said Baker. His words were greeted with total silence.

Israel and its supporters reacted quickly. While Arens issued a statement in Jerusalem saying Israel was "offended" by the speech, AIPAC collected signatures from ninety-four of a hundred U.S. senators to a letter demanding that Baker "strongly and publicly endorse the Israeli peace initiative." The number of signatures that AIPAC was able to gather caught Baker by surprise, and the letter was interpreted as a rebuke to the secretary of state.

The Israelis had won the first round.

Yitzhak Shamir returned to Jerusalem with the classic political problem of a man in the middle. He had to convince his governing partners in Labor and his diplomatic partners in Washington that his peace plan was serious and significant. At the same time he had to portray it to his hawkish antagonists within the Likud as no big deal. And so in May, just four days after the cabinet approved the plan, he derided it to his Likud Knesset colleagues as "just Camp David in a new package." The bottom line, he insisted to them, was that "we shall not give the Arabs one inch of our land, even if we have to negotiate for ten years. . . . We hold the veto in our hands. What could be better than that?"

But his opponents within Likud were not placated. While Shamir and Arens negotiated agreement on the plan with Labor, Levy and Sharon rallied their forces within the Likud central committee. Sharon, who was chairman of the committee, called a meeting for July 5. Shamir's allies insisted to him that he had the votes to win an endorsement of the plan. On the afternoon of the meeting Shamir phoned Sharon to explain the proposal one more time and seek Sharon's acquiescence. When Sharon refused Shamir lost his temper. "The hell with you," he told Sharon. "I will fight you and teach you a lesson today and I will win." Meridor and Olmert, who were in the room with Shamir, nodded their approval. Then Shamir climbed into the back of the prime ministerial car with cabinet minister Moshe Nissim, an arch conservative, for the ride to the Tel Aviv fairgrounds where the meeting was to take place.

Something happened along the way. When Meridor and Olmert, joined by Arens, arrived an hour later, they discovered Shamir ensconced in a back room with Sharon and Levy. They tried to enter but were ordered to wait outside. When Shamir emerged he told them he had agreed to a number of additional conditions to his plan that had been dictated by Sharon. These were designed to make it virtually impossible for the Americans to broker an agreement between Israelis and Palestinians on the election proposal.

Meridor, Olmert and Arens were stunned. Looking back later, all three would see this as the turning point, the moment when it became clear that Shamir was not the man they had hoped he would be. Their leader, the tough guy, had suddenly caved in without warning or consultation.

Finally Olmert spoke up. "Yitzhak, excuse me, but this is a total surrender," he said. "You've sold out on everything." Nissim admonished him: "Don't exaggerate; it's not so bad."

The showdown in the Likud central committee highlighted the divisions between the two circles of advisers around Shamir. The first was a pragmatic, Western-oriented set of talented younger politicians, all lawyers in their early forties, who had been cultivated by Shamir in the days when he served as speaker of the Knesset. There was Ronnie Milo, a Tel Avivan who had entered the Knesset in 1977 and had helped the innately reticent, taciturn speaker navigate the treacherous backwaters of the Likud. There was Ehud Olmert, who at age forty-four had already served for nearly sixteen years in the Knesset and whom Shamir used as a troubleshooter for political and diplomatic crises.

But the favorite son among these crown princes was Dan Meridor, Shamir's justice minister and closest adviser. Meridor's father had been a member of Begin's underground of Jewish fighters and had served in Begin's Herut Party in the 1950s and 1960s. At age thirty-four Meridor had become secretary of the cabinet under Begin, and he was one of the few Beginites to embrace Shamir when he took over from the legendary prime minister.

Meridor had inherited his father's belief in Israel's historical right to the West Bank and Gaza, yet he insisted that Palestinians were entitled to civil rights and humane treatment. As justice minister he sought to ensure that Jewish settlers who attacked Palestinians were prosecuted, calling settler violence "the courage of cowards." He became the target of threatening phone calls and graffiti branding him a leftist and an "Arab lover."

Meridor knew Shamir was stubborn, cautious and skeptical, but he believed that ultimately Shamir would make compromises for peace once the old man was convinced that a deal was in Israel's interests. Meridor and the princes helped sell Shamir to Washington, to the American Jewish leadership and, ultimately, to themselves as a hard but fair bargainer, the right man for the tough negotiations that lay ahead. With his friendly, intelligent demeanor and his growing connections in Washington—he was especially close to Dennis Ross, one of Baker's top aides—Meridor became the intermediary who explained Shamir to the world and explained the world to Shamir. Meridor probably had more fans in the State Department than in the Likud central committee. His own career and his status as the indispensable man were tied to Shamir's. If the prime minister turned out to be something less than Dan Meridor had advertised, then he, too, would stand to lose.

Shamir made sure Meridor got the cabinet post of justice minister in the crowded 1988 national unity government, and he named Olmert and Milo to cabinet positions as well. He believed he was creating a new generation of political leaders who would help keep Likud in power for many years to come. These younger men were his agents and his advisers, and he tasked them as he had his lieutenants in Lehi and the Mossad. "On the one hand he was proud that he had promoted these youngsters," said political aide Yossi Achimeir. "On the other hand he didn't rely absolutely on any of them. He knew their weaknesses."

But for all their intimacy, there was a basic disconnection between Shamir and Meridor. Although they were both staunch believers in Eretz Yisrael, the Israeli-born Meridor was a child of the post-Holocaust, post-independence era. No naïve romantic, he had served as a tank commander on the front lines in both the 1967 and 1973 wars and had been wounded on the Golan Heights in the latter. He had seen friends die, yet his outlook was essentially optimistic; he saw a world in which Israel could compete successfully and self-confidently. He was part of that world and shared many of its values. He had a deep affection for people and tended to trust them unless he had reason not to.

Shamir, of course, came from a different world. He believed Meridor and the other princes were too often soft, moralistic and naïve. "They're nice boys, they're intelligent, they know how to work hard, but they have no steel," he lamented to a close friend. Unlike himself, they were not immune to pressure, not prepared to see the darkness at the core of their rivals. "They never had all their childhood diseases," he quipped.

"Cut into most of these Likud guys and below the surface you find their pessimism isn't very deep, it's a political pose," said author Zeev Chafets, who headed the Government Press Office under Begin. "But take a chainsaw and slice Shamir in half and it's the same thing in the middle as on the outside: deeply cynical, deeply pessimistic. A truly nasty guy."

There was another circle beyond Meridor and the princes—an older, less visible, far more hawkish set of men who were more attuned to Shamir's deepest beliefs. They included Ben-Aharon, a former professional diplomat who served as director general of Shamir's office, wrote his hard-line speeches and set the adamant, uncompromising tone for many of his public pronouncements. A Jerusalem-born Orthodox Jew who was raised in Egypt and spoke fluent Arabic, Ben-Aharon believed he knew more about the

Arabs—their supposed treacherousness, their fanaticism, their disregard for human life—than most Israelis. He played to Shamir's suspicions and pessimism.

A handful of older politicians were also part of this circle. They included Eliezer Gerabin, a former Lehi subordinate who had once shared a prison cell with Shamir and now ran one of Tel Aviv's most successful advertising and marketing firms; Michael Dekel, another Lehi alumnus, named deputy defense minister so that he could keep an eye on Rabin and press for more Jewish settlements, and Nissim, a lawyer from an old Jerusalem family who served in several different cabinet posts and became Shamir's emissary to the ultra-Orthodox. These were Shamir's true soulmates—hardened, intuitively hawkish men who operated from behind the curtains. They were inured to the theatrics of Israeli politics, unfazed by public opinion polls. "Let the dogs bark, the caravan moves on," was Nissim's motto. Their Shamir was devious, unyielding and ideologically pure—a much different political animal than Meridor's hard bargainer.

Who was right about Shamir? His cave-in at the Likud central committee meeting had suggested the hawks and the hard-liners knew him best. Soon there would be another test.

It came early in 1990 when, after months of delays and false starts, the Bush administration pressed anew for Israel to accept a procedure for negotiations between Israelis and Palestinians. In February Arens returned to Washington for another session with Baker. This time Baker put an intriguing offer on the table. The Egyptians were willing to host talks between the Israelis and a delegation of Palestinians from the occupied territories, with no PLO members present. The two sides would discuss arrangements for the local elections Shamir's plan had stipulated. Baker patiently explained that he could achieve Israel's main requirements for the talks but that the Israelis would have to be flexible on details such as who sat in the Palestinian delegation. One of the Palestinians would be a West Bank resident with a second home or an office in East Jerusalem; another would be a non-PLO member of the Palestinian diaspora.

Neither condition seemed a major problem to Arens, whose main concern was that the PLO might try somehow to hijack the talks. The Foreign Affairs Ministry had thirty "nightmare" scenarios, including the prospect that the Palestinian delegation would fly off to Tunis in the middle of the sessions to seek Arafat's public blessing. Despite these reservations Arens acceded, and Dan Meridor's brother, Salai, and Dennis Ross hammered out the details. The next step was to be a three-way meeting between Baker,

Arens and Egyptian Foreign Minister Esmat Abdel Meguid in Cairo to select the Palestinian delegation.

Shamir was suspicious that Baker was working with Egyptian President
Hosni Mubarak to bring in the PLO through the back door. He believed
Arens had caved in too readily, been too soft and allowed himself to be outmaneuvered by Baker. But he led Arens to believe that he would reluctantly
go along with the agreement.

Shamir's grudging acceptance was gradually worn down over the next
ten days. Several prominent Likud hard-liners, including Menachem Begin's son Zeev (known as "Benny") and Benjamin Netanyahu, announced
their opposition. There were also rising tensions with the United States. Appearing before a House appropriations subcommittee, Baker publicly
linked a proposed U.S. guarantee for $400 million in loans to Israel to fund
housing for Soviet Jewish immigrants to a freeze on West Bank settlements.
Money was fungible, Baker warned, and the loan money used inside Israel
proper could free up Israeli funds for settlements.

Later that week Baker phoned Shamir to press him for an answer on the
Cairo terms. It was a brusque, tense dialogue. Baker had boiled the terms
down to one simple question: "Will the government of Israel be ready to
agree to sit with Palestinians on a name-by-name basis who are residents of
the West Bank and Gaza?" Shamir refused to respond, seeking instead a
commitment from Baker that Jerusalem would be kept off the agenda of
the talks. "We'll see," was all Baker would reply. When Shamir further
raised objections about the composition of the Palestinian delegation,
Baker retorted: "Misha [Arens] and I reached agreement already."

At the same time relations were souring between Shamir and Rabin.
Shamir suspected that Rabin was colluding with Mubarak and the Americans to pressure him into agreeing to Cairo. "I was operating on the basis
of a minimum of trust between me and Rabin," Shamir told colleagues. "If
he and Peres are working behind my back, it changes the rules of the
game." For his part, Rabin had come to believe that Shamir was not serious
about negotiating. "He wants the Palestinians to come on their knees," Rabin complained.

The Likud ministers met at the prime minister's residence in Jerusalem
on a Saturday night in early March to hammer out their position. It was a
tense session. Arens described the Cairo formula and insisted it was the
best deal Israel could get. Sharon, who had quit the cabinet in protest several weeks earlier, was not present, but Levy spoke against the proposal. So
did Netanyahu, who said the plan was a gun held against Israel's head to
force them to negotiate with the PLO. Better to call off the process now, he

insisted, because if it went to Cairo, U.S. pressure for a deal with the Palestinians would be "brutal." Nissim also expressed doubts.

Meridor usually kept quiet at such sessions, reserving his opinion for private meetings with Shamir, but this time he felt compelled to speak. Likud had devised the peace plan and advertised its virtues, he said. If the party now rejected the opportunity to pursue one of the plan's key provisions, it would send a clear message to the Israeli public and the Americans that the Likud was not serious about peace. Labor would almost certainly pull out of the government and might well have the votes to bring it down and replace it with a narrow coalition led by Peres. That would be ten times worse than going to Cairo. "It's a turning point," Meridor told the ministers. "If we don't say yes now, our vision and our ideology, everything we believe in, won't survive. This is the test of our principles."

Meridor's passionate remarks seemed to carry the day. By the end of the five-hour session, he thought he could count on eight votes in favor of the plan, with Nissim and Levy the only ministers opposed. But Shamir had not spoken. He thanked everyone for their views and told them they would meet again in two days to settle the matter. But his silence was ominous.

On that day came another unwelcome pronouncement from the United States. Bush had been stewing for weeks over a statement Shamir had made suggesting that Israel would use the new influx of Russian Jews to help settle the occupied territories. At a press conference on the golf course in Palm Springs, California, Bush warned Israel against settling Russians in the territories. He included East Jerusalem, which Israel had annexed in 1967, in his definition of occupied lands. The statement, which seemed to redefine U.S. policy, reinforced Shamir's fear that the United States would not prevent East Jerusalem from finding its way onto the agenda in Cairo.

By the following Monday when the Likud ministers met again, Shamir had made up his mind. Levy was absent and Nissim was the only minister present who opposed going to Cairo. Nonetheless, Shamir told them he wanted to put a number of new conditions on the government's participation in the talks—enough, in fact, to sink the plan. He knew his decision could cause the government to collapse, but he believed Likud could weather the storm. This was a matter of principle and he was not prepared to bend. He knew most of them wanted to go to Cairo. "Go ahead," he told them, "but I will not follow."

The ministers had to go along with Shamir, but Meridor was crushed. Shamir's decision was a vote of no confidence in Arens and himself. And it confirmed Meridor's worst fears about Shamir's inability to take a concrete step toward peace. Shamir had caved in to his right wing in July before the central committee meeting and now he had caved in again, only this time he was going to take them all down with him. Arens, Olmert, Milo—all agreed with Meridor that political disaster was imminent.

When Shamir announced a new set of conditions for going to Cairo, Yitzhak Rabin realized the joint peace initiative was dead. Like the Likud doves, he felt betrayed by Shamir. He was still wary of Peres—the man was an inveterate conspirator, Rabin felt—but when Peres assured him that Labor had the votes both to bring down the government and form a new one without Likud, he was prepared to go along. On March 6 the Labor Party cabinet ministers rejected Shamir's conditions.

But the final architect of the government's collapse was not Peres nor Rabin nor the Americans, but rather an obscure religious party whose leaders believed they were on a mission from God. Shas, the Hebrew acronym for the Sephardi Torah Guardians, had entered the Knesset for the first time only six years before. Most of its supporters were natural Likud voters: hawkish, anti-Arab, working-class Sephardic Jews from Morocco and other Arab states who supported Shas out of ethnic pride and a sense of reverence for the party's charismatic spiritual leader, Rabbi Ovadia Yosef. But Yosef himself and Arye Deri, the party's political strongman, were far more dovish.

Yosef believed the Jewish state could never fulfill its historic destiny without peace with the Arabs, and he believed that peace could not be achieved without territorial compromise. At a 1989 symposium in Jerusalem in which he shared the stage with Rabin, Yosef proclaimed: "To hold or conquer territories in the Land of Israel by force, in our time, against the will of the nations of the world, is a sin. If we can give back the territories, and thereby avoid war and bloodshed, we are obliged to do so."

And time and again Deri had argued publicly that Israel had no choice but to negotiate with the PLO. While he did not describe his vision of a final peace settlement, he pointedly refused to rule out the establishment of a Palestinian state. This put him to the left of even the Labor Party.

Labor helped arrange a trip to Egypt in 1989 in which Yosef and Deri were treated as if they were visiting heads of state. President Mubarak pleaded with them personally to pressure Shamir for the sake of peace. Deri, in turn, helped persuade Rabin that Shas's commitment to toppling Shamir and installing a Labor-led government was genuine and irreversible. Deri, who was a remarkably agile politician, expected that Shas would receive a full range of cabinet posts and benefits from serving as Labor's junior partner, and he himself hoped to become finance minister.

Deri had to be careful; his pro-Likud constituents were not about to sanction betrayal. For months he had conspired quietly with his Labor friends, biding his time, waiting for the right moment. Now it had arrived.

At the last moment, however, Yosef hesitated. The rabbi still believed it was possible to compel Shamir to say yes to Baker and salvage the government. But the prime minister would not back down. On March 13, eight days after Shamir decided he was not going to Cairo, he dismissed Peres from the cabinet for plotting its overthrow. Rabin and the rest of the Labor ministers immediately submitted their resignations. Two days later the Knesset held a bitter twelve-hour debate on the fate of Shamir's government. Near the end, the session was suspended for two hours while Peres, Rabin and Shamir raced to Yosef's modest Jerusalem apartment to hear his final plea for unity.

It was an extraordinary event: the country's elected representatives suspending urgent business while its three top leaders were summoned to the home of a rabbi to compete for his blessing. Yosef handed them a sheet of paper containing his proposed compromise: Shamir would reinstate Peres and Labor and agree to the Cairo talks, while Peres would reaffirm Labor's commitment to a united Jerusalem and its refusal to negotiate with the PLO.

Peres signed on the spot. Shamir refused.

"He spoke to me with great respect but I couldn't influence him at all," Yosef later recalled. "He stood inflexible in all his opinions—'no, no, no.' He didn't give me one positive answer." An hour later, under Yosef's instructions, five of Shas's six Knesset members abstained from supporting the government. Five members of the ultrareligious Agudat Yisrael, hoping to reap rewards from a new round of coalition building, also abandoned the government and voted with Peres. By a vote of sixty to fifty-five the Knesset for the first time in its history approved a no-confidence motion against a sitting government.

Israel's long stalemate, it seemed, was ending. Yitzhak Shamir was on his way out.

The sense of unease and unhappiness in Meridor and the other young princes now turned to panic. All of them were about to lose their cabinet posts and go down with Shamir. And if Labor succeeded in putting together a new government, there was certain to be a bloodbath within the unruly, deeply divided Likud, with all the malcontents ganging up on them and on Arens. All of this, they told themselves, was Shamir's fault. The stubborn bastard had refused to budge an inch. As they worked the phones they found widespread disaffection with Shamir among party colleagues that mirrored their own. "This guy is nuts and we can't keep him in power for one day longer," one Knesset member told Olmert. "He'll destroy all of us." Others agreed. If they could force Shamir out and replace him with Arens, a new unity government might yet be formed that would agree to go to Cairo and thus keep Likud in power.

They met that night after the no-confidence vote in a private room at the Knesset, called together by Mattiyahu Drobles, a close colleague of Arens and former Knesset member. Meridor, Olmert, Milo and Benny Begin were there. Arens was on his way home to a Tel Aviv suburb when Drobles reached him by carphone and called him back to Jerusalem. Drobles sketched out a scenario: They would go to Shamir and demand that he stand aside for Arens. Shamir would offer his resignation, they would formally refuse to accept it, but he would insist. Drobles said they should go see Shamir immediately, but the others said no, let the old man get a night's sleep. They would do it in the morning.

When Meridor spoke to other dissident Knesset members early Friday morning, he told them to hang on, that nothing was lost yet. He pleaded especially hard with Deri. Meridor praised Deri for unseating Shamir but begged him not to throw Shas's support either to Labor or to Levy's rival Likud faction. According to Deri's account, Meridor then said he and the other princes would march into Shamir's office later that morning and demand the prime minister's resignation. Arens would become the new leader. In Meridor's version, there was no such commitment; Meridor only asked for time to come up with a new Likud policy acceptable to Shas. Only the two men know which version is true.

Three obstacles stood in the way of a successful coup against Shamir. The first was the replacement candidate. Even while his closest colleagues were pressing him to take the reins, Arens himself remained passive. He had promised long ago that he would never work behind Shamir's back and he felt uncomfortable about breaking that promise, even though Shamir had deeply disappointed him. When Milo and Olmert spoke privately with Arens, they sensed no enthusiasm for a coup. Of course Arens wanted the job, but did it have to be this way?

The second problem was their own loyalty. Having spent seven years under Shamir, and owing him their cabinet posts, the princes were loath to confront him. "It's like when your father is in charge of the family business and things begin to break down," explained an aide. "You know it's bad and you know he's ruining the business, but it's hard to fire your own father."

The last and most important obstacle was Shamir himself. The conspiracy was less than airtight, and by the time the princes entered the cabinet conference room next to Shamir's office at 10 A.M. the prime minister knew all about their halfhearted coup. He opened the discussion and dominated it for ninety minutes, exhorting his reluctant lieutenants to battle on. "Let's cool off," he told them. "Nothing is lost for us; we're going to prevail." There was no reason to despair. They would prevent Peres from forming a new government, then put together their own coalition without Labor.

The others strained for any hint from Shamir that he was weary, fed up and ready to step aside. There was none. Shamir was firm, clearheaded and insistent. He said not a word about backing down. Olmert suggested that with Labor out of the cabinet Shamir could say yes to the Cairo talks, explaining to Baker and to Yosef that he had been against the plan because he could not trust his own governing partners. This way Shas could be kept inside the government. But Shamir refused to consider the idea. "It was an incredible performance," one of the princes said afterward. "We're lying there dead, certain it's all over, and he's just getting started. I don't know where he got the strength."

Olmert also raised the issue of the Likud Knesset faction meeting scheduled for the following night. Many in Sharon's and Levy's camps were preparing for a showdown. Shamir would have to go to the meeting in Tel Aviv and defend himself, Olmert said. But Shamir only smiled. "You go for me," he told the princes. "It's better that you defend me than that I should have to go and defend myself." After a short discussion he dismissed them. Faced with Shamir's iron certitude, they never spoke the words they had come to say. The confrontation was over before it began. "Take a good look around," Meridor told his colleagues as they left the cabinet room. "It could be years before we get back here again."

Only one person stood up to Shamir. Bemused by the silence of his erstwhile co-conspirators, Matti Drobles told Shamir that he wished to talk to him in private. As the others left, the two men adjourned to Shamir's adjacent office. There Drobles told him to his face what the others would say only behind his back: "With all due respect, Yitzhak, it's time for you to reach the appropriate conclusion to save the government and the Likud." Shamir's face froze and his voice rose. "*Gam atah,* Matti?" he asked Drobles. "You too? After all we've been through?" Shamir ordered Drobles out of his office. There was nothing more to say. It was a ninety-second meeting.

Shamir then demanded a face-to-face meeting with Arens in which he confronted his foreign affairs minister with Drobles's remarks and demanded to know if he could still count on Arens's support. Arens said he could. "I haven't authorized anyone else to talk on my behalf," Arens told him. "My leader is Yitzhak Shamir."

Shamir worked the phones all day Friday and Saturday, repeatedly calling Meridor, Olmert and Milo, using as his agents the same men who he now suspected had conspired against him. He believed that his own people would back him once they knew Arens would not fight. They may have had their misgivings about Shamir, but they shared a far deeper fear of Levy and Sharon. In the end, lacking a candidate of their own, they decided to stay with Shamir.

Saturday, March 17, was a day of ferment. Sharon heard rumors of the coup, as did Levy. The two men did their own quick calculations and determined that if Shamir were deposed, Arens would likely command the votes to take his place. Each decided he was better off with a fading seventy-four-year-old Shamir in the chair than with a fresher sixty-three-year-old Arens. At the meeting of Likud Knesset members that night, Shamir's staunchest supporter was none other than Ariel Sharon, formerly his most vituperative critic. The prime minister had stepped to the brink of disaster by sending Arens to negotiate the Cairo talks, Sharon solemnly told them, but then had stepped back. It was a courageous move, one they must all support. Now was not the time for a leadership change. Sharon's support was the final blow. For now at least, the Likud would stick by Yitzhak Shamir.

The no-confidence vote set off five weeks of some of the most frenzied horse trading in Israeli political history. Likud and Labor sought to line up support among the small, fractious religious parties and to entice, bribe or otherwise shake loose enough malcontents from each other's party to form a new government. Shamir had a basic disadvantage because the small parties had felt used and discarded by him during the last round in November 1988. But the hawkish, more traditional Likud was the more natural partner for these parties than the dovish, socialist-oriented Labor.

Peres had won the support of two ultra-Orthodox parties in overthrowing Shamir. Now he launched a bidding war for their support in forming a new government. Their interest in the peace process was overshadowed by more tangible concerns—power, money and a set of obscure internal rivalries, some of which dated back to the eighteenth century. The state budget prepared during the crisis included a 250 percent increase in allocations to ultra-Orthodox schools and community centers. It was quickly approved by both major parties, each of which was afraid that if it opposed the spending, the small parties would go with the other.

The process was a lethal mixture of comedy and chaos. At one point Rabbi Eliezer Mizrachi, an errant member of Agudat Yisrael, spent several days driving around in his private car after changing his unlisted carphone number in order to avoid politicians seeking to influence his vote. A tear-gas grenade outside an Aguda meeting in Bnei Brak, the ultra-Orthodox suburb of Tel Aviv, injured eleven people. The attack was preceded by death threats against leading Aguda figures for backing Peres and against Israeli President Chaim Herzog for giving Peres the first chance to form a new government.

Peres's first problem arose when Shas's ultimate rabbinical authority, ninety-two-year-old Eliezer Schach, decided to overrule Yosef and Deri and decreed that party members could not support a Labor-led government. Schach was as dovish as Yosef, but he had a deep, abiding dislike of the Labor Party and of secular Jews in general. Eleven days after the government fell, he appeared at a political rally at the Yad Eliahu arena in Tel Aviv, where he launched a scathing attack on secular society, singling out Labor-supporting kibbutzniks for special condemnation. "Can these people be called Jews?" he demanded.

Dropping into Yiddish, he described a blissful scene in a ghetto home in pre-Holocaust Europe. Secular Israelis had "cut themselves adrift from the entire past and are seeking a new Torah," Schach warned. "We must cut ourselves off from the parties that have no link to Judaism. One is better and one is worse, but basically they're the same. They have severed themselves from their forefathers."

The message was clear. Shas would not be supporting Labor.

Coupled with the sleazy coalition follies taking place at the Knesset, the speech compounded the outrage of Israel's secular majority, who saw themselves being held up for ransom by a small army of arrogant bandit-politicos in black hats. The newspaper *Haaretz* ran a cartoon showing Schach at the podium in a military cemetery surrounded by the gravestones of kibbutzniks killed fighting in Israel's wars. "Are these to be called the Jewish people?" he asks, pointing contemptuously at the graves. No one had to be reminded that kibbutzniks had contributed a disproportionate share of the nation's army officers while Schach's yeshiva students claimed military exemptions to study Torah.

After Peres lost Shas he went hunting for stray votes. He wooed Yitzhak Modai, who had been fired from two previous cabinet posts and who was famous for outbursts of crude verbal abuse. Modai once swore he would deny a budget increase to Arye Deri's Interior Ministry, "even if he lets me rape his wife." Peres also approached Avraham Sharir, a disgruntled Likudnik who had lost his seat as tourism minister after allegations, which he denied, that he and his wife traveled widely at public expense for personal enjoyment and used government drivers to run errands and transport the family dog. Despite their shortcomings, Peres promised cabinet seats to both men.

The Likud won back Modai and three other mavericks after agreeing to make Modai finance minister and bestow lesser positions on his three errant companions. Modai, seeing how Shamir had jettisoned without tears the pledges he made to small parties in 1988, insisted not only that all Likud cabinet ministers endorse the agreement in writing but also that it be approved by the party's central committee and that the party post a $2.5 million bond. The Likud signed, said a disgusted Moshe Arens, only because Modai "was holding a gun to our head."

After weeks of wrangling Peres thought he had acquired firm commitments from the five-member Aguda and from Sharir. The six votes were the bare minimum Peres needed and he immediately scheduled a Knesset session for April 11. Members of the prospective new cabinet gathered their families in the gallery that morning, preparing for their ceremonial induction into office. But a few hours before the vote Peres discovered that two members of the Aguda had defied their party's leadership and redefected to Shamir. On the verge of the first Labor-led government in thirteen years, Peres fell short.

Throughout the sordid process Peres doggedly insisted that the end—forming a government to pursue peace talks—justified the means. But even if Peres had succeeded, the gamesmanship and compromises virtually ruled out any chance of progress in the peace process. Peres would have been too dependent on an unstable collection of ultra-Orthodox rabbis and political misfits, all of them under constant pressure from Likud to redefect. Some would almost certainly have jumped ship and scuttled Peres's government at the first sign of progress. Instead of constructing a coalition for peace, Peres succeeded only in increasing the power, demands and egotism of some of the country's most dubious politicians.

The prolonged bargaining process paralyzed much of the government. Appointments for seventeen ambassadorships and senior diplomatic posts—including new ambassadors to the United States, France and the United Nations—were frozen for months.

The Israeli public was appalled by the spectacle. Some 250,000 people attended one of the biggest demonstrations in Israeli history in Tel Aviv to demand that Likud and Labor form a coalition government for the sole purpose of changing the electoral system to eliminate the small factions and provide for direct election of the prime minister. Shamir made a solemn promise that if he was returned to the premiership he would make such reforms a top priority. Like many of his promises, it was to prove unredeemable.

After five weeks of schemes, dreams and frustration, Peres finally admitted defeat. Rabin, who watched with growing incredulity as Peres manipulated and bungled his way to disaster, dubbed the entire affair "the stinking maneuver." He had lost his revered post as defense minister and was convinced that his old rival had sacrificed the unity government and the peace process in the name of blind ambition. "I would say about Shimon, 'He dug a pit . . . and fell therein,' " intoned Labor elder statesman Abba Eban.

Shamir took six weeks to construct the most right-wing coalition in Israel's history. Labor was out, and two hard right-wing parties took its place—Tsomet and Tehiya. Eventually the most right-wing of all, Rehavam Zeevi's Moledet, which advocated the expulsion of all Palestinians from the West Bank and Gaza, joined as well, over the protests of Arens and the princes.

The new government was approved on June 11 after a raucous and acrimonious Knesset session in which Shamir made no attempt to hide his inflexibility on the issue that lay at the heart of the peace problem—the future of the occupied territories. "It would be madness on our part to agree to any concession whatsoever in an area which is the soft underbelly of the Land of Israel while we are encircled by a hostile ring," he told the Knesset, including Egypt as part of the enemy camp. He also made clear that despite his earlier promises there would be no political reforms, criticizing those who showed an "excessive enthusiasm for change."

Peres, bitterly eloquent in defeat, said the new government was based upon "Shamir's unique invention—making peace without Arabs." Turning to the religious parties that had teased and abandoned him, Peres told them, "You will not be entering a God-fearing government. You will be entering a peace-fearing government. Remember, peace is no sin."

Shamir had taught Washington a lesson: he could not be bypassed. Any progress on the peace process had to come directly through him, not through Labor nor even through Arens and Meridor. The Americans, who had prayed privately that Peres would succeed and who had undermined Shamir with their public statements, were chastened but also angered. "You couldn't get Shamir to do even the most modest things because he saw precedents in everything," said an administration official. "We finally came to the conclusion that the Israeli government wasn't prepared to take yes for an answer."

A frustrated Baker was reduced to offering Shamir the White House phone number. "I can only say, take this number: (202) 456-1414," Baker said before the House Foreign Affairs Committee. "When you're serious about peace, call us."

To Meridor it seemed that Shamir had won a Pyrrhic victory. He had jettisoned his Labor partners for a ragtag collection of right-wing extremists and Jewish fundamentalists who frightened many Israelis and outraged the secular majority.

The 1990 experience reaffirmed to Shamir that he could trust no one, not even his closest aides. It confirmed his view that he was the only one with the vision and the will to lead Israel at this dangerous moment. Meridor and the others simply lacked the inner steel to take on a man who had been trained in the hardest and most ruthless of schools. The man who had followed Avraham Stern, who had ordered assassinations and bombings, who had taken on the British Empire and triumphed, was not about to walk away just because a nice Jewish boy like Dan Meridor believed it was time for him to go.

For Israel, the downfall of the national unity government did accomplish one important goal: it ended the political stalemate between left and right that had paralyzed the country since 1984. Israelis now would have a partisan government again, a true political opposition and someone to blame if the government's policies failed.

Within the cabinet, right-wing militants and religious fundamentalists made constant demands, operated at cross-purposes and sought to undermine their government's own weak initiatives. In the face of such forces Shamir's intuitive caution often slipped into paralysis. The government's most pressing historic mission—the emigration and absorption of hundreds of thousands of Soviet Jews—fell victim to such internecine squabbles and to Shamir's unwillingness or inability to lead. Meanwhile, Israel veered sharply to the right, plunging into the most ambitious settlement-building program in the West Bank in the country's history and into deepening conflict with Washington.

Shamir had long sought to avoid such a right-wing government. Now it would sap his own power and increase his innate sense of mistrust not just of his enemies, but of his closest friends. It would set the stage for his political demise—and bring Israel to the brink of sweeping change.

6. Manchild in the Promised Land

Can we find a man like this man, one who has the
spirit of God in him?

—GENESIS 41:38

THE earnest young man in the black skullcap perched anxiously on the edge of an overstuffed chair in the prime minister's waiting room was one of nature's most pathetic creatures: a humbled politician. Arye Deri knew he had miscalculated badly. He had overestimated the power of his friends, underestimated the resources and guile of his enemies and, perhaps worst of all, misjudged his hold over his own party and its rival rabbinical leaders. The imperious godfather of his political movement, ninety-two-year-old Rabbi Eliezer Schach, had shattered his dream, destroying the carefully constructed plot that Deri had hatched to topple Yitzhak Shamir and install a dovish, Labor-led government. Schach's move had left Deri—chastened, embarrassed and humiliated—to make his peace with a triumphant Shamir.

During the last two years Arye Deri had been the golden boy of Israeli politics. Tall, handsome and soft-spoken, with lively brown eyes and a sly sense of humor, Deri was a natural. As the accommodating leader of the ultrareligious yet populist-oriented Shas Party, he had become a powerful and effective agent for reconciliation between warring Israelis—secular and religious, left and right, hawks and doves. Some had even spoken of him as a potential prime minister. It was all heady stuff for a clever yeshiva boy who had been involved in politics for less than a decade. As waves of sycophantic praise washed over him, he began to believe his own reviews and was stricken with arrogance and overconfidence. Now he was paying the price for his hubris. "I never saw him so desperate," said an Israeli reporter who knew him well. "In five minutes he went from Man of the Year to Schmuck of the Year."

Day after day he sat in Shamir's antechamber, his ear glued to a mobile telephone, awaiting instructions from his rabbinical leaders and bowing deferentially to every Likud politician who walked through the door. Shamir and his cohorts were piecing together a new governing coalition and Shas desperately wanted to be part of it. Deri was full of remorse for what he had done and he wanted everyone to know it. "He would have gone for Shamir's dry cleaning if we'd asked him," said a senior prime ministerial aide who could not help enjoying the younger man's pain.

The embarrassment proved temporary. Shamir still needed Shas as much as Shas needed him. With six seats in the Knesset, Shas was the third largest political party, and the party got two cabinet portfolios in Shamir's new government and Deri himself retained control of the influential Interior Ministry. The trust between Deri and Shamir, never strong to begin with, was totally gone. Otherwise, it was business as usual. Arye Deri might have blundered badly at the politically tender age of thirty-one; he was, nonetheless, too pivotal a figure for any Israeli government to do without.

In 1968, when he was nine years old, Arye Mahlouf Ben Eliahu Deri's family came to Israel with a wave of Moroccan Jews following the Six-Day War. They settled in Bat Yam, a struggling, working-class "development town" just south of Tel Aviv. Arye's father had been a prosperous tailor in Morocco, but in Israel such jobs were hard to find. His frustration was intense; at one point he deposited Arye and his other children in the local office of the Jewish Agency for a day to protest its lack of help in his search for work. He ended up as a low-paid fabric cutter in a clothing factory.

Arye had attended a modern French-language school in Morocco and had done so well that he had skipped several grades. But in Israel he was placed with children his own age in an overcrowded, dead-end school. He was bored and unhappy and, after a while, stopped attending classes. For pocket money he and his older brother Yehuda prowled the streets scavenging for discarded bottles.

No one claimed the streets of Bat Yam were paved with gold. Unemployment there hovered in double digits in good times and bad. Many of its residents were crammed into *shikkunim*—drab, prefab, boxlike apartment buildings from the Bucharest school of socialist architecture, featuring paper-thin walls, permanently peeling plaster and windows not much bigger than postcards. There was an air of constant disappointment, of dreams forsaken. Tel Aviv, with its promise of mobility and escape, may have been just up the road, but for many of Bat Yam's residents it could have been on the other side of the moon. They called themselves *d'fukim*—literally, "the fucked-over ones."

Like the Deris, most of those who resided in the Bat Yams of Israel were Sephardim—Jews from the Muslim countries of North Africa and the Middle East. For hundreds of years they had lived in Arab-ruled lands in relative comfort and obscurity, sealed off from the tempestuous trends of the West. Just as the Enlightenment had passed them by, so had Zionism, which was one of the many European nationalist movements that the Enlightenment spawned. While European Jewry was riven by fratricidal warfare between the religious and the newly secular, Zionist and anti-Zionist, socialist and capitalist, life in the Sephardi world continued down a well-charted, less eventful road. Sephardi romantics would look back to a Golden Age of Torah learning, strong family loyalties and stable communities. Realists saw it differently: the price of stability was stagnation, neglect, second-class citizenship and, very often, extreme poverty.

The birth of Israel in 1948 shattered that tranquil world. Life in the Arab states became uncomfortable and often dangerous. Encouraged by secular Zionist missionaries who spoke of deliverance in the Promised Land, nearly 600,000 Sephardim fled to Israel in the first twenty-five years of the state's existence. They came to a country ill-prepared to take them in. Many spent years in immigrant absorption camps, their traditions shattered, their self-respect damaged and derided.

The Labor Zionist establishment, dominated by Ashkenazi Jews from Europe and devoted to a socialist vision of the New Israeli, saw the Sephardim more as a burden than a gift. It was as if someone had shipped over the Middle Ages on a cargo plane. To Labor's social engineers, most of the Sephardim were "human dust"—primitive, uneducated and unable to pull their weight in a young, modern, pioneering society. "We must melt down this fantastically diversified assemblage and cast it afresh in the die of a renewed nationhood," writes David Ben-Gurion. "We must break down the barriers of geography and culture, of society and speech, which keep the different sections apart, and endow them with a single language, a single culture, a single citizenship, a single loyalty, with new legislation and new laws. We must give them a new spirit, a culture and literature, science and art."

During the first decades of Israeli independence, many Sephardim experienced a well-intentioned but ultimately degrading mixture of paternalism and racism. Many of their communities sank into a familiar mire of urban problems: street gangs, petty crime, drug abuse, domestic violence and chronic dependency on the welfare state. Families that had been poor but proud and cohesive in the Old World sometimes crumbled under the relentless pressures of the new one.

"I'll tell you what shame is," an angry Sephardi worker says to Amos Oz in his seminal book *In the Land of Israel.* "They gave us houses, they gave us the dirty work; they gave us education, and they took away our self-respect. What did they bring my parents to Israel for?. . . . Wasn't it to do your dirty work? You didn't have Arabs then, so you needed our parents to do your cleaning and be your servants and your laborers. And policemen, too. You brought our parents to be your Arabs. . . . You exploited us and disgraced us for 30 years. You brought a million donkeys here to ride on."

Arye Deri's mother knew her creative young son would never consent to be a donkey. He was too bright to sit at home. If he was not challenged at school she feared he would find other, more dangerous outlets for his restless intellect. One day two representatives of Yad L'Achim, an Ashkenazi ultra-Orthodox missionary group, knocked on her door. They said they were seeking bright young Oriental Jews to place in boarding-school yeshivas. They were interested in Arye and Yehuda. They told Mrs. Deri, "If the boys stay with you, you will lose control over them. On the other hand, if you give them to us they'll get a good free religious education." Mrs. Deri packed their clothes that night.

While Ben-Gurion's Labor Zionists built the new socialist state, the ultrareligious Ashkenazim, known as *haredim* ("those who tremble before God"), sought to reconstruct in Israel the world of the Eastern European ghetto that Hitler had destroyed. They were contemptuous of the Zionists, who in their eyes were attempting to build an apostate country that replaced religion with nationalistic conviction. Just as the *haredim* had been walled off from the Gentile world in Europe, so they chose to wall themselves off from their fellow Jews in Israel, building separate communities, separate institutions and separate cultures. Many clung to Yiddish, the language of the *shtetl.* They shunned Israeli newspapers and radio stations, rejected the new Hebrew-based culture. Ben-Gurion tolerated them in part because he fully expected their way of life to wither and die in the bracing, challenging atmosphere of the modern Jewish state.

But the *haredim* did not fade away. Nurtured by millions of dollars from relatives and Jewish religious groups overseas, they put down strong roots in the fresh soil of the state they despised. One of the main institutions of their survival was the yeshiva religious seminary. In Eastern Europe only the best and most erudite young men of the community had been sent to the yeshiva. But in Israel, every *haredi* boy was encouraged to go. And when the Sephardim began arriving on Israel's shores, some of the yeshivot, especially those under the control of Rabbi Eliezer Schach's

"Lithuanian" school of ultra-Orthodoxy, began recruiting the brightest Eastern youngsters as a means of rejuvenating these institutions while providing a form of charity to needy fellow Jews.

The Sephardi youths who attended the *haredi* yeshivot became curious hybrids. They wore the black suits and hats that were the regulation *haredi* uniform. Many even learned a Yiddish-inflected Hebrew and adopted Ashkenazi pronunciations and physical mannerisms. But they were treated as stepchildren, never as true equals. Sephardi women might work as servants in Ashkenazi rabbinical homes, but the rabbis never allowed their daughters to marry Sephardi students. Sephardi rabbis were deemed something less than the best.

Arye Deri mastered the yeshiva's demanding oral learning style, which prized quick wit and verbal gymnastics. But it was his social skills that made him stand out after he won admission in 1975 to the prestigious Hebron Yeshiva in Jerusalem, the Oxford of the Israeli *haredi* world. It was a notoriously hierarchical institution—older students on top, younger ones on the bottom and Sephardim, who constituted perhaps 15 percent of the four-hundred-man student body, down somewhere in the basement. Within a few months, however, Arye became a key member. "Arye became the solution for everything," recalled David Yosef, a close friend and fellow student. "He had a soft way of saying what had to be said and no one could resist him. Eventually he became in charge of assigning the most important arrangements at the yeshiva, the *havruta* [pairing off students for Torah study]."

The talents honed at the yeshiva served Deri well in his political career. So did the personal connections he forged. Rav Schach, who oversaw the school, noted his skills and considered him a prized pupil. Even more important was the relationship that evolved between Arye and David Yosef's father, Ovadia, Israel's chief Sephardi rabbi. David asked Arye to tutor David's eight-year-old brother, Moshe, at the Yosefs' modest Jerusalem apartment. Soon young Arye was spending every Shabbat at the house, becoming like another son to Ovadia and his voluble, bustling wife, Margalit. David, his father and Arye talked of many things, of Torah and faith. "My father is a scholar—he loves to study," said David. "If someone important comes to visit, after ten minutes my father is looking at his watch, waiting to get back to his books. But when Arye came, my father didn't care about the time."

He was Ovadia Yosef's ideal yeshiva student: bright, loyal, capable of competing against the best of the Ashkenazim. Yosef ordained him as a rabbi and chose him as an instrument of revenge.

• • •

The Iraqi-born Ovadia Yosef was the most revered Sephardi rabbi of his generation. A silver-bearded man who took pride in wearing the traditional gold-braided purple robes and blue turban of the Sephardi rabbinate, Yosef was a distinguished religious authority yet also a plainspoken man with an uncanny ability to touch the emotions of the Sephardi man on the street.

He was a tireless student of the Torah who pored over prayer books and commentaries until 2 A.M., then rose at seven to begin again. There was nothing impressive about the small, cramped apartment where he and Margalit lived except for the thousands of books that lined the walls and spilled out across tables and floors in unruly, precarious piles. He was famous for his photographic memory and his unmatched command of the Talmud. The Yosefs' eleven children all became rabbis or rabbis' wives and all, he would proudly note, married fellow Sephardim.

Yet Yosef's life mirrored many of the frustrations and resentments of his Sephardi followers. Despite his reputation as a scholar Yosef was never accepted as a peer by the senior Ashkenazi rabbis and was denied a place on the higher rabbinical council, ostensibly because he did not speak Yiddish, the lingua franca of the council. As chief Sephardi rabbi, he was forced to work in the shadow of his flamboyant Ashkenazi counterpart, Shlomo Goren. Many derided Yosef as primitive and unsophisticated—"a donkey with books," they called him—claiming his knowledge was thin and his extraordinary memory merely a parlor trick. They also derided the looseness with which he interpreted Jewish law. He was criticized for his 1973 ruling that the Ethiopian Falashas were authentic Jews, descendants of the lost tribe of Dan, a decision that opened the gate for Ethiopian emigration to Israel.

But the biggest insult came in 1983 when opponents stripped Yosef of his cherished position as chief rabbi, which he had expected to be a lifetime office. A number of Ashkenazi rabbis and politicians who had no particular quarrel with Yosef had decided to jettison the controversial Goren. They passed legislation limiting both chief rabbis to two five-year terms. Yosef was deeply hurt. He had to give up the car, but he would never surrender the title of *Rishon Le Zion*—The First in Zion.

For Deri, Yosef's defeat was a first hard lesson in Israeli politics. He and David Yosef had lobbied intensively for David's father and believed that they had obtained promises of support from several influential Knesset members. Yet when it came time to vote, that support melted away. "Now I can see the truth," Arye told David. "Politically we are deep underground. The politicians talk to us very nicely, they make promises to us, but if you don't have power it is nothing."

As it happened, Yosef's humiliation occurred at a pivotal moment in Is-

raeli political history. Until the early 1980s ultrareligious Jews, who constituted 10 to 15 percent of the electorate, essentially had two choices when
they went to the polls. They could support the National Religious Party
(NRP), a moderate Orthodox party that was Zionist in outlook and had
been part of every governing coalition since the founding of the state; or
they could vote for the non-Zionist Agudat Yisrael, which was controlled
by an uneasy alliance of rival Hassidic and Lithuanian rabbinical sages.
Both parties were dominated by a small Ashkenazi elite, yet both relied
heavily on Sephardi voters. And both were undergoing changes that made
them vulnerable.

The NRP, which for three decades had been the natural ally of the left-
leaning Labor Party, was losing many of its moderate followers to the political mainstream. Among those who remained, the messianic hard-liners of
Gush Emunim, inspired by Israel's stunning triumph in the Six-Day War,
strove to swing the party to the far right. They alienated many of their
Sephardi supporters, who felt unable to break into the party's leadership
and did not share the radicalism of the hard-liners.

The Aguda, propelled by its anti-Zionism, had always stayed on the
fringes of the state. But Begin's watershed electoral triumph in 1977
changed all that. At Begin's invitation the Aguda broke with tradition and
agreed to take deputy ministerships in government departments that controlled the budgets it was most dependent upon. The Aguda's decision
brought a windfall of millions of shekels to its educational and social welfare institutions. But it also thrust the *haredim* into secular political life and
inflamed traditional rivalries within the party. Here, too, the Sephardim felt
marginalized and alienated.

Many Sephardim had gravitated to Begin's right-wing Likud, and they
were the voting base for his landmark victory. Begin's ascension was their
ultimate revenge against the Labor elite, and it opened the way finally for
many Sephardim to attain equal status with their Western brethren. But
even though the gap began to narrow, thousands of Sephardim remained
trapped on the bottom, unable to take advantage of the opportunities the
new Likud-governed Israel had to offer. "The Likud rewarded the most capable Sephardim, integrated them economically and gave them the chance
of their lives," said sociologist Menachem Friedman. "But those who remained behind felt twice betrayed—they saw their friends succeed while
they themselves were stuck in even worse poverty."

In 1983 Sephardi religious activists stunned the leaders of both the NRP
and the Aguda by organizing their own slates of local council candidates in
religious strongholds such as Jerusalem and Tiberias and winning a respectable handful of seats. Deri was not involved in these local movements,

but he immediately saw in them the potential to create a national political force. To bring these disparate local elements together, however, he knew he needed a unifying national figure. He turned to David's father.

Arye and David went to Ovadia Yosef together to plead with him to head the rabbinical council that would guide the new party. "This is the opportunity for the Sephardim," Deri told him. "We can change the country."

At first Ovadia Yosef was furious at his son and his young protégé. He grabbed their arms and hustled them toward the door shouting, "Out! Out! I don't want to hear it! Go away! I've just been through politics. Now you want me to get involved with even dirtier politics?" But Deri persisted. "It's not politics for politics' sake," he told Yosef. "It's new schools and yeshivot, a chance for Sephardim to have real power." Finally, David Yosef recalled, his father acceded.

Deri set out to consolidate the local groupings into a national party known as Shas. Using Yosef as his drawing card, he created something that had almost never been seen in Israeli politics before—a party that melded religious fervor with ethnic populist resentment. Yosef's message, honed by Arye, was a simple one: By denigrating them and robbing them of their religious traditions, the Zionist establishment had stolen from the Sephardim the strength to deal with the onslaught of modern Western culture and created a huge vacuum in their lives. Deprived of that strength, they had become vulnerable to all of the ills of modern society: unemployment, crime, drug abuse, sexual immorality. To become strong again, Sephardim must return to their traditions and put their trust in God's earthly spokesmen. Yosef and the rabbis would lead them back to the glory of the past, when the Sephardi world produced sages, not drug addicts. He would give them back their most precious possessions: their identity, their pride and their past. "God and religion and man's place in the world are all tied up in Shas," said Israeli journalist David Landau, an admirer of Yosef. "It's a party set up to save Jewish souls."

There were two faces to Yosef's argument. When it came to the Sephardim themselves, he was gentle, permissive and understanding. Working-class Sephardim were notorious for observing the laws of Shabbat by walking to synagogue on Saturday morning, then flouting them by driving to soccer games in the afternoon. Yosef tolerated this kind of behavior. He believed that every Shabbat candle lit on Friday night, every prayer, every child's Torah lesson, was a blessing and a step toward the social and religious rehabilitation of a bruised and unhappy people.

When it came to the Ashkenazi establishment, however, Yosef was scathing. Those who opposed Shas's sacred mission were evil, and he attacked them in simple, graphic language that was often both childish and crude. In tape recordings of his speeches to students, Yosef snarled street curses at Attorney General Yosef Harish ("may his home be destroyed") and State Comptroller Miriam Ben-Porat ("that woman who is the enemy of religion"). He condemned Yitzhak Shamir ("a rodent eater") as well as the prime minister's wife, Shulamit ("that wicked woman who would never go to a Jewish restaurant"), for their alleged fondness for unkosher food.

Decked out in Sephardi rabbinical garb and dark glasses (to protect eyes weakened by diabetes), Ovadia Yosef took to the role of political savior like a low-key Jewish Billy Graham. Shas's rallies were revival sessions. Speakers whipped up the crowd into a frenzy and then the chief rabbi quietly entered the auditorium. The crowd often rushed the stage, groping for his touch and for a chance to kiss his hand. Some thrust hastily scrawled pleas for blessings at his aides. Yosef's addresses were usually soft-spoken and soothing, messages of hope and encouragement, a promise of happiness to come once Shas took its rightful place as a major force in Israeli life. And always at his right arm was a smiling, admiring Deri. "Everything I do, I do under the instruction of Rav Yosef," he piously claimed. Ovadia Yosef was the visionary, Deri the human instrument of the vision. Or so he said.

Deri had less than a year before the 1984 general election to build a national party. He knew he needed cadres of disciplined, dedicated workers and he knew the best place to get them: the yeshiva. To mobilize those students, he needed the support of the one man who controlled the dozens of Lithuanian seminaries where most of them studied: Rav Schach, the Ashkenazi head of the famous Ponevezh yeshiva in Bnei Brak, which after Jerusalem was the second capital of the *haredi* nation.

Eliezer Schach was in the midst of a power struggle with the Hassidim over control of Agudat Yisrael. He did not like the growing influence within the Aguda of Menachem Mendel Schneerson, the Lubavitcher Rebbe, a leader with messianic pretensions, and he was equally uncomfortable with the growing messianic fervor of the NRP. Schach was looking for a new political vehicle, and he was fond of Deri, his former star pupil. He had a low opinion of Yosef, whom he privately ridiculed, but he saw the rabbi's value in attracting Sephardi voters. Yosef could be the figurehead as long as he, Schach, made the decisions.

Seeing a possible alliance in the works, Deri took pains to cultivate the most important person in Schach's circle: Yehezkel Schayek, a fellow Sephardi who was Schach's driver and appointments secretary. Together Deri and Schayek arranged the political marriage of two grand and brittle egos with little in common except a shared contempt for their mutual rivals. Yosef and Schach made a very odd couple—it was as if two bright young

American political aides had arranged for Jesse Jackson and Pat Robertson to run on the same ticket.

Yosef became chairman of the Council of Sephardi Torah Sages, the rabbinical body that guided Shas, but its other three members were all graduates of Schach's yeshiva. Yosef was not pleased to find himself effectively under Schach's authority. But Deri convinced him that Schach's support was vital to create the great political movement that Yosef desired. The rabbi swallowed his pride. "When they spit on me I'll say it's raining," he told Deri.

To head the party Yosef and Deri selected Yitzhak Peretz, a handsome but obscure rabbi from Ranaana with a distinguished graying beard, a flowery orator's tongue and a scandal-free past. Deri later boasted that they had chosen Peretz out of a telephone directory of rabbis.

Captivated by the weighty issues of war and peace and 400 percent annual inflation, few analysts in the 1984 election campaign gave much thought to the progress of an obscure group of black-hatted neophytes who mumbled their speeches and spent all of their free television airtime showcasing an aging rabbi in Blues Brother sunglasses. Even the mandarins of the Aguda thought it was safe to ignore these amateurs.

On election day in July 1984, Shas surprised everyone—itself included—by winning four Knesset seats. Better still, from Schach's point of view, the Aguda slipped to just two seats. Schach's vengeance was complete. Shas then surprised the political world by demanding cabinet portfolios that in the past had been the sole domain of the NRP.

In the first months of the national unity government, despite his putative devotion to Yosef, Deri maneuvered between his two mentors, wringing from one what he could not get from the other. When the NRP insisted upon keeping both the Interior and Religious Affairs ministries Deri decided to pull Shas from the government. The night before Yosef was to leave for a trip abroad Shimon Peres, the new prime minister, who was desperate to keep Shas in his coalition, drove to Yosef's yeshiva in Mea Shearim to make a last-minute plea for his support. Amnon Levy, one of Israel's most prominent political reporters, recalled what happened:

"Peres's car pulls into an empty lot and he has to step over live chickens and garbage on his way into the yeshiva. After an hour Peres comes out and tells us that he's managed to convince Yosef to delay the decision.

"I enter the room and it's something amazing. There's Deri making a phone call. He doesn't like Yosef's decision—it's not hardball enough—and he's calling Schach. He tells Schach what's going on, and then he says, 'Here, talk to Rav Yosef and tell him,' and he hands the phone to Yosef. The reporters are asked to leave and thirty minutes later Deri comes out and tells us they're resigning if they don't get the ministry. He was manipulating both rabbis."

Deri's gamble paid off. Shas seized control of one of the NRP's former strongholds, the Interior Ministry. Party leader Peretz became minister. But Deri took for himself the top civil service post. At age twenty-seven Arye Deri suddenly owned a piece of the government.

Interior was one of the most obscure of Israel's twenty ministries, with only 611 employees and an administrative budget of less than $25 million. But it controlled grants totaling nearly $500 million per year to Israel's 251 cities, towns and local authorities. Under the system inherited from the British mandate, local governments were almost totally under the thumb of the central authority; police, schools, revenues, expenditures, land use and planning all fell under its control. No city could spend a penny without the ministry's approval. Nothing could be taxed, built, demolished or altered until it said yes. And it dispensed the huge sums allocated by the central government to local councils—in 1991 a total of $380 million for administrative expenses and another $103 million for capital and development expenditures. It was a vast kitty, one that interior ministers had traditionally used to reward their friends and punish their enemies.

As interior minister Peretz had nominal control over these funds. But it was Deri who made the decisions. Unlike Peretz, Deri was not intimidated by the intricacies of the office; he set about learning land-use planning as if it were another branch of Torah learning, poring over the books night after night. To the surprise of many he proved to be an excellent administrator—informal, straightforward and intelligent. He was a problem-solver, one with a special eye toward the dispossessed. He helped normalize the status of Black Hebrews, a religious sect of some fifteen hundred American blacks who had campaigned for Israeli citizenship for more than two decades. Israeli Arab local councils, which had been blatantly discriminated against and shortchanged during the first four decades of statehood, came to see him as a fair and sympathetic arbiter. He became known in Arab towns and villages as "Sheikh Deri."

Jerusalem, whose pro-Labor leaders had long felt victimized by Likud-led governments, also welcomed his ascension to power. "Deri was the best minister of interior we've ever had," recalled Jerusalem Mayor Teddy Kollek, a legendarily irascible public figure not given to praising government officials. "He learned the situation quickly, he knew it thoroughly, he made decisions and carried them out, even when it was difficult for him. He cared about doing a good job."

Deri changed the entire concept of what a religious politician was supposed to be. In the past religious figures had represented their narrow communities' interests and concentrated on capturing public funds for their constituents. But Deri was an innovator whose vision and concerns transcended his own narrow political base. He pressed for decentralization of some of his ministry's own powers. He also helped local governments consolidate their debts, putting some cities on a firm financial footing for the first time in a decade.

All the while Deri was using the power and purse strings of the ministry to help build for Shas a set of religious and educational institutions to rival those of the NRP and the Aguda. Special allocations flowed to Shas's synagogues, yeshivas and schools, much of it in the name of "affirmative action." The cornerstone was El Hamaayan ("To the Source"), a network of child care centers and after-school clubs that provided low-cost supervision, hot lunches, free transportation and religious instruction for children after twelve o'clock when Israel's truncated school day ended. This was a very practical service for poor Sephardi families, and it gave Shas a hold among voters who cared little about the cosmic issues of war and peace. Shas established dozens of these centers throughout Israel, most of them in poorer urban areas. El Hamaayan filled a vacuum, brought people closer to their faith—and to Shas. Children got help with their homework and were encouraged to learn about Judaism. They were instructed to tell their parents not to violate the Sabbath by watching television or turning on electric lights and to vote for Shas. It was all a blessing—and Ovadia Yosef told his followers that Deri would stand so tall in Heaven that he, the great rabbi, would consider himself fortunate if he could reach up to Deri's shoes.

Deri was an immediate hit with the hardened political journalists who covered the Knesset. He was young, untutored and eager for tips. He had an impish and self-deprecating wit, and unlike most ultra-Orthodox politicians, he spoke the same brand of colloquial street Hebrew as the reporters. "He was playful and he was fun," recalled one of them. "One of the things we could never figure out was where Rav Ovadia ended and Deri began, who was the puppet master and who was the puppet. Deri would always claim total obedience to Yosef—but he'd smile and wink when he said it."

As he learned the folkways of the Knesset, Deri began to take full advantage of its deal-making possibilities. To qualify for the director generalship of the ministry, a senior civil service position, he needed discharge papers from the army, but like many yeshiva students Deri had exempted himself from conscription. Now he arranged to do a quick tour of duty. While other male draftees toiled through three arduous years of military service, Arye Deri strolled through the army in four months.

In the same insouciant fashion, Deri waltzed through the stagnant, ru-

ined structures of the Israeli political establishment. He had something
everyone wanted—a small, nonideological political party that effectively
put itself up for sale to the highest bidder, run by a manchild of charm,
grace and determination. "I was born to be an *askan,*" an exuberant Deri
exclaimed to an Israeli journalist after a particularly intricate political maneuver, using a derogatory Hebrew word for "wheeler-dealer." "This is
what I am. This is what I know. This is what I do best."

Few could resist him. "Here's this kid, with no college education, no
army service—yet he plays with the big boys," said Akiva Eldar of *Haaretz,*
one of Deri's journalistic admirers. "He becomes fascinated with his own
influence and power. Like a kid who's just gotten his driver's license and
here he is out on the road."

Along the way Deri acquired some surprising allies, many of them
young aspiring politicians like himself. Dan Meridor, a new Knesset member himself in 1984, became a friend, as did Yossi Beilin, the chief aide of
Labor leader Shimon Peres. But Deri's best political friend was an ambitious and dovish Labor Party operative named Haim Ramon, whose political skills and wicked sense of humor matched Deri's own. Like Deri,
Ramon grew up in a tough, working-class neighborhood and at an early age
learned contempt for Israel's political mandarins. Just as Deri sought to
break down the status quo among the religious parties, Ramon struggled
against the cartel of fixed interests that dominated the Labor Party. Both
were impatient, clever and iconoclastic, with a generous opinion of their
own talents. They seemed to speak to each other in code; instead of complete sentences, a few words or phrases would do. They basked in the leverage their alliance gave each of them. Deri used Ramon to extort
concessions from rival Likud leaders who feared that Shas would cut a deal
with Labor at their expense, while Ramon used the Deri connection to enhance his own power within Labor.

In time the adulation of his newfound companions on the secular left and
of a smitten press corps began to go to Deri's head. He began to lose touch
with his constituency and took liberties with his expenses. Shas kept a suite
of rooms at the Ramada Renaissance Hotel, a luxury watering hole for the
Orthodox a few blocks from the Knesset. After many a hard night of wheel-
ing and dealing, Deri and his coterie of clever young aides would spend the
early-morning hours drinking whiskey and rehashing their political escapades, recalled an Israeli journalist who knew them well. For many of
them this was far more exciting than returning home to small apartments
and to wives and children they hardly knew. "They were so young and they
had lived a life of so many restraints," recalled the journalist. "Now suddenly the world was in their pocket; they had credit cards with the min-

istry's name on them, cars with drivers, access to hotels and good restaurants. It was all so easy—much too easy, really."

But no matter how far up he went or how sophisticated his deal-making became, the boy from Morocco was still tethered to Sephardi religious life, with its demands and piety and superstitions. Like all religious Jews, he prayed three times daily. He carried on his body *camerot,* little symbolic trinkets to ward off bad luck. Each month before dawn an entourage of cars set out from his Jerusalem apartment to the Tomb of the Patriarchs in Hebron, an hour's drive, where Deri and his wife, Yafa, whom he had married in 1981, offered special prayers. Shuttling between church and state, between the *shul* and the Knesset, Arye Deri moved between two very different worlds. Like a time traveler, each day he crossed the border from the past to the present. Yet as his power and prestige grew, he seemed less and less at home in either.

For Israeli voters, 1988 proved to be the Year of the Rabbis. Mainstream secular voters, confronted with the deteriorating security situation in the occupied territories yet paralyzed by the stalemate between the two big parties, seemed listless and confused. But thousands of *haredim* who had never before seen the inside of a voting booth were galvanized by rivalries among the ultra-Orthodox that saw Brooklyn's Lubavitcher Rebbe enter the fray on the side of the Aguda and his most vituperative critic, Rabbi Schach, form a new Ashkenazi party called Degel Hatorah. Many Israeli citizens who had long ago left Israel for the prosperous ultra-Orthodox communities of New York and London streamed back at the rebbe's behest to vote for the Aguda. Politics reached a celestial plain. In return for a solemn pledge of support, voters were promised intercession with God: fecundity for the barren; miracle cures for the sick; eternal life for the dying. The religious parties transformed God into just another ward heeler.

At first Shas looked in trouble. Schach's new party siphoned off the few Ashkenazi votes that Shas had previously commanded, and it was becoming clear to Deri that Schach wanted to restrict Shas's appeal and keep it weak and dependent. But Deri and Ovadia Yosef decided to make a virtue out of necessity. Using Yosef as the centerpiece, Deri launched a campaign to consolidate Sephardi support. Shas chartered a helicopter to fly the rabbi up and down Israel for party rallies. Watching Yosef descend from the sky, some of the party's more primitive supporters believed the Messiah had arrived. "Return to the Glory of the Past" was the campaign slogan. Yosef and a backup choir of chanting Torah sages dominated the party's free television broadcasts, mumbling incantations and promising great personal rewards for a Shas vote. Secular voters watched in stunned disbelief. It was, wrote Israeli philosopher Avishai Margalit, as if "the TV screen was a Wellesian time machine tuned to a remote medieval station."

Nevertheless, the magic worked. While Labor's and Likud's share of the popular vote declined, the three ultra-Orthodox parties received 11 percent of the total vote and more than doubled their Knesset representation. And the biggest winner was Shas, which jumped to six seats, making it the largest religious party in the Knesset. It was a personal triumph for Yosef and Deri, who suddenly found themselves the objects of even more political wooing.

Shamir offered Shas two cabinet portfolios, two deputy ministries, a deputy prime ministership, a deputy Knesset speakership and membership on countless state bodies, and promised to support a change in the law governing conversion to Judaism. Later, when Shamir opted for a new unity government with Labor, he retracted many of these commitments, but not the two ministries. Peretz, still the nominal head of Shas, was shunted off to the backwater Ministry of Immigration Absorption—a fateful move for Shamir, as it later turned out, when 400,000 Soviet Jewish immigrants flooded the country and came face-to-face with a minister frighteningly ill prepared to deal with them. Deri, at age twenty-nine, became interior minister—the youngest member of a cabinet in Israeli history. His installation was like a bar mitzvah. The young celebrant brought along his parents, extended family and neighborhood friends. There were toasts and music and much good cheer. Arye Deri had come of age.

Deri entered Shamir's new government determined to bring about its demise. He and Yosef were convinced that Shamir was not serious about the peace process. They also believed that Shas was ultimately fighting Likud for the same working-class Sephardi voters. After long, heartfelt discussions with Ramon and Beilin, Deri came to the conclusion that a Labor-led government would provide better financial and political support for the movement. Shas was a party with big dreams and big commitments. There was talk that Peres as prime minister would appoint Deri as finance minister—the ultimate hand on Israel's public checkbook. It was also a chance for Yosef to declare independence at last from Rav Schach. And so what came to be known as the "stinking maneuver" was hatched.

In retrospect, Deri's arrogance and miscalculation were stunning for a man with such sensitive political antennae. Friends contend he was taken in by the soothing, ego-boosting compliments of his Labor Party co-conspirators, who in turn were ecstatic that they had found an authentic and powerful religious politician to join in their plot. With the worthy goal of peace in mind, and with a healthy overestimation of their own talents, they mutually seduced one another. "Don't worry," Deri told Ramon. "I can deliver my people."

Deri did not tell Schach what he was up to. Worse, he did not tell Yehezkel Schayek, Schach's alter ego. With a ministry to run and deals to do, Deri began to neglect Schayek, whose politics were much more rightist than his own. Schayek had deep misgivings about the nascent Deri-Labor alliance and he transmitted those misgivings to Schach.

Schach was just as dovish as Deri on the peace process and just as mistrustful of Shamir. But he despised Labor, the party of the antireligious kibbutz movement. He also wanted to undercut Yosef and keep Shas from spiraling out of his own control. Most of all, Schach did not care for the notion of religious politicians dirtying themselves in the cesspool of secular politics. Israeli political reporter Amnon Levy told the story of a female apple merchant who approached a famous rebbe after thieves had attacked her, knocked her down and stolen all her apples. "I want justice," she told the rebbe. His reply: "Listen, the entire market is full of thieves. The only justice is to go and steal from other people."

This was Schach's attitude toward Israeli politics: Orthodox politicians were permitted to steal apples from the political marketplace, but afterward they must return home safely to the *shtetl* behind the high walls Schach himself had carefully erected. "The difference is that Arye Deri wanted to run the market while Rav Schach only wanted to steal from it," said Levy. "For Schach, the rumors in Labor that Deri would be finance minister, or even vice premier, were a nightmare. He was afraid of too much involvement with secular Zionist society."

Deri had fully expected the Aguda and Degel Hatorah to support the maneuver, since Peres had carefully cultivated both parties with promises of money, power and favored legislation. Shas had hoped to stand aside and not risk alienating its sizable right wing of supporters by voting against Shamir. But at the last minute Schach ordered Degel Hatorah to back away. Shas was forced to abstain on the no-confidence vote in order to defeat Shamir. Peretz bolted the party, alleging that Shas had "betrayed its voters." Schayek quit as well. Shamir's government fell, but everyone knew it was Deri's doing. The reaction among the hawkish party faithful was angry and swift.

Deri became an outcast in the world he had revered. His children came home from school in tears, saying they had been told that their father was a thief and Ovadia Yosef "an Arab." There were death threats, harassing phone calls and medieval-style accusatory posters on the walls of Mea Shearim and Bnei Brak singling out Deri as a betrayer. "How dare you defraud 100,000 Jews who voted for Shas, selling them to the befouled [Labor] Alignment . . . in return for a seat in the government?" one poster demanded. When Deri attempted to attend synagogue that weekend, he was screamed at and roughed up, and had to be rescued by his ministerial driver. To make deals was one thing, but to undermine Likud and then go with the arch dove Peres was another.

In all of this Deri could see the hand of Schayek. He feared his former friend was plotting to isolate Yosef, capture four of Shas's Knesset members and form a new faction under Peretz that would take its orders from Schach. Quickly he and Yosef sought to rectify their mistake, first by announcing they would back a Shamir-less Likud, perhaps led by Moshe Arens. Then, when it became clear that this was not to be, they backed down even further and pronounced Shamir himself acceptable. Deri put the best possible face on his capitulation, saying, "Shamir ought to be given a chance to say yes to Baker." But it was an abject surrender, as Deri's days and nights of penance in Shamir's antechamber attested. Instead of being a pivotal figure in a dovish Labor government, Deri became trapped in the most right-wing government in Israeli history.

Yosef, too, was to taste humiliation. He was invited—"summoned" was a more correct term—to the rally at the Yad Eliahu arena, where he sat silently onstage before a crowd of thousands while Schach denounced the Labor Party and the entire secular Jewish world. It was a ritual degradation performed before a million witnesses on Israel Television: the living vessel of Sephardi pride humbled by his Ashkenazi master.

The acrimonious split between Schach and Yosef weighed heavily on Deri. He had been brought up to revere Schach as the leader of his generation of yeshiva students. Yet his first loyalty was to Yosef, to his own people and to the revolution he believed he was making. As time went on, he became an outcast in the Ashkenazi-dominated portion of the *haredi* world.

Despite the failure Deri's closest political friendships on both the right and left survived. Meridor was not angry. He told friends in Likud that Deri had been honest with him all along and had even warned him that Shas would bring down the government if Shamir refused to go to Cairo. Meridor, in turn, had warned Shamir, who chose to ignore the threat. Ramon argued with his Labor colleagues that Deri had tried his best to keep his word but had simply been outmaneuvered. It was, Ramon insisted, an honest mistake. Arye Deri was still a man you could do business with.

Few could see it at the time, but the humiliation of 1990 was a watershed in the relationship between the religious parties and their secular counterparts. For the first time an ostensibly ultra-Orthodox party had stepped outside the boundary of its narrow religious agenda to take a stand in the existential issues of war and peace that touched all Israelis. Crass and inept as the dealings were, Deri had crossed the border into secular concerns and created a common area of interest with nonreligious Israelis. Some came to hate him because he so successfully manipulated the shaky political system for the greater glory of his party and his mentor, and siphoned off taxpayer money to build yet another network of religious institutions. Yet he believed he was playing by the rules of the game. "The people of Israel are destined to live as tribes," he once told the *Jerusalem Post*. "But to live together peacefully, we must make the tribes feel equal to each other."

This was a new vision for Israeli society. The early Zionists had believed that Israel was destined to take the "human dust" of Europe and North Africa and fashion a New Jewish Man—secular, militant, socialistic, unafraid of physical labor. Religious Zionists later injected a heavy dose of messianism into this vision: their New Man was still an armed pioneer, but one infused with Old Testament piety. Both visions had exhausted themselves, in part because both were based on an impossible model, one that might have been suitable for a small elite but could never be imposed on an increasingly open, democratic and pluralistic society. Arye Deri operated in a world in which competing interests and ethnic groups, rather than seeking to dominate or obliterate rivals, had to learn to live alongside one another in a system of checks and balances. This less ideological, more mature and ultimately more tolerant society was his true gift to Israel.

Arye Deri learned from his mistakes. The chastened young man who emerged from the abortive coup against Shamir was more humble, more inclined to listen and less domineering. But he had become an irresistible target for an Israeli establishment seeking to preserve its power and enforce its rules in the face of sweeping social and political change. Even as the cloud from the 1990 debacle began to lift, Arye Deri came to face a new and far more protracted ordeal in which all of his talent and personal resources were put to the test.

It began with Ornan Yekutieli, a youthful bulldog of a politician who was elected to the Jerusalem City Council in 1989 as a member of Ratz, a small, left-of-center reformist party with a visceral disgust for the machinations and financial shenanigans of religious parties like Shas. Yekutieli had spent several years working in city government and he thought he knew where some of the least attractive bodies were buried. He and fellow councilman Shmuel Meir of the National Religious Party—whose influence was declining in direct proportion to Shas's rise—began to poke around the city's financial allocations. They discovered that some $8 million in city funds had been dispersed to religious schools and charitable organizations connected to Shas without legal justification. In one case the city had converted to institutional use a prime piece of property originally zoned for new apartment buildings and had transferred ownership to a nonprofit charitable organization headed by Deri's wife, Yafa. In another, the city had authorized more than $200,000 for the purchase of a luxury apartment for a religious school headed by Deri's brother Yehuda.

"At first we didn't realize what we were on to," Yekutieli later recalled. "But we sent letters to other municipalities and we found the same pattern over and over again."

What Yekutieli and Meir had stumbled across was a vast system of money laundering in which Interior Ministry funds were funneled to Shas institutions through local governments. Deri would earmark large sums for these governments on condition that a percentage of those funds be passed on to Shas schools, seminaries and social welfare organizations. Yekutieli and Meir estimated that Deri had improperly funneled about $50 million over three years to friends and political allies throughout Israel. Those local officials who resisted feared their own allocations would be cut. It was, Yekutieli charged, a blatant form of public blackmail.

For a time Yekutieli and Meir's allegations were ignored or disparaged, but they persisted. They sent copies of their documentation to Mordechai Gilat, a well-known investigative reporter for *Yediot Ahronot,* Israel's largest-selling daily newspaper, and to State Comptroller Miriam Ben-Porat, whose reputation for independent action made her a lone source of official accountability during the free-spending days of the Shamir government.

In June 1990 Gilat and a colleague, Mali Kempner, published a three-part series headlined "Minister Arye Deri's Reign of Money and Fear." The articles accused Deri of pressuring the Jerusalem religious council to appoint his brother Yehuda as rabbi of the neighborhood of Ramot and his friend David Yosef as rabbi of nearby Harnof. Deri allegedly offered the council a $1 million special allocation in return.

The articles also claimed that Deri had pressed the mayor of Or Akiva, a small town in central Israel, to waive the municipal tax debts of Avraham Shapira, an influential businessman and religious member of the Knesset whose carpet factory was on the verge of bankruptcy. Deri also allegedly coerced a regional government official named Moshe Glazner to grant a $3 million public loan to another town to cover its debts. When Glazner resisted, Deri reportedly had him removed from his job.

The allegations were not extraordinary for Israeli politics, where public graft and political blackmail were not uncommon practices. What was more damaging were Gilat and Kempner's allegations about Arye's personal wealth. A man who had been born poor, who had no private income and who five years earlier had complained that he had trouble paying his bills each month, now allegedly owned four apartments. Arye Deri "dresses elegantly, lives high, travels the world, spends time in luxury hotels, eats in elegant restaurants and takes advantage of his position to grant favors to his associates," the article claimed. A follow-up piece in November alleged that Deri and his family had outfitted their new apartment in Harnof with $55,000 worth of customized carpentry, special fixtures and a Jacuzzi. Sinks, toilets and ceramic tiles from the United States were handpicked by Yafa during a visit to New York, according to *Yediot,* and delivered in the name of Moshe Reich, a wealthy businessman from Brooklyn who was a close friend and neighbor. *Yediot* estimated the value of the two-floor apartment at more than $500,000 and claimed Deri had borrowed $235,000 from Reich to help finance the purchase.

After the articles appeared, police announced a full investigation. Deri was quick to draw a connection between the probe and the failed coup attempt, suspecting that his enemies in Likud—most particularly the new police minister, Ronnie Milo—had leaked damaging material to the newspaper. "The investigation began when we toppled the government," he told reporters.

Appearing on Israel Television, Deri accused *Yediot* of "malicious lies" and waved the results of a lie detector test that he said proved his innocence. He gave interviews to friendly journalists denying the allegations of personal corruption.

Deri denied having blackmailed local officials into cooperating with his ministry, insisting that the instances of public brokering were simply a case of politics as usual. He did not deny intervening to have Yehuda and David appointed as local rabbis, nor did he attempt to defend the system of special allocations. "I didn't invent it or bring it from Morocco," he told reporters. "I improved it. . . . All budget decisions are political; the left wants money for the kibbutzim, the right for settlements. I instituted remedial discrimination for the religious institutions."

Deri insisted that he owned only one apartment and claimed the money to purchase the two-floor flat and its elaborate fixtures had been a cash gift from Yafa's wealthy foster parents in New York, both of whom had since died. As for his purportedly lavish lifestyle, Deri claimed that he, like other young family heads in Israel, was paying off a stiff mortgage. "Does anyone know what I eat at home or how we live?" he asked Amnon Levy. "Does anyone know what clothes I buy? Or where? Is this what we want the press to do to a public servant? Is my blood worth less than anyone else's?"

There were other, even less savory aspects of Deri's "self-defense." In December police arrested a Shas legislative aide and four men whom he had allegedly hired to help wiretap Gilat's phones. One of the phone calls they recorded was between the reporter and Yaacov Terner, who was head of Israel's national police force. According to police, the aide had transported cassettes of the wiretapped conversations to Deri's Knesset office. But investigators could not persuade the aide, Eli Tsuberi, to implicate Deri.

Police in Israel do not play by the American Civil Liberties Union rulebook. When Deri launched his crusade against the investigation, they responded by stepping up their own campaign of newspaper leaks and harassment. In September 1990 they stormed into the homes of six of Deri's closest aides and associates at 6 A.M., ransacking the houses, confiscating records and arresting the six, who were held and questioned for twenty-four hours. They interrogated Deri himself for three hours, but the minister, invoking parliamentary and ministerial immunity, refused to answer questions.

In May 1991 police arrested two more close aides: Yom-Tov Rubin, Deri's former financial adviser, on suspicion of bribery, theft and fraud; and Moshe Weinberg on similar charges. Another of Deri's friends, diamond dealer Aharon Weiner, was remanded in custody on charges of fictitiously buying an apartment from the minister for $200,000, while New York financier Isaac Wolf was held on suspicion of bribing Deri by paying $200,000 for the anti-*Yediot* ad campaign. Wolf's lawyer contended the campaign was not a bribe but simply an expression of Wolf's sincere concern for an embattled public servant.

By July 1991 the more than sixty investigators involved in the probe had questioned more than six hundred people, yet they still could not nail down a corruption case. Police Minister Milo blamed the delay on Deri's own refusal to cooperate, plus the fact that seventeen out of nineteen key witnesses had chosen to remain silent. "It's a conspiracy of silence, like a mafia," Milo told a fellow cabinet minister.

For his part, Deri accused the police of running "a campaign of slander, lies and bloodletting." He refused to suspend himself from office during the investigation, nor did he hesitate to use all of his political leverage against the police.

As time went on, the noose of the police investigation slowly tightened around Deri's neck. In their haste to win for their party the public funding they believed was their due, Deri and Shas had flouted many of the rules. They had risen so quickly, they seemed to believe they were immune, that the regulations were meant only for others. Eventually at least twenty-two people directly linked to Shas were under indictment or criminal investigation, including four Knesset members, three of Deri's relatives and one of Ovadia Yosef's sons. Two people, former Knesset member Yair Levy and his wife, Geula, were found guilty of forging checks and stealing about $140,000 from El Hamaayan. Levy drew a five-year prison sentence, his wife a suspended sentence. Another Shas member of the Knesset, Raphael Pinhasi, faced criminal charges for allegedly concealing the party's illegal employment of dozens of yeshiva students in its political campaigns.

By then Deri stalked through the government like a wounded animal, drained of his energy and his concentration by an investigation that seemingly had no end. It was an embarrassment both for him and the government, but Deri was determined to keep out of prison and prepared to use all of his powers to do so. Time and again he threatened the governing coalition, often on the thinnest of pretexts. The real reason was his effort to deflect attention from his own legal troubles and to demonstrate that unless he got his way he could, like Samson, bring the government crashing down around him.

Through it all he managed to keep control of the Interior Ministry and its special allocations. He still wielded the funds of the very people whom the police needed to testify against him. Shamir, fearing the political fallout, refused to remove him from office. Indeed, when in December 1990 Deri sent an agonized, five-page handwritten letter of resignation to Shamir, the prime minister summoned him and persuaded him to withdraw it. Shamir promised that the investigation would be wrapped up within two weeks; more than two years later it would still be going on.

It was a cruel and tragic fate for a gifted public man and a terrible distraction for the governments in which he served. Deri saw his harassment as the establishment's revenge against Shas for its hubris and growing power. He became obsessed with the probe. Often when he met with journalists or other politicians he would plunge into long, agonized soliloquies. "They want to suck my blood," he told one longtime ally. "They want to kill me."

The scandal seemed to strengthen Deri's position within the religious community he sprang from, which has always seen itself as persecuted and misunderstood by the larger secular world. Deri spent more and more time with his religious friends, who sought to comfort him by telling him what they thought he wanted to hear. He made a pilgrimage to the tomb of the Babi Sali, a holy man who was buried in the Negev Desert. There he prostrated himself, kissing the gravestone and praying for strength and for his enemies to be vanquished.

But while the religious world embraced him anew, the political world he had adopted and sought to conquer grew remote. People who used to mob his table at the Knesset dining room to ask for favors, offer deals or just bask in his brilliance now stayed away. Friendships collapsed. Deri knew he could not get anywhere with Milo, a longtime foe. Instead he pleaded with his old friend Dan Meridor, the justice minister, to persuade the police to wrap up their probe or at least pursue it in a less brutal and public fashion. While personally sympathetic, Meridor refused to intervene. As a new-breed reformist Meridor had taken a strong public stand against political corruption, branding it "the worst public evil" because it eroded the very legitimacy of government. He advised Deri to cooperate fully with the police and to tell his subordinates to do likewise. That way the investigation would speed to completion. Later Meridor gave a speech calling on Deri either to cooperate with the investigation or else resign from the cabinet.

For Deri this was too much. His beleaguered world was increasingly divided between loyalists and enemies, with no room in between for anyone like Meridor. Late one night Deri phoned the justice minister and pleaded one more time for help. "Dan, this can't go on," Deri told him. "I can't take it anymore." Meridor could offer no real comfort. After that Deri stopped speaking to him. For two years there was total silence between them. Even Deri's aides shunned Meridor.

It was a tragedy, thought Meridor, that a politician as bright and talented as Deri should fall so far. He was a brilliant cabinet minister who had made a great contribution to Israeli politics. He had shown remarkable personal resources in continuing to function despite the investigation. Most men, Meridor knew, would have fallen apart within days or weeks. Yet Deri carried on. Israel could ill afford to lose such a talent. But the law had to run its course.

Dan Meridor knew he could no longer help his young friend. Perhaps no one could.

7. The Desert Generation

When the Lord brought back the exiles who re-
turned to Zion, we were like dreamers.

—PSALM 126

WORKING-CLASS Sephardim were not the only ethnic group in Israel to confront the old social and political order. By the spring of 1990, as travel restrictions in the Soviet Union eased and its socialist economy veered toward collapse, thousands of Russian Jews began pouring into Israel.

They turned Ben-Gurion Airport into Ellis Island, piling off airplanes early each morning into the cavernous, humid immigration hall. They came from Russia, Ukraine, Byelorussia, Moldavia and Georgia, trailing thick dark overcoats, cardboard suitcases and pale, exhausted children whose eyes were filled with sleep. They were directed to sprawling, haphazard rows of plastic chairs, where they nestled silently until they were called to a cubicle where a Russian-speaking clerk questioned them, punched their answers onto a computer screen—name, age, nationality, occupation—then delivered brusque instructions on where to go from there, a cash grant of a thousand or so dollars and directions to a cheap hotel. Within an hour or two they would emerge from the drab airport terminal into the brilliant Mediterranean sunlight dazed by the weather and by the fact that their lives had suddenly been turned upside down.

For a country whose defining reason for existence was to provide a haven for Jews, the Russian immigration should have been a Zionist dream come true. The *aliya,* as the immigration is called in Hebrew, was a unique opportunity for Israel to fulfill its destiny as a Jewish state and to revitalize itself. Soviet Jews were a highly educated, talent-laden elite, emigrating from a superpower of 300 million to a small Middle Eastern nation of 4 million. Virtually overnight they added 10 percent to Israel's population and injected billions of dollars' worth of university training into their new country, doubling the number of doctors, engineers and scientists.

It was a time of great expectations not only for the Russians, who were looking for a homeland, security and a sense of fulfillment, but for Israelis as well. Many looked to Soviet Jews for deliverance from all of their society's unresolved dilemmas. The new immigrants would help Ashkenazi Jews reestablish demographic equality with their Sephardi brethren, secular Jews overcome religious ones and Israeli Jews in general reassert numerical superiority over Arabs. The presence of a new and hungry group of refugees from state socialism would lead to more pluralism and economic liberalization. They would provide the missing spark to reignite the stalled Zionist enterprise. "All of a sudden the purpose of this society is renewed," Simcha Dinitz, head of the Jewish Agency and former ambassador to the United States, told the *Washington Post*'s Jackson Diehl. "People remember why we built this country, what it was all for. Suddenly we have a way to reach back to what is clear, what is right, what we are about."

But after the first burst of hope and idealism, the *aliya* collided with Israeli reality. The immigrants hit some of the weakest and most crisis-ridden institutions of the society: its entrenched bureaucracy, its underfunded and demoralized school system, its anemic job market, and its corrupt and chronically inefficient housing industry. There were not enough apartments or classroom spaces for the newcomers and very few jobs. Yitzhak Shamir's new right-wing government had ignored warnings of the impending wave and taken few steps in preparation. And once the influx began, the government's internal divisions and weaknesses, coupled with Shamir's overriding commitment to his ideological agenda of extending Jewish settlement of the occupied territories, meant that in many fields the Russians were left on their own.

Part of the problem was the Russians themselves. Many of them did not consider themselves Jews and fewer still were Zionists. They had decided to come to Israel only after the United States had closed its doors to most of them and it became clear that Israel was the only practical alternative to remaining in the Soviet Union. Many believed their culture, language and training were superior to that of Israel, a younger, smaller, more primitive country. Their landing was fraught with economic hardship and personal pain. Along the way they were forced to develop new calluses and learn how to muscle their way through a difficult, stagnant system.

· · ·

Israelis, who are not known for their volunteerism, responded to the *aliya* with great enthusiasm at first. Thousands made the pilgrimage to Ben-Gurion Airport, greeting the new arrivals with bouquets of flowers and candy. When the Jewish Agency asked for volunteers to host immigrants at seders that first Passover, it received far more offers than it could handle. Volunteers manned information desks, taught language classes, offered orientation classes or adopted a Russian family for meals. They filled warehouses with used clothing.

Yet resentments soon arose. Sephardi Jews feared the Russians would leapfrog over them and significantly retard their own hard-fought climb up Israel's socioeconomic ladder. One working-class Sephardi leader actually wrote to Soviet leader Mikhail Gorbachev and asked him to put a halt to the immigration.

Worse, the feeling quickly took hold among Israelis that the Russians were grudging entries with no enthusiasm or affection for their new homeland or their fellow Jews. Many Israelis came to see them as chronic whiners who were ungrateful for the fact that Israel had opened its doors to them at a time when no other country would. The Russians seemed to expect welfare benefits, treat work with disdain and act as if every employer was an enemy to be outwitted and cheated. "They act like they own the place," complained Israelis living in Yad Eliahu, a tough Sephardim neighborhood in Tel Aviv, to *Hadashot* journalist Michael Kedem. The neighbors were fed up with Russian complaints and hauteur, and were particularly incensed when an immigrant couple was caught stealing canned goods from a local grocer. The accepted rule of Yad Eliahu was that shoplifters should steal only from the nearby chain supermarket. Soon afterward, when a local Sephardi gang began beating up Russian teenagers, many in the neighborhood quietly applauded.

"We've been treated like losers for too many generations to allow some stinking Russians to come and join the Ashkenazim looking down on us," a local Sephardi resident told Kedem. "Where is their self-respect? All the years that we've been screwed, did we say a word? Make a peep? Ask for pity? They show up with the attitude that they have everything coming to them. . . . It seems completely natural to me that seventeen-year-old kids will jump on them and beat them up."

Too often the Russians seemed out of touch with Israeli mores and uninterested in adjusting to them. When four Israeli women were stabbed to death by a crazed Arab in Jerusalem in March 1991, an angry woman approached a band of Russian musicians playing outdoors in the center of town and ordered them to stop. "Now is a time of national mourning," she told them. The trumpeter stopped playing and replied in broken Hebrew:

"Here in Israel not communism. Here capitalism, here freedom"—and resumed playing.

Even their fellow Russians seemed to have little sympathy for their predicament. Ilana Michaeli, who came to Israel in 1971 from Moscow, worked as a columnist for a Russian-language weekly in Tel Aviv, writing advice about jobs, housing and personal matters for the new immigrants. But Michaeli herself had little use for many of them. "People expect too much when they come here," she said. "I get twenty letters a week—they want jobs, houses, social security, but they don't want to work.

"My *aliya* was very different. We wanted to go to Israel. We thought it was our country. Now most of them are just running away from Russia and have no real reason to love this country. They don't feel themselves Jews. They could go to any country in the world. I try to understand and not judge them, but sometimes it's very hard."

After the initial romance most Israelis developed a profound sense of indifference toward their Russian brethren. In a survey of a thousand Israeli-born high school graduates conducted by the social psychology department at Hebrew University, 84 percent said they had few or no social relationships with Russian immigrants and only 5 percent reported "some" or "a lot" of social contact; 74 percent said they would be willing to invite Russians to a party, but only 26 percent were sure they would be willing to marry one; only 23 percent of the respondents believed Israelis had a positive view of the immigrants, while 77 percent said that most people were either hostile or apathetic.

Religious Israelis had their own misgivings about the Russians, many of whom were not considered Jews under traditional law, which holds that Jewish descent can be transmitted only matrilineally. Many of the Russians had no knowledge of Jewish customs or beliefs. Many of the men were not circumcised or bar mitzvahed. Most had qualified under the country's Law of Return, which allowed anyone with one Jewish grandparent or a Jewish spouse to enter the country with full immigration rights. A few lied about their backgrounds. Estimates of the number of Russian immigrants who were not Jewish ranged anywhere from 5 to 30 percent, depending on who was doing the counting.

Either way, it was the largest influx of non-Jews since the founding of the state, and the numbers posed a profound threat to Israel's religious establishment. Unlike in most Western countries, the Orthodox rabbis of Israel held a monopoly over rites of passage such as marriage, divorce and burials. They were forbidden by religious law, known as *halacha,* to marry Jews and non-Jews or to allow non-Jews to be buried in Jewish cemeteries. But what about the Russians? To disqualify large numbers from marrying

Jews was to risk alienating an important segment of the population and to give new impetus to the movement to legalize civil marriage and divorce and remove these matters from rabbinical control. Yet to turn a blind eye was to violate the *halacha* and dilute the religious purity that the Orthodox world strived to uphold.

The rabbinate sought to introduce the Russians to Judaism with campaigns of "spiritual absorption" that included the distribution of 60,000 Bibles, 20,000 Sabbath candleholders and 32,000 Hanukah menorahs at a cost of at least $30 million in state funds. But most of this had little impact on the Russians, some 85 percent of whom came from urban European areas and whose outlook on religion was secular to the point of being openly hostile. "The Judaism I found here was not what I had expected," said filmmaker Leonid Gorovets, who emigrated from Kiev. "It gave me the feeling that time stopped the day before yesterday and still stands there. In Russia you had a Communist Party card in your pocket; here it's a *kippa* and you're supposed to wear it on your head."

Ritual circumcision had been viewed as mutilation and effectively outlawed in the Soviet Union ever since the October Revolution. Most Jewish males had not undergone the operation in three generations. But once in Israel, Russian males were encouraged to submit to the quick but painful procedure. Several government ministries and the rabbinate got together and formed a task force in February 1990 that eventually budgeted more than $5 million for the project. Under unofficial prodding, at least 30,000 Russian men underwent the operation in the first two years of the *aliya*.

The pressures to be circumcised were subtle but significant. Schoolboys did not want their penises to look different from those of their classmates. Young army conscripts felt the same. Those who underwent circumcision often received new Israeli names to go with their newly shaped penises. "It was not only an operation on your body but also on your spirit," said Gorovets, who made a bittersweet documentary on Russian circumcision for Israel Television. As he filmed the patients emerging groggily from anesthesia, Gorovets felt his own sharp pangs of remorse and alienation climbing up his throat: "I understood my own anesthesia had also ended. The euphoria of coming here was over."

The rabbis sought to be accommodating, but some of their compromise solutions inevitably were cruel and even macabre. Olga Haikov, a Russian woman killed by an Arab gunman in an attack on a passenger bus in Jerusalem, was buried in a non-Jewish portion of a cemetery and denied the Jewish prayer for the dead by the rabbi who officiated at her funeral (a Knesset member who attended the ceremony and who was a rabbi went ahead and recited the prayer— "She died a Jewish death and she deserves a Jewish burial," he explained). One local rabbi ordered the remains of Tereza Yankilevitch dug up from beside her late husband because she was not Jewish. Another ordered a circumcision performed on the corpse of a Russian immigrant killed in a traffic accident before the rabbi would allow it to be buried in a Jewish grave. Later it turned out that hundreds of other corpses had been similarly mutilated at cemeteries throughout the country.

All over Israel, Russians seeking to test the parameters of their new freedom found themselves colliding with religious barriers. In Kiryat Shemona, a Sephardi-dominated development town in far northern Israel, three Russian merchants were forced to close their butcher shops because they carried pork and other nonkosher meats. There were demonstrations, physical harassment and vandalism by local residents. A rabbi claimed that 50 percent of the newcomers were not Jewish. "We feel ourselves at war," said one Russian shopkeeper. "The old-timers, the police and the rabbinate are all at one against us."

Still the Russians kept coming. Eventually over the three years between the fall of 1989 and 1992 a total of 410,055 Soviet Jews would emigrate to Israel, along with 66,165 other Jews primarily from Eastern Europe and Ethiopia. The peak came in December 1990, just before the Gulf War began and before the early euphoria had been dissipated and superseded by the sobering truth about housing and jobs. A total of 35,629 Soviet Jews arrived in Israel that month, the highest monthly number of immigrants in the history of the state. Back in Russia hundreds of thousands of others were still contemplating the trip. It was as if the entire population of Canada had suddenly touched down at JFK Airport, with the population of Australia close behind.

On weekdays the Russians filled the sidewalks outside state employment and welfare offices, searching for work, housing and benefits. On Saturdays they filled the parks on the outskirts of the cities. The more successful drove cars that they had purchased soon after arrival in Israel, taking advantage of tax breaks that allowed them to buy at half the price most Israelis paid. While the children quickly adopted the shorts and tee-shirts and sleek haircuts of the locals, their parents still wore frayed flannel shirts and shiny pants, and had homemade haircuts and pasty, wintry complexions. They seemed to bundle up even on the warmest days, looking devastated and listless whenever the thermometer climbed above seventy-five degrees.

The Russians came to Israel without leaders and without heroes. The few grassroots organizers who arose after their arrival seemed unable to connect with or influence Israel's insular power elite. The sclerotic bureaucracy that was supposed to monitor and ease their transition into Israeli society was more concerned with its own interests. But as time went on, many of the immigrants turned increasingly for guidance to a very unusual man, a fellow Russian who sought to become the bridge between the immigrants and their new homeland.

At first many émigrés disliked and distrusted Natan Sharansky. All too frequently he found himself in the position of having to explain and defend Israel to them, just as he had to explain and defend them to Israelis. Neither side much appreciated his mediation—and each suspected his motives and disliked his stubborn streak of independence. Yet as time went on, many Russians came to respect and rely upon his doggedness and his political acumen. Together, they forged an odd but effective alliance: the evolving, reluctant politician and the skeptical but determined immigrants. And together, in the end, they became an angry, embittered but critical force for radical change.

Natan Sharansky was a short man, no more than five feet four in his socks, prematurely bald at age forty and slightly pudgy. He dressed simply in an open-necked shirt, fraying khaki pants and a battered old Army cap to protect his shiny pate from the Middle Eastern sun. His health was fragile, reflecting the ordeal of starvation diets and hunger strikes in prison that had reduced his weight at one point to just seventy-seven pounds. He suffered from myocardial dysfunction, a weakening of the heart muscles, and was gripped periodically by biting chest pains and sharp headaches.

During nine years in a Soviet prison on trumped-up charges of spying for the United States, Sharansky had become the foremost "Prisoner of Zion," the living symbol for Russian Jews struggling for the right to emigrate to the Jewish homeland. He was freed in February 1986 as part of a three-way prisoner exchange and welcomed to Israel as a hero and celebrity.

Within a short period all that he had hoped for in those bitter years of imprisonment came to pass: he was reunited with his wife and family, fathered two children and established a life in his new homeland. He wrote a book about his years of struggle for a high six-figure advance. For many of his admirers, Sharansky's story ended there—the heroic figure, bathed forever in a warm glow of freedom and adulation. But after the spotlight faded, Sharansky was left to come to terms with his new country and to find a new role.

An ardent Zionist, Sharansky embraced his new homeland and was embraced by a nation proud of his struggle and delighted to have him and his family living there. Still, Israel was a hard adjustment for a man used to the purifying silence of a Soviet isolation cell. The country quickly proved far more complicated, more suspicious, more tied to the past and less generous and idealistic than the land he had imagined during all of the years in prison. "I came from an ideal world where every day there was only one choice to make—good or evil, saying yes or no to the KGB—to a much more complicated place," he said. "There the cause was very clear. Here you're always fighting with everybody, and cooperating with everybody. Nothing's clear; not only is there no black and white, but there is no clear enemy and no clear friend."

Israel, too, had difficulty in adjusting to the new Zionist in its midst. This is a skeptical, combative society, one that expects its members to choose sides and enter the arena. There is little tolerance for those who try to stand above the fray, preaching to the crowd while refusing to soil themselves in the dirty commerce of Israeli politics. To many Israelis, Natan Sharansky sounded and smelled a little too much like a saint.

Everyone wanted a piece of the hero, to recruit him to their cause. The left wanted Sharansky to speak out for Palestinian human rights. The religious right hoped he would follow his wife, Avital, into its fold. Both movements were disappointed by his stubborn refusal to choose sides.

In the Soviet Union, Sharansky had bridged the gap between Jewish dissidents and other rights activists. His Jewish identity and his Zionism were his anchor, but his message and struggle were universal. In Israel it was not so simple. For Sharansky to function as a human rights leader beyond his own important but narrow cause, he had to come to grips with the human rights question in Israel's own backyard—the Palestinians. It was an issue he sought to sidestep, but one that inevitably tripped him up. When Palestinians discussed their own grievances, they invoked his name and his story, drawing painful parallels between the treatment he received in the Soviet Union and the way Palestinian activists were treated in the West Bank and Gaza. They also dwelled on the contrast between the warm welcome Israel extended to him and his family and the roadblocks erected to slow or prevent the reunification of thousands of Palestinian families in the occupied territories.

Sharansky refused to accept the parallel. For all its fractious political parties and self-destructive conflicts, Israel was a democratic society, not a totalitarian one like the Soviet Union. If Palestinian rights were being denied, he insisted, it was because Palestinians were not prepared to recognize the right of Jews to live in peace in their homeland. Israel was at war, fighting for its existence, so the standards he claimed to believe in did not always apply.

"Some Israelis on the left are so naïve," he complained one day. ". . . It would be so easy for me to do what people want—to meet with Palestinians and say we Soviet Jews have the same problems they do. Maybe someone would give me a Nobel Prize. But it's such a lie and that is what stops me. It's a serious problem here, but in its roots it is not a human rights problem."

Sharansky voted in his first free election in 1988. It should have been a joyous occasion; the candidates promised economic progress and social change and Sharansky was thrilled by the prospect of altering the course of his new country in this civilized, democratic way. But when the results came in, his exhilaration quickly turned to dismay. The big gains of the non-Zionist, ultra-Orthodox political parties troubled him. So did the speed with which the larger parties moved immediately to jettison their campaign promises and launch an unseemly bidding war for religious party support. The old preelection stalemate reasserted itself with a vehemence that utterly stunned him. "Principles, which I had always thought were more important than portfolios and more permanent than governments, were being auctioned off with dizzying dispatch," he wrote in the *Jerusalem Post*. "It was not a pretty sight."

To Sharansky, the failure of the electoral process to spark change was symptomatic of a larger crisis within Israel. He saw a bruised, unhappy country whose politics and economy had grown stagnant and defensive. Even when things started collapsing in the Soviet Union, bringing the prospect of large-scale emigration, Sharansky could not get Israelis to focus on the problem and mobilize their resources for the coming wave. "Israelis are so desperate and have lost hope that they can attract Jews positively," said Sharansky. "They have no faith in others or in themselves."

The main institution dealing with immigration was the quasi-governmental Jewish Agency. It was a massive bureaucracy, funded largely with money from overseas donors who contributed more than $400 million each year that the agency spent on philanthropy and patronage. Established in 1929, it was a classic Zionist institution caught in an irreversible spiral of decline. After helping to lay the foundations for the state and to fund the economic miracle of Israel's early years, the agency had long since deteriorated into a gigantic patronage plum. It had an immigration absorption department headed by a Likud partisan that duplicated the government's own Ministry of Immigration Absorption, which was then headed by a Laborite. Agency department heads, like cabinet ministers, were entitled to chauffeur-driven Volvos, lots of overseas travel and relatively lucrative pensions.

The agency functioned as a government-sanctioned monopoly when it came to immigration. No other Israeli institution was allowed to raise money or formulate programs without its approval. Its officials were, of course, interested in Natan Sharansky Superstar. Within weeks of his arrival in Israel they asked him to embark on a year-long fundraising tour. Sharansky was willing, but he insisted on a role in determining where the money would go. This, he was told firmly, could not happen. It would be a violation of the process by which the agency allocated its funds. They would pay Sharansky a generous fee—$10,000 per speech, if that was what he wanted. But a say in how the agency spent the money he raised was impossible.

The bureaucrats had a counterproposal. They told Sharansky they would be happy to fund any organization he wanted to establish—on one condition: that he refrain from criticizing them in public. If it ever happened, he would not get another shekel. "The message was very clear—you can be part of us and we'll take care of you, or you can be on your own," Sharansky recalled. "And if you're on your own, you will never succeed."

Sharansky ignored the threat. In prison he had fought a daily battle against his KGB captors with a mental, spiritual and physical ferocity that at times seemed almost suicidal, and he was not inclined to play by anyone else's rules. Telling Sharansky that something worthwhile was impossible was a sure way of convincing him to try it. Together with a group of other prominent former Soviet prisoners, he founded the Zionist Forum in 1988 to represent the interests of Russian Jews already living in Israel and help lay the groundwork for the massive immigration he was certain would soon be coming. For nearly two years no one paid heed to the forum's warnings. Sharansky seemed a man without a mission, leading a paper organization, shouting dire alarms into the thin air.

The *aliya* changed all that, thrusting Sharansky into the position of spokesman. He was the only Russian whom mainstream Israelis had heard of, and the only one whom their leaders felt any obligation to listen to. He was different from many of the Russian newcomers—more affluent, more famous and more respectful of religion. And he believed in Zionism, an ideology that many of them regarded with the same suspicion they had once reserved for communism. At first many saw him as just another bureaucrat making his living from the *aliya,* but eventually many came to accept that he had their best interests at heart and that he was prepared to listen as well as lead.

The Russians should have been a dynamic force for economic growth and pluralism in Israel. Instead, they became a large, undigested lump in the stomach of a country that lacked the political will and the economic strength to absorb them. The immigrants remained largely confined to their own enclaves, where they spoke their old language, listened to the old music and practiced the old culture. For many it was a comfort—a protective coating from the old life that made it possible for them to survive the hardships of the new one. Yet it also enhanced their sense of alienation. The major vehicle of their separateness was their press. Within two years of the *aliya* there were seventeen different Russian-language daily and weekly newspapers, some owned by Russians, others by the large Israeli media conglomerates. They produced a wide range of articles and viewpoints. Yet while the words varied, the theme was always the same: how to beat the system that is beating you.

Israel as portrayed in the Russian press was a dangerous place where slick predators were always seeking to take advantage of poor befuddled immigrants. The Jewish Agency, having enticed Russians to come to Israel by lies and deceptions, ensnared them in red tape and financial clauses to prevent them from leaving. Veteran Israelis were cold-blooded and ruthless, and the authorities were always on their side. When four teenaged immigrants were set upon and badly beaten by a gang of Israeli youths at the beach in Kiryat Haim in May 1992, the real crime was the claim that attendants at the seaside medical service ignored the boys' pleas for help and discouraged them from calling the police. Later the boys said they had been threatened with further assaults if they gave evidence in court.

It did not matter whether all of these grim tales were true. They were published and republished, read and recycled by immigrants all too eager to believe every troubling word. They captured the mood and the desperation of many newcomers, for whom Israel was like living on another planet.

Their world was one of constant humiliations, petty and profound. One newspaper article described how Ernest Gomberg, a noted scientist who was one of the designers of Chernobyl and tens of other nuclear reactors in the East bloc, was adjusting to working as a janitor at a Jerusalem public school. Another depicted the savage degradation of an elderly Russian couple, the husband a crippled World War II veteran, who in October 1992 were evicted from the two-room flat they had occupied without permission at the Gilo immigration absorption center. The couple were handcuffed by police, dragged out of the building and dumped, along with their belongings, onto the pavement. Leonid Sofrin, author of more than twenty books in Russia, at age sixty-six scavenged for his daily bread in a garbage dump outside the Haifa market and said his entire family was talking seriously of suicide.

Others went beyond talk. Seven Russian doctors who could not find jobs in Israel reportedly committed suicide in the first two years of the *aliya*. An article in the biweekly newspaper *Vremya* described the death of an unnamed former top official of the Soviet space program who could find work in Jerusalem only as a school guard for the equivalent of about $2 per hour. One day he took home the Beretta given him at work, put it in his mouth and pulled the trigger. "He was over fifty, and even with Hebrew he didn't have a real chance to get a job," his daughter told the newspaper. "For some time Father had cherished illusions. Then he stopped hoping and living."

Many struggled with economic exploitation. The newspaper *Haaretz* described how the hip restaurants on Sheinkin Street in Tel Aviv exploited Russians trained as economists and engineers by hiring them as dishwashers for far below the legal minimum wage. They were, in fact, lucky to get any pay at all. In an electrical repair shop, five trained engineers were called for an all-day "tryout"—eleven hours at a workbench fixing broken radios, kettles and other appliances. "At the end of the day the owners said that they would notify them later whether they were accepted," wrote *Haaretz*. "They neither notified them nor paid them."

Emma Weinberg's experience was more typical. A forty-year-old former kindergarten teacher from Minsk, she wound up working in a Jerusalem button factory, a dank warehouse with ancient equipment, dismal lighting, filthy walls and floors and grimy windows. She spent nine hours a day in front of a conveyor belt squinting at thousands of tiny white buttons to find imperfections while her nostrils filled with the acrid smell of acetone from open vats on the shop floor. The women beside her on the assembly line were all Russian immigrants—one was a trained dentist, another a computer operator. "The only Israelis in the plant are the managers and office staff," said Weinberg. "Other Israelis refuse to work there because the pay is so low and the work is so boring."

Weinberg's pay was the equivalent of about $450 per month—not quite enough to cover the family's monthly rent. Her husband, Boris, who in Russia had worked as a computer engineer, now earned about $700 per month at a furniture factory. Both Weinbergs came home to Gilo each night drained and exhausted. On Fridays Emma would clean apartments for extra cash.

The Weinbergs had great hopes for their ten-year-old daughter, Lena, who quickly learned Hebrew and made friends at school. But living through her was not enough. The Weinbergs were discovering that in their early forties, a time when their lives and careers should have been peaking, they had little to show and little hope. "We're like people who can't swim and are thrown into the water," said Boris.

Sex was another field of exploitation. Russian women with their light-colored skin and blonde hair were known to locals as "white meat." Taxi drivers would cruise the caravan villages outside Beersheba and other cities offering their clients the opportunity to meet these purportedly loose and provocative women. There seemed to be a constant demand from ultrareligious Jewish men and Israeli Arabs for the chance of cheap, furtive sex with a Russian blonde, natural or otherwise. Women complained to crisis centers about assaults from employers who demanded sex in return for work. Single mothers felt the most pressure, but even high school girls reported sexual assaults by their Israeli classmates. Ella, a former engineering student, told a Russian newspaper that she had once worked as a dishwasher at a late-night restaurant, but "the owner and his friends didn't leave me alone. So I decided to do it without the dishwashing." Ella, who was married, earned nearly $100 per session, half of which went to her pimp. On some weekends she earned more than $700, a small fortune by immigrant standards.

Tel Aviv and Haifa were the centers of Russian prostitution. Some three hundred Russian women were said to be working in massage parlors in the Tel Aviv area. There was much talk about the Russian mafia muscling in, although the police and most crime experts agreed that the brothels were almost entirely under the control of the Israeli mafia and that the Russians worked mostly as low-level managers or hookers. Police data released in 1991 showed that the immigrant crime rate per hundred thousand was nearly four times lower than for other Israelis.

Like the newspapers, Israelis developed their own set of Russian myths. One purported expert claimed that 20 percent of the Russians were alcoholics. Army officers complained that Russian basic training recruits drank too much and showed little discipline. The Ministry of Immigration Absorption hired seventeen nurses to lecture new immigrants on personal hygiene because the Russians allegedly smelled so bad to Israelis and had no experience with deodorants. When Yair Tsaban, the new minister of immigration absorption, did a call-in program on Israel Radio, he spent the entire hour fielding complaints from Israelis about Russian privileges, Russian car accidents and Russian crime.

"The negative perceptions have taken over—the perception that this is a criminal *aliya,* that the Russians are cheating and lazy," said Yuri Shtern, an activist who had emigrated to Israel in the early eighties. "There's destructive media coverage and real defamation. The media started very positive, but then came the backlash. On Israel Television week after week you see Russians in prostitution, or not willing to serve in the army. As a result, there's now a general apathy in Israeli society, as if the *aliya* doesn't exist anymore. The *aliya* is forgotten and the government is leading the process of forgetting."

As their environment turned hostile and indifferent, some Russians dreamed of escape. Newspapers were filled with ads for companies promising reimmigration to the United States, Canada and South Africa. Two young brothers, Anton, twenty-one, and Ilya, twenty-eight, described how they planned to desecrate a synagogue in order to be deported to the West. Arkady I., a shipbuilding engineer, said he had decided to return to Moscow, "that place on earth where I can remain myself. . . . My leaving Russia was inspired by pure romanticism. I acted like an enamored schoolboy, not as a man, husband and father. Half a year I have been washing staircases."

Once it began Yitzhak Shamir saw the wave of Russian immigration through his own narrow ideological prism. In January 1990 he alarmed both the Arab world and the Bush administration by claiming that the country needed "a big Israel for a big *aliya*," implying that he would strive to settle the Russians in the occupied territories. His aides quickly sought to defuse and explain away the remark, but a few months later Shamir reaffirmed that what he wanted was an Israel permanently entrenched "between the sea and the Jordan River . . . for future generations and for the mass *aliya*." *New York Times* correspondent Joel Brinkley recounted Shamir's appearance before a group of Russian Jews: "He didn't talk about jobs. He never mentioned suicides, poverty or plans to address the immigrants' growing difficulties. Instead, the Prime Minister berated the Arabs and spoke passionately about his nationalist dreams. To the immigrants, a few of them hungry, most of them unemployed, Shamir talked about the future of Jerusalem."

When it came to power in June 1990, Yitzhak Shamir's narrow, new right-wing government pledged to place the *aliya* at the top of its agenda. "Considering the united destiny of the Jews in their struggle for existence, and the centrality of ingathering the Jewish people, the Government will make immigration and absorption its primary national mission," read the official statement.

Those were the words. The reality was that the government's "primary national mission" was its own survival; second on the list was Jewish settlement in the West Bank and Gaza. Everything else, immigration included, ran a poor third.

Natan Sharansky discovered this early on when he and his fellow activists sought to persuade Shamir to name a new minister of immigration absorption. Yitzhak Peretz of Shas, who had been given the post in 1988, epitomized for many Russians all that was wrong with Israeli politics. Here was an ultra-Orthodox rabbi placed in charge of a secular, anticlerical wave of immigrants, a neophyte who now had responsibility for a critical moment in Jewish history. He seemed more interested in sorting out who was technically a Jew and who was not than in seeing to it that the immigrants had jobs and housing. He returned from a trip to Moscow in November 1990 saying the Law of Return needed changing because 30 to 35 percent of the immigrants were not Jews, at a time when the Interior Ministry put the figure at closer to 5 percent. Peretz had not bothered to check. Incompetence clung to his shoulders like a prayer shawl.

Shamir knew of Peretz's shortcomings and made fun of him behind his back. But he could not fire Peretz without risking a traumatic rupture of the fragile political peace within his divided cabinet. Like most risks it was one Shamir preferred not to take. He listened to the Russians' complaints about Peretz with understanding and sympathy. But in the end he took no action. The Russians stewed, Peretz stayed.

Sharansky's failure to remove Peretz became part of a pattern. Several times during the course of the next two years he pleaded with Shamir to undertake the kind of political and economic reforms that would attract more immigrants. History would judge Shamir less for what he did about the peace process, which was not totally under his control, than for what he did about the *aliya,* Sharansky told him.

But Shamir seemed curiously unmoved. When Sharansky laid out the long list of immigrant complaints, Shamir addressed them with a smile and a dismissive wave. "It was always like this when new immigrants came," Shamir told him. "We, too, had difficulties. We came anyway. They will come, too."

Shamir decided early on that housing was the key; he wanted to put a roof over every Russian's head in time for the 1992 election so that he would not be met on the campaign trail by homeless immigrants. Jobs would somehow follow. He also saw housing as a tool in redrawing Israel's population map to conform with his vision of Greater Israel. He wanted more Jews in the northern Galilee, where Israeli Arabs were becoming a demographic majority, and in the empty southern expanses of the Negev. He also wanted steady population growth in the West Bank's Jewish settlements. Shamir was not a crusader; he saw these goals in long-run, low-key terms. Despite the occasional spasms of rhetoric he had no desire to flood the West Bank with newly arrived immigrants, knowing that such a move would provoke both the Bush administration and Gorbachev's regime. But he found himself under immense pressure from the right to appoint to the job Ariel Sharon, the one man who would see the settlement drive as a crusade and had the power to act accordingly.

In the summer of 1990 Sharon was a bull in search of a china shop. A former war hero and defense minister, he had seen his influence wane after the debacle of the 1982 invasion of Lebanon. But he still had a solid right-wing constituency and still cherished the hope of one day becoming prime minister. He saw the *aliya* as a vehicle to reestablish his reputation as the man who could get things done.

Shamir had little choice but to acquiesce to Sharon's appointment. To keep peace within the Likud, he had been forced to hand over the foreign affairs portfolio to the petulant David Levy, his chief intraparty rival. He persuaded a reluctant Moshe Arens, his main political ally, to hand over the post and move to the Defense Ministry, largely to block Sharon from gaining that position. But Shamir owed Sharon for siding with him during the bloodless coup attempt by fellow Likudniks in March. Now Sharon demanded the *aliya* as payment.

Shamir named Sharon to Levy's former post as housing minister and also gave him the chairmanship of a new, special "*aliya* cabinet" consisting of Shamir, Sharon, Immigration Absorption Minister Peretz and Finance Minister Yitzhak Modai. Despite the heavyweight roster however, the cabinet was mostly a paper tiger. Sharon fought first with Peretz, who saw his own authority drain away, then with Modai, a much more formidable and vicious foe, whose control over purse strings rendered the *aliya* cabinet something of a joke.

Modai's job was to fix the economy; he believed it would be a mistake to pour government money into housing and jobs for the *aliya,* that it was better to let the free market run its course. Modai said he did not mind if thousands of Russians were forced to spend their first winter in Israel in tent camps. "Living in tents never hurt anybody," he told reporters. But Sharon saw his mission in traditional Zionist terms: if you needed housing, then the government had to build it or at least pay for it; if you wanted people to live in the Galilee and the Negev, then build the houses there. The two men had been allies of convenience in opposing Shamir's abortive peace plan. Now they became bitter enemies. Sharon accused Modai of deliberately trying to sabotage his grandiose housing plans, while Modai claimed Sharon would sink the economy in a sea of debt and hyperinflation by illegally spending millions of shekels on housing.

The real responsibility for the disarray lay with Shamir. He was the one figure who could have imposed order and forced coherent decisions on his recalcitrant cabinet ministers. Sharansky pleaded with Shamir to intervene, but the prime minister refused. He said he understood Sharansky's concerns, that he himself did not sleep nights worrying over how to help Soviet Jews. But he saw his main mission as holding onto power to prevent Shimon Peres and Labor from taking over and destroying the country. He was not prepared to risk a political fight that might bring down the government.

Sharon spent close to $5 billion during his two-year tenure as housing minister between the fall of 1990 and summer of 1992, and built nearly 170,000 dwelling units. He did it by cutting corners and crashing through roadblocks such as budgetary constraints and legal niceties. When he ran out of money in 1991, he kept on spending, overrunning his budget by some $600 million even though an apoplectic Modai pressed the attorney general's office to launch a criminal investigation. The ministry solicited bids from private contractors for specified numbers of units in specified locations, guaranteeing to buy those that the contractors failed to sell on the open market. In central Israel, the government repaid 50 percent of the market value, while in the outlying areas of the Galilee and the Negev the buyback provision was 100 percent. Eager to take advantage of these fail-safe provisions, hundreds of new contractors sprang up, some of them longtime cronies of Sharon or Housing Ministry officials. They built cheaply and quickly and often shoddily, and counted on the government to cover their costs.

Half of the immigrants ignored government threats and incentives and settled in the central region around Tel Aviv and Jerusalem, often cramming two or three families into single-family quarters. Rents for low- and middle-income apartments in the region doubled and tripled between 1988 and 1992. Overall sale prices increased 28 percent in 1991 alone. But by early 1992 Sharon's juggernaut tactics and the sharp fall in projected immigration led to a dramatic oversupply. Prices began to plummet and the government was forced to buy some 26,000 unsold units that nobody wanted.

Sharon declared his housing crusade a great success. But his emergency-style, socialistic approach was more suitable for the Israel of the 1950s than for the 1990s. He succeeded in quickly putting roofs over immigrants' heads, but at an exorbitant cost. Looking back a year later, the *Jerusalem Report* dubbed the Likud's housing boom "The $5 Billion Folly" and reported it had produced 70,000 empty apartments, most of them located in remote parts of the country where no one wanted to live because of high unemployment.

The *aliya* also quickly became another battleground between Arabs and Jews. The influx of Russians alarmed Palestinians in both Israel proper and the occupied territories who feared that the newcomers would gain land, jobs and privileges at their expense. These fears seemed confirmed when many Israeli employers let go their Arab manual workers and replaced them with new immigrants—a move many employers soon regretted when they discovered that most Russians were woefully unsuited for manual labor. Israelis, for their part, viewed these objections as simply another attempt by the Arabs to weaken Israel, this time by challenging one of the most sacred tenets of the country's existence—the right of free Jewish immigration. As usual, neither group seemed prepared to entertain even the remotest possibility that the other had a legitimate point of view.

The *aliya* was supposed to strengthen Israel economically and demographically. But at least in the short run, it made the country far more reliant on the United States. Early estimates suggested that Israel would have to spend $20 billion over a five-year period to absorb the half million immigrants moving through its gates. Some $10 billion of that could be generated locally, but the rest would have to come from outside—most of it from the United States in the form of loan guarantees at a time when the Bush administration was taking aim at Shamir's settlement policy. Suddenly two central Zionist values were in conflict: consolidating Jewish settlements in the occupied territories and successfully absorbing the Russian immigrants. Shamir claimed the government could accomplish both, but the Bush administration forced it to choose.

It was no contest. The settlement movement had a firm constituency, an influential lobbying network and the entrenched allegiance of a powerful group of cabinet ministers. The *aliya,* although much larger in size, had no political muscle. Shamir's government succumbed readily to the settlers.

At first the Zionist Forum tried to influence government policy in quiet, constructive ways. Sharansky attended the first *aliya* cabinet meetings, bringing along studies and experts and proposing pilot projects in job creation and training so that Russians could find work in their own professions or begin training for new ones. But it quickly became clear to him that no one was listening.

During the fall of 1990 Sharansky got his first look at the largest caravan town, Nahal Bekka, located on the outskirts of Beersheba in the Negev Desert. The prefabricated, two-room trailers, pressed against one another in row upon row, were baked in summer and frozen in winter, with rain and dampness leaking through each seam. Sharansky was disgusted and deeply depressed by them. "It's only temporary," Sharon tried to reassure him. Three years later Nahal Bekka was still full.

Frustrated by the politicians, Sharansky decided the forum would have to strike out on its own. He used his prominence to raise some $40 million, including $20 million from a maverick American philanthropist named Joseph Gruss, and poured the money into a home loan scheme and pilot projects for job retraining. The idea was to help the immigrants while demonstrating to the government how these kinds of projects could be done. But Sharansky's financial independence only made government officials more suspicious of him. Here was someone who had not been elected through the parties and who owed them no allegiance. He was, by definition, a dangerous man. "Ultimately, the most important thing for Labor and Likud was that I was not part of either of them," he said. "It was something new to them and they didn't like it."

Unlike the Sephardim, who had decades of experience in Israeli society, the Russians had to start from scratch. Coming from a repressive state, they had no familiarity with democracy and no practice in influencing a democratic system and making it work for them. Many of the heroes of the Zionist movement in the Soviet Union became marginalized, fringe figures in Israel. There was little agreement among them on how to begin to organize and make coherent, effective demands.

Some tried frontal assault. Ephraim Melamed, a combative electrical engineer from the Ukraine, wrote inflammatory newspaper columns, led a protest against primitive conditions at a Hebrew language training center and staged a hunger strike at the Housing Ministry in Jerusalem to gain public attention. After watching construction contractors gouge Russians in the purchase prices for new apartments, Melamed formed a housing cooperative with fellow Russians to build their own apartments outside Haifa in half the time and at 40 percent below the price Israeli builders charged.

The contractors struck back. They got a court order blocking the cooperative from completing the first group of apartments, while the Housing Ministry withheld mortgages from the prospective owners. Equipment at the site was mysteriously sabotaged at night, and Melamed himself was attacked with a knife and beaten with a club. In the end he was fired from his job with a government-run electric power utility, and a court decision forced the hundred families in the cooperative to make mortgage payments for their new, unfinished apartments at the same time they were still paying rent. Melamed became a martyr and folk hero to many Russians, but he was virtually ignored by Israeli newspapers and broadcast media.

Other Russians argued that the only way to make a political impact was for Russians to model themselves on Arye Deri's Shas and form their own ethnic political party. There would be enough Russian voters by the next election in 1992 to get at least five seats in the Knesset. Then they, too, could become part of the great Israeli game of coalition-building and political extortion. Some of Sharansky's Russian friends approached him, hoping he would lead, or at least lend his support to, such a movement.

But Sharansky was appalled by the prospect. He wanted Russians to force changes in Israel, not join in perpetuating the old corrupt system. He flirted for a time with forming a new party, one that would be based on reform, not ethnicity. When the idea failed to garner support, he urged fellow

Russians to choose among the major parties like Labor and Likud rather than form their own. He believed, naïvely perhaps, that this would force the parties to make accommodations with the newcomers rather than write off their votes.

Sharansky saw that Israelis felt more comfortable with Ethiopian immigrants than with the Russians. At first it surprised him; the Ethiopians, after all, were Third World blacks with seemingly little in common with Israelis. Then he realized that that was exactly the point. "The Ethiopians are not a threat. They're lower class, not middle class. It'll take a generation before they threaten anybody. With Russians, Israelis feel threatened immediately. If your daughter wants to go to medical school, she has to wait or study something else because suddenly there are so many Russian doctors here. In school, classes of twenty-five are now thirty-two. Israeli musicians and artists and engineers all feel an immediate challenge."

Increasingly Sharansky came to realize that while Israel may have welcomed the Russians to its shore, once they arrived they were in brutal competition with other Israelis for jobs and benefits. Think tank studies and pilot projects were not enough. People needed to wield power over the government—with their votes, money, protests and anger—before anything would change.

"It was part of his political education—he slowly started to grasp that the politicians here lie as much as they did in the Soviet Union," said Zeev Chafets, a close friend. "Natan had truly believed other people were as Zionistic as he was, and when the politicians said they'd help the *aliya* that they meant it. It was a process of waking up."

Uri Gordon, the bureaucrat in charge of immigration absorption at the Jewish Agency, was an impatient man. A Labor Party operative for three decades, he railed publicly against Shamir's government for its apathy toward the *aliya*. But he saved his angriest remarks for his own constituency—secular Israelis, the backbone of the Labor Party, whom he accused of not rising to the challenge. "Where are those ideological flags of the past?" he wrote. "And why don't we have the same motivation as the *haredim* and the religious nationalists? We, the nonreligious, have lost the Zionist fervor which has always been our guiding light."

In person, Uri Gordon tended to be more optimistic—and more ruthless. "There will be a lot of problems and pain," he argued, "but in some ways this generation of Russians is a desert generation. They will suffer greatly, like the people of Israel suffered in the desert under Moses, but their children will be beautiful.

"You know, in Haifa the other day I met a mathematician, a very serious guy. Now he works in a gas station. It's a tough life, but he says his two sons are happy and so he's happy too. Let's be cruel about it and say that 200,000 of the Russians eventually leave. It would be very sad, tragic even, but let's face it. Those who stay will build the country."

Slowly, painfully but inexorably, Uri Gordon's ruthless vision began to take shape. Some of the Russians were indeed leaving the country to return to the former Soviet Union. By 1993 newspaper reports put the figure at somewhere between 5 and 10 percent, and noted that for $100 cash they could buy back their Russian citizenship from corrupt officials. The annual rate of *aliya* dropped precipitously from 200,000 in 1990 and 1991 to 65,000 in 1992, with a similarly projected figure for 1993. Some Russians were sitting on their suitcases in places like Moscow and Minsk, all packed and ready to leave but unwilling to risk their future in a land with few jobs and little sense of mission. It was a major decline, yet the 1992 figure was still Israel's third-highest annual total since 1951.

Those who stayed in Israel inevitably began to move up. A survey of 1,200 immigrants by the JDC-Brookdale Institute in April 1993 showed that the employment rate among immigrants who had been living in Israel for more than two years was the same as the population at large. Among couples, only 11 percent had no wage earner, and in 45 percent of families both husband and wife were employed. The survey also found that the percentage of those who were working in their desired occupation rose from 23 percent for those in the country less than one year to 54 percent for those who were there for more than two.

Russian entrepreneurs were moving into all kinds of fields. Physicians, shut out by the Israeli medical establishment, began opening "nonmedical" clinics, offering acupuncture and massage. Engineers formed their own firms; bakers began selling rich brown Russian bread unlike anything Israelis had ever eaten before. Trade with the republics of the former Soviet Union was exploding; in 1992 trade with Russia alone increased fivefold.

Predictably, the hardest groups to absorb were those over fifty-five years old, single-parent families and those such as physicians who required massive and sophisticated retraining in their fields. Nonetheless, 94 percent of those surveyed told Brookdale that they intended to remain in Israel.

Beneath these encouraging statistics, however, was a vast reservoir of unhappiness and disaffection. Some 71 percent of those surveyed said they believed their chances of finding work in their chosen field were poor, while 52 percent said job prospects in Israel were much worse than they had expected before coming. Sixty percent said their ability to find a job that fitted their abilities was worse than expected, 75 percent said their financial situation in Israel was worse than it had been in the Soviet Union, and 69 percent believed the chances that it would eventually improve were poor.

Objectively, conditions were improving steadily: the Russians, like previous immigrant groups, were navigating their way into the mainstream with surprising speed. But subjectively, many remained alienated and dissatisfied. They were eager for revenge and they were looking for scapegoats. They were prepared to punch holes in the old political, social and economic arrangements and to help propel Israel toward its date with the future.

8. The Sealed Room

*Come, my people, enter thou into thy chambers,
and shut thy doors about thee. Hide thyself as it
were for a little moment, until the indignation is
past.*

—ISAIAH 26:20

IN coming to Israel, Russian Jews chose to escape from the tumult of history in the making for what they hoped was a more peaceful, stable existence. But history was not so easy to elude. Just as their numbers peaked, Russian immigrants found themselves plunged along with their fellow Israelis into yet another tumultuous historical moment over which they had no control.

On April 2, 1990, four months before his army seized Kuwait, President Saddam Hussein of Iraq accused the United States and Britain of colluding with Israel against his regime. The plot would fail, he said, because Iraq had acquired advanced chemical weaponry, and he swore: "By God, we will make the fire eat up half of Israel if it tries to do anything."

Israel got the message. Moshe Arens, who was then foreign minister and became defense minister in June, told every delegation of American officials that passed through Jerusalem that Saddam was a madman, comparable to Hitler in his delusions and his brutality. Arens even organized an emergency trip to Washington on July 19 with the heads of the Mossad and Military Intelligence to brief Secretary of Defense Dick Cheney on Iraqi purchases of nuclear-related equipment in Europe and to warn that Saddam was very close to assembling a nuclear bomb.

Cheney listened politely and expressed his gratitude. But Arens's overall feeling was that the Americans, who had supported Saddam in his eight-year war with Iran, did not grasp the Iraqi threat. "There was clearly a mind-set that insisted on closing their eyes to all of this," he told Israeli journalist David Makovsky.

Two weeks later Iraq invaded Kuwait.

As George Bush set about constructing the Allied coalition against Iraq, he had one overriding interest when it came to Israel: keep the Israelis on the shelf and out of sight, in order not to jeopardize the participation of Arab states such as Syria and Saudi Arabia. But relations between Bush and Shamir had been sour since the president took office in January 1989. The American strategists who were planning the response to Saddam had no confidence in Israeli restraint. Their main fear in the first weeks of the crisis was that an anxious Israel would launch a preemptive strike, as it had done in the 1967 Six-Day War and again in the 1981 raid on Iraq's Osirak nuclear reactor.

Saddam appeared to be inviting such an attack. Within days of the invasion he equated Iraq's occupation of Kuwait with Israel's occupation of the West Bank and Gaza and proposed an international conference to settle both issues. At the same time U.S. satellite photographs showed Iraqi trucks hauling Scud missiles and their launchers to the far western desert—marked as sectors H-2 and H-3 on Israeli military maps—where they were within range of Tel Aviv. Israeli and American strategists both recognized these moves as an attempt to provoke Israel. Saddam wanted to redefine the terms of the confrontation from Arab versus Arab to Arab versus Zionist and shatter the Allied coalition lining up against him.

When David Ivri, the highly esteemed director general of Israel's Defense Ministry, traveled to Washington in late August, he got a full dose of the administration's anxieties. National security adviser Brent Scowcroft delivered a tough lecture. Israeli involvement would only interfere with U.S. efforts to build a broad coalition, Scowcroft told Ivri. Now that U.S. forces were in the region, Israel had never been safer. It had no need to act. Iraq's defeat would mean a new Middle East, Scowcroft promised, and Israel would be one of the prime beneficiaries.

Richard Haass, Scowcroft's deputy, was even more blunt. The lives of American boys are at stake, he told Ivri, so don't do anything to jeopardize them.

Ivri presented the Americans with requests for F-15 and F-16 warplanes, M-60 tanks and two batteries of Patriot air-defense missile systems. He also indicated that Israel would not directly oppose the massive arms transfer to

Saudi Arabia that the Bush administration was proposing, even though the Israelis remained uneasy at the prospect of an Arab state technically still at war with Israel receiving advanced modern weaponry.

Administration officials promised to supply some of the items on Ivri's list, but they refused to even discuss operational matters such as Israel's military options in the event of an Iraqi attack. They rejected Ivri's plea for the special IFF codes ("Identify, Friend or Foe") that the Israeli air force would need to enter Iraqi airspace without clashing with Allied warplanes patrolling the area. They also effectively denied Ivri's appeal for real-time satellite intelligence data so that the Israelis could monitor movements of Iraqi forces in the western desert. The reason for the denial was simple, a congressional friend told a senior Israeli official: "Israel is not receiving real-time intelligence because you may take the data and decide to act." Washington did not trust Jerusalem.

Shamir understood what Bush was trying to accomplish and made clear early on that Israel had no intention of intervening unless it was attacked. "We live in this storm, but we have no part in it," he told Israel Television on August 22.

Still, Shamir was troubled by American precautions. The moderate Arab states had entered the coalition because of their own self-interests, he believed. Israeli involvement was irrelevant. He did not expect a public embrace from the United States, but he did want recognition of the risks Israel was being asked to take. He felt quarantined and ignored. Every Israeli attempt to establish better coordination was rebuffed by Washington. Cheney and Baker avoided Jerusalem on their many trips to the region. "You're saying to us that America and Israel can't be seen together in public, like being seen on the street with your mistress," Dan Meridor complained to his friend Dennis Ross, Baker's deputy.

The isolation made Israel more bellicose in its public pronouncements. "Whoever attacks Israel won't live to remember it," thundered Foreign Minister David Levy in September. There were dozens of similar statements from Arens, Shamir and other officials. They did not seem to realize that they were saying exactly what Saddam Hussein wanted to hear, and that he presumed Israel would be true to its word.

To assuage Israeli feelings, the administration on September 18 offered a public commitment that the United States would come to Israel's defense if it was attacked. Officials also agreed to set up a direct secure telephone line between the Pentagon and the Kirya, Israel's defense headquarters in Tel Aviv, so that the Americans could pass on instant warnings of Scud launchings picked up on satellite and so that Arens and Cheney could have instant communication in case war broke out. But the Americans did not activate the line until just a few days before the air war began. The first two Patriot missile batteries also did not arrive until mid-January. When they did, the Israelis were surprised to learn that these were the old antiaircraft model, not the new antimissile variety.

Relations were put to a severe test in October when a confrontation between Israeli police and Palestinian demonstrators spun out of control atop the Temple Mount in Jerusalem. Police opened fire, killing nineteen unarmed protesters. Shamir contended that the incident was a premeditated provocation by Palestinian leaders seeking to win support for Saddam Hussein, while American officials were flabbergasted that the Israelis would allow themselves to be drawn into such a clash. There was deep irritation on both sides: Bush rebuked Israel for not acting "with greater restraint," while Israel's acting U.N. ambassador said the country was being made a "sacrificial lamb" to keep the coalition intact. The bitterness was exacerbated by a United Nations Security Council condemnation of Israel that the United States joined in supporting. But remarkably the incident died down quickly, and Bush's coalition held together.

Israeli concerns were somewhat laid to rest in December when Shamir went to Washington. It was his first meeting with Bush since the acrimonious dispute ten months earlier over Jewish settlements. Bush assured Shamir that he had no intention of letting Saddam wriggle off the hook and that the United States would go to war "without hesitation" if Iraq did not withdraw from Kuwait. He also told Shamir that once the war started, Allied warplanes would seek out and hammer Iraq's missile launchers in order to prevent Scud attacks on Israel.

Shamir, in turn, reiterated to Bush that he would not launch a preemptive strike against Iraq. He did not rule out retaliation in case of an Iraqi attack, but he promised not to strike without first notifying Bush.

The two men shared a common goal and a common enemy; on this, if on little else, there would be no conflict between them.

It was not just the Bush administration that made Israel feel isolated and abandoned. Large numbers of American Jews, frightened by the uncertain prospect of war, canceled plans to travel to Israel. In September, more than half of the 350 expected guests—donors, artists, dealers and collectors—did not show up for a gala celebration of the twenty-fifth anniversary of the Israel Museum in Jerusalem. Tourism throughout the fall declined by more than half. The lobbies of Jerusalem's most popular hotels looked vacant and deserted, as if someone had just phoned in a bomb scare.

"Saddam Hussein has fired a shot at Israel and it landed on target: American tourists were wiped out," wrote Bernard Mandelbaum, president emeritus of the Jewish Theological Seminary. When Israelis thanked him for coming to Israel that fall, "I cringed in embarrassment and shame for my fellow American Jews."

Yitzhak Shamir put his view of American Jews who canceled their visits even more starkly. "They are betraying the state of Israel," he told an interviewer.

From the beginning of the Gulf crisis, the generals of the IDF's high command debated, vacillated and fought among themselves. They questioned one another and their political leaders. They offered contradictory advice and undercut one another's arguments. They suffered from the passivity imposed upon them by Shamir, playing a role they had never before adopted in wartime. But in the end they bowed to the prime minister's restraint policy.

Shamir seldom took the generals into his confidence. They were there to give military advice and to follow orders. The old underground warrior carried a reservoir of skepticism when it came to the generals. They always seemed to lean a little to the leftward side of the political establishment, and seemed a little too willing to intervene in matters that rightfully belonged to the cabinet. He did not care for their role in scrapping the Lavi, the multibillion-dollar state-of-the-art jet fighter that the cabinet had narrowly rejected in 1987 after a heavy lobbying campaign by Chief of Staff Dan Shomron and the general staff. He did not appreciate their whining about the difficulty of suppressing the intifada. There was something in their manner that was too clean and too fastidious for Shamir. Some of them were in love with their careers. They did not like to get their uniforms dirty.

As defense minister, Arens was Shamir's main link to the commanders, and the two men talked several times a day. But Shamir believed that Arens, who had never served in the IDF, was not always skeptical enough when it came to the generals. The prime minister came to rely as well on Meridor, a reserve tank commander who was of the same generation and demeanor as some of the younger members of the general staff, such as Deputy Chief of Staff Ehud Barak and the head of Military Intelligence, Amnon Shahak. There were times when these men served as Meridor's back channel, keeping him informed of the debates and power struggles among the generals.

Meridor understood that the generals, like soldiers everywhere, were trained to act in well-rehearsed sequence. In their strategic view Israel was small, vulnerable and undermanned. To deter attack it had always been willing to use preemptive strikes and massive retaliation. The army's strategic doctrine was to seek to transfer the fighting swiftly to enemy territory. The air attack on the Osirak reactor was a prime example of how Israeli military strategy worked: the general staff had identified a prospective threat to national security and, with the approval of Menachem Begin, snuffed it out before it could develop into a real one. World opinion had not been a factor.

Generals tended to fight the last war, Meridor knew. In the wars of 1948, 1956, 1967 and 1973, Israel either had been under attack or on the brink of being invaded. In each case Israel could feel it was fighting not for territory or strategic gain but for its existence.

The Gulf crisis posed a new equation. This was not a case of Israel versus the Arabs. It was the United States and some Arab states versus another Arab state. Israel was a side issue, yet it was also a target of opportunity.

The generals knew that no matter what Shamir said or did, they would be held responsible for Israel's security. If Tel Aviv was attacked, Israelis would expect the IDF to respond. To do nothing would go against the generals' training and their psychology. It would be charged that they had failed their country at a critical moment.

They also worried about Arab reaction. For years Arab leaders understood that if they launched an attack against Israel they would be punished with disproportionate severity. Most of the generals believed this had been a key element in keeping the Arabs from attacking Israel over the past eighteen years.

The army's emergency preparations for the war involved two related areas that were mired in confusion and controversy: intelligence and civil defense.

The biggest uncertainty was over Iraq's chemical warfare capability. Shahak's deputy chief of Military Intelligence, Brigadier General Danny Rothschild, insisted that the Iraqis had chemical warheads and could mount them on Scuds. Air force commander Avihu Bin-Nun said his intelligence experts believed that the Iraqis did not have such warheads in any usable quantity. There were also widely differing assessments of how much damage the warheads could do. Rothschild was withering in his criticism of Bin-Nun's intelligence estimate. "It's the difference between guessing and knowing," he told a general staff meeting. "They're just guessing."

The lack of certainty demonstrated how woefully inadequate Israeli intelligence was when it came to Iraq. While Israel's planners took the Iraqi threat more seriously than their counterparts in other Western countries, they, like these counterparts, lacked both the technical and human intelligence to analyze the Iraqi leader's motives and capability.

The uncertainty also fed into a political dispute over whether to distribute gas masks. Seeking to avoid panic, Arens and Shomron downplayed the need for the masks for as long as possible, while Foreign Minister David Levy pressed hard for nationwide distribution.

In the end Rothschild's assessment forced the cabinet's hand. For the first time in history, a state distributed chemical warfare protection to its entire civilian population. Shomron's calculation was both political and medical. To those who warned that gas mask distribution would cause panic, Shomron replied: "What will happen if not one missile falls or none of them have chemical warheads? So we handed out the gas masks and nothing happens. But if a chemical missile falls and we didn't distribute?" And how much chaos might ensue if the army attempted to hand out gas masks after missiles had already started falling? When the masks were distributed in October there was no panic.

There were other civil defense issues. For a country whose military doctrine had always consisted of attack, attack and then attack again, civil defense had long been a backwater. Many of Israel's thousands of underground bomb shelters were in a sorry state of disrepair, as were many alarm sirens. Because missiles might rain down with only ninety seconds' notice, it was likely that civilians fleeing to shelters would get caught in open ground where bombing would do the most damage. So it was decided that civilians should remain inside their own apartments in rooms sealed with plastic sheeting. Combined with gas masks, these would provide adequate protection for most people against chemical attack—and, perhaps, divert attention from the woeful conditions inside the shelters.

For Shomron, the Gulf War was the last unique act of a thirty-year military career that had encompassed four wars and the Entebbe hostage rescue mission. Nothing had prepared him for the role he now had to play. "I had always been in the front row with the fighters," he wrote later. "Suddenly . . . I found myself dealing with discussions about Magan David Adom [the Israeli Red Cross], the firefighters, the police and civil defense, the local plans for emergencies and local councils. It was a strange feeling. . . . Instead of moving tanks, sending paratroopers and infantry and leading planes to distant targets, I was discussing much more seriously detoxification showers, sealed rooms, gas masks, [and] atropine shots. What a war!"

"Four more days and the hell with it all! Learn to smoke! Collect stamps! Do impressions of people! Try to fly! . . . For my part you can all get up and go to hell! . . . We were an okay country, but you don't have to idealize. We were all pretty crummy!"

While the generals agonized, comedian Doron Nesher's helpful tips on what to do before the apocalypse captured some of the essence of how most Israelis prepared for the war—in the same emotionally contradictory way they lived their lives: with skepticism, idealism, bravado and fear. So did the tangled crowds of Israelis outside local shops clamoring for masking tape and plastic sheeting. Hadassah Hospital set up showers in the parking lot and mobile showers at its central entrance to detoxify people suffering from chemical burns. At the Israel Museum in Jerusalem, workers carefully lifted the Dead Sea Scrolls from their display counter and buried them deep in the earth in special vaults. Orthodox Jews blew rams' horns and pronounced medieval curses on Saddam Hussein, while concerned pet owners fashioned homemade gas masks and protective tents for their cats and dogs. Some shop owners put signs in their windows saying they would no longer accept postdated checks—the signers might not be around to pay.

Weather reports were suspended to deny data to Iraqi targeters. Some two hundred homeless people in Tel Aviv gathered at the bus station for shelter, anxious not to be caught outside when the first missiles hit. At the other end of the economic spectrum, hundreds of people gathered daily at Ben-Gurion Airport ready to pay any amount for a seat on a flight to anywhere. Television cameras caught these refugees in various states of embarrassed denial. "I'm sorry to leave now but my reservation expires," one man told Israel Television. "I'm just going to Rio for the Carnival," said another.

Among those seeking to flee were young American Jews who chose to cut short their academic study programs and kibbutz sabbaticals to return to the safety of the United States. Suddenly the country that was supposed to be a sanctuary had become the most dangerous place a Jew could live. "We have children," was all the explanation one ultra-Orthodox woman holding two toddlers and standing before ten suitcases and three cardboard boxes offered to the *Jerusalem Report* as she stood in line to buy a ticket.

Waiting for the war, Israelis suffered from three levels of shock, quipped the *Report*'s cartoon, *Dry Bones:* "1. Mild shock at hearing what the enemy governments are saying. 2. Serious shock at hearing what our government is saying. 3. Extreme shock at hearing what friendly governments are saying."

On the night of January 17, newspaper presses stopped as if holding their breath, waiting for the air war to commence. When it came, the atmosphere was eerie and silent. School and work were canceled, and Israelis were ordered to remain inside their houses. Yet nothing happened.

Somewhere far away, Allied bombers were raining terror on Baghdad. The first reports were rosy beyond belief. Coalition warplanes had battered Iraq and pulverized the Scud launching sites. Iraq's capacity to strike at Israel seemingly had been destroyed. The nightmare was over before it had even begun. Among soldiers and civilians alike, there was a collective sigh of relief.

It lasted twenty-four hours.

Rivka Sofer, mother of Ilan, Ehud and Yehudit, was sound asleep along with her children when the siren sounded at 2:03 A.M. on Friday, January 18. A few seconds later the first Scud hit six yards from their house in the Ezra neighborhood of south Tel Aviv.

"We heard the siren. I started calling the children's names. I wanted to tell them to get up and get dressed. But then it all happened.

"I heard a bang, it was the Scud falling, then everything exploded. The front door burst into the room. Everything was opening up, everything fell into the middle of the house. The walls, the cabinets, the closets, the books inside the closet, every page in a different place. They didn't just fall, they flew apart. The slats from the shutters, the cupboards. Everything in the kitchen cabinets fell onto the floor.

"Then the whole wall fell on me. The wall between the living room and my bed. The cinderblocks were on my head.

"I could hear the children screaming. I was pinned down. It was dark all of a sudden, so dark. Not even the street lights. For a second there was quiet, then there was so much noise. Things breaking and falling and exploding. And people screaming and running around. And water running. I heard water.

"But I was pinned down. First all the cinderblocks. . . . Then I was covered with glass. There was glass everywhere, from everything, from the windows and from the mirrors and from the dishes and from pictures. Everywhere . . . I felt it cutting me. I was afraid for my eyes. My shoulder, my back hurt. And lots of cuts, from the glass.

"I couldn't breathe. I thought I was going to die, that I would suffocate. I knew I was bleeding. But all I could really think about was, where are the children? I called each of their names, tried to hear them. But there was so much screaming and yelling, from outside, from inside. The walls had opened up. It was like there was no inside, no outside, just me under the cinderblocks.

"When I tried to breathe, I felt the air in my heart. I had no air. My son, together with the neighbor's son, he took me out. . . . We were naked, in our pajamas, running around, total chaos.

"Blood, I was covered with blood.

"The boys ran to check on the old people. Across the street, where the Scud fell, there is an old lady. She was safe, but she was so frightened, she couldn't move. Ilan and my neighbor's boy, they had to take her out.

"I was covered with blood. My dress was soaked with my blood. It was completely dark, no lights anywhere. We were afraid to stand still and we were afraid to move, it was so dark. Then the ambulance came and they took me to the hospital. I was at the hospital a day or two.

"We never thought anything like this could happen. War inside our houses."

The Al-Hussein missile that hit near Rivka Sofer's bedroom was an upgrade of a primitive Soviet Scud. It looked almost comical—a long, thin, metallic cigar, thirty-seven feet long yet less than three feet in diameter. It weighed eight tons and had a range of roughly 400 miles, and it took only seven minutes to make the western Iraq–Tel Aviv run. Its six-foot-long warhead packed 550 pounds of conventional explosives. That amount was just one-eighth the payload of an Israeli fighter bomber, but it was enough to do extensive physical damage to buildings and to terrify their frightened inhabitants.

Seven other Scuds hit Israel early that morning of January 18—five in and around Tel Aviv, two more in Haifa. No one was killed, but forty-seven people were hurt and 1,587 apartments were damaged. At first, civil defense inspectors mistakenly reported that chemical warheads had been used, but the claims were quickly withdrawn before they became public.

The missiles gouged craters in the pavement and alleyways. They shattered roofs, walls and floors, peeling away the sides of apartment buildings to reveal the crumpled intestines within. Balconies dangled precariously. The explosions left massive quantities of broken glass and debris—furniture, appliances, clothing all mingled in a dusty stew.

There was irony in the fact that Tel Aviv, Israel's most modern and cosmopolitan city and the one that seemed farthest removed from the Arab-Israeli conflict, was the first and foremost target. Before the war, Tel Aviv had greeted the prospect of attack with its usual bravado. "It takes five minutes for a missile to fly from Baghdad to Tel Aviv," said Mayor Shlomo Lahat, "but it'll take an hour and a half for it to find a place to park once it gets here."

But the first strike drained all the chutzpah from the city and replaced it with stunned disbelief. "When the sirens sounded, there was a general feeling of unreality," said Linda Gradstein, National Public Radio's Jerusalem correspondent. "People asked how could an Arab country dare launch missiles at Israel? And what happens now? The next day it was panic buying. Like everybody else, I went to the supermarket to stock up. They had run out of milk. So I stopped at a small grocery. Someone saw me walking with the milk and stopped his car. 'Where? Where did you get it?' People didn't need things but they bought them anyway. A real siege mentality took over."

The fear of chemical attack, coupled with the lack of sleep, gripped Israelis. Hundreds of people injected themselves with atropine, the antidote for nerve gas that had been distributed with the gas masks. Many more suffered from maskophobia—they tightened the masks to the point of pain. Youngsters screamed as parents, seized by the nightmarish prospect of their children unprotected, pulled the straps even tighter.

One panic-stricken father tightened a gas mask over the face of his frantic three-year-old daughter. She vomited into the mask and suffocated.

The telephone rang on the night of the first attack just as Brigadier General Nachman Shai, the official army spokesman, was starting to fall asleep. "I pick it up but I can't hear anything," he recalled. "I hang it up, again it rings. No response again. Then a third call—it's a producer at Israel Radio's Tel Aviv studio and she's telling me missiles have hit. I tell her I'll check it. Then we're disconnected. And I can't get through to anyone in Tel Aviv because the lines are jammed.

"I had also a direct line to the Chief of Staff headquarters. I ask them to give me the COS, but I can't understand the woman at the other end—-she's wearing her gas mask and trying to talk to me at the same time. I ask for press liaison—the woman who answers says, 'Nachman, we don't know what's going on.' Israel Radio calls again. We put out an official announcement that missiles have hit the country and everyone should put on their gas mask and wait for further information.

"I try to call my driver to pick me up but I can't get through to him either, so I call Tel Aviv and ask them to call him to come and get me. I'm sitting in my uniform at the front door watching lots of aircraft streaking in the sky and wondering if they're ours.

"The driver comes and by 2:30 A.M. I'm on my way to Tel Aviv. Listening to the radio I realize there is quite a lot of panic. The announcers are very excited. The commander of civil defense is answering phone calls from the audience when he should be out directing his workers and it's all a big mess. So finally I reach the studio and ask them to put me on the air."

Shai had little information to convey. He did not know if the attack was chemical, he did not know how many people were injured or if any were killed. Still, for ten minutes he spoke to Israelis in a slow, calm, soothing voice. "As you all know, missiles have hit Israel," he told them. "It is time for us to defend ourselves. Put on your gas masks. Don't panic. Do it carefully. The IDF is doing everything necessary. I promise that when I have further information, you'll have it, too."

Shai scurried to military headquarters, where he met briefly with Arens and Shomron. "A million of your troops are still in sealed rooms and don't know what to do," he told them. "Not now, Nachman," Arens replied. "Not now?" Shai asked. "It has to be now."

Amid the uncertainty of Israel's worst night since the outbreak of the 1973 Yom Kippur War, Nachman Shai stepped forward. A reluctant, semi-professional general who spoke with the loose familiarity that Israelis use to talk to one another, he became a local hero. Israelis called him The Valium of the Nation.

At age forty-four Shai was a well-known establishment figure who had served as military correspondent for Israel Radio and Israel Television, press spokesman for the Israeli embassy in Washington and the Defense Ministry, and head of Army Radio, the popular music and news station. As IDF spokesman his primary mission was to try to help an army demoralized by two years of intifada mend its battered media image. He took the rank of brigadier general and wore a uniform, but Shai was clearly no general. "Not Every Silence Is Golden," read the poster on his office wall. And in the end his informal, sincere but not too serious style helped him win over Israeli audiences.

At one point a survey by the Dahaf marketing firm showed that 94 percent of Israelis trusted him. With his steel-rim glasses and floppy dark brown hair he had enough boyish sex appeal to tie Benjamin Netanyahu, a local political heartthrob, in a poll of "the man I would most like to be with in a sealed room." But Shai was not sexy so much as he was comforting. At a time when nobody seemed to know very much, Shai was saying, "Calm down; have a glass of water."

It was only common sense, but it was exactly what Israelis needed in the first panicky days of the war. "We had the feeling we were completely cut off from the world," said Linda Gradstein. "And it was hard to breathe through the masks. Israel is a collective society, yet people weren't going through this ordeal together—they were alone, locked in a sealed room with their gas masks on. It was a terrible feeling of isolation." Shai offered a temporary sense of relief. "Suddenly you weren't alone anymore, you were with Nachman Shai."

When the Scuds hit, Israel's leaders were prepared to strike back. "Our first response after seeing the destruction and casualties and seeing reports from the field was natural for any Israeli, almost a conditioned reflex that had developed here during the generation of wars: we have to respond," Dan Shomron recalled. "To hit them, to retaliate, to tear them apart."

Within minutes more than sixty planes took off to defend against a possible Iraqi air attack. Others sat on runways with their engines idling, awaiting the order to take off for Iraq. Arens called Cheney on the newly installed direct line at around five that morning, formally requesting that the Americans clear their warplanes out of western Iraq for a designated block of time so that the Israeli air force could bomb the Scud launchers. He also asked for an air corridor through Saudi Arabia so that Israeli planes would not have to fly over Jordan, a move that might force King Hussein into the war. Cheney insisted that any decision would have to come directly from the president.

A few minutes after Arens got off the phone with Cheney, Bush called Shamir at home. It was the first time they had spoken by phone since the previous February. Bush expressed his anger over the attack and offered his concern and sympathy for Israeli civilians. The president reiterated to Shamir how important it was that Israel not retaliate. Even as they spoke, he told Shamir, American warplanes were combing western Iraq for the Scud launchers. A new set of protective Patriot missile batteries would soon be on their way to Israel, Bush pledged. He recognized that Israel had an undeniable right to retaliate, but insisted that such an action at this time was exactly what Saddam wanted. "Please don't play into his hands," pleaded Bush.

Shamir made no commitment. Israel would probably have to respond, he told Bush, but he would wait to make a final decision until a meeting of the inner cabinet, a twelve-member body of the most senior cabinet members that dealt with national security affairs, later that morning. Meanwhile, the planes were stood down. By going directly to Shamir, Bush had won time.

On the battered streets of south Tel Aviv, Dan Shomron sifted through the wreckage of Rivka Sofer's home and came to his own painful conclusion. "I walked around among the destroyed houses. The scenes were very hard to look at. I bit my lip. I knew that we were ready for any action, that we only had to give the green light and the forces would be on their way. My fingers were itching. I wanted the army to attack Iraq. But a chief of staff has to weigh these things wisely and coldly, even cruelly.

"The dilemma was difficult from the very first minute. I knew the number of casualties would be a major component of the decision on the political level. In the Ezra neighborhood there was much destruction but few casualties. No deaths. That made it easier for me. I decided there was no reason to go out right now. Not yet. We could pull the rope a little tighter. There was no need to act according to the reflex that says they hit you, strike back immediately."

At the inner cabinet session Bin-Nun, the air force chief of staff, said his men and planes were awaiting the order to strike. But Shomron expressed

reservations, as did his soon-to-be successor, Ehud Barak. Shamir demurred, asking the generals to draw up plans for retaliation to be reviewed
by the entire cabinet at its regular weekly meeting on Sunday. When Bush
phoned Shamir that night, the prime minister told him that the cabinet
wanted action but was willing to wait forty-eight hours.

Bush informed Shamir of the specific steps he had taken to meet Israeli
concerns. He said he was ordering the immediate shipment of upgraded Patriot air-defense batteries with U.S. crews and dispatching Deputy Secretary of State Lawrence Eagleburger and Under Secretary of Defense Paul
Wolfowitz to Jerusalem as his personal envoys to ensure full cooperation.
He also ordered a U.S. general to Tel Aviv to serve as a direct liaison between Israel and General Norman Schwarzkopf's Central Command in
Riyadh, Saudi Arabia. All of this was designed to assure the Israelis that
they finally had Washington's full attention. Bush also reassured Shamir
that coalition warplanes were doing everything possible to root out the
Scuds. He expected results within twenty-four to forty-eight hours.

Shamir wanted to believe that the Americans would find and quickly
eliminate the launchers. He had many reasons for not wanting to attack
Iraq. He had met secretly with King Hussein in London a few weeks before
the war and he understood that an Israeli attack using Jordanian airspace
would drag Jordan into the conflict. It could give Saddam an excuse to pull
his forces out of Kuwait and send them westward into Jordan on the pretense of helping a fellow Arab state against Zionist invaders. Shamir also
was not convinced that the Israeli plans for attacking the Scuds would prove
any more effective than the Allied effort. And he hoped that by attempting
to honor Bush's wishes, Israel would regain its place as a trusted American
partner in the region and ease two years of strained relations.

On Friday night and early Saturday morning, January 18 and 19, sirens
roused Israelis three times for false alarms. Then at dawn a fourth alarm
sent a sleepless nation to its sealed rooms just as four more missiles hit.
One landed harmlessly somewhere to the south and three more hit Tel Aviv
but caused little damage. One landed in a city park, while another blew
apart an empty underground bomb shelter in Rivka Sofer's damaged neighborhood.

Israeli author Robert Rosenberg heard the fourth Scud barrel past his
central Tel Aviv apartment. "It sounded like the L.A. Expressway running
right by my window. It fell into the stairwell of a two-story building on Allenby Street, took a sharp left and wound up in the front window of a jew-
elry store. It didn't explode." That morning people came to gape at the
uninvited guest, a disarmed six-foot-long warhead peering blindly out the
shop window like a shiny beached whale on a strange and distant shore.

Following the attack, however, Shamir felt he had no choice but to call an emergency cabinet session for 10 A.M. in Tel Aviv. Minutes before he left Jerusalem for the meeting, he got another call from Bush. The president repeated his plea that Israel not strike back. The Patriots were on their way—the batteries would arrive that evening from Germany. Bush said he would "understand" if Israel felt compelled to strike back, but warned that such a move would weaken the coalition and help Saddam. Shamir did not commit himself.

On the forty-minute drive to Tel Aviv with Avi Pazner, his longtime media adviser, Shamir wrestled with his options. "It's easy for Bush to say not to answer when it's not his cities that are being hit," he told Pazner.

Shamir stared out the window at the rain-streaked hills west of Jerusalem. The car passed the gnarled remains of armored trucks ambushed by Arab partisans in 1948 when Jewish convoys sought to relieve the siege of Jerusalem, left there now as a memorial to the dead and to the fragile birth of a nation. "You know, Avi," he said finally, "I think it would be a great mistake on our part to play Saddam's game. Why is he sending Scuds to bomb Tel Aviv? We've done nothing to him. There's only one reason—he wants to drag us into the war. But I don't have to play Saddam's game."

The streets of Tel Aviv were deserted—like a war zone, Pazner thought. When he and Shamir arrived at the fortified Kirya, they were met by a contingent of heavily armed soldiers in helmets, gas masks hanging from their belts, who escorted them into the compound.

Shamir opened the cabinet meeting by describing Bush's plea for restraint, but he gave no hint of his own views. Bin-Nun spoke at length. Israel could shuttle hundreds of planes through the H-2 and H-3 sectors—far more than the Allied coalition was using in that region—and deliver ground troops by helicopter as well. Anything on the ground that moved would be destroyed.

Shomron offered a number of options. He told the ministers that everything was in readiness for an attack, but he was not enthusiastic. Israel would almost certainly destroy more Scud launchers than American warplanes were finding, he said, but such an attack would undoubtedly damage the coalition. And there was no predicting how Jordan or Syria would react.

The debate that followed among the politicians broke down along predictable lines between the old Israel and the new. Housing Minister Ariel Sharon offered Israel's traditional response when faced with an attack: don't take chances with security; wipe out the threat, then deal with the consequences. "We should go into western Iraq and clean out the Scuds," he told the cabinet. If necessary, the troops could be reinforced and resupplied on the ground through Jordan. Agriculture Minister Rafael Eitan, a plainspoken former chief of staff, backed Sharon, as did Science Minister Yuval Neeman, an ultrahawk.

Foreign Minister David Levy spoke passionately against retaliation. So did Dan Meridor and Arye Deri. These were the voices of another Israel, one that wanted to be an international partner to the coalition and that measured Israel's strength not by its ability to retaliate but by its maturity and restraint. We have made a commitment to the United States and we have much to gain if the coalition succeeds, the proponents argued. Let's not move hastily.

Moshe Arens appeared to waver—he was under intense pressure from the air force to authorize a strike, yet he seemed filled with hesitation. Several other ministers hung back, not sure which way the wind was blowing.

Shamir mostly kept silent. But at one point, when one minister claimed that the Israeli public wanted retaliation, he snapped back: "Don't tell me what the public wants. The public doesn't know what it wants. Whatever we decide, they will agree to."

After nearly six hours Shamir finally spoke. "I am going to surprise you," he told them with a little smile. "I do not think we should react." He described his own desire to retaliate. But for the time being, he added, "we are not going to answer back" and he went on to explain why. "This is what Saddam wants, to transfer the war into one between the Arabs and Israel. What do we gain from this? Just to have the satisfaction that we retaliated? I fully understand those who wish to strike back, but Israel has more to gain from not entering this fight."

He asked for a vote. "There's no need—we all agree," said one of the junior ministers.

No vote was taken.

This was Yitzhak Shamir's finest hour. He had walked into a meeting with the most right-wing cabinet in Israel's history, a roomful of uncertain, jumpy people prepared to go to war for fear of not doing anything. By the force of his own authority, he had walked away with a consensus for self-restraint. It was a shaky consensus. If a Scud plowed into a crowded apartment building and killed several dozen civilians, or if one contained a chemical warhead, he would be forced to order retaliation. But for now, with an assist from Dan Shomron, he had carried the day.

On January 22, three days after the cabinet meeting, the Scuds struck again, this time at Ramat Gan, population 150,000. A former sand dune on the eastern flank of Tel Aviv, Ramat Gan had evolved into one of Israel's most densely populated urban zones. It was on the flight path between western Iraq and the giant, bristling transmission towers of the Kirya, Saddam's primary target.

City officials, aware of Ramat Gan's vulnerability to attack, took extra precautions. Mayor Zvi Baer, a reserve army commander, even remembered to tell the director of the Safari Park Zoo to lock up the lions. Still, because of its proximity to the Kirya, Ramat Gan took four hits. The first occurred on Tuesday evening outside Abba Hillel Silver Street. One of George Bush's newly delivered Patriot missiles hit the Scud but failed to destroy it. No one died from the blast itself but three elderly people died of heart attacks; ninety-six were injured.

The worst night was Friday, January 25. Seven Scuds hit Israel, two of them landing in Ramat Gan. One of them killed Eitan Grunland, a fifty-one-year-old lawyer, the only direct fatality of the war. He was speaking on the phone and had neglected to close his door. The impact of the missile blast outside sent a shock wave through the room that blew his body out a window. In all, 144 apartments were heavily damaged and 400 others were lightly hit; sixty-seven people were injured.

Grunland was the only one to die from an explosion, but Eli Shperling, a retired army colonel who was in charge of the municipal emergency system, believed another twenty to twenty-five elderly people died from trauma during the air raids. Hundreds of others were devastated psychologically by the sudden loss of their homes and possessions. "One man had lived in his place for sixteen years and he had a very long list" of items that had been damaged or destroyed, Shperling recalled. "I asked him, 'How did you put all of that in one little apartment?' And he started to cry. We're talking about a person's life.

"People felt powerless. We had to understand that this was a new kind of modern war. There was a time when men came against men with knives, one to one. Then there was the bow and arrow, the gun, the artillery cannon, men moving further and further apart with each new change. So now you have missiles. Men sit in a room and they push buttons to make war. You see no one. Okay, we must live with it. Now we are all the front."

The sense of powerlessness was not confined to Ramat Gan. All Israelis, from the most senior of generals to the youngest of children, felt it. This was clearly a different kind of war. The enemy was not massed at the border but was somewhere far away, beyond view and beyond reach. The home front was the only front.

"In previous wars men wore the uniforms and did the fighting," said Nachman Shai. "This time women were the commanders. From the first siren, men walked into their sealed room under the command of their wives. You don't wear a uniform, you don't fight, you don't shoot, you don't bomb. Even the generals were like lame ducks, sitting at home making phone calls to their friends, asking what to do."

"Many men were at a loss," said psychologist Eeta Prince-Gibson. "This was war, but not the kind they know. No heroism, no battle dust, just passivity and deep deep fear, eating at all of us."

Despite their new role as "commanders" of the home front, Israeli women did not make many economic or social gains from the conflict. With schools out of session for much of the six-week war, one adult in each family had to do full-time child care. Most of the time it was the mother. When the kids were home, women stayed home as well.

"Women were caught in the conflict between their real role and their ostensible role," wrote Prince-Gibson in an unpublished paper after the war. "Women lost work days, income, status and advancement and, in some cases, they lost their jobs." They also disappeared from the public arena. Television and radio were dominated by male military analysts and commentators. "Women simply aren't authoritative enough," one television editor was quoted as saying.

In one of his few appearances on Israel Television during the first days of the war, Yitzhak Shamir had exhorted Israelis to continue leading "normal lives." But the government's restrictions made normal living impossible. Starting on January 17, most Israeli workplaces and all schools were closed by government order and the economy ground nearly to a complete halt, while Israelis were forced to return periodically to their sealed rooms and gas masks through a series of alerts, most of them false alarms. Gradually the government eased its regulations, but most schools remained closed until the last weeks of the war and most Israelis remained in a state of what was dubbed "routine emergency."

This was, in fact, what government officials seemed to have in mind. Taking a page from the old Zionist handbook, they sought to mobilize public opinion and create a sense of shared sacrifice to help the nation weather the psychological blows that the Scuds inflicted. The gas masks and sealed rooms were a prime tool; all Israelis from Eilat in the south to Kiryat Shemona in the far north were required to use them even after it became clear that the Scuds were targeted exclusively at the country's central urban corridor.

The government also sought to secure a monopoly on news and information. While foreign camera crews roamed freely, the only Israeli crews working the streets during the first weeks of the war were from Nachman

Shai's army unit. Although CNN and other international news organizations broadcast live footage of the Scud damage and victims, Israeli viewers were confined to heavily edited taped accounts. Radio stations were banned from playing anything that remotely sounded like a protest or antiwar song. "This isn't the time for protests but for unity," intoned Arye Mekel, a former Shamir aide who was director general of the Israel Broadcasting Authority.

It worked, to an extent. Polls showed massive popular support for the government and the army. Israelis were willing to put up with a certain amount of discomfort and anxiety as long as they believed the government was doing the right thing, and they were trained in wartime to do what they were told.

There were clear limits, however, to what people would tolerate. Early on many Israelis with military experience—including, most notably, former Defense Minister Yitzhak Rabin—concluded that they and their families would be safer underground than in sealed rooms and took to shelters during alerts in defiance of orders. Soon many others were ignoring Nachman Shai's warnings, abandoning the gas masks and the sealed rooms and venturing onto their balconies and rooftops to watch the spectacle of Scuds and Patriots.

Once the Scud attacks began, officials such as Arens and Shomron (but not Shamir) were on the air nightly promising imminent retaliation. "America knows we'll react if attacked and we were attacked," Arens told one television interviewer. "So we will react?" he was asked. "We certainly will," Arens replied. But he did not, and many Israelis began to suspect that the government lacked either the will or the means to strike back.

But Israelis performed their greatest act of defiance with their cars. By the middle of the war somewhere between 20 and 40 percent of Tel Avivans had cleared out of the city, leaving behind only those too immobile or too poor to move. Entire apartment buildings were vacated. During the day people came back for a few hours, but each night toward evening the road to Jerusalem was clogged with bumper-to-bumper traffic.

This was the first time in Israeli history that residents had fled from their cities, and officials railed against the flight to no avail. Tel Aviv Mayor Lahat, a reserve army general, demanded publicly that the "very small percentage [who] left us" return to the city and "not be deserters. A person who leaves his city during hard times will also leave his country and homeland during hard times."

Lahat hit a raw nerve. He was bitterly denounced by those not inclined to feel guilty over protecting themselves and their families and not prepared to sacrifice their lives for a vague official notion of steadfastness. This was a clash of values between the old Israel—tight-lipped, stoical, self-sacrificing—and the new. There was symbolism in the fact that middle-class Is-raelis fled Tel Aviv each night in late-model Subarus and Fiats.

Roles were reversed. Author Amos Elon noticed that Tel Aviv under Iraqi siege bore resemblance to West Bank cities under army curfew. While the cosmopolitan city became the most dangerous place in Israel, the Jew-ish settlements of the West Bank and Gaza were the safest. They were clus-tered among Palestinian communities that Iraq had no intention of harming. Suddenly the Gush Katif beach resort in the middle of the Gaza Strip, usually a somewhat risky and uncomfortable vacation spot for most Israelis, reported full occupancy. Thanks to Saddam, settlers were, for the moment, back in the mainstream.

Among those who fled were Buki and Etti Sagi of Givatayim, one of the densely populated suburbs east of Tel Aviv. Buki, forty-one, a tall man with thin, graying brown hair and a melodious voice, was a financial adviser; Etti, also forty-one, was a small, delicate-featured schoolteacher. They had been married for twenty years and lived in a large comfortable apartment. They were Mr. and Mrs. Normal Israeli—affluent, intelligent and self-aware, devoted to each other and to their three children.

Buki and Etti considered themselves patriotic, but they were not about to risk their lives and the lives of their children because Shamir or Lahat demanded it. After Eitan Grunland had been killed in nearby Ramat Gan, Buki insisted it was time to leave home. They packed their station wagon with essentials and moved to a hotel in Netanya, a seaside town about fif-teen miles north of Tel Aviv.

"The Scuds were falling very close and we had the feeling that we were in the center of a radius," said Buki. "When the Scud fell on Abba Hillel Silver Street, the noise was deafening. . . . Etti didn't want to go, but she knew that I was right. To stay and pretend that everything was okay, that was wrong. Should we just wait until our house exploded? So we decided to go. Not to gamble with our lives."

The Sagis returned to Givatayim each day in time for the children to at-tend school. "It was very important to me to come home every day, to be in the house," said Etti. "I was worried. I started to have physical symptoms. Food got stuck in my throat. I was very sad. I really didn't want to be so far from my home. We were really opposites. As we got further away from home toward Netanya, Buki would start to brighten. He felt lighter and re-lieved. I felt sad. As we came back to Tel Aviv, Buki would start to feel tense and pressured, fearful, and I would start to feel that I could function again. I felt as though my house was my fortress, not Netanya. Here, noth-ing bad could happen to me."

Each day Etti bought more plastic and tape to secure their sealed room. And she kept supplies of food—rice, sugar, canned milk, pretzels, frozen meat, canned corn, bottled water, bread. "The house was exploding with food," said Etti. "It made me feel safe."

With each alarm the routine was the same. Turn off the gas and the lights, pile into the sealed room with the children and the dog, shut the door tight, seal it with tape and plastic, cover the bottom with wet towels, strap on the gas masks. "Buki would unlatch the extra lock on the front door so that if they had to come in to rescue us, they could get in." Then came the all-clear alarm, followed by the crackling noise of ripping tape as they opened the door.

The Sagis developed an almost blind faith in authority figures, faith they sustained even when it became clear that the authorities had little to say. "We had actually believed the commentators and experts that everything would be over by the end of the first day," said Buki. "We thought that the Americans had destroyed the entire Iraqi army, like they told us. We believed Nachman Shai. We believed in the sealed rooms, in the masks. We believed that the government had done everything it could to make us safe.

"We didn't have a doubt that everything was okay, that we were in the safest place we could have been." Only toward the end, Buki said, did questions begin to creep in. "It never occurred to us that the masks were rotten, that sealed rooms wouldn't have helped, or that maybe we should have gone into the shelters."

The endless official assertions that retaliation was imminent, multiplied by sleepless nights and constant false alarms, left Israelis vulnerable and raw-nerved. The emphasis of official reporting was on the good news, such as the miraculous lack of fatalities, but the constant anxiety took a heavy toll. Hospitals reported a 25 to 50 percent increase in heart attacks. Holocaust survivors were most shaken by the sealed room and gas mask ritual, but other Israelis also could not help drawing the gruesome analogy to World War II.

To help ease sleeplessness the government came up with one brilliant innovation. Beginning at ten each night, listeners could tune their radios to the Silent Station. When an attack was imminent, the station would spring to life sounding an alert and then broadcasting news and instructions until the all-clear was sounded.

Although tourists stayed away, certain visitors flocked to Israel. Some came as mourners. Delegations of German officials, headed by Foreign Minister Hans-Dietrich Genscher, came to view the Scud damage. Genscher walked through the rubble of Ramat Gan whispering of his shame at the role German companies had played in arming Saddam. Germany pledged $600 million in aid for military assistance, rebuilding and rescue work. So many German officials passed through Israel, wrote *Der Spiegel,* that the King David Hotel in Jerusalem seemed "almost like the Bundestag."

Others came as saviors. The Patriot batteries arrived from Frankfurt on the first Saturday night of the war. They failed the following Tuesday to prevent the hit on Ramat Gan, but the next night they succeeded in downing a Scud over Haifa. The first three Patriots missed the Scud, but the fourth tackled it and the collision pulverized both missiles.

That Friday night, January 25, while two Scuds hit Ramat Gan, the Patriots purportedly were able to knock down five other missiles.

By the end of the war there were eight Patriot batteries in Israel: two purchased from the United States, four rushed in on loan from Bush after the Scuds began to fall, and one each from Germany and the Netherlands. While Israelis served as advisers and trainees, the crews were almost all foreigners.

It was the first time Israel had allowed foreign troops to be stationed on its own soil, and for some Israelis the move conjured up the old image of the defenseless Jew forced to rely upon the kindness of Gentiles. But most were delighted to have the protection. The locations of the various Patriot batteries were supposedly a military secret, but thousands of Israelis visited the sites, showering the battery crews with flowers, candy, wine, whiskey and champagne. The minister of tourism announced a free one-week stay for each crew member at a luxury hotel as guests of Israel once the war was over. Israel had finally found heroes for a relentlessly unheroic war.

By early February there was a dramatic drop in the number of Scud launches because of constant pounding by coalition war planes and—unbeknown to Israel—special operations by American and British commando units on the ground. Nonetheless, both Moshe Arens and Dan Shomron believed the Americans were not doing enough to eliminate the Scuds. Schwarzkopf clearly did not take the threat seriously; he told one interviewer, "I frankly would be more afraid of standing out in a lightning storm in southern Georgia than I would standing out in the streets . . . when the Scuds are coming down."

Despite their public praise for the Patriots, the Israelis believed that the missiles were ineffective. Israeli Military Intelligence could confirm only two occasions when the Patriots hit the warheads they targeted. Most of the time they hit the empty missile after the warhead had detached and was heading toward its target. In fact, Military Intelligence concluded that a Patriot did most of the damage to Ramat Gan on January 22, slamming into an apartment after it failed to intercept a Scud. The assessment was kept secret; the generals had no wish to shake the public's faith in the Patriots. But it meant that they could not rely on the missiles if Saddam were to strike again.

And the generals feared a major attack was imminent. Once the ground war began, they reasoned, Saddam would have no reason to hold back and might fire chemical warheads. Israel needed to preempt such an attack, and the generals saw no reason for the United States to object. The war was so far along that the Arab half of George Bush's coalition would hold no matter what Israel did.

Shamir sympathized with the generals, but he remained confident that the Americans would destroy Iraq's fighting capacity and that Israel's wisest role was on the sidelines. He had been told by Eagleburger, during the deputy secretary of state's visit to Jerusalem after the war began, that adhering to the restraint policy would help turn around Shamir's troubled relationship with Bush and James Baker. Shamir was skeptical as always, but he wanted to believe it was true.

Confronted by the IDF's alarming assessment that Saddam might use chemical weapons, Shamir bought time by ordering new studies by the army. But he also agreed to Arens's request to go to Washington to ask the Americans to relent on Israeli involvement and at the same time to reiterate Israel's request for financial aid to pay for war damages. Estimates at the time were that Israel had lost $3 billion mostly because of the loss of productivity and tourism—direct Scud damage accounted for only $90 million of the total.

It was not a happy visit. Arens had been preceded to Washington by Finance Minister Yitzhak Modai, who had deeply embarrassed the Israeli government and its American Jewish supporters by presenting the administration with what amounted to a $13 billion bill for war damages—$3 billion in emergency aid plus another $10 billion in loan guarantees for the absorption of Soviet Jewish immigrants. Modai came away from Washington empty-handed, but he had left the impression that Israel was engaged in extortion.

Arens arrived at the White House on February 11 for a thirty-minute meeting with Bush that rekindled all the resentments and misunderstandings that had marred U.S.-Israeli relations before the war. Bush was expecting expressions of Israeli gratitude. Wasn't the United States ridding the Middle East of Israel's greatest military threat? But Arens, too, was looking for gratitude, for Israel's self-restraint and suffering. He expressed appreciation, but he dwelled on the enormous damage that the Scuds had inflicted—"scenes of destruction that have not been seen in a Western country since World War II," as he put it. He appeared to be softening up Bush for both $1 billion in emergency aid and for a green light to retaliate. He got neither.

When Bush cited the "dramatic decrease" in Scud attacks on Israel, which he said were due to U.S. raids in western Iraq, Arens described the direct hit on Ramat Gan three days earlier. He questioned the effectiveness of the Patriots. Were there any more such hits, he warned, Israel would be forced to retaliate. "People will demand it," he told Bush.

The president was not impressed. He pulled polling data from his vest pocket showing strong Israeli support for the restraint policy.

Arens tried again. "We can do better than the U.S. Air Force because we will use more planes," he said. But again Bush was cool. "Frankly, I don't think you could do any better than we are already doing," he replied. And with that the meeting ended.

At a subsequent session at the State Department, Baker informed Arens that it was "inappropriate to request aid at a time when U.S. soldiers were dying in a war beneficial to Israel." In the middle of his reply Arens was interrupted by news that a Scud had hit his neighborhood in Savyon, a wealthy Tel Aviv suburb. He excused himself and called his wife, Muriel. She told him the Scud had landed a few blocks from their house but that all were safe. Arens returned to Baker and picked up exactly where he had left off. He won points for his coolness under pressure, but both sides came away irritated and hurt.

Arens returned to Israel convinced that now was the time to ready an attack. Shamir stalled anew. He sent the military planners back to their drawing boards to develop a new set of retaliation proposals. He demanded that the plans go through the long, bureaucratic chain of review by the general staff and the inner cabinet. By the time the approved plan reached his desk, the ground war had begun. Four days later the war was over.

For Israel the Gulf War proved a bittersweet triumph. One of its most dangerous enemies was vanquished. Its relationship with the United States was patched. Its other Arab foes—the Palestinians, the Syrians—were either weakened or gained new respect for American global supremacy and awareness of the limits of their own power. All for the price of one dead civilian, 939 injured and 9,000 damaged apartments. Nations pay far more for much less.

But while the Scuds were ineffective militarily, as weapons of terror they were devastating. They showed that having one of the world's best armies was no guarantee of safety in modern warfare, even against low-tech, obsolete weapons. The searing sound of the alarm sirens, the gas masks and sealed rooms, the lack of meaningful information and guidance from the government, the foreign soldiers on Israeli soil and, above all, the gnawing feelings of helplessness and distress—all left a small but indelible mark on the national psyche.

Later, after it was all over, Israelis found out more disturbing information. The state comptroller's office concluded that hundreds of thousands of gas masks had been defective. Moreover, the IDF had found enough defects in the masks it tested in October and November 1990 that it should have been aware of the problem. The tests "should have lit a warning light . . . ," stated the comptroller, "since we are talking about people's lives." Even more alarming was the finding that the plastic hoods and tents fitted for small children and infants were a "severely limited and inadequate means of protection." The comptroller's report concluded that largely because of lack of proper funding, nearly one-third of the civilian population "may not have been adequately protected."

With nothing to do but sit at home and worry, Israelis developed a dulling sense of war weariness, which was captured in an article by Doron Brosh in *Maariv*. Brosh described sitting in a sealed room in the Tel Aviv apartment of his ninety-year-old grandfather, each of them in gas masks. He recalled that forty-three years earlier, during the Independence War, Arabs from nearby Jaffa had fired directly into the same room and that his grandfather had built a brick wall to act as a barrier against the bullets.

"Forty-three years have passed, since then, in that room. Nothing has changed. Instead of a brick wall, we sealed the room with plastic. Instead of bullets, missiles are falling, and nothing in our armed country has changed . . . Three generations of my family, hiding in the same room, changing jobs, building walls, wearing masks."

For Yitzhak Shamir, the war was the one moment when circumstances demanded the precise blend of caution, restraint and steadfastness that were the hallmarks of his personality. For once, doing nothing proved the boldest move of all.

The war marked the height of Shamir's success as prime minister. The restraint policy proved overwhelmingly popular. No one was eager to invade western Iraq and fight a war so far from home. One month after the war ended, 90 percent of Israelis agreed that "Prime Minister Shamir had stood well the test of leadership."

Yet the critics sneered. Just as a broken clock tells the correct time one minute in every twelve hours, one commentator suggested, so had Shamir's congenital paralysis coincided with Israel's security needs for one brief moment. The prime minister had stood firm, but his critics attributed this to a character flaw rather than a strength. What choice did Shamir have? To have defied Washington and launched an attack that might have led to a clash with the coalition's own forces would have been reckless. Shamir had done what he was told to do by George Bush, nothing more.

The critics misjudged. It had been no easy task for Shamir to hold back the hawks in his own cabinet and the wavering enthusiasts on the army general staff. He had, in effect, thrown out forty-three years of strategic dogma and entrusted Israel's fate and his own to a U.S. administration he had long been at rancorous odds with. It took guts to watch Scuds fall on the country's main population center and do nothing. Israel could have unleashed one of the world's most accomplished armies against the missile launchers. No one could say for certain what would have happened. Perhaps the Scuds would have fallen silent, or perhaps George Bush's coalition would have fallen apart. But the fact that it was never tried was attributable to the immovable, imperturbable Shamir.

Shamir himself did not see the Gulf War as a full success. He felt cheated that Bush had called off the war before coalition forces had conquered Baghdad and finished off the Iraqi regime. He knew that gratitude between nations was not a banker's check that could be cashed at will. The Americans had promised their Arab allies that they would press ahead with the Middle East peace process once the war ended. Now that the conflict was over, Bush would surely attempt to deliver on that commitment. The pressure on Israel, Shamir believed, was only just beginning.

Most analysts predicted that the ordeal of the Scuds, combined with Palestinian support for Saddam Hussein during the war, would make Israelis far more hawkish and less willing to compromise on peace. But the first postwar poll commissioned by the Jaffee Center for Strategic Studies at Tel Aviv University drew a much different conclusion. Israelis were still intensely skeptical about Arab goals and intentions, and a large majority opposed an independent Palestinian state. But rather than harden opinion, the war appeared to accelerate a decade-long trend toward territorial compromise. The poll showed 58 percent in favor of ending Israeli rule in the occupied territories, up from 50 percent a year earlier and 46 percent in 1986. If anything, the war had increased the basic predisposition of Israelis to seek a settlement. More than three of four respondents believed a peace accord was possible.

There were several reasons for this. The Scuds had shown that land was no longer a crucial factor when it came to defense. If Saddam could lob a low-tech Scud from four hundred miles away and hit Tel Aviv, then how important in security terms was twenty-five miles of West Bank terrain?

The war also introduced a sense of urgency when it came to making peace. It opened a window on a new kind of warfare—noiseless, odorless, push-button combat in which civilians were the main targets. If thirty-nine Scuds could sow fear and destruction, what might five hundred sophisticated and heavily armed missiles fired from Damascus do? And what might Israel do to Syria in return?

The sealed room was the key. Both Shamir and Saddam, mortal enemies though they were, had tried to force Israelis into isolation. Both had sought to reinstate the siege—to cut off Israel from the rest of the world and return it to an earlier time of war and sacrifice. Saddam tried and failed to demonize Israel, while Shamir sought to return it to a more spartan era when Israelis faced a crisis by mobilizing around their government, following orders unquestioningly and relying solely upon themselves. But the new Israel did not want to remain for long inside the sealed room.

Most Israelis wanted to join the world, not hide from it. They refused to play Saddam's game—or Shamir's.

And so the war became a defining moment for Israelis, a passageway from the past to the future. It tested Israelis—their army, their government, their leaders and themselves—in ways they had never been tested before. It demanded thoughtfulness, restraint and maturity rather than strength, speed and daring. It forced some Israelis to choose between the personal safety of themselves and their families and their obligations to the state. Israel entered the Gulf crisis as one country; it came out the other end of the tunnel as someplace else.

9. "We Are One"

Visits of condolence is all we get from them.
They squat at the Holocaust Memorial,
They put on grave faces at the Wailing Wall
And they laugh behind heavy curtains
In their hotels.

— YEHUDA AMICHAI, "Tourists"

LIKE intruders in the dust, the two silver buses negotiated their way through the gray rubble of Abba Hillel Silver Street in Ramat Gan and pulled up alongside an empty lot. One week earlier a three-story apartment building had stood there. Now it was gone, blown to rubble by a direct hit from an Iraqi Scud.

On both sides of the cavity sat squat, three-story concrete buildings that had also been damaged. Outside walls had been ripped away, exposing staircases and rooms and hallways. Walls, doors and window frames rested at odd angles; utility poles and wires dangled like useless afterthoughts. Piles of broken furniture, books, toys, clothes, kitchen appliances and one forlorn baby buggy lay scattered among slag heaps of plaster, cement blocks and shattered glass.

Some five dozen well-dressed, middle-aged men and women emerged from the buses and began a hesitant, gingerly stroll through the gutted remains. Dangling from their shoulders alongside the usual purses and cameras were gas masks. The visitors were somber and silent. They shook hands with residents, some of whom still looked stunned. One member of the group stopped to have his photograph taken; then another, and another.

After a brief conversation with the town's mayor, who had come out to greet them, they climbed back on the buses and departed.

For the passengers, members of the Conference of Presidents of Major American Jewish Organizations, it was a stark moment, a chance, however fleeting, to share some of the pain and express sympathy and concern for fellow Jews whose homes had been destroyed by a missile dispatched by Saddam Hussein. They had arrived at Ben-Gurion Airport from New York the night before and had been fitted for gas masks even before they left the terminal. They spent fifty hours talking to politicians, generals and ordinary Israelis, and sifting through the rubble of Ramat Gan and South Tel Aviv. They also visited one of the sites where American soldiers were manning a Patriot antimissile battery. After a brief chat the visitors and the troops broke into a spontaneous rendering of "America the Beautiful," many with tears in their eyes. On their second night in Israel, their session at the Jerusalem Hyatt Hotel with Deputy Foreign Minister Benjamin Netanyahu was interrupted by a Scud alert, and they scurried to the basement auditorium and put on their gas masks. The next afternoon they boarded an El Al flight to return to the United States.

Most of them had had no intention of traveling to Israel at this time. The last thing Israelis needed during the middle of a war was to host a bunch of gawking, unctuous visitors. But the representatives in Israel of American Jewish organizations had urged the Americans to come. Israelis were shaken by the missile attacks and angry that they were not receiving more tangible support from abroad. "If you want to maintain your credibility around here, you'd better get on a plane," David Clayman, Jerusalem representative of the American Jewish Congress, had told his bosses.

So Israeli officials welcomed the American Jewish leaders, who arrived a week after the first Scud attacks. The special "mission of solidarity" (American Jewish leaders, it seemed, always came on missions rather than visits) eased Israel's sense of isolation and offered encouragement. But for some of the Israelis standing outside their ruined houses in Ramat Gan, the visit was a bitter farce, an insult from people who did not, who could not, have the faintest notion of what it meant to see your home destroyed by an Iraqi missile. These outsiders from the diaspora had intruded upon their private grief, and for what purpose? For a photograph to take home to America? For a headline? An Israeli reporter scathingly recounted the scene: "One of the women being photographed, wearing a red suit and elegant, black high-heeled shoes, was very careful not to lean, heaven forbid, on one of the destroyed walls, lest the dust stick to her suit.

"Your heart is torn watching such a vision. On the one hand, it is hard not to smile cynically, feeling even a bit annoyed. On the other hand, they got on a plane to demonstrate 48 hours of solidarity with Israel. So for 48 hours of solidarity, apparently, you're entitled to maintain your elegance."

One of the residents, who had returned to salvage enormous quantities of canned food from the ruins of his kitchen, asked no one in particular: "What did they come for? To plant a forest here?"

The scene in Ramat Gan captured the extraordinary emotional gap between Israeli Jews and their American brethren as they sought to cope with the Gulf War. American Jews viewed the live pictures of Scud destruction with great sympathy and alarm. There was an outpouring of support for Israel: American Jews watched CNN, they made phone calls, they wrote checks and attended solidarity rallies. Many felt closer to Israel than at any time since the harrowing days of the Six-Day War. The political and moral embarrassments of the 1980s—Israel's disastrous invasion of Lebanon, its mishandling of the Jonathan Pollard spy affair, its brutal response to the Palestinian intifada, its misguided attempt to restrict the rights of American converts to Judaism—all were overshadowed by the image of a vulnerable Jewish state under the threat of missiles and poison gas.

But Israelis, sitting alone in their sealed rooms, did not share these warm sentiments. They felt angry and betrayed. The cloying sympathy of American Jews just seemed to make it worse. Most Israelis knew they were being a bit unfair, but they were unwilling to conceal just how fed up they were.

Even worse was the fact that to Israeli eyes, too many American Jews seemed to take a certain pride in Israel's vulnerability and defenselessness. Here at last was an Israel they could cheer for, a country that would not shock or humiliate them. Now that Israel was the victim again, American Jews were warm and sympathetic. But the country they were cheering and crying for, the older, less complicated, morally pure Israel of their youth, did not exist anymore. The new Israel—robust, pugnacious, ethnically diverse and morally ambiguous—was not necessarily a country that American Jews understood or felt comfortable with.

In truth, Israeli and American Jews, the two power centers of Judaism, were like middle-aged children still fighting over the estate of a long-dead parent. One child was wealthy; the other colorful. Each depended upon the other. But relations between them were distorted and poisoned by money and history and unresolved differences too painful to discuss openly and honestly.

They claimed to share a common destiny. "We Are One" was not just the slogan of the United Jewish Appeal; it was a moral claim, a promise and a demand. But the fact was that Israelis and Americans did not know each other very well, seldom told each other the whole truth and did not always hear each other when they did. Each group seemed to bring out the worst in the other. Israelis sounded defensive, whiny, alarmist and arrogant when discussing the faults of their American brethren. The Americans sounded pompous, fawning and moralistic. There was a fundamental lack of trust between them.

American Jews were a crucial force in delivering to Israel more than $3 billion per year in U.S. military and economic assistance. They supplied more than $450 million in additional private donations through the United Jewish Appeal. The wealthiest among them also contributed somewhere between $10 and $20 million each election year to Israeli political parties in secret donations that never appeared on the books. And they constructed a political lobby in Washington, the American Israel Public Affairs Committee, that served as an aggressive advocate and renowned enforcer of Israeli interests—the foreign policy equivalent of the National Rifle Association.

All of this was supposed to help Israel prosper financially even while the country spent vast sums on defense. But inevitably it led also to misunderstandings and abuses. Too often American Jews saw Israel as besieged, weak and dependent, unable to fend for itself. Israelis resented this image, even though they helped create it, and they resented the donors who subscribed to it. They saw that American Jewish money increasingly was going to the most entrenched, reactionary and corrupt elements in their society—the political machines and small party interests that sustained Israel's social and political paralysis. American Jews, their money and their power, had become a force for the dying status quo.

Social scientist Steven M. Cohen of Queens College in New York recorded a steady rise in disenchantment of American Jewish opinion with Israel in surveys between 1983 and 1991. But Cohen also noted that levels of "attachment" to Israel remained high. He concluded that while American Jews were increasingly uncomfortable with Israeli policies, their feelings toward the Jewish state itself remained instinctively close. At the same time, however, Cohen uncovered a potentially alarming trend among younger Jews—the younger they were, the weaker their attachment to Israel. Perhaps these Jews would come back to Israel when they grew older and were more involved in Jewish communal life. But Cohen said he feared "a slow and gradual but persistent erosion."

Only a major crisis like the Gulf War, it seemed, could bring back the sense of closeness. This, too, was a problem, for a relationship built only on a shared sense of fear might not endure once the fear was removed. "If it takes these kinds of crises for American Jews to feel emotionally attached to Israel, what's going to happen when the shooting stops and Israel starts

to become a more normal kind of country?" asked Harry Wall, the Israel
representative of the Anti-Defamation League.

A few months after the Gulf War ended a book appeared in Hebrew by
Matti Golan, a prominent Israeli journalist and associate of Shimon Peres.
It was translated and published in English under the title *With Friends Like
You.* But its original Hebrew title is more in keeping with its bitter, dis-
turbed spirit: *Money in Exchange for Blood.* Written as a dialogue between
an American and an Israeli Jew, the book is an indictment of American
Jewry. Much of it is illogical and superficial. Nonetheless, Golan's diatribe
is an authentic cry from the heart; he writes what many Israelis deeply felt.
"In more ways than one, you're my enemy," he tells his American friend.
"A more harmful and dangerous one than the PLO."

Golan defines the relationship between American and Israeli Jews as
corrupt, superficial and deceitful. He finds repugnant the United Jewish Appeal fundraising campaigns that exploit and distort Israel's problems in order to raise money. He mocks the hypocrisy of American Jews, who
sacrifice religious beliefs for personal comfort, make their peace with the
intermarriage and assimilation of their children and grandchildren, and assuage their guilty consciences and their insecurities by donating money to
Israel. He constantly hammers American Jews for their purported timidity
and moral cowardice, contrasting them with their more honest, if cruder,
brethren in Israel.

Golan tells his imaginary American interlocutor:

> The main reason you send money, it seems to me, is that you still don't feel
> safe in the country you live in. I'm your insurance company and you make your
> payments to me.
> The difference between our two mentalities is the difference between some-
> one who lives at home and someone who lives in a rented room. Before you for-
> mulate a position, you ask yourself how it will sound to your non-Jewish
> neighbors. You're very anxious to get across the message that you aren't us: that
> you don't think like us, that you wouldn't behave like us, that they shouldn't re-
> sent you because of us.
> You think that the least I can do for you—the least I should do for you—is not
> to embarrass you in front of the Gentiles. . . . When I see how you live with
> your agreed-on lies and compromises, I know I wouldn't want my children to
> be like you.

Although Golan is a leftist, he has no sympathy for American liberals
discomfited by Israel's tough-guy behavior when dealing with problems
such as the intifada. He does not like to see Israeli soldiers shooting Arab

civilians, but he much prefers it to seeing Arabs shooting Israelis. This, he suspects, is not how his American counterpart feels.

> It's a terrible thing to say but I feel that subconsciously you would prefer that it were the other way around. Because then I would be the underdog, which would make you look better and win you a lot more sympathy.

Toward the end of his diatribe Golan reveals the true nature of his problem—it is not so much American Jews as himself and his fellow Israelis who have failed him.

> We're burned out, we're exhausted. I talk with my friends. All were born in this country. All hold important jobs. All have good incomes. And nearly all are ready to leave Israel. . . . Offer them a good, well-paying job in America and they'll start packing immediately.
> You want a Jewish state? Then please be so kind as to stand guard over it yourself. I've been doing it for dozens of years. Now it's your turn. . . . Because I just can't take it anymore.

Since the days of Ben-Gurion, Israelis had insisted that other Jews should move to Israel or at least recognize Israel's proper place as the moral and political center of the Jewish world. Many held a pessimistic view of the diaspora and believed that even in the United States Jews would wake up one day to find that the prosperity and acceptance they enjoyed had vanished overnight, as it did in prewar Germany. Even the term "diaspora," meaning "dispersion," had a negative and chilling connotation. Israelis were taught in school that the diaspora was a barren and dangerous place. The Holocaust was a major subject of required study, but the achievements of American Jews went untouched in the state curriculum.

As Golan made clear, Israelis demanded that Jews move to Israel largely for reasons of self-protection and self-vindication. The Israeli left wanted American Jews to come add their voices and votes to the peace camp and to reassert Western values such as pluralism and free speech in a country fast becoming "Easternized" by the Sephardi majority. Rightists looked for statistical reinforcements in the never-ending demographic war with Palestinians. Both were angered that the only Jews who ever seemed to move to Israel were those who were endangered or impoverished or both. The affluent and the well-educated—the first-rate "human material" Ben-Gurion had always coveted—remained firmly rooted to their diaspora homes. The one exception was the Russian Jews, who were persecuted back home yet also part of the elite, which was why they were welcomed in Israel and yet were so hard to absorb.

Like Golan, many Israelis believed that diaspora Jews were moral cowards. Still, both sides needed each other. Israel relied upon American Jewry not just for financial donations but for the moral and political support of the U.S. government that American Jews delivered through lobbying, campaign contributions and votes. At the same time, the existence of Israel and its pressing needs gave American Jews a rallying cry and a sense of cohesion that enhanced their political power and their standing in American society. Before Israel's existence, Jews attended White House dinners as individuals. Afterward, they came as Jews.

Israel gave American Jews something crucial as well: a way of preserving their Jewish identity even while fully participating in the freewheeling, assimilationist American culture. Support for Israel became their secular religion and their social gospel, the cause that separated them from other Americans, yet at the same time contributed to their special status in American society. Along with remembering the Holocaust, Israel became the central organizing principle of American Jewish life.

"In a real sense, being involved with Israel made Jewish leaders more truly American than they had ever dreamt of being," said Arthur Hertzberg, rabbi, historian and former president of the American Jewish Congress.

Here was a great paradox for Zionists. Israel, which was supposed to rescue Jews from the diaspora, instead made it easier and more attractive for Jews in America to remain where they were. What's more, as time passed more and more Israelis joined them: by 1992 some estimates put the number of Israelis living abroad at around 500,000. Young Israelis loved the United States; American fast food, movies, television programs and rock music conquered Israeli culture in the 1980s and helped trigger the rise of consumerism. But in some ways this only increased the conflict: American Jews had become more than just a problem; their capitalist economy and their culture were seen as a threat to Israel's way of life.

The roles had become reversed. By Zionist reckoning, Israel was supposed to be the most secure and enriching place for a Jew to live; the diaspora was threatening and draining the human spirit. In reality, however, the opposite was often true. As Shuki Elchanan, an Israeli university lecturer, tells Nathan Zuckerman, an American Jewish novelist, in Philip Roth's *The Counterlife:* "You think in the *Diaspora* it's abnormal? Come live here. This is the *homeland* of Jewish abnormality. Worse: now *we* are the dependent Jews, on your money, your lobby, on our big allowance from Uncle Sam, while *you* are the Jews living interesting lives, comfortable lives, without apology, without shame, and perfectly *independent*. . . . The fact remains that in the Diaspora a Jew like you lives securely, without real fear of persecution or violence, while we are living just the kind of imperilled Jewish existence that we came here to replace."

Every now and then the conflict between Americans and Israelis surfaced with a vehemence that surprised and appalled both sides. In November 1985 a U.S. Navy intelligence analyst named Jonathan Pollard was arrested and charged with selling defense secrets to Israel. The arrest set off alarm bells in the American Jewish community, which saw Israel's recruitment of an emotionally disturbed young Jew as a violation of the long-time understanding that Israel would never put Jews living abroad in harm's way. Angered by Israel's attempts to cover up its role and protect Pollard's handlers, American Jewish leaders publicly criticized the Israeli government and many applauded the life sentence handed down to Pollard.

What was less predictable was Israel's response: While the government cowered and stammered, the Israeli public raised tens of thousands of dollars for Pollard's legal bills. Some lionized him as a new David who had challenged the American Goliath for Israel's sake. A poll for *Yediot Ahronot* reported that 90 percent of those surveyed believed Israel was obligated to help Pollard and his wife, Anne, who was sentenced to five years' imprisonment for her role.

For Israelis, the reaction of American Jews to the Pollard affair betrayed an anxiety and insecurity. Political scientist Shlomo Avineri reflected the mainstream Israeli view when he wrote that American Jews reacted to Pollard in the same way that French Jews once reacted to the Dreyfus Affair, by "falling over each other" to renounce a fellow Jew.

An array of American Jewish leaders paraded through Jerusalem to denounce the Pollard affair and demand that Israel take some action against those responsible. Yitzhak Shamir smiled, thanked them for coming and dismissed their demands until the combination of White House indignation and American Jewish pressure proved too intense to ignore. He then appointed a two-man commission of inquiry that delivered the whitewashed report the government wanted.

Abraham H. Foxman, national director of the Anti-Defamation League, was one of Israel's most ardent defenders. But he found the bitter criticism expressed by Avineri and anonymous government officials too much to take. "If there is any collective neurosis among Jews over the Pollard affair, it exists in Israel, not the United States," Foxman wrote. ". . . . It's the sense of national guilt over using, abusing and then abandoning the Pollards. It's you, not us, whose conscience is troubled by the moral cowardice of the Pollard affair."

Pollard was a trivial matter compared to what came next. Although

Shamir's Likud won a narrow margin of one seat in the November 1988 election, Peres refused to concede defeat. He set off a frenzied round of coalition-bargaining with the three small ultra-Orthodox parties that held the balance of power. To woo them Peres agreed to amend the landmark Law of Return to give Israel's Orthodox rabbinate sole power to decide who among immigrants to Israel qualified to be a Jew. This would have effectively excluded all converts from the Reform, Conservative and Reconstructionist movements from attaining Israeli citizenship. Shamir, not to be outdone, quickly matched Peres's offer.

The Who Is a Jew question was not really an Israeli issue at all. It began as an effort by Menachem Mendel Schneerson, the Lubavitcher rebbe in Brooklyn, New York, to discredit non-Orthodox movements in the United States and gain points in his eternal competition with other *haredi* leaders. The rebbe's agents in Israel insisted, at his behest, that Peres promise to enact the amendment as the price for their support. Thus did American Jews exploit the defects in Israel's damaged political system to wage war against one another using Israeli politicians as their willing pawns.

It seemed at first like a minor issue—the number of converts involved was perhaps a half dozen each year—but it set off an explosion of outrage among American Jews, since 90 percent of them belonged to one of the three movements. They saw the exclusion as delegitimizing their own religious beliefs. The issue quickly became the most intensely personal and yet the most historic of the disputes between Americans and Israelis. It touched upon religion and family as well as on the Law of Return, one of the bedrock principles upon which the Jewish state was founded.

When a high-powered delegation of twenty-nine American Jewish leaders protested the change to Shamir, the prime minister was truly puzzled. "Why get so upset over such a tiny little thing?" he asked. Like Matti Golan and most secular Israelis, Shamir believed that old-fashioned Orthodoxy was the only valid kind of Judaism. His own religion was the Land of Israel, and he had no sympathy for diaspora Jews who had evolved a different form of faith. When the issue arose previously, Shamir had asked David Clayman, "Tell me, Clayman, is it true that the Reform can do a conversion over the phone?"

Shamir was surprised to see Jewish organizations like the United Jewish Appeal and Hadassah, which had always shied away from political issues, sending representatives to warn him that Who Is a Jew could cost Israel a large share of the $450 million it received annually in private donations. AIPAC, which had stayed away from the issue in the past, also weighed in. Executive director Thomas A. Dine, who himself was married to a non-Jew and had children who would not have qualified for Israeli citizenship under the amendment, warned that ultimately Israel's annual foreign aid of $3 billion could be jeopardized if the country broke faith with American Jews.

Who Is a Jew gave American Jews a chance to pay back the Likud for years of abuse. Many Jews had never been comfortable with Menachem Begin's invasion of Lebanon nor with Israel's handling of the intifada, but felt obligated to refrain from public criticism on security issues. Now they had an excuse to unload, and they did so with surprising venom. Shamir wound up taking the brunt of American Jewish criticism, even though it was Peres who had put the issue in play.

It was not a pretty sight. Ehud Olmert, one of Shamir's closest confidants, was well liked by American Jewish leaders. But he wandered the lobby of the King David Hotel early in December 1988 looking disheveled and harassed, a fugitive from a Likud chain gang. After a late-night session of bargaining with the religious parties, Olmert had rousted himself out of bed for an 8 A.M. breakfast meeting with American Jews who had come to Jerusalem to deliver their message of outrage in person. Even as he sat later for an interview in a discreet corner of the lobby, more Americans—some of them financial contributors to Likud's recent election campaign—came up to Olmert to plead, threaten and cajole.

"Don't you people have enough problems without angering your only real allies in the world?" demanded David Schachter, a businessman from Miami.

"You think I don't have other things to worry about? You think this is easy for us?" shot back Olmert, who proceeded to blame Peres and Labor for the mess.

Schachter was not buying. "You better do something about this, my friend, or you'll lose me and my family and a lot of other people as well," he replied.

A few such sessions persuaded the two major parties to forge a temporary truce. The Who Is a Jew amendment was dropped, the issue was declared off-limits politically, and American Jewish leaders returned home bruised but placated. But the issue did major damage to Israel's standing among diaspora Jews. Americans who had always assumed that Israelis practiced the same degree of religious freedom and pluralism that they themselves enjoyed in the United States were stunned to find out that the Orthodox rabbinate wielded a state-funded monopoly over Jewish practice and religious education, and was prepared to attack and defame anyone who threatened its power. They also discovered that a substantial part of the money they donated to the United Jewish Appeal wound up distributed to the schools and institutions of these rabbis. American Jews were paying for the right to be demeaned.

The Who Is a Jew controversy showed Americans and Israelis they had even less in common than either had previously suspected. Even their supposedly shared religious faith was actually quite different and distinct. The values that American Jews took for granted—tolerance, pluralism, civil rights—were all considered marginal to many Israelis, obsessed as they were by existential issues of security and survival. Israel, it turned out, was not a small, Middle Eastern version of the United States, but a very different country.

Yitzhak Shamir was not exactly an easy sell to American Jews. His Polish accent and fractured syntax, his gnomelike appearance, his terse, enigmatic manner of speech and, above all, his strident right-wing views did not endear him to the American Jewish leadership. At private meetings he seemed to listen carefully and he was invariably polite. But there were subtle clues that suggested he viewed American Jews with disdain—the small, dismissive wave of the hand, the half-smile, half-grimace when someone brought up a troubling or unpleasant subject, the occasional biting asides in Hebrew to aides. Above all, there was the way that Shamir constantly evaded direct answers to difficult questions or requests. "We'll see," was the best anyone ever seemed to elicit from him.

Most American Jews held views that were far to the left of the Shamir government. A survey of American Jewish leaders for the Israel-Diaspora Institute by Steven Cohen in 1989 showed that 76 percent favored territorial compromise in the West Bank and Gaza. By 59 to 18 percent they supported the idea that Israel offer Palestinians a demilitarized state to be phased in over fifteen years. Some 73 percent said Israel should talk to the PLO provided the organization recognized Israel and renounced terrorism. All of these views were diametrically opposed to Shamir's.

But the Jewish lobby—led by AIPAC, the Anti-Defamation League and the Presidents' Conference—functioned on a set of principles that made it easy for Shamir to take advantage. First was the tenet that when it came to existential issues such as national security, it was Israel's prerogative to determine its own fate; concerned outsiders should either be supportive or keep silent. "Israeli democracy should decide; American Jews should support," was Abe Foxman's motto. Jews living in Scarsdale and Beverly Hills had no business telling those in Jerusalem or Kiryat Shemona how to live or how to vote.

Second was what some American Jewish leaders called "the *gevalt* syndrome." American Jews were easiest to mobilize when frightened, when there was a whiff of the Holocaust in the air. Time and time again, whenever an issue of importance to Israel arose in Congress, AIPAC and its sister organizations would reach into the closet and pull out a ghost. Whether it was over AWACS sales to Saudi Arabia in the early 1980s or emergency military aid to Israel during the Gulf War, Jewish lobbyists painted Israel as weak, vulnerable and heavily outgunned by the Arabs. They sold The Siege.

This sort of argument played into Shamir's hands. When he addressed American Jews he talked about the Holocaust and history, emphasizing that Israel was a very small country that lived under great threat. Israel needed them; it might not survive without them—or at least that is what Shamir told them and what they told themselves as they lobbied their congressmen for more aid.

In his memoirs, Shamir writes with pride about the warm reception he received from American Jews when he traveled to the United States in March 1988 after the opening of the intifada. He recalls when he arrived at Kennedy Airport in New York seeing "a sea of posters that said 'Hold on' and 'We're with you'; hundreds of faces that smiled encouragingly; a forest of hands that waved a welcome." In Washington, as well, he received a wild ovation from thousands of young American Jews at a United Jewish Appeal Young Leadership Conference. Many of the participants believed they were cheering for Israel and its prime minister, not for the Likud's ideology. But Shamir drew sustenance from this reception, which he interpreted as support for his hard-line policies. "Once these young people understood that I couldn't be forced into acquiescing in any potential weakening of Israel," he writes, ". . . they backed me with relief, with no reservations and with no small measure, I think, of affection."

Shamir's director-general, Yossi Ben-Aharon, had served in Israel's Washington embassy during Golda Meir's years as prime minister, and, like Meir, he had come to believe American Jews were too timid when it came to defending Israel's interests for fear of alienating the Gentile world they lived in. You have to make them work, Ben-Aharon told Shamir. No matter what they tell you, you can always pull the rope a little bit tighter, demand a little more from them and get it. And indeed, by the late 1980s Israel was not only receiving more U.S. foreign aid than any other country but also getting it at more favorable terms than anyone else. While other countries received their economic aid in quarterly installments, Israel got its aid in a lump sum at the beginning of the year, allowing the Israelis to make an extra $75 million in 1991 by investing it in U.S. Treasury bills.

Shamir had other advantages. The Likud boasted a stable of young, attractive and articulate spokesmen who played well in the United States. The main attraction was Benjamin Netanyahu, an Israeli-born but U.S.-educated politician who spoke flawless, American-style English and was a master of the sound bite. A protégé of Moshe Arens when Arens was ambassador to the United States, Netanyahu went on to become Israel's representative to the United Nations and a full-fledged media star. He turned the General Assembly's trademark hostility to Israel to full advantage. Even those American Jews who were most opposed to the Likud's hard-line policies thrilled to Netanyahu's spirited defense of Israel in the face of heavy-handed, uncompromising opposition from the Arab world and the Soviet bloc. Arens, too, was a popular figure in the United States, as were Dan Meridor, Ehud Olmert and Benjamin Begin. Throughout the 1980s they functioned as the acceptable face of Likud, selling pragmatism and realpolitik rather than hard-line ideology.

Likud also benefited from the fact that its dominance largely coincided with Republican control of the White House. Likud used Ronald Reagan's presidency and the climactic years of the Cold War to full advantage. Arens, Ariel Sharon and their colleagues, working closely with AIPAC (with a major assist from Yitzhak Rabin during his six years as defense minister), sought to establish Israel as a stable strategic ally, one that Washington could rely upon in its struggle against the Soviet Union. Using Cold War rhetoric and concepts, the Likud government tried to redefine the conflict in the Middle East. It was no longer a matter of two peoples fighting for the same small strip of land, but rather of East versus West, of totalitarianism versus democracy, of Soviet client states such as Syria versus America's spunky, resourceful ally in Jerusalem.

The high-water mark for these Israeli Cold Warriors was the 1988 memorandum of understanding, signed during Shamir's premiership, that enshrined military and strategic cooperation between Washington and Jerusalem. Yet even while the agreement was being negotiated and signed, the intifada was taking hold in the occupied territories. By concentrating on the superglobal and ignoring what was happening inside Israel's backyard, AIPAC and other American Jewish groups contributed to the Shamir government's complacency and myopia.

Israeli governments had once made the case for American support on values, arguing that Americans had a moral and ethical stake in Israel's survival. Now those values looked askew. A country that enforced a permanent military occupation in the West Bank and Gaza, that denied its Palestinian subjects even the most rudimentary rights of free speech and the vote, and that locked up, abused and expelled Palestinians without formal charge or trial could not claim to wholeheartedly share liberal American values.

American Jewish leaders sought to maintain the illusion that they were not involved in Israeli internal affairs even while Jewish donors poured $10 million to $20 million into Labor's and Likud's campaign treasuries and ultra-Orthodox rabbis like Schneerson sought to manipulate coalition politics. In 1987 Shamir had used the reticence of American Jewish leaders to help sabotage Shimon Peres's attempt to bring about an international peace conference between Israel and the Arabs. Peres spent as much time selling the proposal to American Jews as to Israelis. But the Presidents' Conference and most of its component organizations refused to go along because of Shamir's opposition. They insisted on Israeli unity at a time when unity meant paralysis. And they wound up paralyzed, too. Meanwhile, the status quo—military occupation alongside the steadily increasing construction of new Jewish settlements—continued unabated. Yitzhak Shamir won by default.

Shamir returned to office in December 1988 determined to enforce new limits on Jewish dissent. Netanyahu, in one of his first acts as the new deputy foreign minister, canceled a dinner in the Netherlands in honor of Abba Eban because the former foreign minister had attended a conference at which PLO representatives were present. When a half dozen left-wing Knesset members toured the United States on behalf of Peace Now, Ariel Sharon characterized them as "Jewish informers" who were bent on sabotaging government policy—and Shamir defended Sharon's remarks as "factual."

The ideal American Jewish leader, from their viewpoint, engaged in what author Leonard Fein called "dissent as pillow talk—you whisper it in the ears of Israeli politicians when you visit Israel but you never say it in public."

A Jewish member of the U.S. House of Representatives whom Fein would not identify offered the perfect example. "I go to Israel twice a year and read Shamir out," he told Fein proudly, insisting that this was the way to be truly effective in influencing Israeli policy. Fein responded, "You know what Shamir does when you leave? He calls in his staff and they roll on the floor laughing. They're perfectly prepared to endure your lecture twice a year for fifteen minutes. They have you where they want you."

When Shamir did not get the degree of support he demanded, he would react with anger. He was furious at American Jews who publicly supported the right of Soviet Jews to choose to emigrate to the United States instead of Israel. He denounced as betrayers those who criticized Israeli conduct during the intifada. He was bewildered, then irritated, then deeply angered at the American Jewish revolt over the Pollard affair and the Who Is a Jew issue.

But his worst moment came in December 1988 after George Shultz announced that the United States was changing its long-standing policy and opening a diplomatic dialogue with the PLO. The move caught the Israelis, who were still immersed in political machinations over the forming of a new government, by surprise. Shultz spurned Shamir's attempts to persuade him to reverse the decision. Then the prime minister turned to American Jewish leaders. In an emotional conference call to Presidents' Conference chairman Morris B. Abram, Netanyahu demanded that American Jews pressure Congress to reverse Shultz. Abram rejected the demand. The fact was that many American Jewish leaders had more respect for Shultz's judgment than for Shamir's. They were not prepared to stage a public confrontation with a man widely perceived as the most pro-Israel secretary of state in history.

Shamir was furious. How could American Jews fail to understand what a terrible blow it is to Israel to have our sworn enemies be granted this status? he asked aides. What is the matter with them—are they too afraid to act?

But Shamir saved his angriest words for the five American Jews who had met in Stockholm in early December with Yasser Arafat and paved the way for the Shultz decision by persuading the PLO leader to renounce terrorism and recognize Israel. Four of the delegation were considered fringe figures in the Jewish world, but the fifth, New York lawyer Menachem Z. Rosensaft, was a prominent member of the American Jewish establishment. Born in 1948 the son of Holocaust survivors in a displaced persons' camp at Bergen-Belsen, Rosensaft was president of the Labor Zionist Alliance and a member of the Presidents' Conference. The other four might have been "willing dupes," but Rosensaft knew better, Shamir argued. He was a traitor.

At Shamir's behest Yossi Ben-Aharon phoned Malcolm Hoenlein, executive director of the Presidents' Conference, to demand that Rosensaft be ousted from the conference. The group met to discuss Rosensaft's banishment even before he returned from Stockholm, but Henry Siegman, executive director of the American Jewish Congress, and several other liberals objected, noting that such a move would violate the conference's own by-laws. Rosensaft kept his seat, although he was shunned by many conference members.

The problem was that Rosensaft would not keep quiet. He wrote a column for the *New York Times* Op Ed page in which he predicted (correctly, as it happened) that Shamir's budding peace initiative would prove to be nothing more than a flimsy deception because the prime minister was ideologically incapable of parting with a single inch of territory. For many American Jews, who disagreed with Shamir in private but who wanted to be able to support the Israeli government in public, the column was an even greater sin than the meeting with Arafat. Rosensaft was saying out loud—in the *New York Times,* for God's sake—that the emperor and his supporters had no clothes.

They could not kick Menachem Rosensaft out of the Jewish community, but they could make him feel like an outcast. When Moshe Arens and Ariel Sharon appeared at Presidents' Conference sessions in New York, they demanded to know why members allowed such a "traitor" to remain in their midst. When Rosensaft rose to challenge Sharon at one such session, Sharon eyed him coldly and replied, "At least I would never shake hands with a murderer." Eventually, after two years of this, Rosensaft declined to run again for the presidency of the alliance, citing personal reasons and denying he had been forced out.

American Jews desperately wanted to believe that Israel was actively pursuing peace. For Shamir the 1989 peace initiative might have been only a fig leaf, but it gave American Jewish leaders something to rally around. It also allowed them to continue to make the case—to themselves and to other Americans—that Yitzhak Shamir was a sheep in wolf's clothing, that the hard-line pronouncements and seeming intransigence were a negotiating ploy, that Shamir was a hard bargainer just waiting for a proper Arab peace partner to come and awaken his moderate soul.

Seymour Reich, who took over from Morris Abram as chairman of the Presidents' Conference at around the time Shamir presented his peace initiative, went so far as to suggest that, contrary to his every public statement, Shamir would be willing to make territorial concessions in return for peace. " 'Territory for peace' are words that have been irritating to the government and the prime minister," Reich told a press conference in Jerusalem in March 1989, "but when you come to talk, this prime minister has said everything's negotiable."

Reich and other diaspora leaders had traveled to Jerusalem that month to attend an event that illustrated just how much disdain Shamir felt for American Jews. The prime minister was due to visit Washington in a few weeks for his first meeting with George Bush. He wanted to demonstrate to the administration maximum support for himself and his new initiative, so his government hastily organized, with Labor's reluctant acquiescence, what it called the Prime Minister's Conference on Jewish Solidarity with Israel. It was an occasion for bombast and posturing and a call to diaspora Jews to cast aside whatever reservations they might have held and fall in line.

"There is nothing we need more at this moment than unity, unity of the Jewish people and unity between Israel and the Jewish people," intoned Shamir, managing to slip in the key word three times in a single sentence in his opening speech to the conference. Israel's problem was not the occupation or the intifada, he insisted, but rather the inability of its friends and admirers to give it adequate support in the battlefield of public opinion. "We are now facing all over the world a campaign of slander, of lies, against the Jewish people, against the state of Israel," Shamir insisted. And the biggest lie of all, it seemed, was that Jews were divided or ambivalent in their support of Israel.

"We must dispel the perception abroad that the Jewish people are divided, that there is a weakening of the bonds between Israel and the Jewish diaspora, that Israel's image has been tarnished and that Israel's policies are being questioned even by Jews," said the man who was singularly most responsible for both the tarnish and the questions.

But Shamir was demanding solidarity from world Jewry at a time when even within his own government there was none. During the same week the conference took place, someone in the government leaked a report to the press that Brigadier General Amnon Shahak, then head of Military Intelligence, had told the cabinet that Israel's best hope of ending the intifada was to open negotiations with the PLO. While overstated in press accounts, Shahak's assessment ran directly counter to the position of the government and was an enormous embarrassment to Shamir as he appeared before the conference. The prime minister dealt with the issue by claiming he knew nothing about the assessment. "All was a lie," he told a press conference, referring to the press accounts.

The incident unsettled the conference, but the participants refused to acknowledge its meaning. Speaker after speaker rose to pledge fealty to Israel and to the government. "There's no erosion" in American Jewish support, avowed Seymour Reich, although he conceded that there was "a concern, an anxiety, an eagerness, a sense of an opportunity for peace."

"We wish you well," Reich told Shamir. "We're glad we came. You have our support."

All of the delegates knew they were being asked to rubber-stamp Israeli policies that many of them disagreed with. Still, nearly 1,600 delegates signed the conference's Declaration of Solidarity, composed by the prime minister's office, a document that Henry Siegman characterized as "poorly written, mawkish and incoherent."

"What would you have us do?" asked Burton Levinson, president of the Anti-Defamation League, in defending his own attendance at the session. "Would we rather be used or rather be ignored?"

Levinson confessed that as he sat listening to Israeli leaders exhort him to greater heights of solidarity and support, he could not get out of his head the image of the *shabbes goy*. In the old days Jews hired Gentiles to turn on their lights and perform other menial chores on Friday nights because religious law forbade Jews to do so themselves. Levinson feared that Shamir was exploiting American Jews in the same way—to accomplish something that the prime minister could not achieve on his own.

Another delegate put it more bluntly. "He didn't say come support Likud, he said come support Israel, so what can we do, tell him to fuck off?"

Gradually Shamir's list of American Jewish pariahs grew. Next on it was Siegman, a prickly Holocaust survivor and ordained rabbi who since 1978 had been executive director of the American Jewish Congress, a New York–based organization with a small but loyal following and a traditionally liberal position on Israeli and American issues.

Siegman had been educated in an ultra-Orthodox yeshivot and he was more literate in Jewish terms than many of Israel's own leaders. He spoke their language and understood their thinking. Siegman knew how Shamir talked when he was alone with aides, how he mocked and ridiculed American Jews and non-Jews alike. Siegman understood that for Shamir and his aides, every issue was a survival issue. They saw themselves in a total war; anyone who was not loyal was automatically an enemy. And he knew that Jews like himself, who withheld their support and occasionally voiced their criticism on the Op Ed page or in the letters column of the *New York Times*, were in many ways the worst offenders of all. "For Shamir's people it was always one minute before midnight and crucial that American Jews suspend their own beliefs and side with Israel," he said. "Too many American Jewish leaders bought it, or at least acted as if they did."

Siegman believed that Shamir was leading Israel to disaster. The marriage of Likud's populist base with right-wing ideologues and messianic settlers frightened him. Their desire to hold onto the West Bank and Gaza Strip was damaging Israel's security because it subjugated 1.7 million hostile and rebellious Palestinians to Israeli rule. Ever since the intifada began, Siegman believed, the status quo had become more and more untenable and unsafe for Israel. What's more, he believed that most Israelis agreed with him.

Under the circumstances, Siegman believed all American Jews had an obligation to speak out. "If the status quo were, in fact, to lead to Israel's undoing," he wrote, "it would be scant comfort for American Jews to point out that at least they preserved Jewish unity—while Israel went down the tube! In real life . . . Jews who care passionately about Israel will seek to influence what happens there precisely on issues that affect its existence, because their conscience and guts will not permit them not to."

Siegman did not confine his criticisms to Shamir. He believed that American Jewish leaders like Hoenlein, AIPAC's Tom Dine and the Anti-Defamation League's Abe Foxman did Israel a disservice by refusing to question publicly Shamir's policies. They seemed to view their role as being Shamir's lawyers—advising him on the best way of getting whatever it was he wanted without disagreeing with him on principle. "You're not fucking lawyers, you're fellow Jews," Siegman told Dine. "You have to argue values. Shamir is able to say American Jews agree with him and that's a lie."

Siegman knew he could not openly press for the Likud's defeat; to do so, in any case, would be counterproductive. But he pushed hard and openly for territorial compromise. The American Jewish Congress had been one of the few organizations to support Peres's international conference proposal. Ben-Aharon had responded by accusing the congress of meddling in internal Israeli politics and had briefly banned the organization from meeting with the prime minister.

In 1989, even while Shamir was introducing his new peace initiative, the congress was the main sponsor of a study by Tel Aviv University's Jaffee Center for Strategic Studies that conflicted with key parts of the plan. The study concluded that Israel could live safely next door to an independent Palestinian state, provided that state's military power was severely curtailed. Such a solution might prove a better alternative for Israeli security than the unstable status quo, the report argued. Once again the Shamir government exploded in outrage, with Moshe Arens charging that the report was designed to undermine Israel's bargaining position at a time when it was seeking to sell Shamir's initiative to the Bush administration.

There was a price to pay for this kind of independence, and Ben-Aharon made sure that Siegman and the American Jewish Congress paid it. In 1988 right-wing American Jewish organizations placed a joint advertisement in the Jewish press calling for Siegman's ouster. Siegman was certain that the campaign originated in the prime minister's office. There were names of friends on the list, people who disagreed with him politically but whom Siegman believed would never have called for his removal had they not been pressured by Ben-Aharon. One of the congress's local chapters resigned en masse, citing its disapproval of Siegman's positions.

Two years later, after the collapse of Baker's Cairo proposal, Siegman appeared on Israel Television to warn that relations with the Bush administration were unraveling because of Shamir's intransigence. Ben-Aharon consulted with David Bar-Illan, who had been appointed editorial page editor of the *Post* soon after its purchase by a Canadian publishing house and its conversion from the soft-core left to the hard-core right. The result was a venomous editorial headlined "The Siegman Syndrome." Bar-Illan accused Siegman and the American Jewish Congress of joining hands with "the trendy bash-Israel crowd." Far from expressing principled positions, he wrote, Siegman was merely "expressing his frustration at being persona non grata at the prime minister's office. . . .

"The likes of Henry Siegman," Bar-Illan concluded, should be "assiduously shunned by all proud Jews."

Other congress officials were punished as well. Congress president Robert Lifton was soundly defeated in two bids for the chairmanship of the Presidents' Conference. "Bob Lifton's a nice guy, but frankly there were a lot of people who did not want to see the president of an organization run by Henry Siegman become the chairman of the conference," said a high-ranking American Jewish official. "As a result, Bob didn't even come close."

The Bar-Illan editorial did not shut Siegman up. After the new right-wing government was formed in June 1990, Siegman criticized Seymour Reich and other American Jewish leaders who claimed publicly that relations between Israel and the Bush administration were fundamentally sound. Siegman accused them of telling Shamir what he wanted to hear in order not to jeopardize their own privileged access to the prime minister. "The Israeli people have not been told the truth," Siegman told journalist David Makovsky.

Abe Foxman believed Siegman was adding fuel to a growing and destructive fire. At a time when Israel and the U.S. government were in bitter conflict, the last thing Israel needed was for an American Jewish leader to fan the flames with a hysterical outburst. Israelis and American Jews had to stick together.

If Siegman represented the moderate left wing of the American Jewish establishment, then Foxman was the moderate right. A revisionist who kept a portrait of Zeev Jabotinsky, the Likud's ideological mentor, on the wall of his New York City office near the standard-issue portrait of Ben-Gurion, Foxman was a Holocaust survivor who as a small child had been given to a Polish Catholic family for safekeeping by his Jewish parents. After the war his parents returned to reclaim him and they moved to the United States, where he grew up and got a law degree. Foxman was an energetic activist who had helped transform the Anti-Defamation League from an organization focused entirely on combating antisemitism to one of the foremost components of the Israel lobby. Israel's survival, he argued, was crucial to the existence of Jews around the world. Any threat to its image in the United States could endanger the annual $3 billion package of foreign aid that helped keep Israel afloat and, he believed, ultimately jeopardize the fate of world Jewry.

Foxman had little use for the Henry Siegmans of the world and none whatsoever for Menachem Rosensaft. Nonetheless, as time went on, Foxman found himself increasingly slipping off Shamir's list of allies. It had started with the Pollard affair, when Foxman and ADL president Burton Levinson were vocal in their disapproval. It got worse in the spring of 1990 when the government first denied and then admitted that it had secretly financed the settlement of Orthodox Jews in the St. John's Hospice building complex in the Christian Quarter of Jerusalem's walled Old City. Armed Jewish settlers escorted by Israeli police had occupied the site in the middle of the night during the week before Easter, a move that caused howls of protest from Christian leaders in the United States and Europe and deeply embarrassed American Jewish leaders.

Foxman was especially angry because he had originally repeated the government's claim that it knew nothing in advance about the move—a claim that turned out to be blatantly false. "This government owes an apology for misleading people; somebody should get fired," Foxman told Ben-Aharon. "If you destroy your own credibility, you destroy ours."

But the final breaking point was over the Anti-Defamation League's response to the Temple Mount killings in October 1990. It was the same pattern again: first the ADL wholeheartedly endorsed the government's position, then it had to backtrack when Shamir's people turned out to have been less than truthful. When the CBS television program *60 Minutes* broadcast a report that challenged the official Israel account, Foxman responded with a tough statement denouncing the program and repeating the government's claim that only after their lives were endangered had police opened fire on Arab rioters. Seven months later, however, an Israeli judge issued a report challenging police conduct. Foxman recanted publicly, releasing a letter to *60 Minutes* apologizing for his earlier criticism. This enraged Ben-Aharon and Bar-Ilan. After that, Abe Foxman—despite his credentials as a Betar alumnus and a Jabotinskyite—became another persona non grata, and the ADL became the occasional target for darts from the *Jerusalem Post*'s editorial and Op Ed pages.

As he moved into a confrontation with the Bush administration over settlements, Yitzhak Shamir came to rely upon a smaller and smaller circle of American Jewish supporters, many of whom were not inclined to tell him unalloyed bad news. It would be too strong to say that they told him only what they thought he wanted to hear, but they clearly did not impress upon him the dangers of the battle he was slipping into against the president of the United States. The price of heresy had been made all too clear; Shamir did not want equal partners—American Jewish leaders, in his eyes, did not qualify for such status—but loyal followers. At a time when Israel was undergoing the hard, painful transition from past to future, many of these leaders served the stagnant status quo.

In fact, the relationship between Shamir's government and American Jews was built largely on mutual deception: Shamir misrepresented his willingness to negotiate peace, while they misrepresented their level of support for his policies. None of it mattered as long as no one put either of them to the test. But when George Bush set a challenge, the deception crumbled like a Ramat Gan apartment after a direct hit. Try as they might, Yitzhak Shamir's American Jewish allies could not stop the disaster that was soon to befall him.

10. The Fatal Embrace

*Treat people like rats and they will soon learn to
bite your fingers off.*

— ARTHUR KOESTLER

FOR most of its first three years, the Palestinian intifada had been confined largely to the occupied territories. There had been spectacular acts of violence on Israeli soil—most notably in July 1989 when a Palestinian refugee from Gaza had wrested the steering wheel of a civilian passenger bus from its driver and sent the bus and himself careening down a cliff outside Jerusalem, killing fifteen people; and in May 1990 when a former Israeli soldier who had been discharged for mental health reasons opened fire with an M-16 on unarmed Arab workers south of Tel Aviv, killing seven of them. But these were the solitary deeds of deranged individuals intoxicated by the turbulent political atmosphere they lived in. Appalling as they were, these acts were not contagious.

During the Gulf crisis, however, the violence of the intifada spread to Israel proper in a more sustained and consistent way. The uprising, which began as an act of popular revolt, redefined itself as war. Born in hope, it now wallowed in despair. Innocent lives were lost on both sides. The blood fever, once confined to the West Bank and Gaza, now contaminated the entire country. What's more, many Palestinians, ensnared in their own increasing misery, applauded and embraced the growing violence.

The Gulf War was just as pivotal an event for Palestinians as it was for Israelis. It deeply damaged the PLO, which enhanced its almost unblemished record of failure by supporting Saddam Hussein. The Tunis-based movement paid a heavy price, losing political and financial support from its former Arab benefactors, most notably Saudi Arabia and the Gulf emirates.

As the organization deteriorated, local Palestinians from the West Bank and Gaza, who had long chafed under the PLO's corrupt and unaccountable one-man rule, moved to fill the vacuum. Secular moderates, led by Faisal Husseini and including local leaders such as Jad Isaac, emerged as competitors to Tunis even while they continued to pledge allegiance to Arafat. Another far more radical challenge rose from Islamic fundamentalists grouped together under the Arabic acronym Hamas. The conflict between these authentic grassroots groups and their struggles with both Tunis and with the Israeli army would produce a new wave of grisly collaborator killings and markedly alter the political and social landscape of the occupied territories.

At the same time, relationships between Palestinians and Israelis changed profoundly. The intifada, which had set out to break down the old arrangements between the army and Palestinians in the occupied territories, shattered those same arrangements inside Israel itself. Israelis, who over twenty-three years had come to rely on cheap Arab labor to build their houses, pick their crops, clean their floors and empty their garbage, no longer felt safe with Palestinians around. The Israeli left, which had responded with hesitant sympathy to the intifada's demands for an end to occupation and had conducted a search for genuinely moderate Palestinian peace partners, felt abandoned and betrayed.

A process of separation began that was harsh and bitter for Palestinian workers who had relied on the menial wages they earned in Israel for their survival. But that process, fueled by Israeli fatigue with putting down the intifada, anxiety following the Scud attacks and horror over the killings inside Israel, helped lead inevitably to the historic signing on the White House lawn in September 1993.

When he moved to Israel from Detroit in the early 1970s, one of Zeev Chafets's first jobs was working for the Israeli Foreign Affairs Ministry. There he helped to put together a glossy brochure on Israel's still-young occupation of the West Bank and Gaza. It showed photographs of Arabs and Jews working side by side in factories, shopping in colorful open-air markets and sharing the country's golden beaches. The title was "Coexistence."

In those days, it seemed, there were two kinds of Palestinians. The bad Palestinians, who lived outside the country, belonged to the PLO and staged terrorist raids into Israel. But the good Palestinians—"Our Palestinians"— worked in Israel, were grateful for their new higher standard of living, and came to know, respect and admire Israelis.

The problem with coexistence, as Chafets later conceded, was that it was never much more than a figment of a liberal imagination and conscience. Arabs and Jews never came to know, let alone admire, each other. If anything, the limited contact between the two groups in unequal power relationships such as occupier and occupied, employer and employee, only heightened the tensions between them.

Palestinians who ventured into Israel to work often learned Hebrew and developed some sense of what Israelis were like. But it was a one-way street that led nowhere. Israelis had no particular interest in Palestinians, no desire to know more about them. Palestinians were cheap labor and nothing more. Yoram Binur, an Israeli journalist who posed as a Palestinian worker in 1986, recalled his most humiliating experience: washing dishes in a cramped restaurant kitchen at 2 A.M. when the owner's sister and boyfriend came in, squeezed themselves between Binur and the refrigerator and started kissing passionately a few feet from him. At first Binur lowered his eyes so as not to embarrass the two lovers. Then he realized that they could not have cared less whether he watched or not.

"Those two were not the least bit concerned with what I saw or felt even when they were practically fucking under my nose," he writes in his book, *My Enemy, My Self*. "For them I simply didn't exist. I was invisible, a nonentity! It's difficult to describe the feeling of extreme humiliation which I experienced."

Yitzhak Shamir's government claimed to have abolished the Green Line, the border that before 1967 had divided Israel from the West Bank and Gaza Strip, and to have permanently incorporated the territories as part of Israel. But the line still existed in the minds of those who lived on both sides of it. Except for soldiers and Jewish settlers, most Israelis never ventured into the occupied territories. And the only Palestinians who crossed regularly into Israel were the 130,000 or so Arabs who worked there and returned home each night.

Yet they claimed the same land, shared the same home. Each defined the other as an alien intruder and a threat—as an enemy, not a neighbor. Each saw the other solely through the prism of its own history and suffering. Neither side was about to recognize the legitimacy of the other's grievances or of their suffering. They shared no feelings of grief or intimacy. The only feelings they shared were those of revenge.

The Gulf crisis unhinged both Arabs and Jews, injecting a new, more personal kind of cruelty in an already raw and edgy atmosphere. In the past each side had sought to hide behind its national identity. Palestinian stone throwers claimed they were throwing rocks and Molotov cocktails at Israeli cars, not at individual people. Israeli soldiers contended that even when they were shooting into a crowd or clubbing individual Palestinians face-to-face they were carrying out the orders, however ruthless, of their superiors.

Now all such illusions were stripped away. Just a few days after the Iraqi invasion of Kuwait, the bodies of two Israeli teenagers, Lior Tubul and Ronen Karamani, were found in a ravine north of Jerusalem. Each had been bound and gagged and stabbed so many times in the face that they were unrecognizable. Their grief-stricken families pleaded for calm, but the mob would not listen. Several thousand Jewish residents retaliated in scenes of vigilantism not witnessed in the capital since 1948, burning and stoning Arab cars and beating up Palestinians and—another enemy—news camera crews. A raiding party from the Katamon neighborhood, where one of the boys lived, stormed into the nearby Arab community of Beit Safafa and threw stones at residents, shouting, "Death to the Arabs!" and "Long Live Kahane!" Dozens of groups participated, some in masks similar to those worn by Palestinian activists in the territories. "It's a Jewish intifada," boasted one of the rioters.

It went on for two days until finally someone got killed. A Jewish mob rained stones on a car driven by an Arab motorist named Izzat Halhala. Blinded by a rock to his face, he lost control of the car, which overturned. Halhala was dragged from the vehicle and beaten unconscious. He lapsed into a coma and died two days later. His death somehow seemed sufficient; the riots quickly abated.

But the blood sacrifice was only beginning. A few weeks later an army reservist named Amnon Pomerantz, a civil engineer and father of three returning to reserve duty from his home in Tel Aviv, made a wrong turn while seeking to find his army unit in the Gaza Strip. He turned into the Bureij refugee camp, where his yellow-license-plated car was immediately identified as Israeli (Gaza plates are white) and pelted with stones. He turned around and hit the gas, but collided with a donkey cart carrying two youngsters. Streams of people poured out of a nearby mosque where they had been praying and surrounded the car. What followed was a ritual slaughter. First Pomerantz was stoned until he lost consciousness inside the car. Then someone poured gasoline all over the crippled vehicle and set it ablaze. Pomerantz died inside. The IDF proceeded to demolish thirty-four houses near the site of the killing.

Two weeks after Pomerantz's death came the Temple Mount shootings in which nineteen Palestinians were killed and more than a hundred wounded in Jerusalem's Old City. As with past incidents, the killings set off a new wave of riots in the territories, but this time they also led to deaths among Israelis. The ugliest attack came thirteen days after the Temple

Mount incident when a nineteen-year-old Arab who worked as a plasterer along with his father and two brothers went on a rampage in the affluent Baka neighborhood in West Jerusalem. Amer Abu Sirhan concealed himself in an alley on his way to work, then jumped out and stabbed Iris Azulai, an eighteen-year-old soldier who lived with her parents in the neighborhood. He ran for several blocks, then cornered Eli Alteretz, a forty-five-year-old garden shop owner coming down his front stoop. He chased Alteretz up the driveway and stabbed him in the chest.

A wild chase followed, with Abu Sirhan pursued by a number of horrified residents. He slashed at a thirteen-year-old boy but kept running. Charlie Chalouche, a young soldier who served in an antiterrorist squad, joined the chase. When Abu Sirhan turned on him with the knife, Chalouche first fired a warning shot and then shot Abu Sirhan twice in the legs. It was not enough to stop the Palestinian, who piled onto Chalouche and stabbed him in the chest. Charlie Chalouche's dying body pinned the wounded Abu Sirhan to the ground.

Once again, some Israelis reacted to the stabbings by seeking revenge. Mobs beat up Arab workers and pummeled Arab cars with bricks on the road to Bethlehem. Others stood outside the apartment house where Eli Alteretz had died, which was also the home of Amiram Goldblum, one of the leaders of the Peace Now movement. They taunted Goldblum to come outside. When he did not respond, the mob threw rocks at his windows.

At his funeral Charlie's brother Arye, a nineteen-year-old soldier serving in the West Bank, tried to climb into the open grave with his brother. Two months later he took his automatic rifle and walked to the Hebron Road after dark, where he opened fire on the first car he saw bearing West Bank blue license plates. There were three people in the car—Dr. Faisal Amr, his sister and his sister's baby son. They were returning from a hospital visit to Amr's wife, who had just given birth to their ninth child. Arye Chalouche pumped thirty-three bullets into the car, hitting Amr fourteen times and wounding his sister. When she climbed out of the car pleading for help for her brother, Arye screamed at her in broken Arabic, "Die, you and your brother!"

To stem the violence, Defense Minister Arens ordered the closure of the Green Line, and barred all Palestinians from Israeli territory. Police also threw up roadblocks around Jerusalem and stopped every Arab male who tried to enter the Jewish sectors of the city whether by car or on foot. The mob did its part. Bands of Jewish youths patrolled the old Bucharan market daily, looking for Arab workers. Two shops that employed Arabs were burned. A Jewish butcher shop proprietor who protected an Arab employee from harm was stabbed. Soon after, the same owner, Mordechai Mizrahi, fired all of his Arab workers and hung a sign on his door: "Here Arabs are not employed." It was, he told *Haaretz,* a practical matter: "If we employ Arabs, we will go hungry. People are simply unwilling to buy merchandise when they see an Arab touching it."

At the time of the wave of stabbings, stories abounded of Arab construction workers damaging the houses they were building for Israelis and of Arab employees in food processing plants urinating in vats of Israeli food staples such as hummus and tahini or slipping rat poison into coffee tins. Some of the stories were true, some merely fantasy, but they all added to the sense of popular anger and disgust.

Jerusalem, which under its indefatigable mayor Teddy Kollek had struggled since its reunification in 1967 to avoid becoming Beirut or Belfast, now found itself redivided. It was a stunning defeat for both Kollek, who had little control over the police force's activities, and the Likud government.

Beyond the horror that they evoked, the Baka killings posed a grim warning to Israelis. Abu Sirhan was not some crazed alien who had arrived from nowhere one day with a butcher knife and a grudge. He and his relatives had worked in Israel for many years, earning their daily bread on Israeli construction sites and mingling to some extent with Jews. He was the stranger among them, a man who had concealed and nursed a growing hatred. If Abu Sirhan could one day pick up a knife and slaughter people in a neighborhood where he had worked for years, Israelis reasoned, then every Palestinian worker in Israel was a potential time bomb. Most might never explode, but how could you know in advance which one would?

Zeev Chafets faced that question personally when he decided to remodel his kitchen. "The thought of Palestinian workers with sharp implements wandering around my house frightened me," he wrote in the *Jerusalem Report.* "My concern, I confess, made me uneasy. Most Palestinian laborers are peaceable working men who only want to feed their families; is it fair, I asked myself, to discriminate against everyone for the crimes of a few? Maybe not, I decided, but how do you tell the good guys from the terrorists? I wanted a new kitchen, but not enough to die for one."

Then there was the location. Baka was one of Jerusalem's most affluent and cultured neighborhoods, a home to many transplanted American Jews. It was also home to some of the most prominent activists of Peace Now, the premier Israeli peace movement. It was founded by reserve army officers in 1978, and its members had spent the last decade seeking ways to reach an accommodation with Palestinians. They often had been vilified as bleeding hearts and traitors during the years of Likud rule and felt isolated and marginalized. Yet Peace Now had hung on.

The Baka killings were a chilling blow to the peace movement. Abu

Sirhan had not sought out soldiers or Jewish settlers for his retribution, but had ventured into the heart of the left to commit his deed. In effect he was saying that every Jew, liberal or not, was at risk from every Palestinian. It was a sober and shattering thought, especially because it came at a moment when the first tenuous ties between the movement and Palestinian moderates were starting to unravel.

The 1980s had not been an easy decade for Peace Now. The movement had reached its apex in 1982 when hundreds of thousands of Israelis protested the ill-fated Lebanon invasion and its brutal aftermath, the massacres of Palestinians at the Sabra and Shatila refugee camps in Beirut. But the ensuing years of political stalemate had worn down the movement, which struggled to maintain a toehold in a society jaded by its own political leaders and wary of any kind of contact with Palestinians.

The peace camp was roughly divided into two kinds of doves. There were the idealists, who believed in the possibility of peaceful coexistence between Arabs and Jews and who sought to reach out to like-minded Palestinians. And there were the separatists, who argued that Palestinians would never be reconciled with living or working among Israelis and that the only practical answer for the foreseeable future was to seal them off from Israel in their own political entity, whether an independent state of their own or a confederation with neighboring Jordan. In truth, the two different views coexisted uneasily within many doves.

But the intifada opened new possibilities. Yasser Arafat's renunciation of terrorism and recognition of Israel's right to exist in December 1988 helped open the door. Suddenly, it seemed, there was someone to talk to on the other side. If Palestinians were willing to accept Israel's existence, then the issue between them was no longer one of survival but rather of political accommodation. The conflict was no longer an existential one but simply a dispute over borders and political rights. Some of the more adventurous members of the peace movement began to search for Palestinian partners.

One of the places they came to was Beit Sahur. With their tax revolt crushed by the army and their economy seriously damaged, Jad Isaac and his neighbors were searching for another, less risky outlet for their rebellion. Previously, they had concentrated on themselves and their own institutions. Now they began looking to their enemy.

They started with Shlomo Lecker, a dovish Israeli lawyer who had taken Isaac's case and those of other detained Beit Sahuris at the behest of the Association for Civil Rights in Israel. Encouraged by the moderate political views he heard in Beit Sahur, Lecker suggested that the Palestinians open a dialogue with sympathetic members of the Israeli peace camp. A dozen people got together in Beit Sahur in August 1988 for a session marked by mutual skepticism and suspicion. "We tried to be polite but we avoided specifics," said Ghassan Andoni, a physics professor at Bir Zeit University who led the Beit Sahuri side of the group. "Could you be open with them? Everyone was listening hard, trying to discover, to understand the character of the other side."

More people attended the next meeting, held at Andoni's house. There followed other sessions, as the two sides found themselves drawn in despite their reservations. Gradually, after much tentative dancing around the subject, they began to get to the basics of what lay between them. "We finally started talking honestly about what we believed—about historical rights, the Zionist movement, Palestinian nationalism," Andoni recalled. "There were real arguments and hot discussions. We told them, 'This is our land, you came here illegally and because you are powerful you managed to defeat us.' They talked about two thousand years of history.

"Finally we managed to draw a picture of who each other was. When we spoke of politics, of the occupation and human rights, the gap between us was not that big. But when we spoke of things that are more important—history, ideology, culture—the gap was very very wide."

Each side had their underlying agenda: The Beit Sahuris wanted to spread the word among Israelis about the army's abuses and to buy some protection for themselves. The doves wanted to communicate to Palestinians that not all Israelis were settlers or soldiers, that a moderate Palestinian leadership would find allies among moderate Israelis.

"That was the whole issue. We'd been fighting these people for decades and yet we didn't know them. We thought we could learn. The intifada made it possible by creating a sense of power inside us, a sense of equality with them. It wasn't master and slave anymore. We could talk."

Jad Isaac returned from Ketziot prison at the end of November 1988 to find the dialogue well established. Each week there were three or four sessions. Sometimes as many as two dozen Israelis would make their way around army roadblocks on back roads or by foot to get there and participate. Isaac, who was hungry for more contact with Israelis, began hosting some of the sessions at his house. Over sweet tea and dark Turkish coffee, often with small children underfoot, the two sides would grope toward communication.

The army tried to intervene. Andoni was arrested four times in 1989 and sent to Ketziot for three months. Isaac was summoned by the military governor and warned not to get involved. When the army got word of a joint prayer service or a weekend retreat in which Beit Sahuris hosted Israeli families in their homes, it sealed off the town. But many Israelis slipped through the porous cordon.

One of the most frequent participants was Hillel Bardin, a fifty-two-year-old American-born Israeli who had become increasingly disturbed by the naked hatred that members of his reserve army unit felt toward Palestinians. Once in the West Bank town of Jericho an officer explained to soldiers how to force striking merchants to open their shops. To demonstrate his point he drove his jeep into a storefront, shattering glass and smashing the goods in the shop window.

Bardin kept returning to Jericho after his reserve duty ended to see if he could come to terms with the Palestinians he had overseen. One day he arrived at the front door of a young man whom he had guarded in jail. Dressed in his civilian clothes, Bardin began awkwardly, "You may not want to let me in but . . ."

"No, no, come in," the man replied.

Soon, of course, they were discussing politics and the man was expressing support for a two-state solution—Israel and Palestine, side by side. Bardin was stunned and disbelieving. "But what would your neighbors say?" he asked.

"My neighbors say the same thing."

To prove it the two men headed out into the street, stopping people at random. The conversations were amicable. People were surprised to see an Israeli out of uniform asking them earnest questions. Then someone took Bardin to a small clay house. Inside was an old Arab lying on a bed. The man looked wasted, as if he were dying. But when someone whispered in his ear, he pulled himself off the bed, stood up and embraced the Israeli. "We've been waiting for you for so long," the man said. He had tears in his eyes.

Bardin was an idealist, but he was no fool. At the first Beit Sahur session, Andoni had told the Israelis that the intifada was a message of peace. "We almost fell off our chairs," recalled Bardin. "If it was a message of peace, it was in a language we couldn't understand at all. Later we came to realize that the intifada really had two messages: (1) we're sick and tired of occupation, and (2) we could live side by side in two states. The second message had never really arrived."

"To us the intifada is a war against Israel to throw us into the sea with stones and Molotovs," Bardin told Andoni. "Even the nonviolent activities like the flags, demos, strikes, graffiti—we can't distinguish between them and the violence." The intifada was seen by all Israelis as a challenge to their legitimacy, he told the Beit Sahuris. That was why the tax strike had triggered such a brutal response. The army was angrier at people challenging its authority than it was at the stone throwers.

But the sessions had an effect on Bardin. "It completely changed my thinking. I'd always thought of Palestinians as dangerous people. Now I was beginning to trust them. With enemies it makes sense never to give an inch. But I no longer thought of these people as enemies."

The dialogue participants on both sides were a minority of a minority with little influence on their respective societies. But they were important because they were breaking a basic taboo. Communication could not solve the Israeli-Palestinian dispute, but it could at least give each side a better understanding of the other's fears and demands.

Nothing was easy for the would-be peacemakers. They had to cope not only with each other's complex feelings but also with the army. At one point Bardin sought to organize joint Arab-Jewish jogging sessions. He printed up tee-shirts with the message in Hebrew, Arabic and English: "We want peace—between Palestine and Israel—each free and secure." But the military commander of Bethlehem banned the runs. Only after lawyers petitioned the Israeli Supreme Court did the army back down.

On the day the first run took place, the army sealed off Bethlehem and banned the press, supposedly to prevent disturbances. The jogging session was limited to nine participants. Later, after the Israeli runners left, soldiers beat up some of the Palestinians and arrested one.

A few weeks later, a new, more liberal commander took over the area and agreed to allow open runs. It was a small step but a symbolic one. The first run was scheduled for early August 1990. Thanks to Saddam Hussein, it never took place.

The Iraqi invasion of Kuwait set off an explosion of popular support among Palestinians for Saddam. The Iraqi leader had conquered another Arab state, an unprecedented breach of Arab unity, but he had quickly sought to recast his aggressive act in terms that Palestinians could endorse. He equated his occupation of Kuwait with Israel's occupation of the West Bank and Gaza, and suggested that he would be only too happy to withdraw once the Israelis did the same. He also wrapped himself in Arab populism, portraying the oil sheikhs as greedy, money-hoarding tools of Western and Zionist imperialism.

It was a transparent ploy. But for Palestinians frustrated by the lack of political gains after nearly three years of the intifada and outraged by the army's heavy-handed crackdown, it was effective. Saddam offered deliverance by other means. Yasser Arafat rushed to Baghdad to kiss the Iraqi leader, and Palestinians in Jordan, Lebanon and the occupied territories embraced Saddam as their new hero. There was nothing very rational about their embrace. Even liberal intellectuals, who almost certainly would have been executed for treason had they lived under the brutal Baathist regime in Baghdad, became ardent supporters and apologists. Local leaders got caught up in the fervor and the fury on the streets, or at best stood aside, offering rationalizations for a stance that at its core was both irrational and ultimately self-destructive. With the exception of marginalized figures like Bethlehem Mayor Elias Freij, no Palestinian stood up publicly to condemn the Iraqi leader. Most applauded Saddam's message even if, privately, they abhorred the messenger.

For the PLO itself, the endorsement of Saddam completed a process of reradicalization that followed directly from Arafat's frustrated diplomatic efforts. By renouncing terrorism and recognizing Israel's existence in December 1988, Arafat had played the American card in the hopes that Israel's closest ally would force the Shamir government into negotiations over the future of the territories. But the move had led nowhere. Eighteen months later Arafat had nothing concrete to show skeptical Palestinians either inside or outside the occupied territories. If anything, conditions had regressed. The economic plight of those under occupation had worsened during the intifada, and by March 1990 the Israeli government had been captured by its most hawkish component.

In June 1990 the Palestinian dialogue with the United States collapsed after Arafat refused to discipline Mohammed Abbas, the PLO operative in charge of an abortive terrorist sea raid into Israel. It was a short step from there to the embrace of Saddam Hussein.

Palestinians argued that they had nothing to lose by siding with Iraq, but in fact they lost much. The fragile bridges they had built to the Israeli peace camp crumbled within days. On the weekend following the invasion—and before the extent of popular Palestinian support for Saddam was clear—local Arab leaders held an unprecedented public meeting with sixteen dovish Israeli Knesset members. The two sides were supposed to draft a joint platform for peace, but the meeting went nowhere. The Israeli side wanted the Palestinians to condemn Saddam, while the Palestinians wanted the Israelis to denounce American efforts to evict Iraq by force. The two sides never met again.

The Beit Sahuris were no different from other Palestinians when it came to Saddam Hussein. Jad Isaac did not support the invasion of Kuwait, but once Saddam linked it to the occupation, Isaac too became enthusiastic. He had no faith in Saddam's rhetoric, but he clung to the hope that an Arab strongman, no matter how despotic, would bestow upon Palestinians some of the political leverage they lacked.

Isaac and his fellow Beit Sahuris sought to rationalize their support for Iraq at the dialogue sessions with Israelis. "Almost every Palestinian has a personal grudge against the state of Israel so don't expect him to start crying when Scuds hit Tel Aviv," Ghassan Andoni told his Israeli guests. "You have a serious misconception. To you Palestinians are either very bad terrorists or super peace lovers. But in reality we are neither. You have to learn to see us as we really are."

At a bitter session in September the Palestinians lashed out. "Many Palestinians feel that Israelis do not want moderates, they want collaborators," said Andoni. "I don't see how what Saddam did is any worse than what Israel did in 1967. . . . I don't think that having a powerful Arab state in the area is anything bad." Saddam, he added, "seeks a peaceful solution to the Palestinian conflict."

Tami, an Israeli woman, was disbelieving. "Saddam says he wants to destroy Israel. If you want dialogue and you want to recognize our mutual rights, Saddam is not the partner you'd choose."

Mazin, a Palestinian, rejected her reasoning. "I'm discouraged. You haven't tried to understand us and we have tried to understand you. All the time in all these meetings it is we who have been blamed. You should know us very well and you don't."

"No one can deny that we share sympathy with your situation," Tami replied. "That is why we are here."

A young Palestinian girl interjected, "But we don't want your sympathy. We want action."

"I thought that people who had converted to the peace camp would not stand against us. I feel that for the last two years I've been building a castle on sand. . . . I no longer know where to look. Perhaps I should no longer look," Mazin concluded.

Israelis felt the same despair. Levi Weiman-Kelman, an American-born rabbi who had spent two years in dialogue sessions with various Palestinian groups, felt that the Gulf crisis had not just set back the cause of reconciliation but had destroyed it. He quit the sessions after a meeting that fall at his synagogue in Baka. About three dozen Israelis attended, but only one Palestinian, a young journalist, who told them, "We see Iraq as a victim of imperialist colonial Christian crusaders."

Kelman recalled, "People argued with him, but the image I remember was of thirty-five Israelis, some of them hard left people, sitting there with their heads in their hands saying, 'We haven't gotten anywhere.' We were right back where we started—worse, actually, because of the time and energy spent and wasted—and we were back under the same threat."

One of the Israelis told the Palestinian, "You guys are like Samson pulling down the temple. Don't you understand how tactically wrong this is? You'd rather keep your ideological purity and lose everything than compromise and win something." And the Palestinian replied, "You're right, we'd rather be on the losing side than win with the imperialists."

"I found myself wondering: am I supposed to share feelings and values with this guy?" Kelman continued. "It led to a real sense of suspicion and betrayal. It was a hard lesson to learn, and I say it full of sadness."

Yossi Sarid, a maverick left-wing politician, summed up the sense of anger and betrayal in a column for *Haaretz*. "One needs a gas mask in order to overcome the poisonous and repulsive odor of the PLO position toward Saddam Hussein," he wrote. The impact on Israeli public opinion was "ruinous. . . . If it is all right to support Saddam Hussein, maybe it's not so terrible to support the policies of Shamir, Sharon and Rabin. In comparison with the crimes of Saddam Hussein, the sins of the Israeli government are white as snow."

When Scuds started falling, Sarid's attitude hardened further. In a second column, he condemned "the moonstruck sleepwalkers" who were applauding missile attacks on Tel Aviv. "When a stray bullet killed a child of theirs, it pierced our hearts as well. When a missile—not at all stray—is sent to kill our children, it fills their hearts with joy."

Seeking to monopolize the moral high ground, Sarid wandered from the facts. Not all the Israeli bullets that hit children were strays, of course, and not all Israeli hearts were pierced. Even so, he had come a long way from his former dovish views. Palestinians, he warned, "should not come looking for me . . . because they won't be able to find me. I don't have a telephone in the air-raid shelter, and in the sealed room I don't hear their rings. The thunder of missiles is deafening my ears at the moment. It's hard for me to speak while wearing my gas mask, and my speech is breathy and unclear. After the war, when Allah will be less *akhbar* ["great"], don't call me, I'll call you."

Once again the argument was about Israel's survival, not about its borders. Palestinians had regressed, taking the already anemic peace process as their sole hostage. "For 40 years they talked about wiping us out; then they talked about two states," wrote liberal columnist Yoel Marcus in *Haaretz*. ". . . But all it took was one statement from Saddam and their hope of our destruction awakened anew."

It is said that when Palestinians saw the bright arcing trajectory of a Scud pass overhead on its flight to Tel Aviv, they danced on their rooftops. No one has a photograph to prove it ("I searched and searched, but I never could find one," confessed a senior Israeli intelligence official), but there is no question that, whether on the rooftops or on the streets, many Palestinians cheered on Saddam's missiles.

Saddam played to the gallery. He named his missiles The Stones to commemorate the rock-throwing youths of the intifada. On the eve of a Muslim feast he announced a special "holiday gift" to the Palestinian people. That night two more missiles struck the Tel Aviv area.

In his book *The Sealed Room* Raja Shehadeh, a prominent Ramallah lawyer who founded the Al Haq center for human rights and who has many Israeli admirers, sums up the Palestinians' elation and their dilemma. Shehadeh is an aristocrat from an old Ramallah family whose gentle, courtly manners belie great passions that he is scarcely able to conceal. He loathes Saddam Hussein, yet he is impressed by Iraq's military strength. When the Scuds hit Tel Aviv he takes grim satisfaction.

> On our side, we are jubilant that Tel Aviv was hit, not once but twice . . . Why jubilation? Because they [the Israelis] have destroyed thousands of our homes in the occupied territories and have pounded our refugee camps in Lebanon for years. Maybe this will make them realize what it means to lose one's home.

Shehadeh cannot help sympathizing with Israeli suffering during the war. But in the end he admits to mixed emotions.

> What about me? Do I not also have the right to live my life normally? Why should it cost us so dearly for the Jews to live in their state? The intifada has made our position clear: We are willing to compromise, to share our land with them. They refuse. What then do they expect of us . . . ?
>
> And then having come to the point where we know that the way of diplomacy, of nonviolence and of compromise is not working, we turn our hopes to the only other alternative: war and destruction of one of the two parties. Then they point an accusing finger at us and say: "See how evil they are. They like to see us hurt."
>
> Of course we like to see you hurt. You have refused to make peace; you take our land, kill our people and defame our name. Your unbridled power dictates our lives and fate; is it any wonder we now relish your vulnerability?
>
> . . . Yes, I will say these words that so ill-become me: I would like to see your cities under siege, your soldiers crushed, and your arrogant noses stuck in the mud.

It did not turn out that way. Israel was damaged, but it was the Palestinians who were defeated.

Inside the West Bank and Gaza, the war was a stalemate. Anticipating rebellion on behalf of Saddam, the IDF sealed off the territories. The army warned that any outburst would be dealt with according to "wartime rules," not by those of the peacetime occupation. To underscore the point, the authorities arrested leading pro-PLO activists such as Sari Nusseibeh, Radwan Abu Ayash and Ziad Abu Ziad—all of them journalists and academics—and a Gaza physician, Ahmed Yazdi. They also slapped a four-week curfew on the territories, the longest since the Six-Day War. No one starved, but the lack of income from employment in both Israel and the territories devastated the Palestinian economy and made harder lives that were already on the edge. Compounding the pain, the army imposed a new permit system that tightened the number of Palestinians allowed to resume work in Israel after the curfew was lifted.

Even after Palestinian workers were allowed back into Israel, police were given orders to crack down, sweeping up Palestinians waiting at bus stops and street corners, arresting even those with valid work permits. The only sure way to avoid arrest was to be picked up by an Israeli employer at the Green Line and returned there at the end of the day. "Basically every Palestinian is seen as a danger," said Tamar Peleg, a human rights lawyer who defended workers in court. "So if they want to work, they must be unseen." Worker's Hotline, an Israeli group that provided legal aid to Palestinians, estimated that such tactics reduced the number of Palestinian workers from 120,000 to something like 80,000.

The measures produced a curious confusion inside Israel's usually rigidly divided political camps. There were Israeli leftists who welcomed the separation and others on the left who passionately opposed it. The same was true among right-wing nationalists. Palestinian leader Faisal Husseini welcomed the trend, as did the extreme anti-Arab Tsomet party. The Israeli army, fearful that it would exacerbate the already desperate economic squalor of Gaza, was vehemently opposed.

One of the most fervent opponents was Dan Meridor, a passionate but rational nationalist who believed Israel had to demonstrate to Palestinians and to itself that Jews and Arabs could live together and that it was committed to Palestinian economic well-being. Separation, he argued in cabinet meetings, would prove the beginning of the end for the Likud's territorial aspirations. "But the public likes it," a fellow cabinet minister once argued. "That's exactly the problem," Meridor replied. "They will like it too much and they will want it to last forever."

But the biggest loser from the Gulf War was the PLO. Arafat had led Palestinians down a dead-end alley, and the movement paid a huge price both financially and politically. Before the Gulf crisis Saudi Arabia gave the PLO $90 million a year and Kuwait sent nearly $50 million. After the war they cut off all payments. The moderate Arab states of the Gulf also suspended payment of funds they had collected through a 5 percent tax on Palestinian workers in their countries. Financial aid and diplomatic support from the former Soviet bloc had already ceased.

The PLO's budget was cut in half. Its salary checks and payments of social welfare benefits to at least 150,000 Palestinian families in the territories were slashed. The institutions that were the bedrock of its power—universities, labor unions, hospitals, newspapers—deteriorated for lack of funds.

For years the central PLO based in Tunis had used money to maintain control over local Palestinians in the territories. The Tunis PLO was the master; the locals were pawns, preyed upon by Tunis, Israel and Jordan, who held the purse strings and benefited from the status quo. By asserting Palestinian independence, the intifada had destroyed Jordan's role—in August 1988 King Hussein had severed Jordan's financial links to the territories. And when the money dried up, the chains that bound the locals to Tunis loosened as well. New forces were emerging that were critical of the old Tunis-based hierarchy and willing to be more pragmatic in their dealings with Israel and with the world's sole remaining superpower, the United States. These same forces sought to reclaim an intifada that had slipped out of popular control and fallen into the hands of local thugs and street gangs. In the months following the Gulf War they killed three times as many of their fellow Palestinians as did the Israeli army.

For the first time, criticism of the PLO and Arafat appeared in the Palestinian press, most notably in *Al-Fajr,* an East Jerusalem daily that was funded by Fatah and generally held to be its mouthpiece. *Al-Fajr*'s maverick publisher, Paul Ajlouny, who directed the newspaper from his home in the United States, led the way in an article entitled "Revolution" in which he complained about the lack of accountability of PLO leaders. "Financial corruption is rampant and only seems to get worse," he wrote. "The outside leadership have no one to blame but themselves.

". . . We now have Palestinian representatives living in the most expensive neighborhoods in the cities of Europe and entertaining as lavishly as the embassies and consulates of the richest states. . . . The leadership seems to have studied the Marcos regime for tips on nepotism." He denounced the "incredible waste" and spending spree habits of unnamed "P.R. perkies" abroad who always flew first-class, treated PLO funds as their personal budget and barely bothered to conceal their sexual escapades. "The personal and even private lives of some representatives have come to resemble the smell of the open sewer running through the streets of a refugee camp on a hot August day," he asserted.

Ajlouny called for "spring cleaning" and asked readers to send him examples of PLO corruption. "We are not subjects looking for a king, or a dynasty," he concluded. "From now on, leadership will be earned by those who can lead."

The leader Ajlouny had in mind was not Yasser Arafat but a balding, fifty-year-old scion of one of Jerusalem's best-known Palestinian families. Faisal Husseini had been a Fatah member since the early 1960s and was considered one of Arafat's most loyal and trusted lieutenants. Husseini had spent most of the 1980s under house arrest or inside Israeli prisons, where he had studied Hebrew, read Israeli newspapers and conducted long discussions with his captors. He had listened and he had learned much about Israelis, their motives and their fears, and when he emerged from administrative detention in June 1988 after a six-month stint he began talking earnestly about a two-state solution.

No one could question Husseini's nationalist credentials. His uncle had been the notorious Mufti of Jerusalem, a politician of inflammatory rhetorical gifts who backed the Nazis during the Second World War. His father, Abdul Khader Husseini, was a guerrilla chieftain who fought against Israel in the 1948 Independence War and was killed in the battle for a strategic Crusader castle on the western edge of Jerusalem. Arafat himself was said to be a distant cousin and had often visited the Husseini household in Cairo during the 1950s when he was an engineering student and Faisal was growing up. After a brief army career in Syria, Faisal returned to Jordanian-ruled East Jerusalem in 1964, where he became an organizer for the fledgling PLO. After Israel took control Husseini spent one year in prison for possession of weapons.

Husseini had experienced firsthand the wounds of occupation. When his mother died in London in 1983, officials cited reasons of state security in denying him permission to bury her in East Jerusalem (later, after intervention from Israeli friends, the decision was reversed). During the early days of the intifada, his teenaged son was badly beaten by soldiers. Husseini himself was jostled and spat upon by a mob of Jewish extremists outside police headquarters in Jerusalem while a dozen policemen stood by.

He was an unusual blend of aristocrat, ward heeler and social worker. His living room was always crowded with supplicants, some arriving by donkey cart, who sought his counsel for burying a martyred son, paying the electric bill or finding a good match for an unmarried daughter. More than once he put aside his political work and ventured to some remote West Bank village to settle a blood feud between rival clans.

But Husseini had a sense of historical mission. He was in the crowd on October 8, 1990, when Israeli police opened fire on Palestinian protesters atop the Temple Mount, and he had held some of the victims as they died.

Since that day he had taken a more religious and more fatalistic view of his role and his destiny. "I know there is a bullet waiting for me somewhere but there's nothing I can do about it," he once told Janet Aviad, an Israeli friend. There was too much work to be done to worry about the personal consequences.

Few Israelis knew who Husseini was, so it was something of a surprise when this tall, dignified Arab with an easy manner and sincerity appeared before Israeli groups speaking in heavily accented Hebrew about two states, one for Israelis and one for Palestinians, coexisting side by side. "There has to be mutual recognition by both sides," Husseini told a Peace Now rally in West Jerusalem. "The Palestinian side has to recognize the existence of Israel. The Israeli side has to recognize the Palestinian right to self-determination." While he dreamed of one secular democratic state in all of Israel and the territories, Husseini told them, "I am not prepared to impose my dreams on others, just as they cannot impose theirs on me."

For the Israeli authorities, this kind of rhetoric was more dangerous than an army of stone throwers. It gave a political meaning to the intifada that no act of violence could. They responded to Husseini as they had reacted to the rebel moderates of Beit Sahur. Three days after the Peace Now rally Husseini was arrested again.

It was not only the Israelis who were made uneasy by Palestinian moderation. The PLO in Tunis had a major stake in the status quo. Its main constituency, the Palestinian exiles, had little interest in a two-state solution that might satisfy the needs of the 1.7 million Palestinians living in the occupied territories but do little to redress the claims of the 3 million others living abroad. Yasser Arafat had long presided over the PLO as a tribal chieftain. He wielded sole control over the movement's $200 million annual budget and $5 billion reserve while cautiously searching for the broadest consensus on political and diplomatic matters. It was a recipe for paralysis: Arafat and his aides may have sought to steer the organization toward more moderate positions, but at the same time they effectively had granted a veto to the most radical elements within it, while the Palestinians in the West Bank and Gaza had little influence.

The intifada had shifted the balance of power. Local Palestinians were rebelling not only against occupation but also against their own powerlessness within the Palestinian movement. The intifada had become a struggle of inside versus outside, East Jerusalem versus Tunis. The inside was less experienced on the world stage, but it was more pragmatic, more attuned to public opinion and more inclined to seek practical ways of easing the burden of occupation, even if that meant coming to terms with Israeli demands. Arafat, who was not unsympathetic to their plight and their politics, began invoking the insiders in his struggles with the radicals. When emerging leaders like Husseini pressed him to recognize Israel, Arafat told the doubters in Tunis, "If this is what our struggling brothers in the occupied territories demand, who are we to deny it to them?"

Of course, Arafat needed Husseini and the insiders to validate his diplomatic moves and to ward off the radicals. But Husseini and the pragmatists needed Arafat to grant them political protection and credibility. No one had elected Faisal Husseini leader of the West Bank. When his legitimacy was questioned, he evoked Arafat. "I am not the leader," he would reply, pointing to Tunis on the map. "The leader resides there."

Their relations were cautious. Arafat was a volatile and jealous ruler who basked in ambiguity and enjoyed playing off his subordinates. Husseini accumulated power gradually and quietly, but his every decision had to be cleared with the Old Man, and Arafat would not tolerate rivals. It took more than two years for Husseini to convince Arafat to allow the reopening of Orient House, a stately villa in East Jerusalem that came to serve as unofficial headquarters for local Palestinians.

Over the course of the intifada power shifted between the two Palestinian capitals. Husseini and the pragmatists rose on the crest of the rebellion. By the fall of 1988, with Husseini back in prison and the intifada running out of steam, Arafat seized the initiative and launched his diplomatic campaign to transform the energy of the intifada into concrete gains.

Because of Yitzhak Shamir's intransigence, American reluctance to intervene, and sabotage by Arab radicals, Arafat's initiative quickly stalled. His Gulf War blunder once again sapped his power and thrust forward Husseini and the locals. Privately, Husseini had condemned the invasion of Kuwait and criticized the PLO's support for Iraq. Publicly, he spoke in cautious terms and expressed regret for the Scud attacks on Israel. When the war ended badly for Arafat, Husseini was there to pick up the pieces.

More than anyone else in the Palestinian community, Husseini and his chief adviser, Palestinian intellectual Nusseibeh, understood that the world had changed following the Gulf crisis and the end of the Cold War. Although on the surface conditions looked glum for a movement that had lost two of its most powerful sponsors, Moscow and Baghdad, Husseini saw a unique opportunity for Palestinians to make progress toward their goal of an independent state. But they had to modify their tactics and show a willingness to compromise in ways they had never done before.

"We are facing a stage which follows many catastrophes," he told an audience of Palestinian supporters. "Now new regimes have come and there is a new world order. We must understand the rules of the new game so that we can face the challenge and reach our goal."

When James Baker came in March for the first of what turned out to be nine trips to the region, Husseini and a delegation of local Palestinians were there to meet with him. They claimed to be emissaries of Arafat, who had given his last-minute blessing to the session, but in fact they were, for the first time, calling some of the shots themselves. While PLO officials in Tunis at first issued statements rejecting the idea of a regional peace conference and then insisted that the Palestinians attend as a separate delegation, Husseini accepted the conference and the idea that Palestinians would be part of a joint delegation with Jordan. He considered these demands an unavoidable price to pay for admission to an event that might restore Palestinian stature following the Gulf War debacle.

Jad Isaac was not part of the delegation that met with Baker, but he was a key participant behind the scenes. Husseini and Nusseibeh appointed Isaac as head of the technical committees whose role was to begin drawing up plans to deal with problems such as commerce, agriculture, water and environment. In a real sense these groups, which started as a handful of technocrats meeting in a room, were laying the groundwork for a future Palestinian state.

"The peace process gave us a new momentum," said one of Husseini's closest advisers. "After nearly four years of intifada, we were readier than Tunis for the change. We had new figures, new ideas. We knew how to talk to the media. We were strengthened and the outside was weakened."

Faisal Husseini's secular pragmatists were not the only forces moving to fill the vacuum left by the weakened PLO. Islamic fundamentalists were also on the rise. They did not have the funds to substitute for Arafat's movement, but they offered Palestinians something that money could not buy—dignity, self-respect, incorruptibility and a sense of religious certitude that played well among people who had been battered by their enemy and had lost faith in their own institutions and leaders.

Kemal Abu Arer's story was not unusual. A thin young man in wire-rimmed glasses and neatly trimmed beard, he had been an active and loyal Fatah member as a teenager in Gaza City until 1988, when Yasser Arafat had renounced terrorism and recognized the state of Israel. Abu Arer's teachers had taught him the gospel of Palestinian irredentism, and nothing he had heard over the years had prepared him for this sudden turnabout. "They had taught me to work for the liberation of all of Palestine," he recalled. "They taught me that we were not terrorists but freedom fighters. So what was Arafat doing?

"I began to question other things as well—the finances, the tactics, the morals. One day I asked my cell leader for a match and I found hashish in his matchbox. What kind of revolution was this? There was mixing between girls and boys and there was dirty talk. Some of it was disgusting."

In 1989 Abu Arer was arrested and thrown into Ketziot prison for twenty months. There he saw a real contrast between the cynical, corrupt ranks of local Fatah leaders and the younger, more devoted cadres of Hamas, the Islamic resistance movement. "When I was released from the interrogation section and put in with the other prisoners, I found a big difference between Hamas and Fatah. During the holy days of Ramadan the Fatah leaders did not fast, did not pray. Yet they criticized Hamas and Islamic Jihad as if they were the enemy, not the Israelis. The Fatah tents had their own groups and rivalries. No one welcomed me, no one cared about me. There was no community.

"On the Hamas side there was more cooperation and good feeling. They made me feel welcome. They offered me food and clothes. I felt that they cared about me and I started becoming Islamicized, praying and listening to religious lessons. Islam became everything to me."

When Abu Arer got out of prison, he could see that Hamas's support had grown back home in Gaza. Islamic blocs had won elections in trade unions and universities. Women had taken to wearing veils in public. Liquor shops had closed, as had movie houses. "You could feel Islam in the street. It existed everywhere."

Young men like Abu Arer were long on emotions, if short on political logic. They said they wanted peace, but they also seemed prepared to wage endless war against Israel. "We can live with the Jews, but not in their own state," Abu Arer said. "We will never surrender. It doesn't matter if it goes on another hundred years."

But, he was asked, how would the Palestinians defeat the Israelis, who had won every war they had fought and who were so much stronger militarily and economically? Wasn't there really no choice but to do what Arafat and Faisal Husseini were seeking to do—cut your best deal and make peace? "It's true that so far the Jews haven't lost a war, but maybe things will be different in the future," Abu Arer replied. "Remember, the Soviet Union collapsed as a superpower almost overnight. So you never know. Israel isn't as strong as you think. The Jews have always won because we Palestinians have been weak and divided. That won't always be true."

Hamas was dangerous because it had simple answers to complicated problems. Palestinians like Abu Arer had grown up on the easy answers they had learned from the PLO. But now the PLO was speaking a more complex and nuanced language. Especially in Gaza, which had always been poorer and more Islamic-oriented, many could not accept the new words. Hamas, with its rhetoric of Allah and blood and the Koran, attracted fanatics, but it also attracted conservatives who were offended by the PLO's deteriorating morals and motives and were ready for a change in leadership. Like Yitzhak Shamir's Likud, the PLO was a movement that had been in power too long. It had grown fat and distant from people's concerns and fears. Hamas became the unofficial opposition.

The Islamic movement's strategists aimed their fiery rhetoric at Israel, but they understood that their first enemy was the PLO. Before he was deported in 1992, Abdel Rantisi, a Hamas leader in Gaza, spoke about the movement's strategy with Brigadier General Danny Rothschild, who had left his job as deputy head of Military Intelligence to become the military coordinator for the occupied territories. Rantisi spoke cautiously with the Israeli general, but over the course of six hours he explained that Hamas's goal was to replace the PLO as the sole legitimate representative of the Palestinian people. The movement had no intention of shooting its way to power, Rantisi insisted. Islamists had tried that course in Egypt with the assassination of Anwar Sadat in 1981 and it had backfired.

"We're not a gun-type revolution," Rantisi told Rothschild. "We're not interested in shooting the head of the pyramid. So how will we do it? By establishing a very wide base at the bottom of the society and pushing upward. And then when there's a vacuum at the top, we will fill it."

It was a shrewd, rational analysis. But there was a side to the fundamentalist movement that was more visceral, that celebrated vengeance, not patience, and took solace and joy in the blood of its enemies. It was this side of the movement that arrived in Jerusalem soon after the Gulf War ended, carrying an eighteen-inch butcher knife.

Mohammed Mustafa Abu Jalala was twenty-six years old and he hailed from Jabaliya, the Palestinian refugee camp in the Gaza Strip where the intifada had begun three years and three months earlier. A tall, heavyset man, he had worked as a nursing attendant in an East Jerusalem hospital and he had recently become engaged to another nurse. They were due to be married in six months.

March 10, 1991, was a crisp, bright afternoon, nearly spring. Abu Jalala wore a black leather jacket and dark brown pants, and he carried a package of clean, ironed clothes—a beige shirt and pants—that he carefully laid on the side of Henrietta Szold Street, which winds along a high spine of western hills to Hadassah Hospital. He held the butcher knife under his jacket and carried a second, nine-inch jagged-edged blade taped to his chest with bandages.

The first thing anyone heard was the piercing scream of *"Allah Akhbar!"* ("God Is Great!") as Abu Jalala grabbed Benita Mercedes, a kindergarten

teacher and mother of four. He swung one arm around her neck and pulled
her to the ground. She was so stunned, a witness recalled later, she could
not even scream. He rammed the butcher knife into her chest and stomach
three times, puncturing her lungs and her heart.

He dashed to a nearby bus stop, moving so fast that two middle-aged
women sitting on a bench, Rosa Elispur and Bella Levitzky, had no time to
react. He plunged the knife twice into each one with such force that the tip
of the blade emerged from their backs.

Passersby who saw what had happened scrambled for cover. A motorist
tried to run Abu Jalala down, but his car rammed into a metal traffic barrier. An off-duty police detective named Moshe jammed on his brakes and
jumped from his car. He pulled out his service revolver and took aim with
both hands, but he could not get a clear shot through the fleeing pedestri-
ans. He chased after Abu Jalala on foot, firing in the air and shouting at the
man to halt.

Moshe was too late to save Miriam Biton, a slight twenty-one-year-old
factory worker who was crossing the street. Abu Jalala ripped at her chest
with a single blow. Then as he turned toward an old man on the sidewalk,
Moshe fired five low shots, hitting Abu Jalala four times in the legs and
lower body. He collapsed on the pavement.

Bystanders turned on Abu Jalala, screaming "Murderer! Murderer!"
Moshe pried the knife from his hand, then shielded him from the crowd.
Within moments a patrol car pulled up and took Abu Jalala away. The inci-
dent took no more than two minutes.

Two of the victims were beyond hope. The other two were rushed to
Hadassah. Both died within hours. They were treated in the same emer-
gency room as Abu Jalala. Witnesses said that he seemed to be in a trance.
The only words he uttered that day: "This is the Palestinian answer to
Baker"—the U.S. secretary of state who was about to arrive in Jerusalem
for a first round of post–Gulf War shuttle diplomacy.

Ironically, Abu Jalala's cry was echoed by some of the hundreds of enraged Jewish Jerusalemites who took to the streets that night, burning tires
and garbage. They chanted "Baker Go Home!" on nearby Guatemala Street
as they threw rocks at Arab cars bearing blue West Bank license plates. Fifteen men broke into a grocery store near the scene of the stabbings, looking for the Arabs who worked as clerks inside. Police arrived in time to
rescue the workers. Disturbances went on past midnight. Yitzhak Shamir
called the murders "the act of a rabid dog."

But what was more disturbing was the way Abu Jalala's act was received
in Jabaliya. It was endorsed by graffiti writers on the walls of the refugee
camp and invoked with approval by fundamentalists. They saw the deed as

suitable vengeance for Israeli killings of Palestinians in the occupied territories. The stabbings were more than one Palestinian's statement of who he was and who Israelis were. They were an outcry from a maimed, bitter community that no longer seemed to care who lived and who died.

Hamas was an Israeli nightmare come to life. Just as the PLO was beginning to move in more pragmatic directions, Hamas arose to take its place. It was a product of political frustration and economic squalor, and the long process of brutalization that scarred relations between Arabs and Jews.

Tamar Peleg, a Tel Aviv lawyer working with the Association for Civil Rights in Israel, saw that process close at hand. Peleg spent much of her time in Gaza defending Palestinian detainees in military court. Over the course of the intifada she had seen a steady deterioration in the way her clients were treated. Despite the 1987 Landau Commission report that purportedly set strict limits on the use of what it delicately called "physical pressure," Israeli interrogators were using more and more physical abuse to extract confessions. No acts were unrelated—the increase in Israeli abuses fueled the increase in Palestinian violence. And, of course, the gruesome stabbings and acts of murder by Palestinians were a green light to interrogators to intensify their own worst techniques.

"Interrogation is held on a gradually increasing scale," Peleg explained. "First they request cooperation from the prisoner and warn him, if he doesn't talk then what comes next will be his own fault. Then at the next session they slap and kick, tie his hands, maybe choke him or squeeze his genitals. The system is so deeply rooted and the people involved have their habits and routines. No one can change it. They do it to people who don't exist to them, who aren't real. To people we don't know and to a community where the only thing we know about them is that they hate us."

Torture and physical abuse were the invisible factors in the Arab-Jewish equation. Despite the best efforts of Israeli human rights groups such as Btselem and the Public Committee Against Torture to document cases, most Israelis preferred not to know about it. Such abuses were part of the unpleasant price of occupation and of combating terrorism. The less said, the better. Even physicians and senior military people never ventured into the isolation wings of military prisons where interrogations took place.

James Ron, a researcher for Middle East Watch, was one of the few who tried. He found a twenty-eight-year-old army reserve sergeant who had served in the interrogation wing at Faraa prison in the West Bank during the intifada. The soldier estimated he had beaten between 250 and 300 Palestinians during his month-long duty in 1988. Ron withheld the man's name from the transcript of his interview, parts of which follow:

SOLDIER: They took me inside a room and there was an interrogator there, he was in an army uniform, but he was Druze. . . . There was a detainee there, and they told me to hit him. I did.

Afterwards I didn't like it. I said, "Look, this is not for me, thanks a lot, I don't want to do this." So they showed me the detainee's file and said, "This guy is a terrorist, he killed Ofra Moses,* now you see, we need to do this. . . ." And then you are willing to keep doing it. So I kept going, until the end of my reserve duty.

My job was to guard the interrogator. I stood inside the room with the interrogator and the detainee. . . . And they would talk, talking in Arabic. I don't understand Arabic. And then, when the interrogator didn't get the answer he wanted, he made a sign, and I hit the detainee.

RON: What did you hit him with?

SOLDIER: With a club, my hand, foot, anything. . . .

RON: Were there any orders about how to beat?

SOLDIER: No, nothing. They would just say, "Try not to kill him." That's all. We hit them everywhere: head, face, mouth, arms, balls.

RON: Did everyone talk?

SOLDIER: Everyone talked in the end. Some, it took ten minutes. Others, it took three days of going in and out of interrogation. In the end, everyone talked.

RON: Describe the beating to me.

SOLDIER: The beating? What, are you kidding?. . . . Have you ever seen a broken arm before?

RON: No. What does it look like?

SOLDIER: The arm is all straight, up until a certain point, and then just collapses, goes down, at an angle, just hanging there.

RON: Did you break many bones?

SOLDIER: More than I can remember. . . .

RON: Was there much screaming?

SOLDIER: Screaming? Everyone screamed, all the time. From almost the first minute they came into the room, they were crying, screaming. You could hear the screams in the cells and in the yards, that was part of the whole idea. They wanted them to see and to hear.

Taher Shriteh, a thirty-year-old Gazan who worked as a news stringer for Reuters, CBS News, the *Washington Post* and the *New York Times,* was not beaten during his brief spell in jail. His imprisonment was unremarkable, just one man's humiliation inside a system geared to break down and humiliate thousands. But Shriteh's arrest and mistreatment—for the crime of

* The Jewish settler killed along with her son in a firebomb attack on her car in April 1987.

using a facsimile machine—was another window on how unhinged Israeli methods had become.

Shriteh was a slender, handsome man with short-cropped, curly brown hair, a coffee-with-cream complexion and a trim mustache. His best feature was his smile, a wry, open grin that lit up his face.

The son of a pharmacist refugee and one of twelve children, Shriteh had graduated with honors from Cairo University and had studied graduate engineering for three years at the University of Wisconsin. But he returned to Gaza in 1987 to find his education a useless ornament. He answered an advertisement in an Israeli Arab newspaper seeking a Gaza correspondent for $200 per month, and he eventually parlayed that into better-paying stringing arrangements with Reuters, CBS News and the *Washington Post,* among others. Shriteh quickly won a reputation for being fast and reliable. "Don't make things up; the truth is bad enough!" he had been lectured by Daoud Kuttab, one of the West Bank's foremost journalists, and Shriteh had taken the advice to heart.

After the intifada began, Shriteh became indispensable to his overseas clients—and a thorn in the flesh of the army. His first day on the job with CBS News on December 9 coincided with the first day of the uprising. Shriteh ended up ferrying Bob Simon and his camera crew through an urban battle zone. It was stunning television and, thanks largely to Shriteh, CBS got some of the best shots.

When Simon returned to Gaza City the next day, Shriteh took him and his crew to Omar Mukhtar Street, the city's main shopping district, where merchants were honoring a strike called by the activists. Israeli troops were going door-to-door ripping off the metal security grates of shop owners who refused to open, sometimes dumping merchandise out on the sidewalks. When the military commander of Gaza City saw Shriteh and Simon's crew working together, he exploded.

In Arabic, he screamed at Shriteh: "You! Come here! It's unbelievable! What the fuck are you doing here? Give me your ID! I'm going to blow up your fucking house! Arrest all your brothers! Fuck you, you come with me!"

Shriteh got off easy that day—Simon accompanied him to military headquarters and insisted on staying with him until he was released. But he was now on the army's list. In January soldiers ransacked his house, breaking windows and tipping over bookshelves and furniture. In February he was arrested a second time and held for several hours blindfolded and handcuffed in the rain. Later that month soldiers dumped a concrete block through his car windshield and slashed his tires.

In October 1989 soldiers raided his house again, confiscating his phone book and other materials he used as a journalist. The military investigator who ordered the raid telephoned Palestinian names he found in Shriteh's book and ordered them to appear at military headquarters to explain why they were helping Shriteh gather information. The investigator stopped after there was a query from the *New York Times,* one of Shriteh's clients.

But Shriteh's real troubles began in January 1991, when the Israelis mounted a crackdown on Hamas. Among those arrested in the early sweeps was Yusuf Haddad, a lawyer who was a neighbor and old classmate of Shriteh. Haddad had given Shriteh his most precious possession for safe-keeping, his facsimile machine, and Shriteh frequently used it to transmit news to Reuters in Jerusalem. This was a crime under Israeli law. Fax machines had been restricted in Gaza since August 1989, when the authorities had issued an order requiring written permission to own one. After three days of questioning Haddad had broken down and told the Israelis where he had stashed the fax.

Soldiers came for Shriteh on the afternoon of January 28 and hauled him away to the Gaza City prison known to the locals as *al-Maaslah* ("The Slaughterhouse"). They handcuffed his arms behind his back and slipped a foul-smelling gray canvas hood over his head, stripped him of his civilian clothes and gave him a pair of rough brown pajamas. Then the questions began.

"I decided not to hide anything," he recalled later. "I thought they would hold me only for a few hours. They asked me, 'Do you know Yusuf?' I said, 'Yes, he's my friend, an old college classmate, a neighbor and a junior leader of Hamas. Yes, he gave me his fax machine, and yes, I do use it.' Don't you know it's illegal? 'Of course,' I told them."

The Gaza City prison included "The Bus," a long corridor between interrogation rooms where men were kept hooded all day with their hands cuffed behind their backs, sitting on child-sized chairs. Between sessions Shriteh sat there in the darkness. His hood, which stank from sweat and urine, came down to his shoulders and blocked out all light. He gnawed tiny holes into the fabric, producing small rays of light. No one was allowed to move or speak. Notes were slapped on the prisoners' backs saying when they had last been taken to the toilet or been fed.

At the end of the day Shriteh was taken to a small boxed cell known as "The Grave." He had no window, no blanket and no heat, just the cold tile floor in a cubicle of about five by two and a half feet. February was the coldest month of the year in Gaza, so he huddled and shivered. Every hour a guard would bang on the door to keep him awake. "I felt so frightened. I remember that I just wanted to die. No one beat me—I was a special case because of my connection to foreign journalists. But I could hear the screams of other prisoners. The first day I wet my pants because they would not let me use the toilet. The urine spilled into the hallway. They screamed at me and gave me a dirty rag to clean it up. They humiliated me."

The treatment continued for eleven days. "They had a thick file on me that must have come from informers: Taher was at this demonstration, Taher was with that journalist. They wanted to know who I had sent faxes to. And they wanted to know which faction I belonged to. They also wanted to know my sources and my contacts. I insisted I was an independent journalist. This angered them greatly. But on the eleventh day the interrogator asked me, 'Do you want to see a lawyer?' I knew then it was over—you only get a lawyer after the interrogation is over."

Shriteh's interrogation was finished, but he spent ten more days in solitary confinement before he was taken for a bail hearing. Many of his colleagues from the foreign press came to see him. As he spoke to them before the military court convened, he tried to hold back tears. The hearing was conducted in Hebrew, a language Shriteh does not speak, without an interpreter.

The prosecutor said that by sending off facsimiles of the Hamas leaflets to Reuters, Shriteh was "giving aid to an enemy organization." When asked by the judge, the prosecutor conceded that Shriteh himself was not a member of Hamas, "but his activities are assisting it." He had allegedly violated Egyptian Law 32, last revised in 1948, which granted the authorities the power to regulate telephone and telegraphic equipment.

Shriteh insisted he was nothing but a journalist. "I am neutral. I am Palestinian but I don't work for any group. This is my job."

But the judge said that in accepting the fax machine Shriteh had crossed the line into illegality. He also cited classified evidence that supposedly linked Shriteh to Hamas. Neither the defendant nor his Israeli lawyer was allowed to see the evidence. Bail was denied.

After nearly a month in solitary confinement Shriteh was transferred from The Slaughterhouse to the tented beach camp known as Ansar Two. The prison guards there kicked and screamed at recalcitrant prisoners, the nights in the tents were often freezing cold, and the food was meager and badly cooked. Nonetheless, compared to The Slaughterhouse it was heaven.

Twelve days after Shriteh's transfer the court reversed its decision and he was released on $5,000 bail, paid by Reuters. Eventually he was charged on four counts: illegal possession and use of the facsimile machine, illegal publication of a book on Palestinians killed during the intifada and failure to report to the authorities on illegal activities of fellow Palestinians.

Shriteh had spent thirty-eight days in prison, twenty-six of them in solitary confinement. When he was released on bail on March 7 he had lost thirty-three pounds.

More than two years and seven hearings later, Shriteh's trial was still pending.

In his memoir in which he recounts his experiences as deputy mayor of Jerusalem, Meron Benvenisti recalls an exchange he once had with a visiting South African official who was interested in Israel's scheme for allowing Palestinians to manage their own affairs. "How would you react if we were to invite you to advise the new regime in Transkei?" the South African asked him.

Benvenisti was shocked. The question implied that the South African considered Israeli policy comparable to apartheid. The official was bemused by his indignation. "I understand your reaction. But aren't we actually doing the same thing? We are faced with the same existential problem, therefore we arrive at the same solution. The only difference is that yours is pragmatic and ours is ideological. Yes, we are all in love with our own compromises."

Like black and white South Africans, and Catholics and Protestants in Northern Ireland, Palestinians and Israelis had become locked in what Albert Camus called the "fatal embrace" of two peoples sealed by history and hatred, who could neither live together nor live apart. Each group viewed the other not as political opponents but as mortal enemies. Negotiation with such an enemy was a form of betrayal. Security forces operated at the edge of legality and often well beyond—all in the name of survival. Yet despite the abuses, state power had its limits. Governments had to answer to a limited extent to outside forces and to critics within their own ranks. They could suppress revolts but could not totally silence opponents. Both sides became locked in a process of brutalization; the abuses meted out in the name of the state were echoed, and at times exceeded, by the abuses the oppressed dealt out to their rulers and to each other.

The Gulf War had been a terrible blow to the Israeli peace camp and to moderate Palestinians as well. But when the dust settled, both sides actually appeared to have gained strength. The war had given Israeli doves new arguments for relinquishing the occupied territories. And it had given Palestinian pragmatists new power within their own beleaguered and divided community.

An open letter written soon after the Iraqi invasion of Kuwait had captured a small piece of the truth. In it the sixteen dovish members of the Knesset who had tried and failed to come to terms with Faisal Husseini and his followers over the invasion of Kuwait issued a prophetic warning:

"Those who think that the aggression of Saddam Hussein and the serious errors of the Palestinian leadership can lend credence to the perpetuation of ruling over another nation are mistaken. After the dust settles and the Gulf has calmed down, there will still be two peoples in this land. Two peoples who will find themselves living in a hell unless the conflict between them is resolved by peaceful means."

11. Farewell to the Kibbutz

*Once upon a time the pioneers of Palestine wore
khaki shorts and lived on crude settlements. They
spoke the language of ideals and lived for redemption through toil. Their grandchildren wear khaki
only for gardening or washing the car, and their
notion of self-improvement runs to Italian lessons
and Weight Watchers.*

—ZEEV CHAFETS

As the decade turned and the 1990s began, Israel's public record was dominated by large, wrenching events: the intifada, the stalled peace process,
the Russian *aliya,* the Gulf War, the slowly gelling confrontation between
Washington and Jerusalem, and the collapse of the Soviet Empire. But a
second, less dramatic narrative was unfolding offstage. Hidden from the
headlines and the sound bites, Israel's centralized, socialist-oriented economic establishment was slowly crumbling, giving way piece by piece to
new institutions, new ideas, and new ways of making and spending money.

It was like the thawing of a huge glacier. And in many ways it was the
real story of Israel, a change more profound and irreversible than anything
that happened on the battlefield or in the polling booth.

Israelis could trace the shift in the explosive growth in consumer spending, in the dramatic increase in unemployment and in the appearance on
the shelves of a wide range of foreign products. They could see it in the
huge increase in the number of privately owned cars on the road, in the de-
cline of public transportation, in the mushrooming of a vast service econ-

omy and in the increase in foreign travel. And they could see it in the declining economic and political power of the *ancien régime* and in the rise of new elites.

No place was more evocative of the old Israel than the kibbutz. It was here that the Zionist pioneers had first combined their dream of returning to the Promised Land with their vision of a socialist community. It was here that the founding fathers had built their liberated New Man—a Jew freed from sycophantic mercantile pursuits to work the soil. But no place was more shaken and damaged by the convulsions that marked the transition from the old centralized economy to the new, slowly emerging, free-market Israel. Just as the kibbutz had once been a symbol of a bright young nation, so it became a metaphor for the collapse of the old order and the death of an ideology and a way of life.

Gonen means "defender." Kibbutz Gonen started in the early 1950s as a desolate outpost about five hundred yards below the Syrian border on the western slope of the Golan Heights, sandwiched between Syrian artillery to the east and the stagnant, malarial Hula Valley swamp to the west. The idea was to settle aspiring young farmers with military training who could both develop the land and defend it against attack. Slowly Gonen and other kibbutzim in the picturesque Upper Galilee region made their mark on the Hula. Over a seven-year period they drained the swamp, uprooted its thick papyrus jungle and transformed it into farmland, artificial fish ponds and fruit-tree orchards—a multimillion-dollar project that symbolized the youthful vigor and pioneering spirit of the new Jewish state. They fought to a standstill the Syrians, who periodically shelled the area or staged infiltration raids and whose snipers always sat on the first ridge, taking potshots at cows, sheep and herders. The kibbutzniks also built a paved road to connect Gonen and the other settlements below the brow of the Golan to the main highway. But the settlement's main purpose remained military; with the Syrian threat so close, its economic prospects were grim.

Haim Goren came to the kibbutz in 1964 as a nineteen-year-old member of a paramilitary unit known as Nahal. The son of Jews who had fled prewar Germany, Goren was attracted to the kibbutz ethic of socialism and self-reliance. When his Nahal duty ended he stayed on at Gonen as a regular member. Ayala Brodsky arrived two years later in a similar army unit. Theirs was a typically utilitarian kibbutz romance: On the first night they met she accepted Goren's invitation to join him while he sprayed the orchard with pesticides. Two years later they were married.

Goren's day would begin at 4 A.M. bathed in darkness. He would stumble blindly out of bed, pull on sweater and pants, and drag himself up the dirt path to the dining room for a hunk of yesterday's bread and a cup of muddy coffee. Then it was off to the waiting truck and a jangling fifteen-minute ride to the orchard. There he would struggle to coax the cold, sullen motor of the picking machine into life, clamber on and set to work, pulling dew-coated fruit from its branches and depositing it in thick canvas sacks that hung like nests from his perch. He and his fellow kibbutzniks were tough, hardy and permanently tanned men who knew how to start engines and fix tractors, how to tell which trees were ready for picking and which needed a few more days, how to pick five sacks of pears in an hour without bruising the fruit or losing their balance atop the tall young trees.

There was nothing about him that stood out physically. He was not tall or powerfully built, and he wore the same ridiculous floppy hat, torn shirt, surplus shorts and makeshift sandals that were standard issue for kibbutzniks. But he exuded an air of self-confidence, intelligence and resourcefulness, a sense that whatever the problem was, he could solve it. And people believed in him. At twenty-one Goren was put in charge of a key part of the orchard, the economic backbone of the kibbutz. Indeed, in many ways Goren (everyone called him by his last name, even Ayala) was the kibbutz and the kibbutz was Goren.

American journalist Gertrude Samuels, who journeyed to the Hula at around this time, portrays Gonen as the model kibbutz. What struck her most was the selflessness and idealism of its members. Her romantic description in her book *The Secret of Gonen* might easily have fit Goren: "The kibbutznik by nature and by choice is a solitary person and a visionary. He is motivated by a vision of a communal society, peopled by idealists like himself who seek a truly democratic way of life on the land, fighting a hostile nature and hostile neighbors. . . . With immense inner resources he is typically a quiet man who has given up material values for higher aspirations in his life and his work."

For the kibbutzniks of Gonen, the Six-Day War started as trauma and ended as triumph. Like Goren, who served in the paratroopers, most of the men were called up for reserve military duty and shuttled south to the Sinai, where Israel launched its opening strike against Egyptian forces, leaving almost all of northern Israel shorn of defenses. The remaining men, women and children at Gonen, Ayala included, huddled in underground shelters to escape Syrian shelling. Had the Syrian army chosen to attack, it could have overrun Gonen within hours. The Syrian fighters were known for their cruelty, and the kibbutzniks knew they could face mass slaughter.

Still, not one kibbutznik chose to flee to safer ground. They stayed to set an example—to each other and to the country as a whole. "I think the worst effect of all, if mothers and children are evacuated, is not only the impact on those who remain behind, but also on the country itself," Yigal Gil, Gonen's head of security, explained to Samuels. "For people everywhere might begin to think that Israel was losing its borders. This was our home. Our wives and children and babies stayed."

The Syrian assault never came. Instead, on the final day of the war the IDF pushed its way up the heights and evicted the Syrian army. The new cease-fire lines gave Gonen fifteen more miles of breathing space from the siege guns and allowed the kibbutz at last to become a thriving farm community.

In those first years after the war, Gonen was bathed in an air of optimism, power and pride. When the kibbutzniks knocked off early one Friday and took their foreign volunteer workers to Jerusalem for a weekend sightseeing tour, they insisted on taking the winding road through the West Bank, stopping just north of the Holy City at the half-built, hurriedly abandoned summer palace of King Hussein. There, from a once-forbidden hill, they could see across Israel's narrow waist to watch the sun set over the Mediterranean, a sight that had once belonged solely to the Arab ruler of Jordan, now possessed by the proud young kings of Zion.

The kibbutz movement was just one component of a ruling Labor Zionist establishment that had wielded enormous economic and political power since the birth of the nation. It was as if in the United States the Democratic Party controlled not only the AFL-CIO, but Wall Street, Main Street and General Motors as well. When an Israeli went to work, when he went to the bank, when he shopped at a supermarket or downtown department store, when he bought a liter of milk or a newspaper, when he took out insurance or bought an apartment, chances were better than even that he was dealing with a Labor-owned firm.

Forged by David Ben-Gurion, Yitzhak Ben-Zvi and Israel's other founding fathers, the Labor establishment was a web of institutions—including a political party, central land agency, militia and school system, as well as the kibbutzim—that in the 1920s became the foundation of a state-in-the-making. The founding fathers sprang from the same soil as the Bolsheviks, and the system they built, while far less brutal than that of the Soviet Union, was no less centralized. As one annual guide noted, it included: "One farm-produce exporter. One beef importer. One television station. Twenty-three industries dominated by sanctioned monopolies. Plenty of near-monopolies: in health maintenance, confections, pasta, dairy products. . . . Cartels, trusts and guilds: in hotels, auto mechanics, publishers, even among writers and translators. Big, united enterprises in a small, fractious country. . . . Governments that nurtured the system with multiple exchange rates, preferential credit terms and towering trade barriers. Agriculture regulated to the last orange. A telephone? Order one for your unborn children."

At the center of the web was the General Federation of Workers in the Land of Israel, known as the Histadrut, a combination trade union and industrial conglomerate. As a labor federation it boasted the membership of nearly half the country's population. As an employer it accounted for 25 percent of the country's gross national product. It owned Israel's largest bank, construction firm, insurance company, department store chain and dairy cooperative. It also owned the country's largest health-clinic network, to which 85 percent of the population belonged.

When the community had been a small, struggling society, the Histadrut saw to it that no one starved or went without work. When in the late 1940s the new state was inundated with nearly a million refugees, the Histadrut and its factories absorbed the newcomers and became the central engine of a remarkably productive economy. Growth rates averaged 6 to 8 percent per year through 1973. Labor also helped develop from scratch one of the world's most sophisticated defense and armaments industries. It controlled land, jobs, housing, schools, even the price of bread. Its bosses decided who got good jobs and who got no job at all.

Along with the production lines and the collectives and the socialist ideology, the Labor establishment helped create something else: the predominately European pioneer elite. Paternalistic, self-confident, and hierarchical, its members walked more erectly, spoke with a more cultured accent, wore simpler and tasteful clothes, listened to better music. These were the "Real Israelis," the bearers of the Zionist faith. Working-class Sephardim from North Africa and the Middle East were somehow less authentic. In the classless society there were, in fact, two distinct classes.

The kibbutzniks were card-carrying members of the elite. The way they lived in Israel was a rejection of their ancestors' European past. They lived in collectivist settlements where they pooled their savings, resources and profits. The early Zionists had an almost mystical belief in the redemptive qualities of physical labor. Through their sweat they would come to own the land, and the land would own them.

The Six-Day War marked the apex of the Labor establishment's power and glory, a time when the freshly conquered West Bank seemed a treasure rather than the time bomb it would become. The kibbutz had supplied many of the war's heroes and was in the vanguard of victory. The kibbutzim and their cousins, the moshavim cooperatives, constituted 4 percent of the workforce, but they produced 12 percent of the country's gross national product and a substantial chunk of the army officer corps.

The orchard became the centerpiece of the new Gonen. Goren worked there for nine years, the last three as manager. But the war that had liberated the kibbutz as a farming enterprise also held the seeds of its destruction. The cooler heights atop the newly captured Golan turned out to be ideal for growing apples, and the kibbutz's primary agricultural product soon lost its competitive edge.

Then came the 1973 Yom Kippur War and the Arab oil embargo. The oil crisis damaged Israeli agriculture in ways it never recovered from. Those who could not compete were soon wiped out, Gonen's orchard among them.

The war damaged Goren as well. After several days of chaos Goren and his army unit found themselves on the western side of the Suez Canal, driving north toward Ismailia as part of the IDF's daring counterattack. His battalion was ambushed and some of his friends were killed. On the second day the shelling started again. Goren found himself shaking uncontrollably and wandered shell-shocked through the battlefield.

The IDF's commanders had no time for victims of battle fatigue, and the army's methods of coping with it were primitive. "They gave me an injection of some sort of tranquilizer and sent me back alone to the other side of the canal," Goren recalled. "I spent a day back at Gonen, but I couldn't stay away, I had to go back. I found my unit sitting in front of Ismailia. There were raids and bombings every day. I started shaking again. This time they took me to the regimental clinic. There they told me to go home and not come back."

In some ways the kibbutz was the ideal place to recover. Goren was among friends, a valued member of an extended family that paid for his medical treatment and protected him. Yet he felt smothered and restless. Gonen could not hold him any longer. He developed a passion for travel, becoming an expert on geography and historical sites in Israel, exploring every nook and cranny. When Israel itself proved too small to contain his energy, Goren focused on the captured Sinai Peninsula, taking charge of the kibbutz's volunteer workers and organizing two trips a year to the vast, empty desert kingdom.

While Goren was changing, so was Israel. In 1977 the victory of Menachem Begin and Likud marked the end of Labor's twenty-nine-year political hegemony, even though economic power shifted more slowly. Despite the lip service he paid to free market reforms and his sniping at "millionaire kibbutzniks," Begin made no real attempt to undermine the Histadrut or the kibbutzim. The Histadrut's problems stemmed instead from socialist arteriosclerosis, from featherbedding, rigid union work rules, phony bookkeeping, favoritism, nepotism and managers who were petty bureaucrats or party hacks.

Begin's government contributed to the damage with its inept economic policies. In 1981 Finance Minister Yoram Aridor created an artificial boom to help assure the Likud leader's reelection, printing millions of new shekels and drastically lowering customs duties on cars, televisions and other luxury items. The result was a burst of triple-digit inflation and an explosion of consumer debt. Suddenly, it seemed, every family had a foreign-made color television set in its living room and a car in the garage. Inflation became so manic that people spent any cash on hand immediately because they knew it could be worth 20 percent less by the next morning. Yet because virtually all salaries were indexed to the inflation rate, Israelis suffered little direct economic pain. They learned to adjust and began living on borrowed time and money.

By 1984 the damage to the economy was so massive that voters finally called a halt, forcing the two large parties into a national unity government with a mandate to tame inflation. Israelis absorbed an effective 25 percent cut in salaries virtually overnight in an effort that, combined with the liberalization of credit controls, quickly brought inflation down to a 20 to 30 percent annual level. Government restrictions were eased and cheap credit vanished. Those who had borrowed heavily faced punitively high interest rates and a bottomless pit of debt.

Many of the Histadrut's companies found it impossible to adjust. They were designed to serve their managers and workers, not the market. As trade barriers were lowered and their products were forced to compete against higher-quality, lower-priced foreign goods, many Histadrut firms lost their customers and could not pay their debts. Koor, the country's largest manufacturing conglomerate, tottered on the edge of bankruptcy after its largest foreign creditor, Bankers Trust Company, demanded immediate payment of $20 million in overdue loans. The government spent millions each year in bailouts for Histadrut-owned defense plants, insurance companies and construction firms. The country's major banks—all of them controlled by Histadrut, other quasi-public institutions and political parties—were caught manipulating their share prices on the Tel Aviv Stock Exchange in a scandal that eventually cost Israeli taxpayers a staggering $7 billion.

The kibbutzim were also trapped in the crisis. They had borrowed enormous sums during the Begin boom to build new housing for their members and embark on hundreds of commercial projects. Some had plowed their profits into the stock exchange in an effort to stay one step ahead of the soaring inflation rate. When the bottom fell out the country's 290 kibbutzim were left with a $4 billion debt and double-digit interest rates. They were forced to plead on their knees to an increasingly hostile Finance Ministry.

The proud, self-reliant socialists of the kibbutzim became one of Israel's biggest welfare clients.

Gonen was not immune. A new wood-products factory proved unprofitable, and the general collapse of agriculture virtually finished off what was left of its farm. As their debts rose and their world began to collapse, the kibbutzniks turned inward and restrictive. Gonen stopped paying for members to take long-scheduled overseas trips, yet refused to allow them to set aside private money or use cash gifts from relatives. Members who asked for permission to work outside the kibbutz were criticized. This policy was especially tough for women, who were largely confined to working in Gonen's laundry or children's nursery and often denied opportunities for more interesting work outside the kibbutz. And like many kibbutzim, Gonen was growing older and more stagnant because the grown children of the first- and second-generation members were leaving for better opportunities in Israel's cities.

Goren watched it all with growing sadness and then despair. As a true believer in the kibbutz ethic, he had first become disgusted with the selfishness of his fellow members when he had been put in charge of housing construction and observed the way purported socialists fought for bigger living rooms and better refrigerators. Now he became disillusioned with their doomed efforts to maintain a facade of collectivism in an increasingly capitalist environment. He was so fed up that he refused to appear before the governing committee to ask permission to attend university courses or to use a kibbutz car. After all he had done for the kibbutz, who were these people to tell him what he could and could not do?

Ayala, trapped by her dual loyalty to the kibbutz and to Goren, would go in his place to make the requests. People made excuses for Goren—he was sick or he was too busy to appear himself—but everyone knew what was really happening. Goren was drifting away. "They were still playing pioneers," Goren recalled later. "They were committing communal suicide because the situation was getting worse all the time, and instead of solving it by opening up the kibbutz and giving people more freedom to do what they want, they were like a porcupine, closing themselves up."

He began looking for a way out. First he got the kibbutz's reluctant permission to enter a three-year undergraduate program in historical geography at Haifa University. When he graduated cum laude, he went on immediately to a master's program and started working toward his Ph.D. He knew it was time to leave the kibbutz, but it took him five years to convince Ayala, who loved her job as a music and piano teacher and had no wish to go. Finally, however, afraid that Goren would decide to leave with her or without her, she acquiesced.

When they appeared before the governing committee to announce their decision, the members were stunned. The heart of Gonen was leaving and there was nothing they could do to stop him. "People didn't shout, they simply cried," Goren recalled. "I was determined to go but it was still touching. The hardest thing they told us is, you don't leave a sinking boat. Well, I told them, it's been sinking for seven years and I'm forty-two and I can't wait anymore."

What happened to Haim Goren in those painful years happened in different ways to hundreds of thousands of Israelis as old institutions slowly crumbled and new ones struggled to be born. The Israel that Goren reentered in 1988 was becoming a very different country—more open, more capitalist, more self-reliant, more selfish and more Americanized. It cared more about money and less about social welfare. An economy that for years had been fettered by socialist restrictions and harnessed to the demands of the state was beginning to burst free, carrying on its shoulders new promises and new demands. It saw itself as strong and independent, and had little patience for the old excuses that Israel was too weak or too vulnerable to take risks. Risks and innovation were what the new economy was all about.

There were many ways to measure the change: the explosion of late-model Japanese cars; the slimming down of the workweek from the old six-day socialist model to the five-day American-style one; the fact that by 1992 virtually every household boasted a color television set, and that 60 percent had access to forty channels of cable television. The frozen-yogurt shops, the American pizza franchises, the shopping malls, the rock concerts, the multiplex cinemas—all were evidence of a revolution in the way Israelis thought about themselves, their money and their culture.

Neither Likud nor Labor welcomed the transformation. They were both creations of the old Israel, and they represented the interests of the ruling elite and the bureaucrats. They could retard change, but they could not stop it. A government that for years had kept a stranglehold on the economy with high trade tariffs, punitive taxes and mountains of red tape was slowly forced to loosen its grip.

"Since the mid-1980s there has been a gradual and reluctant government pullout from economic activity," said Eli Sagi, an economist who was director of Economic Models, a Tel Aviv consulting firm. "In the long run economic forces are stronger than political ones. It's a very slow process—too slow for many people—but the powers making it happen are stronger than the government can withstand."

The changes were not all positive. The old Israel had been a cohesive community that had taken care of its own and had imbued its members with a shared sense of purpose and self-sacrifice. There was a strong, reassuring sense of egalitarianism. The gap between rich and poor was narrow. The driver of one of Israel's largest computer firms served in the same reserve military unit as his boss. In the mess hall and on patrol in the Gaza Strip they were equals. The crime rate was low; unemployment was minimal. Paternalism was the rule: the founding fathers had banned the Beatles from appearing in Israel in 1965 for fear of the impact that decadent rock music would have on Israel's youth; the advent of television was delayed for a decade and then tightly controlled for the same reasons.

The new Israel was inclined to let the market rule and to allow people to make their own decisions. As population growth soared, economic growth climbed as well, but so did unemployment, and wages stagnated. The gap between rich and poor widened and the crime rate began to rise slowly. The ambience of the old Israel began to fade. "Some of the provinciality is gone," notes the *1993 Israel Yearbook and Almanac*. "A measure of Western worldliness—and alienation—has set in. You can get service with a smile in Israel today, but the smile is delivered by a stranger. Israel never used to be big enough to have strangers."

There was a dramatic shift in Israel's economic profile. Production and sales in defense-related industries plummeted as the Cold War ended and arms merchants from the former rival East and West blocs competed for a shrinking world market. Agricultural products, which twenty years before had been the country's main export, now fell to less than 5 percent. Israel was too expensive to waste large parcels of land for growing fruits and vegetables, too dry to export its own water in the form of cheap citrus.

The new economy was based on high-tech electronic goods, computer software, telecommunications, drugs, machine tools and other high-quality, innovative products that flowed from the country's only real natural resource—its brainpower. Its reservoir of trained talent was swelled by those half million Jews from the Soviet Union. Israel had more scientists, engineers and doctors per capita than any other country, and one of the highest rates of literacy and math skills. High-tech incubators, supported with government funds, were blooming around the country.

There was an opening of markets and borders. In part because of free trade agreements with both the United States and the European Community, Israel's net exports and imports doubled between 1984 and 1991. Thirty-two countries established or restored diplomatic relations with Israel between 1988 and 1992. Meanwhile, Saudi Arabia, Kuwait and the other Gulf states quietly dropped their secondary economic boycott, setting off the arrival of dozens of foreign companies, many of them Japanese, that for years had been afraid to do business there. Suddenly Toyotas and Hondas and Mitsubishis took over the streets. Pepsi, which had honored the Arab boycott, competed with Coke, which had not. And Israelis found they had certain advantages of language and cultural familiarity in the newly opening markets of Russia and Eastern Europe.

By the early nineties, some of Israel's largest and most troubled companies began to slim down and some disappeared into receivership. Under the watchful eye of a steering committee of foreign bankers, Koor eliminated 20,000 jobs, sold off its withered branches and jettisoned others, and in 1992 recorded the largest profit of any company traded on the Tel Aviv Stock Exchange. It completed a recovery plan originally projected for twelve to fourteen years in less than two and started turning a profit again.

Other companies showed marked improvements. Bezek, the bloated national telephone monopoly that was famous for its rude operators and endless waiting lists, was removed from direct ministerial control in 1985 and became a public utility. Its efficiency and profitability jumped. Before 1985 it took so long to get a phone that the value of an apartment increased by as much as 15 percent if it was sold with an existing line. Now it took a week or less to get a new line installed. After closing down for four months in 1982 and being slapped into receivership, El Al, the state-run airline, fired one-third of its staff and forced its thirteen unions to combine into one. It recorded its first profit in 1987, the first of six straight years of profits, including a record $38.6 million in 1991, a year when most international airlines lost money because of the Gulf War.

During a time of lingering recession in the West, Israel's growth rate exceeded 6 percent per year for three straight years, higher than any other industrialized country. Much of the growth resulted from the sudden wave of Soviet Jewish immigration, which caused the country to undertake Ariel Sharon's massive housing boom. But even after the wave receded and housing construction tapered off, the growth continued at nearly the same pace. By 1992 inflation, for the first time in twenty-three years, was reduced to single digits (although just barely at 9.4 percent).

The biggest winners were a new generation of high-tech firms that arose, like green shoots from dying tree trunks, from the old, heavily subsidized state industries such as defense and health care. Using research and development skills and innovations from the old top-heavy industries, the new firms created innovative products and a distinctive way of doing business that had never been seen before in Israel. One group of companies, the Digital Signal Processing Group, used military technology to become the world's largest manufacturer of customized computer chips for the latest generation of cellular and cordless telephones and digital telephone answering machines.

The biggest and most successful company of this new generation did not even have its own parking lot. Most of Scitex was crammed into a half dozen buildings in a crowded corner of the Herzliya industrial zone, a mile or so from the Mediterranean Sea. Parking was impossible and security almost nonexistent. It was a modest setting for Israel's fourth largest exporter, but then that was the idea. Scitex prided itself on its nonhierarchical, innovative atmosphere and its sense of informality. More than a thousand people worked at the Herzliya location, yet there were only six senior managers. Each one sat in a modest cubicle behind a plate-glass window visible and accessible to employees. Anyone could walk in at any time and often did. Its mental outlook was a mixture of Silicon Valley and Japan with a strong Israeli accent.

Founded in 1968, Scitex started out making specialized computer equipment for the military. Like many Israeli firms, it established itself with the army connection for its first few years, then branched out. In the early 1970s it developed computer-automated designs to produce color fabric printing for the textile industry. Its biggest breakthrough came in the late 1970s when it used the same innovative technology to jump into publishing, revolutionizing the graphic arts industry with computerized digital imaging systems that allowed publishers to enhance, retouch or otherwise manipulate color photo images and layouts.

Scitex's high-priced systems swept the publishing industry. From 315 workers and $14 million in sales in 1979, the company grew to $550 million and 2,500 employees worldwide by 1992. It set patterns that many Israeli firms tried to follow. The most successful companies either downgraded their defense business or abandoned it altogether, seeing only limited horizons there. They made high-cost, high-quality products that they sold not to consumers but to large industrial or commercial users. They decided early on that Israel's domestic market was far too small and branched out overseas to the United States, Europe and often Japan.

In the mid-1980s Scitex suffered three years of losses and almost went under. Part of the problem was the staggering Israeli economy and part of it was within the company itself, which had to make the painful transition from golden childhood to middle age. Scitex had started life as a technology-driven innovator in a small, protected market, but to compete in the global economy it had to become a market-driven producer. To help make the transition, Scitex hired a new generation of managers, one of whom had a most unusual pedigree.

Yair Shamir looked a lot like his father—the same compact, powerfully built frame, the trim mustache, the half-smile/half-grimace expression and the trademark shrug. Yair had been an underground baby, born at the end of World War II while his father was on the run from the British and his mother was a Lehi courier. Soon after his birth the authorities hauled in his mother for questioning; she brought the nursing baby along and shamed them into letting her go. Yair spent twenty-five years in the Israeli air force before leaving to become general manager of Scitex in 1988.

In the same way that Scitex was a classic second-generation company, Yair Shamir was a classic second-generation Israeli, with many similarities yet a different outlook from his famous father. Yitzhak Shamir had one obsession—the security of the Jewish state. Like most prime ministers before him, he treated economics as a luxury; it commanded little space on his narrow agenda. Interviewing the prime minister one time, an Israeli journalist threw in a question about the economy. "Were you trying to embarrass the prime minister?" an irate press adviser asked after the interview. "You know he doesn't know anything about economics."

Yitzhak Shamir believed his son was compromising his ideals by quitting the air force to go to work for Scitex, giving up a socially responsible public sector job in order to make money. But to Yair, economics was the new Zionism and he patiently tried to explain this to his father, with limited success. "People say Zionism is only to go build new settlements and roads like the pioneers did," Yair explained. "People believe Zionism is a hundred years old. That's why the word has become obsolete. I say no, building Scitex is Zionism."

Yair Shamir was both a pleasant, reasonable and charming man and a ruthless perfectionist. When he stalked the factory floor he insisted that cracked tiles be replaced and that the floors be spotless. Yet the atmosphere was relaxed—open doors throughout the work areas, no locks, very light security. Engineers and researchers and assembly line workers all mixed freely in a multidisciplinary style, moving between their various shops unself-consciously.

"I want to keep the same values, to keep the ethic of a small company while we grow bigger and bigger. My drive is to be a billion dollars in annual sales but to remain small. We still want to give people the feeling we're the best place to work for. There's a woman responsible for social activities and she reports directly to me. There are gifts and family activities so that workers will consider themselves Scitex families. We opened five child care centers during the Gulf War, and every bomb shelter held twenty to forty kids ages four through ten. We kept functioning and reduced tensions at home. We wanted people to feel part of an organization.

"You know, we lose people to Silicon Valley but we also get people from there—Israelis who are ready to return home, surprised at all that we have to offer."

With the help of its new managers, Scitex got back on its feet. It tripled its productivity per worker between 1986 and 1991 and nearly tripled its output without adding new staff. Scitex remained every Israeli entrepreneur's role model. But by the beginning of the 1990s it was being outstripped by a new generation of younger, more innovative firms led by talented, restless entrepreneurs. They operated tiny export companies that made highly specialized products from computer chips to telephone parts to specialized software to sophisticated medical products. Having quickly saturated the Israeli marketplace, they shifted their attention overseas, prowling markets in Europe, the United States and, increasingly, the former Soviet bloc and the Far East, looking for opportunities and niches. Often they formally incorporated abroad to look "non-Israeli," and often when they found a market they would hook up with local investors who would handle marketing and sales. They looked and operated much as Scitex had twenty years before.

It was a high-risk, high-pressure type of business and it attracted people with raging hormones and unhealthy egos. Yair Mendels, who operated a small, high-tech medical products firm, grew up in Tel Aviv in the 1950s and 1960s, the son of first-generation Israelis who arrived there from Holland before World War II. He was brilliant and he was impossible. A restless, disobedient student, he was expelled from one public school and bounced around several more until at age fifteen his parents shipped him to a kibbutz school up the coast where he learned to live with hard teachers and rigorous learning. At eighteen he joined the paratroopers, fighting constantly with his fellow troops and commanders and, it often seemed, with himself as well. "When is it possible for you to control yourself?" one frustrated officer asked him. It was a question that all his life Mendels had never satisfactorily answered.

Mendels eventually became a captain, but the army bored him just as much as school had. He quit and forced himself to go to college, eventually graduating from Hebrew University with advanced degrees in biology, isometrics and physics. He was accepted at the Massachusetts Institute of Technology and Harvard for a joint Ph.D./M.D. program in neurobiology. He stayed three weeks in Boston, bought a camper with a friend and took off to explore the United States for six months. Then he returned to Hebrew University and spent two years in a Ph.D. program but quit again. Mendels did not want to study. He wanted to make things.

He found himself back at home with no job and very little money, working out of a basement. All he had was a table and ideas that flowed from the nightmarish experiences he had lived through in two wars. During the Six-Day War he had watched in terror as an officer in the command car in front of him keeled over from a bullet in the chest. "We ran over to him, and as we stood there he just got paler and paler and paler and in two minutes he was dead," Mendels recalled. "The blood had drained from his body." During the Yom Kippur War six years later, Mendels's unit came under shellfire in the Sinai Desert and he saw firsthand the huge gaping wounds that shells can make in the human body. "The wounds were horrible—nerve cells and blood vessels ripped all to hell."

Mendels concluded that a device that could quickly transfuse blood into a wound victim during the first crucial minutes after injury might have saved the lives of some of his comrades. He started working with blood pressure packs and catheters and rapid transfusion sets. It was in a sense a typical Israeli innovation: take an experience you'd had in combat and turn it into an idea, an improvement and, finally, a product.

He called his company Biometrix Ltd. In a small factory on the outskirts of Jerusalem, he started making high-tech, high-quality disposable surgical and cardiovascular devices that could compete locally with expensive imports. He designed a disposable bag for wound drainage that he manufactured for 40¢ each and that functioned better than a U.S. competitor that cost $1.80. He designed a closed drainage system that could remove, store and measure fluids in a more sterile and accurate manner than systems that had to be opened and poured out. Based on his army experience, he also designed a pumping device that could warm and deliver a liter of blood in seconds. "I'm a vampire," he leered. "When I see blood my eyes grow big."

Mendels found the medical supplies market very conservative: hospital purchasing officers wanted to buy only from well-established manufacturers. But there were certain advantages for a newcomer. The Israeli market was so small that many foreign manufacturers simply did not bother to service it. And because Israel is a place where everybody knows everybody else, it was not so hard for a brash upstart with obvious talent to begin to make a small name for himself.

"It was a learning process," he recalled. "I learned to be hungry and smart. I found out that having a good idea wasn't enough, that to produce an actual product I had to have engineering, materials, electronics and chemicals. Israel was a good environment to start with. It can absorb many mistakes. It gives you the ability to stabilize and define your product line. We had things to offer. We were more ambitious and more flexible than the bigger companies."

Biometrix quickly saturated the local market as sales grew from $360,000 in 1988 to $2 million in 1992. Mendels started to look abroad. At first he had few bites. The markets were huge and complicated and hard to penetrate. He was told over and over again, "You're interesting but you're too small." In the United States, for example, he learned that he could not sell directly to individual hospitals as in Israel but to four large hospital associations. To compete he needed a product turnover not of $2 million per year but $200 million.

Like Scitex and others before it, Biometrix began the search for foreign investors and partners. This was the big challenge—it would either make or break Yair Mendels's company. "Biometrix will either vanish in the next two years or make a big jump," he said ruefully. Either way, he felt on the cutting edge of a new way of doing business for a country that had kept its economy sealed off and insulated. "Entrepreneurs," he had read one day, "are people who bend reality." That's me, Mendels thought, trying to bend Israeli reality.

After he left Gonen, Haim Goren quickly found a job supervising adult education courses and a school for gifted children at a regional college in the Upper Galilee. He got a cash settlement of about $40,000 from the kibbutz—not much compensation for twenty-four years of work, but enough to buy a used car and rent a house in Rosh Pinna, a small crossroads town some ten miles from Gonen. He and Ayala bought a small piece of land and eventually saved enough to build their own house. Two former kibbutzniks bought parcels alongside his; they jokingly called their little neighborhood "Gonen B."

Ayala taught music at the area kibbutzim just as before, only now the money she earned went to the family instead of to Gonen. For a while she and Goren and the children were invited to every kibbutz event, and people got angry if they did not attend. But gradually the ties faded.

Everyone's life changed in curious ways. Goren had to adjust to quiet nights at home without committee meetings or constant demands on his time. After the first few months the only time he ventured to Gonen was to get his car repaired. Ayala, who never made a hot meal for fewer than 120 people during her years at Gonen, learned for the first time how to cook for a small family. The years of forced sharing were over, and in reaction, a certain enlightened selfishness took hold. "For twenty-two years Ayala never sat and played the piano for herself because she never had the time," recalled Goren. "Now for the first time she does."

One big difference was money. Goren had never needed or wanted much, but after he left Gonen money became central to his life and thoughts. For a time he was obsessed by how much he made and how much he spent, and amazed by how much money other people had. At the kibbutz a man's worth was measured by the respect he commanded from his fellow members and the amount of responsibility they bestowed upon him.

But outside Gonen a man's salary and bank balance seemed more important than his values. The kibbutz had been Goren's safety net and his buffer from economic reality. Now that it was gone, his preoccupation with money betrayed his insecurity.

The fact was that although Goren had left the kibbutz, he was still in many ways the same kibbutznik—resourceful, generous, self-aware and enthusiastic. His first dream had died of causes, both natural and unnatural, so he set about building a smaller, more realistic one. He liked the freedom of his new life, the sense that his decisions and his fate were in his own hands. He struggled not for idealism, but for normality, to come to terms with an Israel he no longer felt totally comfortable with, yet needed to make peace with.

Kibbutz Gonen changed as well. As Goren was leaving a new generation was taking over, people who had looked to him and other early kibbutzniks for leadership and guidance but who now realized they had to do it for themselves. One of the new leaders was Shabtai Glass, a former bank manager from Tel Aviv who had moved to Gonen in the early 1980s to escape the urban rat race. Not long after Goren left, Glass became the chief financial officer of the kibbutz and helped devise a tough economic plan to help Gonen pay off part of its massive debt. Gonen's wood-products factory made something of a comeback and the kibbutz opened a car-repair shop to service the region. Gonen also followed in the footsteps of many kibbutzim by opening a bed-and-breakfast guesthouse in the old dormitory where Gonen's teenagers had once lived.

The entire Upper Galilee faced similar adjustments. As farming and light industry died out, the kibbutzim struggled to find new ways to make money and escape from under their debt mountain. Physically the valley was also going through changes. The peat bog that had been drained forty years earlier was losing its fertility after years of intensive farming, and species of plants and wildlife were vanishing from the remaining wetlands. Pollutants from the dried peat and from chemical fertilizers washed downstream into the Sea of Galilee, poisoning Israel's most scenic freshwater lake. As the peat sank, the old swamp was slowly reasserting itself. Lush and beautiful as it looked, the Hula Valley was becoming both an economic and ecological disaster area.

The kibbutzniks sat down and coolly analyzed their predicament. They decided that the answer lay in tourism—both from foreign visitors with their hard currency and from Israelis who with the coming of the two-day weekend had more leisure time and money to spend. Already the Hula, once dominated by agricultural settlements, had become dotted with fish restaurants, guesthouses, adventure playgrounds, shopping centers and even a baptismal site on the Jordan River. But now the kibbutzniks decided to go one giant step further: they voted to turn back the clock and undo what their parents had done by digging a new network of waterways and dams and reflooding the valley. The new project, initially planned for 2,000 acres, would cost $25 million and constitute one of the biggest environmental enterprises undertaken in Israel since the original reclamation project forty years ago. It would revitalize the old nature reserve and restock the area with birds, fish and other wildlife. The original drainage of the valley had become a great Zionist legend; the reflooding would be a powerful symbol of what the new Israel was about: pragmatism, profits and a willingness to challenge the sacred truths of the past.

For the kibbutzniks, the old values of collectivism and hard manual labor were gradually being superseded by marketing skills and the ability to service a new breed of tourists who were descending upon the region. People who had once tilled the soil now took breakfast orders and made beds. "I didn't come to the Hula to be a waiter," one farmer complained. What choice was there? Shabtai Glass responded.

Socialist values faded as well. Kibbutz Ein Zivan in the Golan Heights closed its communal dining hall, symbol of the old collectivist way of life, saving more than $300,000 per year. In an even greater heresy, the kibbutz began paying its members differential wages according to the value of their work. The move brought censure from the United Kibbutz Movement, but it mirrored changes in the movement throughout Israel. In many kibbutzim, members were receiving bigger personal budgets and fewer free services; many paid their own electricity, phone and heating bills. Some two dozen kibbutzim turned their dining halls into restaurants where members paid for meals. Kibbutz factories and other enterprises were increasingly operated by independent boards of directors who were more concerned with the profit-and-loss sheet than with the well-being of the community. Several kibbutzim paid their members extra for overtime work; one even issued credit cards.

Traditional kibbutzniks complained that the movement was shifting from the old Marxist adage of "From each according to his ability to each according to his need" to a more hard-edged, American-style ethic: "He who doesn't work, doesn't eat." Ben-Gurion, the old socialist warrior, might be spinning in his grave, but the kibbutzniks of the Hula Valley knew there was no going back.

Old habits died hard. While some Israelis strived to create something new, others fought grimly to hold onto what they had. Every now and then, just when it seemed the free marketers were winning, the past reasserted itself with a vigor and range of support that showed it was far from dead and that the contest for Israel's economic soul was far from over.

Sometimes they fought over weighty, existential issues. Histadrut leaders battled fiercely against the efforts of successive health ministers to reform and streamline the bloated and desperately inefficient Kupat Holim health-care network that was one of the last vestiges of the federation's fading power. Bezek's powerful trade union undermined attempts to create a modern telecommunications network by opposing the government's plans to privatize various parts of the company. Defense workers at the giant state-owned military and aircraft industries staged violent strikes against layoffs and reforms that would have saved the government millions in wasted subsidies but cost thousands of workers their jobs.

And sometimes the fight was about little symbolic things. Like frozen french fries.

The first American fast-food franchises that made their way to Israel's shores in the late 1980s were pizza outlets. Pizza was easy—it was cheese, crust and tomato sauce plus a few toppings, all ingredients that could be readily bought from Israeli suppliers. When the rabbis insisted that the franchises serve only kosher food, it was a simple matter to eliminate the pepperoni and sausage. Domino's and Pizza Hut arrived simultaneously in the early nineties and made fast profits. The Domino's franchise in Ramat Gan was said by its owners to sell more pies than any single store in the United States.

Cheeseburgers were another matter. Cheese combined with meat was a fundamental violation of the laws of kashrut. But how could you make a Big Mac without cheese? And how could Israeli kosher beef, which tended to be dry and tasteless, do for a Quarter Pounder? Nonetheless, when an Israeli entrepreneur announced plans to open the first McDonald's in Israel, the problem was not the rabbis or the meat. The problem was the french fries.

Israeli frozen french fries were manufactured by one food processor, Tapud, which was owned by four kibbutzim that grew potatoes in the Negev Desert not far from the Gaza Strip. Like Gonen, these kibbutzim had been originally settled not for economic reasons but for security ones. Their water and their crops were heavily subsidized. But the real problem was taste. By American standards, Tapud's fries were limp, gray, watery and tasted like oil-saturated cardboard. They also cost twice as much as the Idaho Russet-Burbank frozen fries that McDonald's wanted to import from the United States. This demand by a foreign giant deeply alarmed the cartel of local potato growers, who knew that if McDonald's won the right to import cheaper, better fries, Israeli fast-food chains would quickly do the same. The trade minister, who wanted to placate the local growers while not alienating McDonald's, hit upon a compromise that satisfied no one: The frozen fries could be imported, but with a tariff of about twenty cents per pound, which would nearly double their cost. The money would go into a fund to help local growers develop the right kind of potatoes to service McDonald's within a few years.

The growers were not interested. "The minute the first frozen french fries enter the country, we'll block all the major junctions in the Negev with potatoes," the head of their local council told the *Jerusalem Report*.

The growers got support from the agriculture minister, himself a kibbutznik, who forced the matter into the ministerial economic affairs committee. After much deliberation eight of eleven ministers on the committee sided with the growers. It's our fries or no fries, they told a flabbergasted McDonald's. Inevitably the four little growers won and the giant American hamburger chain lost; McDonald's bought from Tapud.

For many Israelis this was a matter of national pride. Why should a capitalist giant from the United States be allowed to ride roughshod over local workers and play havoc with a small but proud Israeli company? But the victory came out of everyone's pockets in the form of higher prices for lower-quality fare. The little guy won, but other Israelis paid the price.

"It's a perfect example of what happens when one company has a monopoly," said Zeev Golan, spokesman for the Institute for Advanced Strategic and Political Studies, a Jerusalem-based economic think tank that monitored these kinds of struggles. "It's like the divine right of kings, only here it's the divine right of monopolies. This is a country that says it is crying for foreign investment and every Israeli wants McDonald's in here, and then one small part of the agricultural lobby raises a stink. And the government gives in."

The institute was a collection of economists, businessmen and former bureaucrats, many of them American Jews transplanted to Israel, who saw their mission as teaching the fundamentals of free enterprise to a recalcitrant band of recovering ex-socialists. Its main guru was economist Alvin Rabushka, a senior fellow at Stanford University's Hoover Institution, who journeyed to Israel twice yearly to check the student's progress. Each year Rabushka issued a report card on the economy in which the government received failing grades. Despite cosmetic reforms Rabushka argued that Israel remained overly centralized and government-controlled.

"It may be rotting away from within, but it's still your basic old-fashioned Bolshevik economy," Rabushka contended. "Where there has been transformation, it's been done out of sheer necessity. They're not putting in place a set of policies that will encourage investment. They're not laying a foundation for sustained growth, but just temporarily fixing the system until it breaks down again. A bag of disconnected parts is not a coherent policy."

Rabushka peeked behind the sunny economic figures of the early 1990s and found shadows. He attributed Israel's high growth rates to the rise in population caused by the Russian immigration; growth per capita remained stagnant. Productivity rose because unemployment was in double digits and wages were suppressed. Rabushka pointed out that the government still owned and operated some 160 companies, about one-fifth of Israel's industrial output. The Histadrut owned another one-fifth. Some 25 percent of goods and services still functioned under price controls. There were more than sixty companies like Tapud that functioned as protected cartels turning out low-quality products at high prices while cheaper products from abroad were either banned outright or so highly taxed they could not compete. Taxes consumed 50 percent of the gross national product and the government slapped import duties of 100 percent and higher on new cars.

Part of the problem, Rabushka confessed, was that things were not quite bad enough for Israelis to insist on changes. "It's not the United States, but it's not as bad as Russia. It's about half the standard of living of the United States, comfortable enough that most people figure it's more important not to lose what they've got than to risk it for something better. The half a million who insist on something better have moved to Los Angeles."

Ultimately, Rabushka believed, Israel suffered from an economic Catch-22. "It's impossible to reform anything unless you reform the whole thing. And it's impossible to reform the whole thing so you can't reform anything."

For Rabushka, the most distinguishing characteristic of the Israeli economy and its most singular failing was its inability to attract direct foreign investment. Despite the astonishing growth of export industries, imports still exceeded exports by $5.5 billion. Without investments of foreign capital, Israel was compelled to make up the shortfall with American foreign aid, American Jewish charity and loans, all of which accounted for about one-eighth of Israel's gross national product. Indeed, Israel had become the largest per capita recipient of grants and philanthropy in the world—around $1,000 per year for every Israeli man, woman and child.

Most Israelis were grateful for the aid, which helped defray the massive cost of security for a small, resource-poor country living in a hostile region. But an increasing number questioned its economic impact. Aid had served to soften the blows caused by the costs of the Yom Kippur War, runaway inflation and Begin's consumer-spending binge. It had permitted economic inefficiencies to survive and delayed necessary reforms. Aid, in other words, had become part of the problem; it helped prop up Israel's stagnant status quo.

In lobbying for high levels of aid, American Jews argued that the money was vital for Israeli security. In fact, the IDF had become increasingly adept at squeezing more security out of less money. Like any smart business, the army learned to adjust to new economic realities. It cut staff, reduced operating costs, and concentrated its spending on high-tech weaponry and the other big-ticket items that it needed to continue to dominate the competition. Despite a steady growth in the defense budget, military spending as a proportion of the gross domestic product had actually declined by half since the mid-1970s, and analysts expected the trend to continue. But the savings to the government had been wiped out largely by state subsidies to inefficient producers and social welfare payments, which by 1991 accounted for more than half of Israel's annual budget.

Nonetheless, the cost of state security continued to be a major drain on Israel's resources. That cost went far beyond the defense budget itself, as Bank Hapoalim economist Nadine Baudot-Trajtenberg pointed out. It exacted a price in Israel's trade relations, labor productivity, competitiveness, standard of living and a host of other economic factors. The 1991 defense budget of $7.8 billion accounted for 14 percent of Israel's GDP, more than twice that of the United States and four or five times what the typical Western European country spent. There were damaging ripples such as the three years every Israeli male sacrificed for military service and the month in work time lost each year to reserve duty. Eighty percent of Israel's spending on research and development went to military industries, compared to 35 percent in the United States and just 5 percent in Japan. This military spending strapped Israel to a fading business in defense exports. Israel also suffered from a relatively poor credit rating despite its unblemished record of paying its debts on time. The reason was simple: a country that had faced six wars in forty-four years was no one's idea of a good credit risk. "We're still paying for the burden of yesterday," said Baudot-Trajtenberg.

To reach its full economic potential, the new Israel needed peace. It could not continue to pour billions into defense spending, billions more into the Russian *aliya,* and millions beyond that into housing and roads and security for 100,000 Jewish settlers and still afford cable television and a spending spree at the shopping mall. At some point it had to make choices. For years Likud-led governments, cushioned by American aid dollars, had avoided facing that decision. U.S. governments may have disapproved of

Menachem Begin's adventurism in Lebanon or Yitzhak Shamir's settlements policy in the occupied territories, but they had never been willing to
penalize Israel financially.

Emerging from the Gulf War, Shamir was confident he could still have it
both ways. The American Jewish lobby was stronger than ever and firmly
under his control. In the weeks following the war, AIPAC and other groups
flooded Congress with lobbyists, guaranteeing passage of an amendment
granting Israel $650 million in emergency aid as compensation for war
damages and the added costs of defense. Shamir fully expected American
Jews to deliver again when the issue of loan guarantees to help finance the
Russian *aliya* came up later in the year. After all, what could possibly stand
in his way?

12. "It Will Not Be a Problem"

> *In the fabric of human events, one thing leads to another. Every mistake is in a sense the product of all the mistakes that have gone before it, from which fact it derives a sort of a cosmic forgiveness; and at the same time every mistake is in a sense the determinant of all the mistakes of the future, from which it derives a sort of a cosmic unforgivableness.*
>
> —GEORGE F. KENNAN

FROM the moment he arrived at the White House, George Bush seemed fated to clash with Yitzhak Shamir. The tall, wealthy, Wasp preppie with the polished résumé and wide circle of friends and companions lived in an entirely different world from the diminutive, secretive underground commander who wore his suspicions on his sleeve. Bush believed in personal communication and treated the telephone as an instrument of diplomacy, while Shamir was an awkward conversationalist who could not make small talk and seldom said what he truly believed even to his closest advisers. Bush was an American optimist, Shamir an Israeli skeptic. Bush held no particular ideology, but believed in fairness and personal honor; for Shamir ideology was crucial—he would cut any corner, shade any truth, anger any friend, defy any foe, to secure the Land of Israel.

Shamir was no fool. He understood that the United States was the world's most powerful nation and Israel's only real ally. He knew he would have to make concessions, that he would have to bend to try to fit in with the new president. He desperately wanted to get along. "This is the situation: today the United States is the only superpower, with all its advantageous and detrimental implications," he told an Israeli television interviewer. "We must live in their world and with these circumstances."

Yet at the same time, once Shamir concluded that the administration was hostile to his goals, he adopted his old familiar stance. He would outwait and outsmart the president and fall back on Israel's loyal allies in the American Jewish community and in Congress to outmaneuver Bush. At times he even managed to play off James A. Baker III against Bush, using the pragmatic secretary of state as a cushion against Bush's hard-line approach.

The personal and stylistic differences between Bush and Shamir were important. But behind every miscommunication, spiteful exchange and inadvertent insult there lay a fundamental conflict. As he had made clear from the first days of his presidency, Bush believed that in order to achieve peace with its Arab neighbors, Israel ultimately would have to withdraw from much of the territory it had occupied since 1967. But Yitzhak Shamir believed that the retention of territory was crucial to Israel's future and therefore even more important than a peace accord. On this they never did and never could agree. All of the conflicts, misunderstandings, mistakes and miscalculations flowed from this one basic disagreement.

Over the years a series of circumstances had combined to give Israel power and leverage over U.S. policy far beyond its size or importance. Shamir had presided over Israel's ascendancy and had come to take it for granted. Indeed, it had become the centerpiece of his strategy. You can always pull the rope a little tighter, demand a little more, argued Yossi Ben-Aharon, his chief ideologist and point man with the Americans. When push came to shove, Shamir believed he would always win because he cared more deeply and was more patient than anyone else in the game. He had outwaited and outwitted George Shultz, Shimon Peres, Ariel Sharon, David Levy, Arye Deri and his own closest colleagues when they had sought to overthrow him. Surely the same tactics would work with George Bush and James Baker.

This time, however, to his great surprise, the tactics and strategies that had served him so well for so many years finally betrayed him.

George Bush saw the Gulf War as a turning point in Middle Eastern affairs, and he believed that it opened a "window of opportunity" to end the Arab-Israeli conflict. Saddam Hussein was defeated, while Yasser Arafat and the Arab radicals who had backed Iraq were in flight, and their old sponsor, the Soviet Union, was in eclipse. Bush believed that the same Arab moderates who had been persuaded to hold together against Saddam could also be brought to the peace table with Israel. But in order for it to work, both sides would have to be prepared to make concessions: Bush believed the Arabs should suspend their economic boycott of Israel and the Israelis should freeze Jewish settlement in the occupied territories. Bush knew that Shamir would resist; he expected Jim Baker to find a way to overcome that resistance. Before the war Baker had made eight trips to the region to put together the Arab coalition to wage war. Now that it was over, Baker set about constructing a diplomatic dragnet so sturdy and resilient that even Shamir, the Houdini of political escape artists, could not cut through it.

Shamir and his people had few illusions about Baker. They had watched him slice and dice Moshe Arens during the foreign minister's two trips to Washington in 1989 and conduct a relentless but ultimately fruitless campaign to corner Israel into going to Cairo in 1990. They saw him as cold, ruthless and mean, a Texas lawyer of no scruples and no loyalties who believed only in the art of the deal. Ben-Aharon kept a copy of a 1989 *Time* magazine cover story on Baker in his desk drawer in which the incoming secretary of state had described his technique for hunting wild turkeys. "The trick is in getting them where you want them, on your terms," Baker had said. "Then *you* control the situation, not them. *You* have the options. Pull the trigger or don't. It doesn't matter once you've got them where you want them."

Shamir knew that he was Baker's prize turkey.

Shamir did not share the administration's sense of optimism about Arab moderation. The Arabs were the same Arabs. If they emitted peaceful signals it was not so much because they were prepared to live in peace with Israel as because they wanted to impress and remain on good terms with the United States. Shamir was also troubled by the fact that, with the Cold War over, the United States was shifting from being Israel's patron and chief ally to the new, more neutral stance of "honest broker" between Arabs and Israelis.

Nonetheless, Shamir could not help being intrigued. The prospect of reaching arrangements with some of the Arabs—most especially with Hafez Assad, the Syrian strongman—was too enticing not to be pursued. Besides, like the Arabs, Shamir needed American good will. The wave of Soviet Jews descending from passenger planes at Ben-Gurion Airport each morning meant that Israel would soon have to return to the capital markets to borrow vast sums for immigration absorption. To get $10 billion in U.S. loan guarantees that would substantially ease interest rates, Shamir knew he would have to welcome Baker despite all of his misgivings.

Many of the diplomatic raw materials Baker worked with had been used before by George Shultz, his predecessor as secretary of state, and others without much success. Now Baker's Middle East team, led by policy planning director Dennis Ross, sought to refashion them. Baker pressed for a two-track negotiation—simultaneous talks between Israel and its neighboring Arab states and between the Israelis and a joint Palestinian-Jordanian delegation. After his first trip in March, Baker seized upon the idea of opening such talks with a regional conference. The proposal bore a marked resemblance to Shimon Peres's 1987 proposal for a U.N.-sponsored international event, but it was modified to meet some of Shamir's concerns. Baker suggested a truncated, symbolic meeting—an opening session that would segue into direct, bilateral talks that could not reconvene without the consent of all the parties and that would have no power to impose a solution on any of them. One year earlier the Arab side would never have accepted such restrictions. But the Gulf War had dramatically shifted the power equation. Baker found Palestinians and Jordanians, Saddam's former allies and two of the war's biggest losers, to be the most flexible.

The weakest of all the parties, the Palestinians, had the most to gain. Devastated financially and diplomatically by the PLO's embrace of Saddam, they were willing to entertain compromises that in the past they had emphatically rejected. They suspended the embargo they had maintained since June 1990 and opened talks with Baker in March 1991 despite U.S. refusal to reinstate its dialogue with the PLO. At Israel's insistence, Baker and the Palestinians conducted a flimsy charade. The United States denied it was negotiating with the PLO, while local Palestinians insisted that they were Arafat's agents. Everyone said what they needed to say; everyone heard what they wanted to hear.

Slowly but surely over the course of 1991 the Palestinians acceded to Israeli demands, shedding their national symbols and their long-term goals in order to get a seat at the table. They reluctantly agreed to enter negotiations that would center not on statehood but rather on the interim step of autonomy. They agreed to exclude PLO members and political exiles from their delegation and were even prepared, ultimately, to keep East Jerusalemites off the list.

The Israelis told themselves that this process would help further the break between local Palestinians and Tunis. But in the end Shamir's tough line actually helped drive the two parties back together. Faisal Husseini and the locals, who were elected by no one, did not have the authority to accept independently the humiliating terms that Shamir imposed. For that they needed the political cover that only Tunis could provide. Husseini had forced Arafat to allow the negotiations with Baker to go forward. But once the talks began, the delegation made no moves without first firing off a fax to Tunis and awaiting its approval. In the remarriage between the locals and Tunis, Yitzhak Shamir was the unwitting matchmaker.

Baker treated the Palestinians with patience and a touch of condescension. He was the mentor and they the neophytes at the grand game of diplomacy. He told them repeatedly that they had the most to gain from any peace process and therefore they had to be prepared to make the most concessions. On more than one occasion when faced with what he considered to be obstinacy from the Palestinians, he folded his notepad and announced he was quitting. One of the participants at the meetings recalled how Baker, with a look of half-pity, half-disgust, would tell them, "You know, I feel sorry for you people, I really do, because you don't know how to help yourselves. And if you're not willing to help yourselves, then I can't help you either." The Palestinians, both angered and shamed by these displays, eventually gave in.

Baker worked in slow, incremental movements. Determined to avoid Shultz's fate, Baker offered no formulas of his own or grand schemes that the parties could target and pick away at. His sessions with Middle East leaders were often one-on-one, with no aides or note takers in the room. Baker and his high-flying entourage were so tight-lipped that American diplomats in the various capitals were often reduced to pleading for briefings from traveling reporters. Baker could be charming, impatient and irritating. In one-on-one sessions he relentlessly challenged Shamir to explain how it could hurt Israel simply to come to the bargaining table. How could Shamir allow technicalities to stand in the way of the opportunity to sit down with countries that had been in a declared state of war with Israel for forty-three years? Isn't this what he always had wanted?

It was tedious, grinding work. Baker made eight trips to the region between March and October, shuttling between Damascus, Jerusalem, Amman, Cairo and Riyadh. Some of the sessions went for six hours or more without a break. Baker had to sit once for nine and a half hours of bargaining with Assad, with only a pitcher of warm lemonade to sustain him. Finally, he had to interrupt one of the Syrian leader's sustained soliloquies to ask permission to use the men's room.

There were many disappointments. The Saudis, whose dazzling ambassador in Washington, Prince Bandar Ibn Sultan, had promised to recognize Israel in return for American Jewish support during the Gulf War, suddenly contracted diplomatic amnesia. At best, after much cajoling, they agreed to attend a regional conference as an observer, not a participant. The Arab states demanded a settlements freeze but refused to lift the economic boycott in return. For his part, Shamir continually seemed to erect new procedural obstacles in Baker's path.

Each time Baker believed that he had finally made some headway with the Israelis, he found himself undercut. In April he induced Foreign Minister David Levy to agree that the regional conference should reconvene for a progress report every six months, only to have the idea vetoed by Shamir. But a bigger obstacle than Shamir himself was the prime minister's Doctor No, Yossi Ben-Aharon, who seemed to define his role as making sure that nothing positive happened.

Shamir wanted to ensure that no PLO members or East Jerusalemites were included in the Palestinian-Jordanian delegation. Baker agreed, but argued that Shamir ought not to insist upon personally approving every single Palestinian delegate because it would be a kiss of death for those whom he did approve. Just set the parameters, Baker told him, and let the Palestinians pick among themselves. Shamir saw the logic; in their one-on-one session in late May, he reluctantly agreed. Baker submitted an informal joint paper in English summing up their areas of agreement. Shamir made a few minor editing changes, then approved it.

A few weeks later, however, Ben-Aharon visited Washington and told Ross the paper was unacceptable. Shamir, he said, had "not been paying attention to details"; besides, the prime minister's English was not very good. Baker was trying to trick Shamir, Ben-Aharon claimed. He and Ross got into a shouting match.

Baker came away convinced that Ben-Aharon personally was undermining the talks. A few days later, however, a letter arrived at the White House from Shamir that seemed to affirm Ben-Aharon's position. At this point it became clear to Baker that no matter what he might be saying in public, Shamir did not want to attend a peace conference.

At Baker's behest Bush wrote to Shamir suggesting that if the prime minister was not willing to freeze settlements, he must be prepared to compromise on other points, such as allowing the peace talks to reconvene with the assent of all the parties and with a U.N. observer present. These were, at best, technical matters, argued Bush. It would be hard to understand why Shamir would forgo a chance to achieve a longtime Israeli dream—direct, bilateral talks with its Arab neighbors—for such trivial pursuits.

But Shamir believed these issues went to the heart of the matter: The Arabs wanted an international conference so that they could evade direct talks with Israel. They wanted a settlement freeze so that they could deny Israel's right to exercise sovereignty over the land. Their first objective may have been the West Bank and Gaza, but their real goal, as always, remained the destruction of Israel itself. They had not even begun to take steps to prove otherwise. And Bush, by playing the role of "honest broker" rather than staunch ally of Israel, appeared prepared to help them get what they wanted. It looked to Bush and Baker as if Shamir was just playing games to avoid going to the talks. But his objections were much deeper. The two sides were operating on entirely different levels: Bush and Baker were on the Middle East's upper floor conjuring up a rosy portrait of the future, while Shamir and Ben-Aharon were rooting around in the gloomy, window-less basement where the foundations lay.

In stalling the Americans, Shamir always believed that the Arabs would be his unwitting allies by sticking to their maximalist demands, as they al-ways had in the past. But this time the game had changed. Baker managed to persuade Assad that Shamir was counting on the cagey Syrian leader to say no to a peace conference. "Why let Shamir off the hook?" Baker asked.

Assad agreed. In July he dispatched a letter to Bush making clear that he was willing to put some of his own reservations aside and attend the con-ference. Armed with this windfall, Baker returned to the region, held a marathon bargaining session with Assad and then ventured to Jerusalem. In an intense one-on-one meeting Baker managed to persuade Shamir that As-sad was indeed prepared to recognize Israel and conduct bilateral talks. This was a breakthrough that not even Shamir could shrug off. Shamir even spoke about Assad as if the Syrian leader were another Sadat—an Arab leader prepared to make a remarkable change in direction. Shamir told Baker that he, too, was ready to attend a conference. Finally, the Americans had manipulated Shamir into a position where he could not say no.

There were still many procedural hurdles. Baker implored Shamir to leave the hardest issues—the status of Jerusalem, the question of land for peace—for later. He offered the device of composing letters of assurance for each party. Each letter consisted of a broad restatement of American policy in language that appealed to the recipient. There were phone calls, faxes and occasional press leaks. Sometimes it was Washington hardball, sometimes Texas charm. At one point when Baker was trying to convince Shamir to accept the notion of a U.N. silent observer attending the confer-ence, he muzzled his mouth with his hands and mumbled, "Tell me how this hurts you." Shamir could not help himself—he broke out laughing and Baker knew he had made his point.

Later Baker would tell Israeli journalist David Makovsky: "People have the wrong idea. They think that I didn't have a good relationship with Shamir. I had a great relationship with Shamir. I respected him and I still respect him. . . . I always leveled with him, and his word was always good. He was the one person in the Israeli government that I could confide in and never have it leak."

But while Baker scraped away, attempting to break through the wall of

Shamir's resistance or tunnel under it, the prime minister's inability to control his own government and the issue of Jewish settlement in the West Bank and Gaza remained constant obstacles in Baker's path.

The government that Yitzhak Shamir and his lieutenants had patched together in the aftermath of the failed 1990 coup had the distinction of being both the most narrowly right-wing and the most politically incoherent of any in Israeli history. It came to power with a mere sixty-two seats—a majority of two in the 120-member Knesset—and consisted of seven different parties and factions plus three maverick legislators (later, after considerable legislative and financial promises from Shamir, the ultra-Orthodox Agudat Yisrael and ultra-rightist Moledet would join as well). In effect, Shamir had traded the Labor Party's solid thirty-nine seats for the chronic instability of his new governing partners, a crazy-quilt assortment of nationalists, fundamentalists and pragmatic Sephardim who had nothing much in common beyond a disdain for the prime minister who ostensibly led them and a keen desire to wring every conceivable material benefit out of him.

Whenever they made demands Shamir would accede. Funds that were supposed to go to the ailing state school system instead were channeled into the various religious school networks run by Aguda, Shas and the National Religious Party. In the 1992 budget the ultra-Orthodox received a 43 percent increase for their schools and cultural institutions, then wrung an additional $30 million in "special allocations." Bills banning the sale of pork and sexually provocative billboards made their way through the Knesset with Likud support. Some 18,000 ultra-Orthodox yeshiva students were exempted from military service.

Shamir could not bear to meet with many of his coalition partners face-to-face, dispatching Moshe Nissim to deal with the ultrareligious parties and Benjamin Netanyahu to talk to the rightists. Cabinet meetings, which had been perfunctory at best in the previous national unity government, now became farcical. The few issues that Shamir truly cared about—state security and foreign policy—became the domain of an increasingly tighter circle of confidants and advisers, including Arens, Meridor, Olmert and Ronnie Milo. The rest was left to individual cabinet ministers. Finance Minister Yitzhak Modai, who now headed a bitter four-member faction of ex-Likudniks and whose public pronouncements grew increasingly erratic, wielded almost total control over economic decisions. The small religious parties turned the Labor and Social Services ministries into feudal duchies of religious intolerance and petty graft.

But the largest duchy of all belonged to the warrior-king, Housing Minister Ariel Sharon. Besides launching an enormous construction drive to house the 400,000 Soviet Jewish immigrants who were pouring into the country, Sharon presided over the most ambitious expansion of Jewish settlement in the West Bank and Gaza Strip in Israel's history. He oversaw a growth in population from about 90,000 settlers in 1990 to 126,000 over a two-year period.

The building program was undertaken behind a dense smokescreen of deceptive figures and public statements. At the launching of his new government in June 1990, Shamir had stated that he had no intention of increasing expenditures on settlements. The following February he sent a letter to George Bush insisting that there was no formal government decision to build new housing units in the territories. The Housing Ministry in its official publications reported only 3,385 housing starts there over an eighteen-month period. But left-wing Knesset members Dedi Zucker and Haim Oron reported that the government had already constructed or was planning a total of some 21,000 housing units between April 1990 and December 1991. Peace Now counted 13,650 under actual construction.

Sharon's goal was to get as many housing starts on the ground as quickly as possible, and every time he made the case he presented a higher set of figures. He told the Knesset finance committee in December 1990 that only 2,500 housing units were planned for 1991. But three months later he took Israeli journalists on a tour of the West Bank during which he claimed that Israel was committed to building 13,000 new units over a two-year period. Six months later officials in Sharon's Housing Ministry told the *Washington Post*'s Jackson Diehl that more than 22,000 new units were either already under construction or approved for the West Bank, Gaza Strip and Golan Heights. Once completed, the units would double the Jewish population in the occupied territories.

Sharon may have hid the numbers, but his goal was plain: to settle enough Jews in the territories to alter the political geography and demography of the West Bank, permanently eradicating the possibility that the land could ever be redivided and that any independent Arab political entity could be established. He envisaged a protective ring of Jewish settlements around each Arab urban center—from Jenin and Nablus in the north to Ramallah in the center to Bethlehem and Hebron in the south. The Arabs of these cities ultimately might aspire to a limited form of political autonomy, but they would be small, disconnected, vulnerable islands in a Jewish sea. Similarly, Sharon planned a belt of settlements around the Arab population centers in East Jerusalem to seal off the area from the rest of the West Bank and permanently enshrine Israel's annexation of the city.

Sharon also wanted to erase the Green Line by building twelve new Jewish towns in a north-to-south line along the edge of the pre-1967 border.

296   Beyond the Promised Land

The new towns were to be paired with settlements that lay just a short distance across the border. The idea was to create a series of urban blocs, known as "stars," that would extend across the old border and connect more than two dozen settlements directly to central Israel.

It is clear, in retrospect, that Shamir knew of and approved most of Sharon's plans for expansion. He agreed with Sharon that it was important to push through as many housing starts as possible now that there was no Labor governing partner to put limits on the growth and before the Bush administration could pressure Israel into a settlements freeze. Still, Shamir expected Sharon to follow certain guidelines and to be discreet, a character trait Sharon never overvalued.

In effect, Sharon did the same thing to Shamir over settlements that he had done as defense minister to Menachem Begin a decade earlier over the Lebanon invasion: he proposed a grand scheme, won the prime minister's approval, then carried it out well beyond the point where his leader expected him to stop. Begin had expected Sharon to halt the troops twenty-five miles north of the border, but backed him when he went all the way to Beirut. Shamir hoped that Sharon would build settlements with less speed and more discretion, but he was not prepared to interfere when the housing minister, nicknamed "The Bulldozer," did neither.

At first Shamir's office denied the truth of reports of expanded construction, then fell back to denying that it had known about the moves. But by September, Shamir and his aides were defiantly endorsing Sharon's program. Unlike Sharon, however, Shamir wanted it done quietly, with no headlines or fanfare. He had no wish to provoke the Bush administration, no desire to call attention to himself. He somehow believed that Sharon could go ahead stealthily with the biggest settlement-building program in the twenty-four-year history of the occupation, as if all of Israel were Lehi, a clandestine underground society. But Shamir could not conceal such a program from friends or foes, both of whom had reasons to exaggerate its size and importance.

Zucker, Oron and Peace Now issued periodic updates disclosing the various new settlements in order to raise the alarm in Washington. At the same time the settlers themselves announced new communities—some of which amounted to no more than a dozen empty mobile homes, with no running water or electricity, hauled before sunrise to a barren hilltop—as a means of inflating the size and strength of their movement.

"New" settlements began popping up on the eve of each of Baker's visits to the region. In April, in time for Baker's third trip, there were Revava, a "private community" erected on a hilltop outside Nablus, and Talmon B, a new "neighborhood" built two miles from an existing settlement near Ramallah. Shamir's aides claimed to know nothing about these new developments; settlement leaders claimed that Shamir's office had granted prior approval. "This is our land," a settlement official told Joel Brinkley of the *New York Times*. "It doesn't belong to Baker or to George Bush."

In May, just in time for Baker's fourth visit, settlers opened Givon B, a collection of thirty-one mobile homes about eight hundred yards up a hill from another settlement near Bido, an Arab village north of Jerusalem. And in October, timed to coincide with Baker's final trip to the region, settlers seized a half dozen houses in the Arab neighborhood of Silwan in East Jerusalem. The government at first denounced the move as needlessly provocative, but later the cabinet endorsed it.

Shamir was adamantly opposed to provoking Baker and the administration with such blatant moves. There were times when he ordered Arens to delay settlement openings and when he even ordered the Shin Bet internal security service to investigate whether Sharon was exceeding his authority. But when a furious Baker demanded that the prime minister put a stop to Sharon's building spree, Shamir responded with his trademark shrug. It was nothing, he told Baker, only a public relations ploy by extremists on both the right and left and by Sharon, who tended to get carried away. Pay it no heed, Sharon was firmly under control, Shamir assured Baker. But Shamir refused to condemn Sharon. He felt Baker had no right to poke his nose into internal Israeli affairs—and settlements, built on soil that he considered part of Greater Israel, were an internal Israeli affair. He would not give in to Baker by publicly ordering a halt to the new settlements.

Baker was deeply frustrated. "I don't think there is any bigger obstacle to peace than the settlement activity that continues not only unabated, but at an enhanced pace," he told a House of Representatives subcommittee in May. "And nothing has made my job of trying to find Arab and Palestinian partners for Israel more difficult than being greeted by a new settlement every time I arrive."

Baker said he felt stuck in a Catch-22 situation. "We're not going to get any movement on settlement activity before we have an active peace process going, and it's going to be just that much more difficult to get a peace process going if we can't get any action on settlement activity."

Nonetheless, when questioned about settlements at a press conference in June, President Bush denied that he planned to link a settlement freeze to the granting of new loan guarantees to Israel for settling Soviet Jews. "I don't think it ought to be a quid pro quo," he told American Jewish leaders who came to lobby for the aid.

He would soon change his mind.

. . .

In the growing conflict over Jewish settlements, the Bush administration held a $10 billion hostage. Loan guarantees had first been requested by Labor's Shimon Peres in 1989 when he served as finance minister. In an appalling underestimation of the size of the wave of Soviet Jewish immigration about to inundate the country, Peres had asked for $400 million to help Israel build housing and create jobs for the thousands of immigrants pouring through Ben-Gurion Airport. Israel was not asking the United States to lend it the money directly but rather to guarantee private loans so that Israel would receive a lower interest rate. The cost to U.S. taxpayers was nominal—about 3 percent of the loan in a cash reserve—provided that Israel made its payments on time. But within weeks of the request it was clear that the $400 million was only a first installment; Israel needed billions.

Congress approved the $400 million in the spring of 1990, but the Bush administration, disturbed by the right-wing orientation of Shamir's new government and by the prime minister's grandiose "big Israel" statement in January, wanted ironclad assurances that the money would not be used to build new settlements or install Soviet Jews in the West Bank and Gaza. It held back the guarantees for almost nine months while Baker negotiated terms with the new Israeli foreign minister, David Levy. After much hard bargaining Levy submitted a letter in October 1990 pledging that the government would not settle any Soviet Jews "beyond the Green Line," nor use the borrowed funds there. When Ben-Aharon read the letter, he erupted. By using the term "Green Line," Levy had employed a phrase that the government considered obsolete, and he had effectively ruled out allowing Soviet Jews to live in annexed Jerusalem communities such as Gilo and Ramot where many were, in fact, settling. Embarrassed Foreign Affairs Ministry officials had to withdraw and rewrite the letter, which did nothing to enhance Israel's credibility with Washington.

Baker delayed the guarantees for several more months, using them as leverage to help keep Israel from launching a preemptive strike against Saddam Hussein during the Gulf crisis. He was preparing to approve them in early February when a Jackson Diehl article appeared in the *Washington Post* reporting charges by Zucker and Oron that Sharon was planning to build 12,000 new homes for settlers. Now it was Baker's turn to erupt. He ordered Ross to contact Shamir's office, which informed the Americans in writing that no such plans had been approved by the cabinet (the letter neglected to mention that formal approval was not needed). After receiving the letter Baker authorized the $400 million. Three weeks later Sharon told Israeli reporters that the real figure was 13,500 and that he already had all the authorization he needed to go ahead.

To Washington, it appeared as if the Israelis had once again gone back on a commitment. They had taken the $400 million, then gone ahead with the largest settlement program in history. Only a child could pretend that the money they were spending on settlements had not been freed up by the loan guarantees. To make matters worse, Israel also reneged on a pledge, contained in the Levy letter, to provide detailed information on Israeli settlement activity. When he approached the prime minister's office U.S. Ambassador William Brown was told to look up the numbers in the annual report of the Israeli Bureau of Central Statistics. We don't recognize any difference between Israel and the so-called occupied territories, Ben-Aharon told Brown; therefore we don't keep separate numbers. "Not what you'd expect from an ally who wants us to be forthcoming with even larger sums later on," said a U.S. official. The United States was forced to resort to using satellite photographs of the West Bank, spying from the sky on its own purported ally.

None of this stopped Israel from requesting that the United States guarantee an additional $10 billion in loans over a five-year period. At the behest of administration officials Shamir agreed in March 1991 to a 180-day delay in making the formal application, but he was so confident Israel would receive the guarantees that he allowed Modai to factor the first $2 billion into his 1992 budget. By early summer, lobbyists for the American Israel Public Affairs Committee were boasting to Israeli and U.S. officials alike that they had the votes in Congress to pass the guarantees even if Bush decided to veto the bill. "It's all over," one of the AIPAC people told Dennis Ross. "We've got the votes, so let's find a way to make it go down easy."

Seemingly assured of victory, Shamir decided to press ahead. As the six-month delay drew to an end he began receiving signals that Bush was changing his mind and might demand yet another delay or else reject the request altogether. Shamir did not seek a confrontation, but he would not back down again. If necessary, he was ready to challenge the president of the United States head-on.

Many people claimed later to have warned Shamir, but if so the warnings were muffled, both because the speakers were inclined to soft-pedal their advice to the prime minister and because Shamir was not inclined to listen. Dine, Hoenlein and Presidents' Conference chairman Shoshana Cardin all advised Shamir at various times that summer that he could face a bruising battle if he confronted the president. Cardin chided him for incorporating the first $2 billion of loan guarantees in the 1992 budget—he was taking too much for granted, she said.

Even Zalman Shoval, Shamir's loyal ambassador to the United States, could see the Hobson's choice that was shaping up. He told Israel Radio in June: "The Israeli government . . . may have to decide whether the issue of settlement is a priority or that the issue of aid is a priority." Shoval was ordered to fall into line by his superiors. Although there were staffers at both the embassy and AIPAC who predicted disaster if the issue came to a vote in Congress, they were overruled by their superiors. The assessments sent to Shamir generally were enthusiastically positive.

There were other warnings. Vice President Dan Quayle, a staunch supporter of Israel, cautioned Arens against challenging Bush during the defense minister's visit to Washington that summer. Another Republican ally, U.S. Senator Phil Gramm of Texas, visiting Jerusalem as a guest of the Anti-Defamation League, warned, "I've known George Bush for twenty-two years in public life and I've never seen him as upset on anything as on the settlements issue."

American Jewish leaders gave Shamir the numbers, but not the entire truth. Dine, Hoenlein, Ben-Aharon and Benjamin Netanyahu had become a charmed circle; they fed one another's self-concept of Israel's righteousness and invincibility in Congress and ultimately fed that concept to Shamir. No one, it appears, explained to Shamir that forcing a confrontation with the administration would be a huge mistake even if Israel won, that with Bush seemingly heading for reelection, a showdown could damage the power of the Jewish lobby and set back the cause of Israel in the United States for years to come. And although several pleaded with him to suspend new settlements, all of them made clear they would support him even if he did not. No one in Shamir's shrinking circle of advisers was prepared to tell the prime minister to his face or to declare publicly what many of them believed privately—that he was sacrificing the great cause of Soviet Jewish immigration to the narrow ideological agenda of more settlements.

Shamir listened to all of them but, in fact, he heard nothing. He believed strongly in Ben-Aharon's concept that the rope could always be pulled tighter, that Israel's supporters tended, if anything, to underestimate their power to deliver. Shamir saw the guarantees as Israel's due, insisting in a radio interview that the United States "is obliged, from a moral point of view, to give Israel this aid. . . . If the Arabs are handed such a gift without even asking for it, they will dance on the rooftops and make new and even bigger demands, and the peace process will become impossible."

Shamir's advisers may have had their numbers correct, but their reading of President Bush's determination on the issue was just plain wrong. Once they had the votes, they believed that Bush would fold without risking a confrontation. After all, the president himself had said there would be no linkage between the guarantees and settlements. But something was happening to George Bush that they failed to see.

All through the summer of 1991, Bush was losing patience with Shamir and Israel. Reading the satellite data, the headlines and Ariel Sharon's public statements, he and his staff concluded that Israel had launched a large-scale settlement program even while Shamir was telling Washington that no such buildup was taking place. Bush grew increasingly furious—at the way the Israelis had tried to deceive him, at the way they had stiff-armed his ambassador over settlement data and at the way they treated his personal envoy, Jim Baker. And now AIPAC and Shamir and their allies in Congress were telling the administration that the loan guarantees were no longer in Bush's power to grant or deny. To George Bush it felt as if Israel and its friends were spitting in his face.

Bush was at the height of his prestige following the Gulf War. His poll ratings on domestic matters might be slipping, but he was still highly rated as a calm, collected manager of foreign affairs. He felt he had tried as hard as possible to work with Shamir. But he was persuaded from their first meeting in 1989, from that first enigmatic wave of Shamir's hand and that first claim of "it won't be a problem," that Shamir had not dealt honestly with him. Bush had stated several times that he would not link loan guarantees to Israel's settlement policy. But now a larger issue was at stake: as far as Bush was concerned, Israel and its allies were challenging the authority of the president to make foreign policy.

Bush did not want to reject the loan guarantees request outright. But he wanted another postponement so that the issue would not interfere with Baker's efforts to get the Arab states and Israel to attend a Middle East peace conference. And, no doubt, Bush also wanted to let Shamir know, in plain terms, who was in charge.

Baker, who was attempting to put the finishing touches on the Middle East peace conference, wanted to go easy on Shamir. A confrontation on loan guarantees at this late stage might scuttle six months of painstaking diplomatic work. Richard Haass recommended that Bush invite Shamir to his summer home in Kennebunkport, Maine, put his arm around the prime minister's shoulder and ask him to hold off on the loan guarantees request for another four months. Baker was interested; Bush was not. Just call Shamir and inform him that we want another delay, he told Baker.

Shamir told Baker he would think it over. Then the prime minister consulted again with AIPAC's Dine and the Presidents' Conference's Hoenlein. They told him that they already had signatures from nearly seventy senators in support of the loan guarantees and that Senators Daniel Inouye and Robert Kasten, respectively the Democrat from Hawaii and Republican from Wisconsin who were joint sponsors of the amendment, were very optimistic. The House of Representatives was already in Israel's pocket: in mid-June the House had voted 387 to 44 to reject an amendment to cut aid to Israel by $82 million in response to settlement activity. There was no reason to believe that a vote on loan guarantees would be any less decisive.

So Shamir called Baker back five days later to inform him that Israel was going ahead. It was a matter between the administration and the Congress, the prime minister told him disingenuously. A few hours later Ambassador Shoval arrived at the State Department bearing Israel's formal request for the guarantees.

Most American Jewish leaders believed the guarantees were a fait accompli. But a businessman named Gordon Zacks, a longtime friend of Bush, returned to New York after spending Labor Day weekend at Kennebunkport and asked to meet with a select group from the Presidents' Conference. He told them he had hit a stone wall when he raised the issue with Bush, that the president was angry and was preparing to fight. They listened, but they did not heed. "Look, Gordy had been point man ten years ago but he was now totally out of the loop, not representing anyone, not delegated by anyone," said a participant. "Frankly, no one took him seriously."

At Shamir's behest, AIPAC, the Presidents' Conference and the National Jewish Community Relations Advisory Council had set up a "task force" in June to lobby Congress for the guarantees. It conducted a well-oiled campaign of letter writing and personal visits. The message was that loan guarantees were a humanitarian issue involving the freedom and safety of Soviet Jews and should have nothing to do with either the peace process or a settlement freeze. And the Holocaust was invoked: Soviet Jews were in danger from antisemites, it was said; they needed to be rescued and "brought home" to Israel.

It was one of the biggest and most emotionally powerful lobbying campaigns American Jewish groups had ever organized. Rescuing Soviet Jewry was an issue that went to the very heart of what Israel was about. During the Rosh Hashanah holiday rabbis around the country urged congregants to call their congressmen and lobby for the guarantees. A special toll-free phone number (1-800-92-ALIYA) was established to send prepared messages to lawmakers.

The task force had long-standing plans to make Thursday, September 12, a day of public lobbying. Some five hundred supporters from around the country were due to arrive on Capitol Hill to meet with their congressmen and explain why the loans were so important for Israel's future. Hoping to cut them off, Baker invited AIPAC's leaders to his office on September 6 to offer a six-point compromise that would give the administration a 120-day delay. There was no firm commitment that the administration would support the request at the end of that period, but the compromise did commit the United States to helping Israel secure the lowest possible interest rates on the loans if approved. No deal was struck, but Baker asked the lobbyists to hold off for two weeks while he journeyed to Europe and the Middle East. He would offer the compromise personally to Shamir in Jerusalem; after that, if Shamir said no, the Israel lobby could resume its effort.

Baker left Washington believing he had won a respite. But AIPAC's leaders made no attempt to call off the gathering; indeed, by Wednesday afternoon the numbers had swollen to more than a thousand. Some of the campaign's leaders were meeting at AIPAC's office when the phone rang. It was Dennis Ross calling from Moscow to ask about Thursday's gathering. Dine was not reassuring. Dennis, we've got seventy senators who say they support us, he told Ross.

The White House believed it had been double-crossed. Bush fielded phone calls from senators who warned that they could not resist American Jewish pressure to approve the guarantees without a strong public stance by the president himself. Bush tried in vain that evening to reach the president of AIPAC, Mayer Mitchell, to head things off. By the time Bush met with AIPAC officials the following morning, his mind was made up. The president was blunt. He saw the AIPAC lobbying effort in Congress as an attempt to subvert his authority. This was not a question of loan guarantees and settlements as much as a constitutional dispute between the president and Congress. Since he could not reach a compromise with AIPAC, Bush said, he was prepared to take his case directly to the American people.

While Bush and the AIPAC leaders were meeting, the loan guarantees campaigners gathered at the Washington Sheraton for National Leadership Action Day. Some forty heads of major American Jewish organizations joined Shoshana Cardin onstage. Cardin spoke of the campaign as a moral crusade that could not and should not be turned aside. American Jews were going into battle for Israel and their fellow Jews. The session had the atmosphere of a military operation. The troops received their marching orders—schedules of the lawmakers each was to visit, plus a computer printout detailing the arguments to be made. A dozen buses ferried the troops to Capitol Hill for the assault.

Two hours later George Bush counterattacked. Using remarks scripted by Haass, the president appeared at a press conference to talk about American-Israeli relations and why he wanted Israel to wait on the loan guarantees. "Just months ago," he told reporters, "American men and women in uniform risked their lives to defend Israelis in the face of Iraqi Scud missiles, and indeed Desert Storm, while winning a war against aggression, also achieved the defeat of Israel's most dangerous adversary."

Now the United States was in the midst of delicate negotiations to bring about a dream that Israel had held for forty-three years—direct talks with its Arab neighbors. But that effort could be undermined by a drawn-out dispute over settlements and loan guarantees, Bush contended. So the president had attempted to persuade Israel's supporters to accept a new delay so that the peace process would not be jeopardized. Bush told the press that he had "worn out" one of his ears making calls to congressmen and would now "move over to the other ear and keep on it."

Then, in unscripted remarks, Bush took direct aim at the Jewish lobby, saying he was "up against some powerful political forces. . . . We're up against very strong and effective, sometimes, groups that go up in the Hill. I heard today there were something like a thousand lobbyists on the Hill working on the other side of the question. We've got one lonely little guy down here doing it."

In his trademark fractured syntax Bush tried to explain his reasoning. "It is my best judgment that a rancorous debate now is literally miniscule in importance compared to the objective of peace. . . . Who is going to get hurt? What possibly could work against that reasonable request from an administration that's brought this thing from square one right up to a peak that nobody really believed we could achieve, getting these countries together, and the work that's gone into it."

Striking the podium with his fist, Bush pledged to put the cause of the peace conference ahead of political considerations, even if it damaged his 1992 reelection chances. "I'm going to fight for what I believe, and it may be politically popular but probably it's not. But that's not the question here, that's not the question, whether it's good 1992 politics. What's important here is that we give this process a chance. And I don't care if I get one vote. I'm going to stand for what I believe here, and I believe the American people will be with me."

Bush's remarks punctured National Leadership Action Day like a shotgun blast through a helium balloon. Some of the participants wanted to call it quits immediately, but Hoenlein and AIPAC officials insisted that they carry on. Afterward Shoshana Cardin held a damage-control press conference in which she praised the president and said nothing to acknowledge the blow he had just struck.

Yitzhak Shamir was on an official visit to Paris when Ehud Gol, his newly appointed media adviser, knocked on his hotel door. Gol, Ben-Aharon, Avi Pazner and Ovadia Sofer, the Israeli ambassador to France, all gathered in the front room of Shamir's suite. They missed the live feed of Bush's press conference on CNN but watched reruns of the critical segment over and over in silence, as if they were watching a train wreck repeat itself before their eyes. Everyone knew what it meant. The president of the United States had just declared war against them.

Shamir stayed cool. He analyzed the situation calmly and with an almost impersonal detachment. It was 6 P.M. Paris time and he was scheduled to attend a dinner. He refused to cancel. He issued a very cautious statement emphasizing, as he always liked to in times of trouble, that despite occasional disagreements, Israel and the United States remained close friends and partners. There was no point in taking up Bush's challenge with inflammatory remarks of his own, Shamir felt. Indeed, he was furious when members of his cabinet—Ehud Olmert and Deputy Police Minister Rehavam Zeevi—denounced Bush as an antisemite. With his house on fire, Shamir had no wish to throw more gasoline on the blaze.

Shamir believed he still had the votes on Capitol Hill and the lobbyists to deliver those votes. But he quickly found Israel's support had melted down. Congressional backing, even among Israel's traditional Democratic allies, had been wide but not very deep. Most congressmen were unhappy about Sharon's settlement drive. They did not want to undermine the administration's efforts to get Arab-Israeli peace talks under way. They also were not happy about extending more foreign aid to any country at a time of economic recession and neoisolationism at home. Many had been prepared to go along with AIPAC until Bush drew the line. Now Speaker of the House Thomas Foley and Senate majority leader George Mitchell used Bush's hard line as their excuse to back away. They urged AIPAC and the Israeli embassy to reach some kind of compromise with Bush.

But what surprised Shamir and his aides much more was the rapid defection of American Jews. Suddenly Jewish leaders were urging compromise and warning that the votes were no longer there. Many were stunned by Bush's condemnation of the Jewish lobby—to them it was a blatant appeal to antisemitism, a claim that Jews were too powerful and too shadowy, that they needed to be confronted. They also did not like being portrayed as serving the interests of a foreign power in opposing the president. Traumatized by his strong attack, they quickly folded. "It clobbered the Jewish community, left us in a state of shock," recalled one senior leader. "People were deeply hurt and offended, and it also scared the shit out of us."

Later, when he heard of their objections, Bush met with Jewish leaders and apologized. "I did not understand before how hurtful my words were," he told them. "I never intended to cause pain." But the damage was done. "One lonely little guy" entered American Jewish lore as the worst attack by a president on organized Jewry since the 1950s.

In a meeting at Ambassador Shoval's house a few nights after Bush's remarks, the leaders of AIPAC asked that Israel formally withdraw its loan guarantees request. Shoval passed on their plea to Shamir's office, but the answer came back no. Yossi Ben-Aharon railed at what he called the "*galut* mentality" of American Jews, who had collapsed in fear the moment they were attacked by Gentiles. But many American Jews saw Shamir as jeopardizing the guarantees and undercutting their efforts by his insistence on the settlement program. Settlements were not their issue and they were relieved to walk away from it. Within days the matter was settled. Israel did not formally withdraw its request, but congressional leaders gave George Bush his 120-day postponement.

Shamir seemed stunned and incredulous. "This is not the reality; this is not the American people," he told Israel Radio. "The American people will return to their senses." Israel's relations with the United States had become "a bad dream."

At first Shamir seemed caught unaware that his support had drained, that he was now facing the administration without his allies. He delayed and deferred, assuming that support in Congress would grow. Meanwhile, his rhetoric on settlements became even more inflammatory. He made no pretense now of distancing himself from Sharon. The expansion program became his own. In late September he personally inaugurated a new Jewish settlement on the border of the Green Line, declaring that "all the territories that we have available for construction will be populated by Jews up to the horizon's edge."

When he finally realized he had lost Shamir lashed out ineffectually. Bush had struck "against the deepest foundations of Jewish and Zionist consciousness," he told reporters. "I would like to believe that if the leaders of the United States knew of our great sensitivity on this matter, and if they were aware of the scope of the struggle of our enemies since the beginning of the century, precisely against Jewish immigration to the Land of Israel, they would have thought twice before pursuing the course that they did." But Shamir got it wrong: Bush was more than aware of Shamir's "great sensitivity" when it came to settlements; that is why he struck the blow he did. As for Jewish immigration, it was Shamir, not Bush, who sacrificed this sacred mission on the altar of the settlements.

Abe Foxman of the Anti-Defamation League visited Jerusalem and was saddened and alarmed by what he heard. Even the so-called Americanists like Dan Meridor and Ehud Olmert spoke of the administration in terms of betrayal and antisemitism. Washington was the enemy: liars, cheaters, bastards who wanted to destroy Israel. Meridor noted recent leaks of disparaging reports about the economy, implying that Israel was not creditworthy, that it might default on its loans and leave the United States to pay the bills, an outrageous accusation considering that Israel had always been a model borrower. Meridor told both Foxman and Howard Squadron of the American Jewish Congress that he was convinced not only that Bush wanted to drive Israel back to the pre-1967 borders, but that the president also wanted to destroy the country's nuclear capability—to cripple Israel, render it toothless, defenseless against its enemies. Foxman and Squadron believed this was a dangerous fantasy on Meridor's part, but they could not persuade him that he was wrong.

American Jewish leaders and Israel's closest allies in Congress—Republicans and Democrats alike—sought to fashion a compromise that would allow the loan guarantees request to go forward in January 1992, when Bush's 120-day delay expired. But the battle was already over. Baker for a time indicated he would entertain a compromise provided that Israel was prepared to freeze new housing starts in the occupied territories and deduct from the amount of the loan guarantees any money used to finish those units already under construction. He and Shoval held three fruitless meetings in late January and February 1992 to see if they could reach an accord. But each time they met Baker offered a shrinking set of numbers for how many settlements Washington would allow Jerusalem to complete and showed a decreasing interest in reaching a deal.

Two weeks later Baker gave a blunt public warning, telling a House subcommittee that Israel must stop building settlements or forgo the loan guarantees altogether. "The choice is Israel's," said Baker in a take-it-or-leave-it ultimatum. With public disenchantment with foreign aid at an all-time high and with almost no public support for settlements, it was a battle that the administration could not lose. Israeli elections were due to be held in June, and the White House was now content to sit back and see who won. In the meantime, the loan guarantees were on hold. George Bush could not freeze settlements, but he could freeze the money to build them.

While all of the parties involved took some time to realize it, the loan guarantees issue was decided the moment that George Bush went public. Israel simply did not have the economic or political wherewithal to defy an American president. For the first time in the history of their relationship, the United States had demanded that Israel change one of its key policies as the price for economic aid and had inflicted the penalty when Israel refused.

• • •

A man who for his entire life had been anchored firmly to one vision, Shamir now seemed lost and adrift. When it came to settlements he followed behind Sharon's provocative lead; when it came to the peace process he caved in increasingly to Baker's conditions. He still raised obstacles, most particularly around the makeup of the Palestinian delegation to the international conference Baker was engineering. But his heart was no longer in it. On the question of the U.N. observer and on the reconvening of the conference, Shamir gradually abandoned positions that he earlier had claimed were based on unyielding principle.

He had no desire to go to the conference that Baker envisaged, but he saw no way to escape it. Some of his colleagues wanted to retaliate against the administration by linking Israel's participation to the loan guarantees, but Shamir refused. For years Israel had been on record stating that it was prepared to talk peace with its Arab neighbors at any time and any place. Israelis, Shamir knew, expected him to honor that pledge. He had no choice.

Still, he forced Baker into one last marathon session of negotiations in October. Baker had just completed a twelve-hour final round of talks with Syrian Foreign Minister Farouk Sharaa in Damascus. Arriving in Jerusalem, the secretary of state now underwent a five-hour session with Shamir that centered mostly on the composition of the joint Jordanian-Palestinian delegation and on the text of the letter of assurance Baker planned to present to Israel. Shamir wanted the Americans to attend the conference as a declared ally of Israel, committed to walking out alongside the Israelis if the Arabs violated the spirit of the conference—if, for example, the attending Palestinians declared themselves to be members of the PLO. But Baker insisted that the United States could best serve everyone's interests by continuing to act as an honest broker. Because it was hosting the conference, it could not play favorites. Israel was on its own.

That Friday afternoon, October 18, the clock ticked down toward the Jewish Sabbath while Baker and Shamir played out one more tug-of-war. The secretary of state insisted on Shamir's approval for a still-incomplete list of Palestinian delegates, while on the other side of town the Palestinians stalled finishing the list—they could not reach final agreement on the names with PLO headquarters in Tunis—and Boris Pankin, the new Soviet foreign minister, waited at the King David Hotel. Pankin had arrived the previous day to bestow upon Israel the final prize for going to the conference—the restoration of Soviet diplomatic recognition after a twenty-four-year break. In any other context this in itself would have been a milestone event; now it played a subordinate role in Baker's grand orchestration.

Pankin cooled his heels until Shamir signed off on the Palestinian delegation. Then, with only an hour or so to go before sundown, Pankin's limousine dashed to the Israeli Foreign Affairs Ministry for a flurry of signatures and a toast with Levy, while Baker headed home triumphantly with the agreement on a peace conference firmly in hand.

As he met with Israeli reporters that afternoon, Shamir looked pale, depressed and disoriented. In effect, he had gotten almost everything he demanded—a conference with no role for the United Nations or East Jerusalemites, no settlement freeze and an agenda that dealt with Palestinian autonomy rather than territorial compromise. Nonetheless, he told them that he was still unhappy about the terms of the conference, which was scheduled to take place in Madrid, and doubted very much that it would bring positive results. But he added, "In any case, I think I will recommend to the government to choose this way because I don't see a better alternative."

"Ain alternativa," he told them, shaking his head with a slight grimace. "There is no choice."

Menachem Begin would have treated the Madrid conference like the historic spectacle it was, would have risen to the occasion with fiery rhetoric and sweeping gestures. Yitzhak Shamir treated it like a trip to the dentist. He did not trust the pomp and circumstance. He was certain that the Arabs were there only to please the Americans, not because they wanted to make peace with Israel. And in fact, Shamir was there for much the same reason. An Israeli reporter asked him after the opening session how it felt finally to sit down across a table from Israel's Arab enemies. "It was a regular day," Shamir replied with a shrug.

A few days before the conference began Shamir had cast aside David Levy and installed himself as the head of an aggressively hawkish delegation. He had put his own aides in charge of the two most important bilateral meetings—Ben-Aharon would lead the negotiating team with the Syrians and Eli Rubinstein would deal with the joint Palestinian-Jordanian delegation. At the time Shamir's decision to go to Madrid himself was interpreted as a sign of his personal enthusiasm. In fact, it was only a measure of his disdain for Levy, his main Likud rival, and his fear that the inexperienced foreign minister would give away the store in negotiations.

Shamir's opening speech to the conference, penned by Ben-Aharon, was cautious and uninspiring, invoking the Holocaust and the many other historical tragedies that had befallen the Jewish people, restating the exclusive claim of the Jews to the Land of Israel and warning that "the quickest way to an impasse" was for the negotiations to focus "primarily and exclusively" on territory. The root cause of the conflict, Shamir insisted, was not a dispute over borders but rather the Arab refusal to recognize Israel's legitimacy.

After the opening addresses on Thursday, the conference quickly deteriorated into a mudslinging match. The American notion that putting all of the parties in a large room and having them hear one another talk would begin to break down decades of mistrust proved to be naïve. For months Baker had acted as an acoustic barrier, absorbing their harshest attacks against one another and communicating their demands in the dry, neutral language of a diplomatic translator. At Madrid the barrier was suddenly removed and the two sides faced each other directly. It was not a pretty sight.

During the second-day responses Shamir and Sharaa traded accusations and insults. Shamir called Syria "one of the most oppressive, tyrannical regimes in the world." Sharaa angrily waved a 1946 British Wanted poster of Shamir and accused him of murdering peace mediators such as Folke Bernadotte. Western diplomats, including Baker, scrambled to keep the opposing parties from walking out before the landmark bilateral sessions scheduled for two days later. The delegations stayed on, but it was clear that rather than erode the psychological barriers between the warring parties, the conference had reaffirmed the deep, emotional divisions between them. The hard-liners outshouted the healers. The spectacle ultimately was more hysteric than historic.

The one exception was Palestinian representative Haidar Abdel-Shafi, who presented a dignified address that eloquently laid out the Palestinian case while calling for reconciliation with Israel. The speech put the Palestinians back on the diplomatic map and gave them, at least for the duration of the first round of talks, a status on a par with Israel and the Arab states.

Dan Meridor watched Shamir's performance with grave misgivings. The prime minister gave the impression that he did not take the conference seriously. Meridor wanted Shamir to reach out to Palestinian moderates, take some initiative that would give real momentum to the autonomy proposal and outflank the PLO and its sympathizers. Instead, the government assumed a static, defensive crouch. The only fireworks came when Benjamin Netanyahu, brought to Madrid by Shamir to serve as his public relations man, held a press conference for Arab journalists. The session, a first in the annals of the Arab-Israeli conflict, enhanced Netanyahu's reputation as a verbal scrapper but did nothing to further Israel's policy goals.

Even while they were skeptical about the Arabs, Meridor knew, most Israelis desperately welcomed the Madrid conference and hoped against hope for some kind of breakthrough. They wanted their government to seize the opportunity and demonstrate to the world that Israel was truly interested in reaching peace. But this was more than Shamir was capable of producing. He gave his speech, offered a belligerent response to Sharaa, then flew home almost immediately.

The downfall of Yitzhak Shamir began in Madrid. When the curtain was raised on the diplomatic gala, Israel was deprived of its longtime enemy. Suddenly the issue was no longer legitimacy; for all their hopelessly hostile rhetoric, the presence of the Arabs at the table across from Israel was de facto recognition of its existence. And all of a sudden Israelis saw Shamir as pursuing a strategy not of survival but of ideology—one that most of them did not share.

Two days before the conference opened, a different kind of exchange between Arabs and Jews took place in the West Bank on the main road to Nablus. Four buses had left the Jewish settlement of Shiloh that evening to travel to Tel Aviv to attend a right-wing rally denouncing the conference and calling upon Shamir to stand fast in Madrid. As the bus climbed the winding road north of the settlement, gunmen opened fire, killing the driver of one of the buses and Rachel Druck, a mother of seven who sat directly behind him. Six other passengers were wounded, five of them children. Rachel Druck died almost instantly from a bullet in her chest.

Rachel's husband, David, decided to bury her at Shiloh. Hers was the first grave since the settlement had been founded thirteen years earlier. Sitting in his modest stone house atop a windswept hill, surrounded by relatives who had come to help him grieve and by his seven motherless children, he explained his decision this way: "A grave is stronger than a house. A house you can move. A grave you can't move. This is my answer to the killers."

Yitzhak Shamir knew about Rachel Druck's death when he left for Madrid. When he returned he wrote to David Druck that her death had been constantly on his mind at the conference. When Druck phoned the prime minister after the conference to thank him for his tough stand there, Shamir was so moved with emotion he could not speak. Yitzhak Shamir's heart was in Shiloh, not Madrid.

Shamir hoped that Israel's attendance at Madrid would help induce Bush to change his mind and accede to the loan guarantees. But the president's position actually hardened—No Settlement Freeze, No Loan Guarantees became the administration's unspoken mantra. Shamir was so cowed that he did not even raise the subject when he met with Bush for thirty minutes at Madrid. "It was as if the issue didn't exist," said a Shamir aide. "No one wanted to spoil the mood."

Later in November Shamir visited the United States in a vain effort to shore up support among American Jews and to discuss the matter again with Bush. First the administration humiliated the prime minister by not agreeing to a face-to-face meeting until the last minute. Then the fifty-minute discussion focused on another issue entirely—Israel's seemingly petty refusal to attend the next round of bilateral talks in Washington. The Israelis wanted a Middle Eastern venue for the talks and Shamir patiently explained why. By the time the discussion was complete, the fifty minutes were up and Shamir and his working group were ushered out the door. The loan guarantees never came up. Shamir was angry, claiming Bush had steered the conversation to a dead end. The Americans claimed that Shamir had wasted the time on minor issues. Shamir left the White House embittered and totally exhausted.

It was one scene from a frustrating trip. Shamir succeeded in raising hundreds of thousands of dollars in Los Angeles, New York, Boston and Washington for the Likud's reelection campaign. But the day before he spoke at a meeting of the Council of Jewish Federations in Baltimore, an opinion poll was released of the views of more than two hundred council board members and other Jewish community leaders. It showed that 88 percent were prepared for territorial compromise "in return for credible guarantees of peace" and that 85 percent disagreed with Shamir's refusal to return "not one inch." Seventy-eight percent supported a freeze on settlements, and 79 percent agreed to the eventual emergence of a Palestinian state within the context of a peace accord.

The poll was another embarrassing blow, but Shamir claimed not to get the message. "I am not surprised, but I don't believe it," he told *Face the Nation*. Wherever he went in the United States, "people have applauded me." The rank and file of American Jews "supports my views and my opinions."

It was not true. Most American Jews believed in territorial compromise and believed that sooner or later Israel would have to sit down and talk to genuine representatives of the Palestinians, whether PLO members or not. They were deeply uncomfortable with Shamir's ideology, yet they did not confront him directly or publicly. Instead they looked on as he went up against Bush and Baker and lost.

The Bush administration, Shamir knew, had done a lot of positive things for Israel during its four years in office. It had played a key role in helping nearly 400,000 Soviet Jews and 15,000 Ethiopians emigrate to Israel and in expunging the hated "Zionism is racism" resolution from the United Nations. It had prodded China and the Soviet Union to open diplomatic relations with Israel. It had fought a war that vanquished Israel's most powerful enemy, Iraq, and left Israel more secure militarily than at any time in its history. The relationship between the Pentagon and the Kirya in Tel Aviv had grown more and more extensive. And Jim Baker had brokered the first face-to-face talks between Israel and its Arab enemies in forty-three years. These were solid accomplishments that led many Israelis to conclude that the Bush years were good ones for Israel.

Yet at the same time Shamir and Bush had staged the most serious confrontation between an Israeli prime minister and an American president since the 1956 Suez crisis. Both men knew going in that they could pay a high price for their conflict, and both eventually did. The rejection of his request for loan guarantees cost Shamir popular support among Israelis, who believed he had mismanaged relations with Israel's most important ally. Bush's role in defeating the request deeply alienated many American Jewish voters, who helped elect his Democratic opponent, Bill Clinton, in November 1992. Neither man walked away unscathed.

Looking back, Shamir would explain the clash in conspiratorial terms. Bush and Baker had been out to get Israel and cut it down to size from the moment they took office, he insisted. His aides pointed to Bush's denunciation of Jewish settlements back in 1971 when he was U.S. ambassador to the United Nations and to Baker's senior thesis at Princeton on the Arab world. They recounted the words of former cabinet secretaries in the Reagan administration who recalled how Bush had bitterly opposed Israel's 1981 air raid on the Iraqi nuclear reactor and its role in the 1985 Pollard spy scandal. Bush, they claimed, believed he was set up by the Israelis in 1986 when Amiram Nir, Israel's operative in the Iran-Contra affair, insisted on meeting him secretly at the King David Hotel during a vice presidential trip to Israel and briefed him on arms-for-hostages dealings that he would just as soon not have known about. And Shamir's aides saw the hand of Bush and Baker behind George Shultz's decision in the waning days of the Reagan administration to open a diplomatic dialogue with their hated enemy, the PLO.

If only we had done our homework better, and if our friends in AIPAC had done theirs, we would have seen it coming, or at least we would have known what we were up against, Yossi Ben-Aharon lamented.

Missing from all of these explanations was any sense that Israel itself was to blame as well, that with a little less arrogance and a little more willingness to compromise Yitzhak Shamir could have ducked the final confrontation. The truth was that Shamir had badly miscalculated his own power and the power of Israel's American Jewish allies, that he had overplayed his hand by forcing Israel's supporters into positions they did not agree with and ultimately could not defend, that he had maneuvered himself into a confrontation with the leader of the strongest country on earth and turned a potential friend into a determined adversary.

The confrontation put to rest the maxim that you could not pressure Israel into concessions. For one solid year Bush and Baker did exactly that. They squeezed and cajoled Shamir into going to Madrid. Then when they could not extract anything more, they isolated him and speeded his downfall.

In some strange way Shamir still longed for Bush's respect and approval.

He told Meridor that his only regret was that he had not been able to sit down and talk to Bush one-on-one about why the settlement issue was so important to Israel. If only he had been able to explain the history and the background, Shamir felt certain, he could have won the president's support. But the two leaders were never to meet again.

An aide recalled Shamir's euphoria a few months later when Bush phoned to wish him a happy Passover holiday. The conversation was light and friendly and it went without a hitch. "Fifteen minutes we spoke!" he told the aide. "You see, he likes me." Shamir bubbled with delight, as if the episode proved something important to him. Perhaps it was not too late. Once the Israeli election was out of the way, and Shamir was safely back in the prime minister's office, he would approach Bush again. Next time, perhaps, it would all go differently.

13. "Israel Is Waiting for Rabin"

*The old is dying, and the new cannot be born; in
this interregnum there arises a great diversity of
morbid symptoms.*

—ANTONIO GRAMSCI

BEERSHEBA is a tough, working-class city on the rim of the Negev Desert,
populated largely by Sephardi Jews. Many of its neighborhoods are rugged,
treeless and unkempt, dominated by raw concrete and half-paved boule-
vards. It had long been prime Likud territory; in 1988 a crowd of thousands
had welcomed Yitzhak Shamir when he made a campaign appearance. Despite his dogmatic, unmodulated rhetorical style and his decidedly un-
charismatic personality, they had cheered him lustily, mobbed him as if he
were a film star. They had endorsed the formula that had brought Likud to
power in 1977 and had kept it there despite countless setbacks and disappointments: the populist economics, the tough line against the Arabs and
the vilification of the left-of-center Labor opposition as the party of elitism
and sellout.

Shamir came back to the same park in May 1992 to help kick off his reelection campaign. But this time things were different. The crowd was tiny,
no more than three hundred hardy souls, and it was passive. The security
people, expecting a mob scene, had cordoned off fifty yards of space
around the speaker's platform. Shamir was isolated from the small group of
listeners so far away. The stage seemed too high, too remote, and he really
could not see the crowd. What he could see was a small group of protesters
standing at the front with signs: "Likud Is Corrupt" and "Shamir, You've

Cheated Us." And he could hear one of them, an angry bass booming into the thin, evening desert air: "Shamir, you're corrupt! You're a liar!"

Shamir was used to troublemakers bused in by Labor to cause disruption. In the past they would not have lasted very long; neighborhood enforcers would have moved in, even broken a few heads if necessary. But this time nobody made a move. The crowd just kept quiet. And it soon became clear that the hecklers were not imports, but local people from the neighborhood that had always gone 70 to even 80 percent for Likud.

It made no difference to Shamir. He was not to going ignore this little challenge. Soon he was waving his fist, pointing his finger and screaming back at the lone voice, trading insult for insult. "You are violent! You are a criminal! No one will listen to you!" he shouted. "These terrorists who are heckling us want to destroy our democracy! They've been paid by Labor to come here!" Most of the crowd standing behind the heckler could not hear what Shamir's antagonist was shouting. All they could hear was their own prime minister, the leader of Israel, firing off frenzied accusations into the empty desert air. He sounded out of control, almost hysterical, a little man lost in his own tangled anger and syntax.

Later, on the helicopter going back to Jerusalem, Shamir seemed shocked. "This is the first time in my political career that this has happened to me," he told *Yediot* columnist Nachum Barnea. He continued to insist that the hecklers were ringers imported to sabotage the campaign. Real Israelis would never turn against him and the party.

Still, he had seen and heard it, and he must have realized deep inside that things were not the same as before. His favorite political son, Dan Meridor, the adviser he deemed his most intelligent, was warning that unless things turned around quickly Likud would be lucky to win thirty seats in the new Israeli Knesset, a plunge of 25 percent in its support. Benjamin Netanyahu, lean, hungry and full of American-style electoral stratagems, came to him with a private poll projecting disaster and pleaded for sweeping measures like a cabinet reshuffle and a tax cut. Moshe Arens, once his closest ally, would not even speak to him. And David Levy was sulking on the sidelines, unwilling to help deliver the big Sephardi vote that was always such a crucial component of Likud's electoral base.

And now, even while Shamir continued to shrug off all the bad tidings with a thin, all-knowing smile and a dismissive wave of his seventy-six-year-old hand, he knew it was all true. In a country that for so long had been stalemated politically, where Shamir and his party had always been able to rely on their strongholds and their faithful, something had changed.

• • •

The Likud and Shamir had come out of the Madrid conference with bright prospects for reelection. Polls in late 1991 showed the party winning as many as forty-eight seats in the Knesset (it had won forty in 1988), with Labor, its strongest competition, trailing by at least a dozen seats. Good fortune seemed to be smiling again: just as Menachem Begin had been able to make peace with Egypt while retaining full control over the occupied West Bank and Gaza Strip, so had Yitzhak Shamir launched direct peace talks with the Arabs while tightening Israel's grip on the territories. Despite the bitter opening speeches and the quick stalemate in the negotiating sessions, Madrid seemed like a brilliant stroke. Netanyahu, following his agile public-relations performance at Madrid, had become one of Shamir's favorites. He pleaded with the prime minister to call an early election. We've got the momentum so let's capitalize on it, he told Shamir. But the prime minister demurred. We don't need to rush things, he replied. Time is on our side.

But the polling numbers, pumped up by the short-term euphoria of Madrid, were a momentary phenomenon that masked a deep-seated disaffection with Likud in general and Shamir in particular. Part of the problem was economic: largely because of the influx of Russian immigrants, unemployment had climbed into double digits for the first time in anyone's memory and remained stubbornly at 11.5 percent. Not only were Russians suffering from joblessness; so were the traditional *d'fukim*—the Sephardi underclass—who were the first to lose their jobs in hard times and who felt themselves in direct economic competition with the Russian newcomers. The sudden spurt in housing prices caused by the mass immigration drove up their rents as well. The *d'fukim* were traditionally part of Likud's voting base. Their alienation was a danger sign.

Another was the growing sense that after fifteen years in government Likud had been corrupted by power. The annual report of Comptroller General Miriam Ben-Porat's office blasted several cabinet ministers, but zeroed in on Housing Minister Ariel Sharon's handling of the government-financed construction boom, contending he had dramatically overspent his budget, paid too much for prefabricated homes, and rewarded cronies and party donors with dubious contracts at the public's expense. Voters also saw Shamir's constant attempts to placate the various small religious parties within his governing coalition with "special allocations" for their schools and religious institutions as bribes. The new annual budget, which the Knesset passed in January 1992 over Labor's objections, reinforced Likud's image as the party of the corrupt status quo, doling out kosher pork to its governing partners.

Then there was Shamir's repudiation of electoral reform. Following the 1990 debacle reform was the most popular issue in the country among secular Israelis on both the right and left. After much debate the Knesset had come up with a proposal for direct election of the prime minister to give the position stronger executive powers and loosen the grip of the smaller parties. Shamir originally encouraged the proposal, but when it came to a vote in January 1992 he caved in to the demands of his small party partners and adamantly opposed it. Nonetheless, it eventually passed, making Likud and Shamir again look as if they were on the side of the most corrupt and narrow-minded forces in Israel's fractured political society.

Ever since he had opted for a narrow, right-wing government in June 1990, Shamir had struggled to hold together his disparate coalition of populists, nationalists and fundamentalists. One of the right-wing parties, the reformist-oriented Tsomet, pulled out in disgust in December 1991. Two others, Moledet and Tehiya, followed a month later to register their opposition to the autonomy talks that had begun in Madrid. As a result Shamir lost his parliamentary majority and was forced to move up the election date from November to June 1992. Still, looking at poll after poll, he believed he had little to fear.

The move immediately set off a brutal faction fight within Likud. Arens had expected Shamir to step down in 1992 and allow him to take over leadership of the party. But Shamir was determined to hang on through one more election. A succession contest now, he argued, would lead to a bloodletting among the various followers of Arens, Sharon and Levy. Besides, he did not believe that Arens had the necessary toughness for the top job. After running and winning again Shamir hoped to bypass all three and hand off the premiership to one of the younger generation of Likudniks, such as Meridor, Olmert, Netanyahu or Benjamin Begin.

Arens, Sharon and Levy had no intention of being bypassed. Seeing how the game was about to go, Arens and Sharon secretly joined forces to ensure that their own loyalists dominated the party's new Knesset list. When the Likud chose its list in late February 1992, they caught Levy's camp by surprise. Levy, who had held second place on the old list, was reduced to eighteenth place, and virtually all his allies were eliminated from the top forty places. A younger generation of Likudniks, most of them allied with Arens and the party establishment or with Sharon, vaulted to the top.

Levy was outraged. He saw an Ashkenazi conspiracy within Likud against himself and his fellow Sephardim. He told his followers at an emotional gathering that Arens and Sharon looked upon him as "a monkey who just came down from the trees." Then he announced his intention to resign from the cabinet.

This was a political disaster for Shamir because without Levy's supporters Likud stood no chance of hanging on in office. The day after Levy's speech Shamir called his threat of resignation "a joke" and sought to downplay it. But in the end Shamir believed he had no choice but to accede to Levy's demands.

On the day Levy was supposed to tender his resignation, Shamir met with him privately for twenty minutes. Arens was not informed of the meeting. When the two men emerged Shamir told the cabinet that Levy had been reinstated in the second slot on the list and that some 30 percent of the slate would be reserved for the foreign minister's supporters.

The deal won Shamir little. It further alienated Arens and it scarcely assuaged Levy. Many Sephardim saw the arrangement for what it was, an attempt to buy cooperation from one of their most prominent political leaders. The ethnic card, which Likud had always played so deftly against Labor, had now been played against it. "Shamir, you don't like Moroccans?" one of the protest signs at the May 1992 Beersheba rally asked. "We are all Moroccans here."

The factional fight cost Likud an entire month that should have been spent on getting ready for its new opposition, because as Likud refought old battles, Labor was remaking itself with a new image, new candidates and, most important of all, a new leader.

Yitzhak Rabin had been stalking Shimon Peres ever since his old Labor Party rival had misled him into supporting the abortive political coup attempt against Shamir. The defeat had cost Rabin the Defense Ministry, the one job he truly loved.

Since his return to the ministry, Rabin had enjoyed higher poll ratings than Peres, largely because of his leadership of the army in the legendary Six-Day War and the tough-guy image he had projected during the first grim days of the Palestinian intifada. But it was one thing to win public opinion surveys; it was another to oust Peres from control of the party he had been entrenched in for nearly fifteen years. Peres commanded intense loyalty among many of the party faithful. His dovish views were more in line with those of the new Labor mainstream—the largely Ashkenazi but growing professional class of white-collar workers—which had moved increasingly to the left and was in favor of negotiations with the Palestinians. He spoke their language and paid attention to their concerns. Rabin, by contrast, appeared arrogant and supercilious. He gave the impression that the party was lucky to have him, that it was something of a burden to him. He seemed to expect Labor's support as his birthright.

Indeed, Rabin had only one real advantage over Peres: he could win a general election. Peres had a solid base within his party, but Rabin commanded much wider support within the country at large. The wary Israeli electorate, bruised by professional politicians who seemed slick and dishonest, had come to equate eloquence with insincerity and bluntness with credibility; so the taciturn, inarticulate Rabin seemed both sincere and credible. Rabin was stiff, awkward and shy. He clearly did not enjoy politics and just as clearly was not very good at it. He had an anticharismatic authenticity, not unlike Shamir's. His prickly toughness made him especially popular among the same working-class Sephardim who usually voted for Likud or Shas. They dismissed the smooth-talking Peres as the epitome of the Labor establishment that had shut them out for years. But Rabin, although he was a child of the same establishment, held their respect.

After fifteen years of disappointments even Labor's most hardened apparatchiks had grown tired of losing. They could see that with Peres they were going nowhere. The same was true of some of the younger Labor doves—Haim Ramon, Avraham Burg—who were even talking of breaking away and forming an alliance with the new left-wing Meretz coalition.

After the 1990 disaster Rabin had forced Peres to agree to suspend his long flirtation with the small religious parties and commit the party to electoral reform. The following year the party had adopted internal changes, scrapping the old smoke-filled-room method of choosing a leader and a Knesset list for a system of party primaries similar to those in the United States. Instead of 3,000 central committee members choosing the next leader, Labor now threw the contest open to 156,000 registered party members, their ranks reinforced by thousands of Russians and young voters. By one estimate, 49,000 of the members were under thirty-five. It was the fresh blood that Israeli politics had needed for so long—and that Likud conspicuously lacked.

Before the vote on February 20, 1992, some of Peres's most dovish allies defected to Rabin. Two dark horses who entered the race took more votes from Peres than from Rabin. A candidate needed to get 40 percent of the vote to avoid a runoff, and Rabin snuck through with 40.6 percent to Peres's 34.5. The new system had produced a candidate who could win.

The Labor Knesset primary that followed also produced a major upheaval: fourteen new faces made it to the top forty on the list, including a number of Sephardim and several recently retired generals. It was a decidedly left-wing collection; the third-place finisher behind Rabin and Peres was Burg, a Peres ally and prominent liberal who antagonized the religious parties with his demands for separation of church and state. But it was young and fresh and, most importantly, free of the backroom taint and internal feuding that infected the Likud list. Rabin, the supercentrist hawk, found himself atop a flock of doves.

For the most part, he simply ignored them. Heeding what the polls told them about his own high popularity ratings, Rabin and his strategists devised a highly personalized campaign to persuade voters that they were choosing a leader, not a party. They even changed the party's name on the ballot to read "Labor Party Headed by Yitzhak Rabin." It was American-style presidential politics: Rabin was telling voters that he, not Labor's Knesset members, would be running the country. The campaign slogan was: "Israel Is Waiting for Rabin."

Because Rabin was Labor's shield, he quickly became Likud's target. Its television advertisements called attention to his emotional breakdown two weeks before the Six-Day War and his chronic drinking. Rabin defused the first issue early on by granting an interview to *Hadashot* in which he frankly discussed the breakdown and attributed it to lack of sleep, nicotine poisoning and deep anxiety. He noted that he had come back to work after thirty-six hours and had proceeded to lead the army to victory. Although he said nothing new, his perceived candor helped persuade voters it was a non-issue. As for his drinking, he simply denied that he drank too much or that it impaired his judgment. Since Likud could offer no concrete evidence to the contrary, the issue quickly withered.

It was also hard for Likud to open up much political ground between itself and Rabin. He and his aides operated from the basic principle that the floating voters who would determine the outcome of the election were fundamentally Likud-oriented on the issues—hawkish on security and populist on economics—but not in ideology. And he offered himself as the embodiment of that approach: the Likud program without the Greater Israel ideology or the political incompetence.

At times Rabin and Shamir seemed like an Israeli version of The Sunshine Boys—two old men, with a combined age of 146, who had long ago forgotten what it was they were supposed to be arguing about. Their one televised debate reminded *Haaretz* columnist Yoel Marcus "of two old people sitting in chairs along the shore in Miami Beach conducting a calm conversation while looking at the horizon." Many commentators complained that the campaign would put Israelis to sleep. Most expected Labor's poll lead to collapse as it had in the previous two elections and that Likud would find a way to close the gap. The result, many glumly predicted, would be another dreary national unity government with the two big parties chained to each other and to their smaller allies.

But under the placid surface a very different result was taking shape. Shamir and Rabin may have looked and sounded alike, but the voters saw that they were different. Rooted in the Old World of Eastern Europe, a psychological prisoner of the Holocaust, Shamir increasingly wrapped himself in a cloak of historic, mystical inevitability. He understood that most Israelis did not support his ideological goals in settling the occupied territories, but he believed they would acquiesce in the drive to build Jewish settlements because it was the one way of ensuring that there would be no Palestinian state there. When hundreds of thousands of Jews lived in the West Bank, he told a campaign rally in Jerusalem, "the notion of territorial compromise will fade away like a bad dream."

Rabin was a native-born, pragmatic Israeli. He made it clear to the voters that he was prepared to change course, to bend with the times. Despite his dour personality and his disdain for others, he seemed more optimistic and more willing to recognize and seize an opportunity than Shamir. Like a good military strategist, he believed in improvisation. He might move with extreme caution—but he moved.

Rabin and Shamir were campaigning in a changing landscape when it came to issues of war and peace. The long, hard freeze that had gripped Israel through most of the 1980s had begun to thaw. Both the Gulf War and the Madrid conference had increased the guarded optimism and the urgency of mainstream Israelis toward the peace process. The intifada and the spate of Arab stabbings inside Israel proper had persuaded a large majority that the status quo was not viable, that they must find some means of separating themselves physically from Palestinians in the territories.

Pollsters Elihu Katz and Hanna Levinsohn of the Guttman Institute of Applied Social Research in Jerusalem tracked a slow but steady increase in dovishness. Most Israelis did not want to return to the 1967 borders, but at the time of Madrid, Katz and Levinsohn found that 81 percent were prepared to relinquish Gaza and 58 percent at least some of the West Bank as part of a peace arrangement. Few mainstream Israelis were pure hawks or doves; most were a little of both. For many the question was not whether there would be territorial compromise, but how much.

To lead them through this complicated period, Israelis wanted a militant negotiator—someone they could trust to be tough, to understand their fears and not yield when it came to their security, yet at the same time to not allow a genuine opportunity to pass them by. Many had hoped that Yitzhak Shamir was such a man, but the confrontation with George Bush had revealed him to be an ideologue for whom settlements and territory were not negotiable. They turned to Yitzhak Rabin.

Not all the analysts believed in the dovish trend. Pollsters Hanoch and Rafi Smith were persuaded from their own survey readings that the basic hawkish slant of the Israeli public had not changed. They calculated the hard-liners at 40 percent or above and moderate doves at 30 percent, with another 30 percent hovering somewhere between. But even the Smiths detected the sense among voters that Shamir was blocking the peace process at a time when the public—hawks included—wanted it to go forward. As Shamir had been the appropriate custodian for the frozen Israel of 1987 so Rabin became the appropriate leader for a country that was ready to inch cautiously forward. And even the most hawkish of voters seemed comfortable with Rabin's style, if not with his policies. By late spring of 1992, after Likud's long month of internal feuding, a Gallup Poll gave Rabin a much higher approval rating than Shamir even among right-wing voters.

Rabin had sat on the political sidelines for nearly two years since leaving the Defense Ministry in 1990 and had watched the world change dramatically. He saw the threat to Israel's existence easing because of the demise of Soviet power and the subsequent weakening of Moscow's radical Arab allies, because of the wave of Russian Jewish emigration to Israel and because of the Gulf War, which had sharply reduced Iraq's power. He believed these changes gave Israel a window of opportunity, perhaps as long as five years, to make deals with its neighbors. If the process stalled, if Israel failed to capitalize on this moment, it could be faced by 1997 by an Iran with nuclear weapons, by a hostile, frustrated Syria and by a rebuilt Iraq. Better to move now, Rabin believed, while the opportunity was there. "We have a true hour of grace and it must not be allowed to pass us by," he told supporters.

Unlike Shamir, Rabin could draw a sharp distinction between compromising over security, which he told voters he would never do, and compromising over territory. "I am unwilling to give up a single inch of Israel's security, but I am willing to give up many inches of sentiments and territories." Indeed, as far as Rabin was concerned, holding the 1.8 million Palestinians of the occupied territories was ultimately a security risk. He was happy to cede much of the West Bank and Gaza because he wanted to be rid of the Arabs who lived there. Nonetheless, he promised that he would not initiate negotiations with the PLO and would not allow an independent Palestinian state in the occupied territories.

When it came to the Golan Heights, Rabin was even more cautious. Unlike their West Bank counterparts, many of the 13,000 Golan settlers were Labor supporters who had moved to the area at the encouragement of various Labor-led governments between 1967 and 1977. When Rabin visited them two weeks before the June election he praised their achievements and promised them his full support. He said he did not believe that Israel needed to retain "every meter" of land on the heights, but he added, "Whoever even thinks of leaving the Golan wantonly abandons the security of Israel."

While he was vague about his own policies, Rabin was specific in his indictment of the Likud. He accused the government of severely neglecting

Israel's domestic problems, losing the momentum of Russian immigration, endangering relations with the United States, wasting funds on the settlements and squandering chances for a deal with the Arabs by stalling at the peace talks. He linked spending in the territories to the lack of development and growing poverty within Israel proper, and he promised to invest in education, infrastructure and employment. "In the current erroneous and distorted order of priorities, political settlements in the territories precede everything else: immigration absorption, the future of the younger generation, the war against unemployment, and social and economic progress," he said in his opening address as party leader. Shamir, he said, was "subsidizing parasites in the territories."

He was also able to link Likud's ideology to the issue of personal security. Shamir's insistence on retaining all of the West Bank and Gaza inevitably increased frustration and anger among Palestinians at the same time it allowed them access to Israeli cities and towns. The result was an increase in the number of Palestinian stabbing incidents. One of the Labor Party's campaign spots, "Gaza Inside Tel Aviv," was a gruesome display of bloodstained Israeli victims of Palestinian knife attacks.

On an early morning in May, Labor's point was driven home at a bus stop on the streets of Bat Yam, south of Tel Aviv, when fifteen-year-old Helena Rapp was slaughtered by a young Palestinian with a butcher knife. The killing set off a nasty round of anti-Arab retaliation as gangs of Israeli youths spread out over Bat Yam, wielding sticks and iron bars from construction sites, chanting "Death to the Arabs," beating up Arab laborers and overturning cars with Gaza license plates. The rioting continued for five nights.

Throughout the spring Rabin campaigned like a man possessed, determined to make up for the fifteen years of lost time. He seemed somehow to grow in stature as he realized that he could be popular with voters. He even showed warmth. Following the recommendation of campaign adviser Binyamin Ben-Eliezer, Rabin loosened up a little, smiled now and then, showed a willingness to listen and a sense of personal concern for the poor, the new immigrants and the unemployed. In every speech he spoke sympathetically of the humiliation of not having a job. Rabin realized he had blown his first term as prime minister. Now he was pleading for something that politics seldom provides: a second chance.

For years Shimon Peres had been heckled and bombarded with rotten eggs and fruit when he ventured into working-class areas. But Rabin got a much warmer welcome. He surrounded himself with a group of rough-and-ready toughs led by top aide Shimon Sheves, who protected him from street thugs and occasionally played the role of self-enforcer. When a far rightist yelled obscenities at Rabin during a campaign stroll through the Mahane Yehuda market in Jerusalem, Sheves punched the young heckler in the face.

Two weeks after Shamir's tepid Beersheba performance, Rabin's campaign staged an electrifying rally there before a full-throated audience of three thousand that shattered the city's reputation as a Likud stronghold. The highlight was the candidate himself, who gave a passionate speech that summed up his argument to the Israeli people.

"The Likud took your money, the money you paid in taxes, and threw it away in the territories," he told them. "They built villas, not for you, people of Beersheba, but for their cronies, who keep their flats in Tel Aviv too. In fifteen years they have not built a single factory in Beersheba. They spit in your face, and some of you still think it's rain. Well it's not."

Labor had recaptured the street.

From the moment they arrived, Russian immigrants had been assumed to be in the pocket of the Likud. They were, after all, vehemently opposed to state socialism, hawkish about security issues and supremely uninterested in Palestinian rights. An April 1991 poll of Russian immigrants by the private research group Tazpit had given right-wing parties their support by a ratio exceeding two to one. From the beginning of the aliya, however, Natan Sharansky had warned Shamir not to take the Russians for granted—that they were impatient and politically pragmatic, and would punish the ruling party if it did not at least make a good faith effort to meet their expectations.

As election day approached the Russians began moving to the left. Those without jobs felt the same sense of disappointment and alienation as the Sephardi underclass. Those with jobs often found themselves on the lowest rung—engineers sweeping streets, Ph.D.s pumping gasoline. Rabin was offering a sweeping new agenda while Shamir proposed patience. "In half a year the immigrants will be doing much better," he told a gathering of skeptical Russian voters in Ramat Gan. "We're preparing places of work, factories. It's only a matter of time."

With few concrete achievements to offer, Likud tried to scare the Russians to its side by tying Labor to the discredited socialism the immigrants had fled. One Likud television commercial showed Labor members singing the Internationale and marching on May Day. Rabin was presented as an Israeli Ceausescu, collectivist and militaristic. But most of the immigrants were not buying. "We've experienced Likud," one anonymous Russian voter told Israel Television. "Now we'll see what Labor can give us."

By February 1992 a poll conducted for Likud showed Labor and the left polling 32 percent of the Russians compared to 16 percent for the right. Dahaf president Eliezer Gerabin, an old Shamir crony, pleaded with the prime minister to take steps to co-opt Natan Sharansky and pour more funds into the *aliya*. But Shamir was certain the numbers would reverse themselves.

When that did not happen Likud leaders belatedly began to realize that they were dealing with a new kind of immigrant with different demands. "This is a spoiled *aliya*," Housing Minister Sharon told a meeting of Likud ministers. "The *olim* [new immigrants] are making all kinds of demands. . . . What bothers them is not national issues but personal, material matters. I miss the past *aliyot*, the *olim* of the fifties."

As election day drew near and polls continued to show the Russians growing more and more anti-Likud, Shamir met one last time with Sharansky and offered him the cabinet post of minister of immigration absorption if Sharansky would break his long-standing personal policy of nonpartisanship and publicly urge his fellow Russians to vote for Likud. But Shamir seemed more angry than forthcoming. When Sharansky politely declined his offer, Shamir warned, "If the Russians vote for Labor, you yourself will be blamed for betraying the Jewish people." Sharansky shrugged it off. Whatever Shamir said, whatever he did, it was simply too late.

The religious parties were also unprepared for the new wave of change. Many secular Israelis, upset by the naked influence that the *haredim* had wielded in the discredited Shamir-led government, flocked to two vocally anticlerical, reformist parties, Tsomet on the right and Meretz on the left. The influx of new Russian voters further diluted the voting power of the ultra-Orthodox. The rabbis performed their usual tricks, promising blessings and God's help for those who voted for them, despite a new law against such celestial electioneering. But the campaign's major rabbinical pronouncement was a profound misstatement by Rabbi Eliezer Schach, now age ninety-four, who brought ridicule upon himself and a bounty of votes for Arye Deri's Shas Party with his condescending remarks about the Sephardim. Schach told religious voters that the Sephardim were "not ready for spiritual or political leadership. . . . They need a few more years, they still have time to learn."

Schach had helped Shas rise to prominence in 1984 and had kept it under his influence during the 1988 election and the abortive 1990 coup, despite the strong misgivings of the party's Sephardi spiritual leader, Rabbi Ovadia Yosef. Now Schach's verbal blunder gave Yosef the opening he needed to declare Shas's independence from Schach and the rest of the Ashkenazi religious establishment. For Deri this was a painfully difficult move. He agreed with Yosef, but he still felt a sense of loyalty and reverence for Schach, who had been one of the first to recognize Deri's potential when he was a green student in the yeshiva. But in the end the seasoned politician won out over the yeshiva boy. Deri helped steer Shas toward its political independence.

While the Russians and the religious Sephardim were consolidating, the settlers and their allies on the Israeli right were falling apart. Rather than formulate a coherent strategy to counter Rabin's relentless attack on the government's spending on Jewish settlement in the territories, the settlers took to warring among themselves. Moshe Levinger, the prominent rabbi who served as the unofficial mayor of the Jewish quarter in the West Bank city of Hebron, decided the Gush Emunim settlement movement had become too soft and he divided it further by forming a political party of his own. He ran a series of outlandishly aggressive television ads featuring himself as a kind of Jewish Clint Eastwood dressed in black, with skullcap and dark glasses, and carrying an assault rifle stalking Arab terrorists through the mean streets of Hebron. "Only an iron fist will solve the intifada," he intoned. The spot ended with a pistol shot sending his party emblem spinning.

Radicals like Levinger were so intoxicated with their own power that they could not see how deeply they had alienated mainstream Israelis. But others could. One of the most thoughtful of the settlement movement's leaders, Rabbi Yoel Bin-Nun of Ofra, wrote an article in the monthly *Nekuda* that predicted the defeat of pro-settlement forces two months before it occurred. The movement, he wrote, "has succeeded in establishing numerous glorious settlements but has totally failed in the spiritual dimension, of which it was so proud; that is, we have failed to settle into the hearts of the people, to bring our opponents—our brothers—into our fold, to soften their resistance, to convince them. . . .

"It is a spiritual distortion to say that the real problems are with the Arabs or the Americans; it all stays within us, with the divisions among us." Bin-Nun bemoaned that the settlers had become just another selfish, self-righteous, special interest group. They had achieved great material success, but "if the people aren't with us, no number of houses will save us." It was a cry from the heart and a chilling analysis of what had gone wrong.

The suspense did not last long on election night, June 23. At one minute past ten Israel Television's Haim Yavin announced that Labor was on its way to victory, Likud to abject defeat. It was, pronounced Yavin, a "second upheaval" comparable in size and meaning to Begin's triumph in 1977. For a moment there was stunned silence from the crowd at the Labor Party's gathering. They could not quite believe what they had heard. Then came an explosion of cheers and, for many, tears. Avraham Burg sobbed. "You don't know how it feels to finally get your country back," he told National Public Radio's Linda Gradstein.

The victory, when the votes were tallied, was not quite as large as first projected. Labor squeaked in with forty-four seats plus twelve for the left-wing Meretz and five for two Israeli Arab-dominated parties, giving the left a bare one-seat majority of sixty-one. Another big winner was the rightist Tsomet, which like Meretz drew support from young voters fed up with politics as usual. It took eight seats. Finally, Arye Deri's Shas withstood the challenge from Rabbi Schach and the taint of a two-year police investigation to win six seats, making it the largest *haredi* party in the new Knesset.

But the real story was Likud's collapse—down to just thirty-two seats, a loss of 20 percent of its support over four years. Voters were tired of many things, but above all, they were tired of Yitzhak Shamir. He had worn out his welcome. The world had changed; he had not. The cruel verdict on election day was that this humiliating defeat was basically all Shamir's fault. "For nine years the Likud has been without a leader," wrote commentator Dan Margalit in *Maariv*. "That's why it lost."

In fact, Shamir's failure as political leader was only one part of a singular set of circumstances that brought about Likud's defeat. The crippling divisions on the right as well as Likud's unusual weakness were part of it, as was Labor's good fortune in having changed its nominating process and chosen Rabin. Another factor was the first-time participation of an influx of Russian voters prepared to cast a protest vote for the opposition (*Yediot* calculated that 47 percent of the Russians voted for Labor and only 18 percent for Likud). Even with all of these one-time advantages, Labor barely won. Whatever else the 1992 election was, it was not a ringing endorsement for the Israeli left.

But it was an upheaval in a deeper sense. For years Israelis had been as tethered by bonds of loyalty and blood ties to political parties as they were to their own families. To switch one's vote was a betrayal of ethnicity and class. For the first time many Israelis broke those bonds. They punished Likud, held it responsible for doing a poor job in office and voted it out. They could readily do the same to the new government. It was a process that had begun with the 1977 election but that now reached a new level of maturity and sophistication; at age forty-four Israeli democracy had finally grown up.

Most of all, Israelis had voted against deadlock. The biggest loser on election night was the status quo.

The euphoria at Labor headquarters faded slightly when Rabin stormed in. Looking haggard and agitated, he insisted that he and he alone would decide on the new coalition and the cabinet. He wanted a strong centrist government with coalition partners from both the left and right to balance each other and allow him, as chief executive, a free hand. This was his own personal triumph—the party should just sit back and follow orders. "Alone and egocentric, cranky and overheated, with the friendliness of a pickled eggplant, Rabin angrily snatched the victory wreath," wrote Doron Rosenbloom in *Haaretz*.

Impassive and motionless, Shamir watched the early results sitting straight up in an armchair in his suite at the Tel Aviv Hilton. Yet as the night wore on he seemed to grow more comfortable. Being on the losing side did not trouble him. To be small and beleaguered and misunderstood was a familiar feeling for the underground man. "We've never been spoiled by history," he later told the morose crowd at Likud headquarters. "Everything we have ever achieved we achieved with great difficulty and with agony."

Shamir noted that this was the same room in which they had celebrated Begin's triumph fifteen years earlier. In a hoarse voice he exhorted them to stand firm and remain united. This was no time for surrender: "There are people all over the world and in the Middle East who are joyful that their dangerous enemy is going down. I tell them, 'Your joy is premature.' The Likud is alive and well."

After the debacle Likud dissenters spoke out. Meir Sheetrit, a member of the younger generation of grassroots Sephardi politicians, spoke for many when he blamed the party's emphasis on ideology at the expense of social and economic issues. "With all due respect, the Land of Israel is not a religion," he told a television interviewer. "What brought the Likud to power is the social issue. Likud didn't grasp the message. Our leaders forgot where they came from."

In the days following the election, Shamir insisted that he had presided over a golden age of Israeli progress and that history would vindicate his rule. At his cabinet's final meeting he boasted of the government's achievements in getting Israel to direct talks with its Arab neighbors, expanding diplomatic and trade ties with dozens of new countries, overseeing the absorption of more than 400,000 Soviet Jewish immigrants, transforming the economy and, perhaps most important of all, strengthening the Jewish hold over the occupied territories through increased settlement. Had he stayed in office, Shamir confessed to *Maariv*, "I would have carried out autonomy talks for ten years and meanwhile we would have reached half a million people in Judea and Samaria." He later denied the quote—but not the sentiment behind it.

"I doubt that any other Israeli government ever has made such achievements," Shamir told the cabinet, and the funny thing was that he was almost right. The accomplishments had been impressive, but many of them were a tribute to Israel's momentum and to changes in the world over which Shamir had no sway. They happened for the most part despite Shamir, not because of him.

On his last day in office he addressed a warning to the new Israel that had sent his government to defeat. "The Jewish state cannot exist without a unique ideological content," Shamir told the Knesset. "We will not exist for long if we become just another country that is mostly devoted to the welfare of its residents. . . . We must provide our sons and daughters with a motivation of value and challenge."

Rabin's opening speech to the Knesset that day, written by longtime aide Eitan Haber, argued for a much different country. Israeli voters had changed more than their government, he told the Knesset; they had changed their entire way of looking at the world:

"In the last decade of the twentieth century, the atlases, history and geography books no longer present an up-to-date picture of the world. Walls of enmity have fallen, borders have disappeared. Powers have crumbled and ideologies collapsed, states have been born, states have died, and the gates of emigration have been flung open. And it is our duty, to ourselves and to our children, to see the new world as it is now—to discern its dangers, explore its prospects and do everything possible so that the state of Israel will fit into this new world. . . .

"No longer are we necessarily 'a people that dwells alone,' and no longer is it true that 'the whole world is against us.' We must overcome the sense of isolation that has held us in its thrall for almost half a century. We must join the international movement toward peace, reconciliation and cooperation that is spreading over the entire globe these days—lest we be the last to remain, all alone, in the station."

Getting out of the station was easier said than done. Rabin's hope of forming a broad-based government of right and left was soon crushed by political realities. Once he made a deal with the left-of-center Meretz, which with twelve seats would be Labor's biggest and most important partner, he found it impossible to attract a right-wing partner. He hoped to recruit Tsomet leader Rafael Eitan, a former general, but Eitan wanted the education portfolio, one that Meretz also coveted. The Meretz people viewed Eitan as a cryptofascist and used their weight to deny him the post. Eitan and Tsomet then decided to stay outside the government.

Arye Deri and Shas made the opposite decision. During the campaign Deri had made his usual promise to support a Likud-led government. But with Labor, Meretz and their Israeli Arab partners already controlling sixty-one seats, Deri felt free to sign on, arguing that he was simply assuring that his constituents got their fair share of patronage out of what was a fait accompli. Rav Schach was livid. No government that included the anti-Orthodox Meretz was fit for Jewish participation, he insisted. But Ovadia Yosef was no longer taking orders from the Ashkenazi establishment. When Deri hesitated, Yosef put the coalition agreement in front of his young protégé, held out a pen and instructed him to sign. The deal was done.

By leading the only ultra-Orthodox party to join the new government, Deri gained control over a vast stream of political spoils. His participation also gave him ministerial protection at a time when police investigators were breathing down his neck. The reformists in Meretz were outraged that a man under criminal investigation was allowed to resume holding the cabinet position he allegedly had abused. But Shas proponents pointed out that there was, as yet, no indictment. Deri submitted a letter promising to resign from the cabinet if and when he was charged. That was good enough for Rabin. He needed Shas just as much as Shas needed him, not for its votes so much as for the legitimacy it provided. Without Shas, the government would be forced to rely for its majority on the five votes from the non-Zionist Israeli Arab parties. It could survive, but it could not govern with authority.

The dealings with Meretz and Deri were not the only cases in which political reality forced Rabin to settle for less than he had promised. He had run as the candidate of the future, but he was stuck with the government of the past, a heavily bureaucratized structure in which the smallest factions still held the whiphand. To satisfy the opposing forces within his own party as well as his governing partners, Rabin was forced to scrap his pledge to streamline government and instead created nine deputy cabinet ministers—each one getting a stipend, car and driver, and a dollop of power. He also had to placate many of Labor's own traditional interest groups—the Histadrut, the senior bureaucracy, the kibbutzim—whose agendas were very different from his own.

His administration was presidential in the sense that he took for himself the Defense Ministry as well as the premiership. His best days were those he spent at the Kirya, defense headquarters in Tel Aviv, where he could concentrate on security issues and geopolitical strategy. His worst were back in Jerusalem, coping with petty political problems and the competing factions within his own cabinet, people he had little respect for and little patience with. Most of the infighting was between Meretz and Shas, the opposite poles in Rabin's new government. They fought at first over the provocatively anticlerical remarks of Shulamit Aloni, the Meretz leader and education minister; then over Arye Deri's continuing attempts to thwart police investigators and avoid indictment.

But when it came to security issues, Shas and Meretz formed an oddly coherent alliance. In November Rabin brought to the cabinet a proposal for a major military operation in southern Lebanon to punish Hezbollah, the Shiite fundamentalist fighters. Most of the Meretz ministers were unhappy with the plan, which they feared would cause civilian casualties, but they were too intimidated by Rabin to speak up. Deri, however, was not. At a late-night cabinet meeting that lasted more than five hours, he spoke out, raising objections and demanding a precise assessment of the goals and the means. After he spoke a number of Meretz ministers also raised their voices in opposition. Rabin, who had expected the meeting to rubber-stamp the plan, took a vote in which a compromise version of the operation passed by only nine to seven. He understood that such a controversial action would prove unsustainable with such a narrow majority, and he chose not to pursue it. *Haaretz* branded the decision, "The Doves' First Coos."

The odd alliance of the ultra-Orthodox and the anticlerical was not as absurd as it might have seemed. Both Meretz and Shas were, in effect, post-Zionist parties that did not share the traditional Israeli outlook on security issues. They were both more concerned with improving the quality of life of their constituents than in pursuing old-fashioned Zionist goals. When it came to the peace process both were prepared to cede territory, including the Golan Heights, in return for a genuine, sustainable accord. Although volatile and disorganized, both parties were harbingers of a new Israel. They sat uneasily, but they sat together.

One campaign promise Rabin moved quickly to fulfill was to repair relations with the United States. Before the end of his first month in office Rabin announced a partial settlement freeze and won quick approval from George Bush for the $10 billion in loan guarantees that the American president had long denied Shamir. Bush, who was trying to shore up support among American Jews during a tough reelection campaign against Democrat Bill Clinton, emphasized Israel's strategic reliability. He met with Rabin in Kennebunkport, his Maine summer home where, a year earlier, he had refused to invite Shamir.

And Rabin resolved another matter in Washington. He had never been a fan of AIPAC. He believed American Jewish lobbyists had usurped Israel's role in steering diplomatic and military relations with the United States. As defense minister he had felt insulted when AIPAC's lobbyists sought to advise him on which weapons systems Israel should be requesting from Washington. Now, in a closed-door meeting at the Madison Hotel with senior AIPAC leaders, Rabin made his feelings clear. He accused AIPAC of steering Israel into a needless confrontation over the loan guarantees and of overstepping its authority. In the future, he made clear, Israel would take charge of managing its own relations with the United States. AIPAC would have to learn to play a subordinate role. To drive home the point, Israeli officials leaked word of the lecture to the press.

Stunned by the dressing-down, AIPAC's leaders privately complained that the blame for the loan guarantees debacle lay far more with Shamir and his top aides than with them. It was unfair, they argued, to blame AIPAC for its increasing dominance in U.S.-Israeli relations during the Likud years when it was Shamir who had strongly encouraged AIPAC to assert its influence. With the growing policy gap between his government and the Bush administration, someone had had to play the role of intermediary. AIPAC had simply filled the vacuum.

Both sides were correct. AIPAC had overstepped its bounds, but it had done so at Shamir's behest, becoming in effect Israel's lobbying agent with the administration and with Congress. It had accepted too many marching orders from Yossi Ben-Aharon and from a right-wing government with a slim majority of support in Israel. Worse, it had come to identify itself with the Likud's narrow, paranoid vision of the world and of Israel's fate. With Likud's defeat, AIPAC and its sister organizations faced what Dean Acheson described as Britain's predicament after World War II: having lost an empire, they were searching for a role.

While Yitzhak Rabin pressed forward with negotiations in Washington, the Israeli army and the Palestinian warriors of Hamas and the PLO's Fatah movement were turning the Gaza Strip into a combat zone. By 1993, year six of the intifada, the army had reduced the uprising to a hard core of Palestinian activists, many of them armed and boasting long records of violence against purported "collaborators" as well as against soldiers. Now the two sides waged an increasingly violent war on each other, a conflict in which Arab civilians were caught in the middle.

Rabin's new government started out with a flurry of hopeful gestures. In its first weeks in office the government released hundreds of political prisoners and tore down dozens of the concrete-and-razor-wire barriers the army had previously erected in various refugee camps in the West Bank and Gaza. These good-will measures were designed to demonstrate that the new administration wanted rapid progress at the bargaining table and better relations on the ground as well. But the actions seemed tokenistic and half-hearted to most Palestinians, who saw little or no tangible improvement in their daily lives, and the peace offerings were rejected by a radical minority whose goal was to undermine the process altogether.

Rabin the strategist believed in "marching with two feet"—coordinating diplomatic and military moves so that one strengthened and complemented the other. He saw no contradiction between offering better terms in Washington at the same time that the army stepped up its assault in the territories; like a general, he thought in terms of softening up the enemy, forcing him to the table. "If you continue to pull the trigger," Rabin warned Palestinians, "it will be unfortunate because your fate will be bad and miserable. We say to you: consider your deeds well. . . . You will bear the consequences of your mistakes."

But Palestinian society did not function as one coherent organism, with gunmen and negotiators serving as different arms of the same body. The army's tactics enhanced the stature of the Palestinian fighters while undermining the negotiators. A moderate like Faisal Husseini had staked his life and reputation on his claim that participating in negotiations would make life better for Palestinians and bring about an end to the occupation. Rabin's tough tactics suggested that Husseini was wrong on both counts.

Throughout Rabin's first year in office the gunmen launched repeated assaults on the army. Using semiautomatic rifles and grenades fired from civilian cars or roadside positions, Hamas activists staged at least a dozen ambush attacks on Israeli army patrols and outposts. And at least six undercover soldiers were killed during attempts to seize wanted men.

The IDF responded with combat-style search-and-destroy operations, sealing off neighborhoods where gunmen were suspected to be hiding, evacuating civilians and shelling their houses with rocket-propelled grenades and other heavy weapons. Btselem, the Israeli human rights organization, counted at least fifteen such assaults between September 1992 and April 1993 in which 102 houses were damaged and hundreds of people were rendered homeless. The IDF also put greater emphasis on roving undercover units whose tactics and methods of operation seemed more appropriate to a battlefield than to the civilian-filled streets and alleyways of Gaza.

The undercover units had been created before the intifada began, but their status was upgraded and their ranks increased after Lieutenant General Ehud Barak took over from Dan Shomron as army chief of staff in April 1991. Barak, a graduate of the elite Sayeret Matkal unit, had personally carried out such special operations as the 1973 raid on Palestinian guerrilla leaders in Beirut and had overseen the 1988 assassination of PLO deputy Khalil Wazir. Barak did not like to sit back passively and react to events. He believed in quick, dramatic operations that showed flair and initiative and made an impression on supporters and enemies alike. Rabin was one of his biggest boosters. "If this boy doesn't make chief of staff, there is something wrong with the system," Rabin reportedly said about him back in 1962 when Barak, then only twenty, completed his first officers' training course. Thirty years later the two men were in full agreement about how to cope with the intifada. Together, they dramatically increased the use of undercover units. According to Btselem, the units killed forty-three Palestinians in 1992, more such killings than in the first three years of the intifada combined.

Under Barak's guidance the army effectively redefined the intifada as a war. It was a much easier concept, tactically and ethically, for the IDF to handle than the popular civil revolt of the late 1980s. Policing their way through a tangled thicket of rebellious, rock-throwing civilians had always been fraught with painful difficulties. But fighting a war against an armed enemy was straightforward and unambiguous.

As a result of intensified combat on both sides, Btselem reported that seventy-six Palestinians were killed by soldiers during the first six months of the Rabin government, a 20 percent increase from the last six months of Shamir's. Later in 1993, Btselem reported that the army had killed thirty-eight children age sixteen and under between December 1992 and June 1993—more than double the number killed in the entire previous year and a magnitude of killing unprecedented since the intifada began.

It was not that the army had a deliberate policy of killing children. Instead, the rules for opening fire had gradually been relaxed to the point where soldiers were often allowed to use their guns in situations in which their lives were not endangered. In hundreds of incidents, soldiers had opened fire at escaping rioters or defiant stone throwers even when they mixed with innocent bystanders. Btselem also faulted the lack of investigations and punishment of soldiers who broke the rules. The army spokesman's office replied that in all the incidents either children were near or among rioters or armed people or else the army had not been aware of their presence when it opened fire. It also stated that the increase in deaths over the six-month period was due to an increase in riots and attacks on soldiers.

The army arrested hundreds of Hamas activists, but it failed to make significant inroads into the movement's popularity or ability to function. Indeed, as time went on, Hamas's loosely organized cadres intensified attacks on both Jewish settlers in the territories and on soldiers.

Over a six-day period in December 1992, Hamas gunmen staged two ambushes in the territories, killing three soldiers riding in a jeep through Gaza, and shooting dead one soldier and wounding two others in a similar attack in Hebron. In the predawn hours of the following Sunday morning, a Hamas gang operating far from Gaza kidnaped a Border Police sergeant named Nissim Toledano near his home in Lod as he was heading for work. The gang demanded the release of Sheikh Ahmed Yassin, Hamas's imprisoned leader, in return for Toledano's freedom.

From the moment he heard about Toledano's abduction, Yitzhak Rabin was determined to strike back. At a crisis-management meeting that day, Barak proposed the mass expulsion of alleged activists. When Barak had made a similar proposal to the Shamir government, Dan Meridor had shot it down on legal grounds. Rabin was more amenable, but he noted that designated expellees could appeal to the Israeli Supreme Court, a process that could last months. Barak replied that his advisers had found a way to circumvent the legal requirement: set the expulsion for a fixed time period. The expellees could still appeal, but only after they had been deported. Meridor in the past had rejected such a stratagem. Rabin leaped at it.

On Monday the security forces began rounding up some 1,200 Palestinians identified in Shin Bet files as Hamas activists or sympathizers. The next morning Toledano's body was found in a roadside ditch east of Jerusalem; he had been stabbed and strangled with his hands tied behind his back. Rabin ordered the security services to sift through the 1,200 names, plus 300 purported activists already being held, and identify the worst potential offenders. The hasty process produced 475 names overnight.

Rabin convened the cabinet early Wednesday morning. First he spent a half hour with the ministers from Meretz, who in the past had been the most opposed to expulsions. Hamas was a serious threat, he told them, because its influence threatened moderate Palestinians and its violent attacks could derail the peace process. He described operations that Hamas was allegedly planning, including the assassination of Faisal Husseini and an abortive attack on an Israeli elementary school. Temporary expulsion was less harsh than alternatives such as blowing up houses or introducing the death penalty for terrorism, he told them. And finally there was a threat: with the Israeli public clamoring for retaliation, Rabin warned Meretz, he would feel compelled to offer the right-wing Tsomet party membership in the government and cabinet seats if he could not take action. Otherwise, he feared public pressure would cause the government to fall.

What he did not tell them was how many Palestinians he was planning to expel. Meretz leader Shulamit Aloni later said that because Rabin had spoken about Hamas "leaders," she assumed the number to be between twenty and thirty. She and her two colleagues did not ask; they just gave Rabin their approval.

The full cabinet meeting was short and to the point. Justice Minister David Libai was the sole abstention. No one else dared to defy Rabin in a moment of national pain and anger. Even after the cabinet's approval, however, things did not go smoothly. It took several hours for military commanders in Gaza and the West Bank to check the list of deportees. Plans to fly them north in helicopters collapsed because of bad weather. Instead, they were bused overnight to the border.

Meanwhile, despite a blanket censorship ban, news of the expulsions leaked out. Human rights lawyer Leah Tsemel, soon joined by two lawyers from the Association for Civil Rights in Israel, went searching for a duty judge from the Israeli Supreme Court. At 2 A.M. they obtained a restraining order stopping the buses outside Metulla in northern Israel and delaying the expulsions for twenty-four hours until the full court approved the move. Finally at six-thirty on Thursday night, the buses pulled over the border and dumped 415 activists at Zumriyya, a point just north of Israel's self-declared security zone.

When the Lebanese government, under orders from Syria, refused to let the deportees pass through its military checkpoint or to allow outside aid to be delivered to them, 415 hungry, tired, miserable deportees were left sitting on a frozen hillside with nothing to sustain them but camera crews from CNN and other international news networks, all of them eager for a hardship story during the slow Christmas season. The Palestinians looked like innocent victims, Yitzhak Rabin like a heartless, arrogant giant.

Much of this might have been avoided had Rabin consulted with some of his own experts before he acted. He never called Shimon Peres, who was on a diplomatic mission to Tokyo. He did not speak with Danny Rothschild, the army general in charge of administering the occupied territories, nor with Uri Lubrani, the Defense Ministry's highly respected Lebanon expert. Nor did he speak with the leaders of his negotiating teams at the peace talks. It was a one-man show all the way, and when it began to backfire Rabin lashed out. He decried Justice Minister Libai as a bleeding heart minister and pressed unsuccessfully for his resignation. He branded the Association for Civil Rights in Israel as the "Association for Hamas Rights." Such people were endangering Israel's security, he charged.

Red-faced and raw, Rabin scrambled, denouncing the Palestinians, the Lebanese government, the media and the United Nations. For three weeks he refused to allow the Red Cross to provide humanitarian relief to the deportees, a decision that the cabinet narrowly sustained by an eight to six vote. Doron Rosenbloom in *Haaretz* compared Rabin's performance to Shamir's disastrous confrontation with Bush over settlements. "Suddenly we had another Captain Ahab, completely enamored of some colossal mistake that carried with it a great principle, a mighty idea for which he was prepared to endanger everything," Rosenbloom wrote.

The move also caused much discomfort for the Clinton administration, which upon entering office in January 1993 faced an immediate Middle East crisis. Warren Christopher, the new U.S. secretary of state, was forced to put the matter at the top of his agenda. The Middle East became his first stop on his first official tour. He managed to persuade Rabin to allow a hundred of the deportees to return home immediately and to permit the others to return after one year rather than two, in exchange for the United States blocking what otherwise could have been an embarrassingly harsh U.N. resolution of condemnation. The deportees rejected the arrangement; it was all or none, they insisted. Their intransigence helped put the matter to rest, as did the fact that few Arab governments, under threat from their own fundamentalist movements, had genuine sympathy for the deportees. The issue quickly faded from international consciousness.

It remained a serious problem, however, for Palestinian moderates such as Husseini, who was forced to suspend Palestinian participation in the autonomy talks. He desperately wanted them to go forward, but he could not be perceived as acceding to the Israeli action. Rabin's argument that the deportations helped Husseini and other moderates by weakening their fundamentalist opponents demonstrated a profound misunderstanding of Arab society. How could Rabin fail to grasp that just as he was leader of all Israelis, not just Labor Party members, so must Husseini act as leader of all Palestinians? Husseini could not be seen rejoicing, nor would he rejoice, over the troubles of his rivals.

Yet Rabin did well with the audience he was most concerned about—the Israeli electorate. More than 90 percent endorsed the original expulsion decision. The number dropped to somewhere around 70 percent after the blundering. Still, it was high enough for Rabin to argue that only he understood the security aspirations and fears of his people. Clumsily executed, the expulsions nevertheless had sent the message to Israelis and Palestinians that while Rabin was prepared to be more forthcoming than Shamir in negotiations, he also intended to be far tougher when it came to security. This, he believed, was exactly the blend that Israelis wanted. He also believed it was a combination that made sense to Arab leaders like Hafez Assad, who respected power and force, nothing else.

The deportations actually helped Hamas; they gave the movement martyrs and a legitimacy that its moderate opponents lacked. And they did negligible harm to the Hamas infrastructure because the movement had little. Many of the people Rabin ordered arrested and deported were middle-aged professionals with no direct involvement in the ambushes and shootings Rabin sought to combat. The people responsible for the violence were for the most part younger and barely recognizable to the authorities. The four

Palestinians accused of killing Toledano had no known connection to Hamas when they decided to kidnap the police sergeant, according to Israeli investigators. They had used their old Subaru sedan to run him down because they owned no guns. They had strangled and stabbed him for the same reason. Only after they had killed Toledano did they make contact with a known Hamas activist.

Israeli intelligence analysts depicted Hamas as a well-organized network of armed cells funded by Islamic extremists operating out of Saudi Arabia, Iran and the United States. But by Israel's own estimation, Hamas received from outside sources no more than a few million dollars per year, most of which went to finance mosques, schools, social clubs and other above-ground institutions. By contrast, the PLO had been receiving an estimated $500 million per year from the Arab Gulf states until the Gulf War.

Hamas thrived precisely because it was a homegrown movement that attracted angry young men with nothing to lose. It was driven not by money but by fervor. The deportations shut down the peace talks for four months but failed to stop the violence. They set off a week of intense rioting in Gaza. On one brutal day six residents of Khan Yunis were killed, including Rana Thawrat Abu Tyour, a ten-year-old girl who was shot in the back by soldiers while fetching a pail of milk during a two-hour lifting of the army's curfew on the city. Four more died over the next three days. And on January 30 a Hamas gang ambushed and killed two soldiers in Gaza.

The riots and killings confirmed the feeling of the Israeli public that Gaza was a trap that Israel would be well rid of. Rabin expressed the wish that Gaza would "sink in the water," although he added that he knew it was not possible.

Gaza would not be contained; its young fanatics kept bringing their knives and dreams of martyrdom to Tel Aviv and Jerusalem. Finally in March 1993 after fifteen Israeli soldiers and civilians were killed in one month in a dozen separate incidents (twenty-six Palestinians also died that month), public anger overflowed. Rabin reacted first by cutting short a trip to the United States—in marked contrast to his response to the beginning of the intifada in December 1987—and then ordering Gaza and the West Bank sealed off. The army strongly opposed the move; the generals feared it would cause an unbearable buildup of anger and tensions inside the occupied territories. The left-wingers of Meretz also expressed misgivings. But Rabin overruled the dissenters and ordered roadblocks erected at every possible entry point. No Palestinians, workers or otherwise, were allowed to cross into Israel.

The stabbings stopped. Personal security improved, and Rabin's standing in the polls shot up. Best of all, the closure demonstrated to Israelis the concrete benefits of separating themselves from Palestinians. Certain sectors of the economy where Arab workers predominated suffered. Spring crops spoiled, and houses sat half finished. The Gaza economy suffered enormously from the cutoff of Israeli income. But most Israelis felt it was a price worth paying. They were not concerned about the Gaza economy. They wanted security and closure seemed to promise it. Polls showed some 75 percent of the public favored the measure.

Rabin was amazed at his unexpected success; he had seized a deep longing of Israelis and transformed it into government policy. The closure seemed to reverse the terms of the political debate within Israel. Whereas before, each terrorist attack was one more reason Israel should hold onto the territories, now each stabbing was a further reason to let them go. Rabin was able to portray the closure as a dress rehearsal for the autonomy deal he wished to strike with the Palestinians. He did not hesitate to appeal to the most racist longings of Israeli Jews. "We must see to it that Palestinians do not swarm among us," he declared in one speech, using a Hebrew verb associated with animals and insects.

Rabin scored another security success in July when he responded to Katyusha rocket attacks on northern Israel with a massive aerial assault on southern Lebanon designed to punish Hezbollah. Operation Accountability was in essence the same plan that Arye Deri had succeeded in defeating the previous November. This time, however, Deri was too weakened by his legal troubles to oppose Rabin, and no other cabinet minister dared take the lead in criticizing the plan. The Israeli bombardment forced some 150,000 Lebanese civilians to flee northward from their villages—which was exactly Rabin's intention, he told a Knesset committee. Their plight forced the Lebanese government and its Syrian sponsors to rein in Hezbollah.

Rabin took some public criticism for punishing civilians to achieve military aims. But the plan worked. After seven days of shelling Rabin won his cease-fire. He compelled U.S. Secretary of State Christopher to become personally involved in mediating between Israel and Syria to end the campaign. The cost was low—no Arab grouping walked out of the peace talks. Both Rabin and Assad came away looking like tough winners. And as columnist Zeev Chafets noted, "Anytime Israel and Syria both emerge victorious from the same war, something new and different is happening in the Middle East."

The events in the north illustrated something new in Israeli society as well. In the past, when Katyushas rained on Kiryat Shemona, a predominately Sephardi development town of 15,000, residents who fled had been condemned for not riding out the shellings in bomb shelters and wearing a brave face for the nation. This time, in the wake of the Gulf War, when some 70 percent of the population fled to safe havens to the south, no one criticized them or called them deserters. The old Zionist stalwarts, determined to enforce self-sacrifice in the face of danger, were gone. Let the army fight the war. The new Israelis considered themselves civilians; they felt society owed them protection, not the other way around. Prosper Azran, the mayor, told *Haaretz* that his people did not have to be heroes; it was better to be smart. "It sounds so right, it's as though the ethos of 1948 never was," commented *Haaretz* columnist Tom Segev.

Yitzhak Rabin had promised to lead Israelis into a new era of peace and prosperity. Instead, his first year in office was a troubled interregnum in which Israel straddled the border of socioeconomic and diplomatic change with one foot firmly planted on each side of the line. Rabin wanted to be the vehicle of reform, yet he was the leader of a political party deeply rooted in the status quo. Labor's traditional leaders in the Histadrut labor federation, the banks and the bureaucracy had no intention of allowing themselves to be reformed out of their jobs. They struggled against changes in the health care system, in the economy, in the defense industry. Gradually many of them grew estranged from Rabin. Yet they could not, would not, get a divorce. Each still needed the other.

Labor was not the only party suffering from political schizophrenia. Likud made a dramatic change in leadership after the election, replacing the retired Yitzhak Shamir with forty-three-year-old Benjamin Netanyahu. "Bibi" was the ultimate American-style candidate—young, handsome, articulate and, according to his many critics, more than a touch superficial. He was very much a champion of the new bourgeois Israel, preaching free market economics and consumer choice. He was master of the sound bite and the fundraiser. Indeed, America helped make him—he traveled to the United States at least four times a year to tap his wealthy financial supporters in the American Jewish community.

But although Netanyahu was an apostle of the politics of modernity, he also worshiped at the altar of the siege. He believed that Israel was surrounded by enemies and needed to maintain a strong military edge. He argued that it could not afford to give back an inch of territory in the West Bank for security reasons (Gaza, Netanyahu said privately, should be released immediately—indeed, he had tried to sell Shamir on announcing a break with Gaza before the disastrous 1992 election). He saw the Middle East as functioning on the Cold War model—the best Israel could hope for was to reach a modus vivendi with its hostile Arab neighbors based on Israel's overwhelming deterrent capacity. As long as the Arabs know that we can blow them to kingdom come, Netanyahu argued, then we can live with them in peace, the same way that the United States lived with the Soviet Union for forty-five years.

It was a recipe for permanent stalemate and for massive amounts of defense spending, and Netanyahu had trouble reconciling this with his vision of a modern consumer society. He welcomed the advent of cable television; indeed, he called it one of Likud's most important breakthroughs, proudly noting that the Shamir government had passed legislation ensuring that the various franchises would be privately held, a break with the socialist past. But innovations like cable were certain to undermine the zeitgeist that Netanyahu believed necessary to defend Israel from an unchanging Arab threat. Bourgeois democracies and couch potatoes were not so good at constant mobilization or at staying armed to the teeth. Israel could not pay for huge amounts of smart weapons and for the latest in Japanese electronics as well.

Bibi Netanyahu wanted to be the new Likud. But like the old Likud, he wanted to have his ideological cake and eat it, too. Somewhere, somehow, someone had to make a choice. Netanyahu seemed unwilling and unable to decide.

Israel under Rabin remained a complicated mixture of self-confidence and vulnerability. Increasingly it found itself integrated into a new world political and economic order. It cultivated trade links with the newly independent Muslim republics along the southern tier of the old Soviet Union and with Indonesia, the world's biggest Muslim country. Yet at the same time Rabin constantly warned of the relentless march of Islamic fundamentalism, which he said threatened Israel from within and without. After the series of stabbings in March he complained that Israeli teenagers were not prepared to defend themselves with hand-to-hand combat and wondered aloud whether Israelis had lost "their ability to react." Reminding listeners that he belonged to "the generation of 1948," he stated, "If we were of [today's] kind, I'm not sure the country would have been established."

Rabin himself embodied the contradictions of his country. In his inaugural Knesset speech he had declared the lifting of the siege, yet his face was etched with lines of anxiety and suspicion. He was still the angry lone wolf, unhappy with the bureaucrats, impatient with fellow politicians, withering with his own aides and supporters. After a year in office, no one dared question him; no one challenged him to his face. He treated the Labor Party and the Knesset as hostile enemy territory. He seemed able to communicate his flashes of anger, but little else. The successful closure of the territories had reinforced his belief that only he knew what was best for Israel. No one else knew what he really thought—how much territory he was willing to cede on the Golan or how far he was willing to go with the Palestinians. Would his caution and fear lead to continuing paralysis, or was he ready to take a truly bold step? Was Rabin prepared to launch a new era, or would his premiership merely lower the curtain on the old 1948 generation that he, as much as Shamir, embodied?

One year after his election, Israel was still waiting to find out.

14. "Enough"

Sometimes the wildest notion, the most apparently impossible idea, takes such a firm hold of the mind that at length it is taken for something realizable. . . . More than that: if the idea coincides with a strong and passionate desire, it may sometimes be accepted as something predestined, inevitable, foreordained, something that cannot but exist or happen.

—FYODOR DOSTOYEVSKY, *The Gambler*

YITZHAK Rabin had never been enthusiastic about the Madrid formula for talks between Israel and the Arabs. He believed that by staging four separate negotiations simultaneously, the formula effectively chained all of the Arab parties together—no one could afford to move faster than the other three for fear of being branded a sellout, so the slowest and most intransigent set the pace. The formula had been designed by Yitzhak Shamir as a recipe for stalemate, Rabin believed, and stalemate was exactly what it had produced. Instead of the slow accumulation of good will, trust and respect that their American sponsors had hoped for, ten rounds of talks over twenty months had succeeded in freezing each side's negotiating position, while producing for each a fresh list of grievances and disappointments.

Rabin hoped that with Labor's return to power and its more flexible bargaining position, the Arab side would loosen up and things would get moving. First he tried the Palestinians. They were the party most desperate for change and with the most to gain from a settlement. But he could not overcome the obstacles built into the process, beginning with the question of just who it was that the Israelis were negotiating with. The Palestinian delegation, which consisted of locals from the West Bank and Gaza, had one set of priorities and needs; the PLO bureaucrats in Tunis had another. The two were in constant conflict, which meant that the Palestinians offered virtually no flexibility—they could not move beyond the lowest common denominator, which was invariably hard-line. And faced with a more accommodating Israeli negotiating partner, the Palestinians actually toughened their position. They insisted that Arab East Jerusalem be part of the autonomy agreement and that Palestinian refugees be allowed to return to their homeland just as Jews enjoyed the "right of return" in Israel. They also demanded that their ultimate goal of Palestinian statehood be irrevocably linked to the interim autonomy arrangement. All of these demands were unacceptable to Rabin.

Not that Israel was particularly forthcoming in other areas. The new government dropped the word "autonomy," which the Palestinians detested, and replaced it with "interim self-government arrangements." The government released a few hundred political prisoners and tore down a few dozen security barriers. But it offered no basic change in principle from the bargaining stance of Likud. Rabin, like Shamir, was offering a very truncated form of interim self-government to Palestinians, with no guarantee of what the final settlement would look like. He even kept on Shamir's head negotiator, cabinet secretary Elyakim Rubinstein, a lawyer and civil servant who was good-natured and impeccably evenhanded but congenitally legalistic. Indeed, it was not a true negotiation at all, so much as a transaction. The Palestinians had nothing to give—Israel held all the power, all the land and all the cards; the only option the Palestinians had was to accept or reject whatever the Israelis chose to offer.

When he took office Rabin had predicted that an interim agreement with the Palestinians would take six to nine months to complete. But he soon lost patience with their inflexibility and disorganization and turned to Syria. Here there were clear lines of authority and only one person to deal with, Hafez Assad. But Assad perplexed Rabin. Was the Syrian leader ready for a real agreement or was he toying with Rabin, waiting for the Americans to compel Israel to return the Golan Heights? Assad seemed in no hurry for a deal; worse, in his few public remarks he displayed no awareness of what he would be required to give in return—not just a cessation of hostilities, but a full-scale peace accord with open borders, exchanges of embassies, trade and tourism, and lots of demilitarized territory between the Israeli-Syrian border and Damascus. Assad expected to get the same terms Sadat had gotten from Begin—the restoration of all occupied territory up to the last square inch. But in return he proposed none of the offerings Sadat had given Israel, most especially the gift of recognition that Sadat had bestowed by stepping foot on Israeli soil.

Rabin understood that dealings with Syria would be long and drawn out. What's more, Israelis across the ideological spectrum were opposed to withdrawing from the Golan because of its obvious strategic value and because the 13,000 settlers who lived there were not messianic fanatics but hardworking, middle-of-the-road pioneers, many of them card-carrying members of the Labor Party. Settlers in the West Bank and Gaza, hoping to hitch their own faltering movement to a more popular, mainstream cause, organized a campaign of mass demonstrations, road signs and posters against withdrawal from the heights. Thousands of apartment windows and balconies displayed the slogan "The People with the Golan." Rabin knew it would be a hard sell.

Jordan and Lebanon were on the sidelines. King Hussein was ready for a deal—the terms of the negotiation were agreed upon within the first few sessions—but he could not afford to sign anything in public until the Palestinian issue was settled. Lebanon followed the dictates of its Syrian overseer.

Rabin was frustrated and disappointed. He could feel the pressure of the clock. His term would end in 1996, perhaps sooner if his fragile coalition fell apart. At age seventy he still smoked two packs of cigarettes a day and drank scotch, and there were days when his face looked hollow and haunted. He could not afford to waste time, nor to allow others to waste it for him. Yet that was what was happening. In February 1993 he conceded that he would not be able to meet his deadline with the Palestinians. "I imagined it would be simpler, and I admit it appears to involve more difficulties," he confessed.

Desperate for progress he turned secretly to many parties, Israeli, American, European—anyone who might be able to break through. Especially after the Knesset repealed the law banning contact with PLO members that winter, there was a flurry of secret activity. There were back channels, side channels and third-party contacts. Most were pipe dreams—someone who knew someone who knew someone else. Mostly they led nowhere. But there was one improbable channel that did lead somewhere. Ironically for Rabin, it was developed by two of his most hated political opponents.

Yossi Beilin had worked for Shimon Peres since the dark days of 1977, just after Peres lost the watershed election to Menachem Begin. A former journalist with a Ph.D. in political science and plainspoken left-wing views, Beilin had stuck with Peres through good times and bad—he was cabinet secretary when Peres served as prime minister, and director general of the

Foreign Affairs Ministry when Peres became minister. Along the way he had incurred Yitzhak Rabin's wrath in 1987 when he led the effort to sever Israel's long-standing military relations with South Africa. The defense minister pinned one of his bitter designer labels on Beilin, calling him "Peres's poodle." Nonetheless, in 1988 Beilin won his own Knesset seat.

When others abandoned Peres after his defeat by Rabin in the February 1992 primary, Beilin stayed loyal. And when Rabin reluctantly bestowed the Foreign Affairs Ministry on Peres after the June election, Beilin became the deputy minister. But Rabin sought to ensure that his longtime rivals could not get in his way. He kept the bilateral negotiations with the Syrians and Palestinians under the control of the prime minister's office and doled out the more sporadic multilateral talks to Foreign Affairs.

This did not stop Peres. Like Rabin, he was eager to atone for past misjudgments and lost time. He was still aggrieved that Shamir had shot down his efforts to convene an international peace conference in 1987. Had the conference been held, Peres believed, the intifada might never have occurred and Israel might not have wasted five years. Now he was playing a subordinate role in a government whose leader feared and despised him. The two men had declared a joint truce after the Labor primary—neither wanted to be blamed for another general election defeat. But when Rabin looked around the cabinet table, he saw no one else whose experience and stature approached his own, except for his old adversary. When they met alone there were two prime ministers, two defense ministers, a foreign minister, a finance minister, a chief of staff and an ambassador to the United States in the room. Virtually no government on earth could boast such a duo. They hated each other; they needed each other. Author Amos Oz compared them to two bickering old women who needed to hold hands to cross a busy street. Beilin understood the relationship. When the time came in 1993, he would manipulate both men to achieve the signing of the PLO accords.

After the signing, Israeli officials disclosed bits and pieces of what would become known as the "Oslo connection"—how Beilin, backed by Peres, authorized an old friend, Haifa University professor of Mideast studies Yair Hirschfeld, to conduct secret talks with Yasser Arafat's director of finance, Ahmed Suleiman Khoury, first in London and then in Norway under the auspices of the Norwegian Foreign Ministry and the Norwegian Institute for Applied Science (FAFO). But the accounts were incomplete—they overstated Peres's role and underplayed Rabin's decisive one. This was how the various Israeli parties wanted it for domestic political considerations; Peres was happy to take the credit, while Rabin wanted to distance himself from the controversial document.

The truth was far more complex. The talks were improvised, fragile and intuitive. None of the parties knew exactly where they were going until they got there, and Beilin and Peres's achievement was both in manipulating the back channel to the Palestinians and in persuading the crusty, cynical, often hostile Rabin that this was the real thing and that it was worth pursuing.

Hirschfeld's first meeting with Khoury, known as Abu Alaa, in London in December 1992, was not authorized by Beilin or anyone else. But the professor, who had held secret meetings with Palestinians in the past, decided on his own to forge ahead. Beilin knew nothing about the meeting until after it had occurred, although he then encouraged Hirschfeld to continue.

Armed with Beilin's tacit approval, Hirschfeld and an academic colleague, Ron Pundik, journeyed to Oslo for two more sessions with Abu Alaa, and in February 1993 they presented Beilin with a seven-page draft declaration of principles. Some of it was pie-in-the-sky: it proposed that the United Nations administer Gaza as a trusteeship for an interim period and it granted Palestinians self-government in East Jerusalem. Rabin would hit the roof, Beilin knew, if he saw this. Still, Beilin was pleasantly surprised to see that the document also contained basic agreement on an autonomy arrangement that would begin with the Gaza Strip and gradually expand to the West Bank, and that the Palestinians were not insisting that the plan be formally tied to eventual statehood. He believed that the draft, defects and all, should be pursued.

He took a version of the draft to Peres, and Peres eventually took it to Rabin, informing the prime minister at one of their weekly private meetings that "two *meshugoim*" ("crackpots") were talking to the PLO at Beilin's behest. "Yossi is playing with his toys," Peres told Rabin. But Peres said he was inclined to let them go ahead—there were some promising elements in the draft; anyway, it could always be disavowed later. Rabin gave his reluctant consent.

From the beginning Rabin had his doubts about the document that was evolving in Norway. But it contained one element that he found irresistible: Israeli withdrawal from Gaza. For years Israel had been searching for someone to take Gaza off its hands; the Egyptians, the Jordanians, even the Saudis had all been offered control or special privileges but had turned it down. The PLO was far from Rabin's first choice, but it was better than nothing. He would be getting rid of Israel's biggest burden, the place he had said he wanted to "drop in the water." And Gaza would be a good test of the PLO's ability to run its own affairs and maintain order.

And so Rabin decided to let the Oslo connection go forward. "If Peres wants to fool around with this, let him," Rabin told his aides. No one believed in it, which was one reason it was allowed to develop without interference.

Hirschfeld and Pundik, now operating under detailed instructions from Beilin, held five more informal sessions with Abu Alaa between February and May. Still, Israeli officials remained skeptical. Their intelligence files held only four and a half pages on Abu Alaa, and they had no idea if he was truly authorized to speak for Arafat and the PLO. They decided on a test. Abu Alaa had told Hirschfeld that he was secretly in charge of the various multilateral talks in which the Palestinian position had been uniformly hard-line. Now Hirschfeld asked Abu Alaa for an easing in those positions. Sure enough, at the next two multilateral sessions in Rome and Oslo in May, Palestinians sounded more conciliatory.

Abu Alaa was equally skeptical about Hirschfeld. From the beginning he constantly demanded that Israel send an official representative to the sessions. In May he threatened to shut down the back channel unless the demand was met. Peres wanted to attend himself, but Rabin insisted that they dispatch a subordinate. Eventually Beilin designated two men for what became the first formal contacts ever held between the Jewish state and the PLO. One was a Peres loyalist: Uri Savir, a forty-year-old diplomat who had been Israel's consul general in New York and had just been named director general of the Foreign Affairs Ministry. The other was an acquaintance of Rabin: Yoel Singer, a lawyer who had worked on the Camp David accords and had been a senior military prosecutor during Rabin's term as defense minister.

The two men were in many ways a fitting embodiment of the new Israel. Baby-faced yet serious, Savir had few ideological hangups and displayed a passionate sense of purpose. Singer, by contrast, was brusque, businesslike and unrelenting. Their Palestinian interlocutors quickly warmed to Savir, but they soon learned that they could not bypass Singer.

When it came to co-opting Rabin, Singer, who still held the rank of reserve army colonel, was an inspired choice. Rabin seemed comfortable with him and relied upon him as a reality check on Peres, Beilin and Savir, none of whom Rabin trusted. Singer's entry marked the beginning of more intense involvement by both Rabin and Peres, who began meeting weekly with Singer and Beilin, then twice- and sometimes thrice-weekly. Rabin raised all kinds of questions: Who would control roads, settlements and unused state land under the proposed arrangement? What kind of security safeguards would Israel receive? Who would operate the border posts? What about the army's right to strike preemptively or to pursue terrorists into Palestinian-held areas? As Beilin listened, it became clear to him that

Rabin had turned a corner. The prime minister was still skeptical, but it seemed to Beilin that he was no longer looking for a pretext to shoot down the arrangement—he actually wanted it to succeed.

Rabin had always believed that no deal was possible with the PLO because it would never accede to anything less than an independent state and because Israelis abhorred the organization and its terrorist record. It had been his idea back in 1988 to take advantage of the shift in power caused by the intifada and build up Faisal Husseini and other local Palestinians into a credible alternative to Tunis.

The strategy never quite jelled at the bargaining table. Under the Likud's stringent terms, Husseini was not allowed to participate directly in the negotiations because he was an East Jerusalemite and Shamir was unwilling to negotiate the future of the city. Husseini could only advise and instruct from the corridor outside. The biggest problem, however, was the delegation's lack of legitimacy. No one had elected it; instead, its members had been selected in a drawn-out negotiation between Tunis, Amman, Washington and the locals, with Israel wielding a veto from the sidelines. Its credibility with Palestinians back home in the West Bank and Gaza depended strictly on results. As the talks dragged on and conditions in the occupied territories continued to deteriorate, the delegation's standing in its own community plummeted and its room to maneuver narrowed.

Arafat continually manipulated and undercut the delegates. He wanted the negotiations to continue, so each time they sought to walk away he ordered them back to the table. At the same time he knew that an agreement reached without him would undermine his own power, so he halted progress anytime a deal looked possible.

The Arab delegations had cut off the talks during the deportees' crisis, a move that caught Rabin by surprise. He was forced to admit he had miscalculated the diplomatic consequences and should have consulted with Peres, his top diplomat. As a result, he had no choice but to allow the foreign minister to become more involved in the faltering peace process. Peres first sought to open a back channel to Husseini, meeting secretly three times with the Palestinian leader in an effort to get the talks restarted. But although they reached personal agreement on many issues, there was no apparent easing of the official Palestinian position. Husseini was not calling the shots, Peres concluded.

The Israeli foreign minister tried other doors. He floated to the Egyptians the idea of including Jericho as part of the autonomous zone, along with Gaza. This would give the Palestinians a foothold in the West Bank.

The Egyptians took the proposal to Arafat, who then presented it publicly as his own.

Jericho was perhaps the sleepiest and most stable Palestinian town in the West Bank. It straddled the main route north through the Jordan Valley, but it did not intersect any of the strategic highways atop the West Bank's hilly spine. Best of all, through strenuous efforts over the years, the army had managed to keep the Jericho area off-limits to right-wing Jewish settlers. There were a handful of settlements along the Jordan Valley route, but these were strategic enclaves populated by former soldiers, many of them Labor Party loyalists. It would be relatively simple to turn the area over to a Palestinian authority.

In the ninth and tenth rounds in May and June, Israel tried to outmaneuver Arafat by allowing Husseini to take formal charge inside the negotiating room. American diplomats also for the first time proposed their own draft declaration of principles, which outlined the areas of self-rule Palestinians would be granted under an interim agreement while retaining for Israel overall authority for security in the territories. Neither ploy worked. One year of battering from the Hamas deportations, the army's crackdown in Gaza and the March closure of the territories had destroyed whatever independence Husseini once had possessed. As for the American "bridging proposal," to the Palestinians it looked too much like the Israeli position— they didn't even bother to attend the joint meeting that the Americans called to discuss it.

The Palestinians went home from the tenth round in June depressed and rebellious. Privately they blamed not only Israeli intransigence and American faintheartedness, but also Arafat. None of them except Husseini knew about the Oslo connection, but they were convinced Arafat was playing a double game—insisting that the delegation take a hard line in Washington while offering many hints that he would personally be more forthcoming if only he were allowed to participate openly. Yet back home in the territories it was the delegates who were held responsible by their fellow Palestinians for the lack of progress. The delegates feared Arafat was setting them up as scapegoats; if the negotiations failed, they would take the blame. This was not an academic exercise. Arafat's blessing had provided them with a certain degree of physical protection. If he abandoned them, they could not only lose their positions, but also their lives.

Haidar Abdel-Shafi of Gaza, a fiercely independent veteran politician who was leader of the delegation before Husseini's elevation, was the first to resign. Then the core of the local leadership—Husseini, Hanan Ashrawi and Saeb Erakat—decided that they, too, would quit. They journeyed to Tunis in early August for a showdown with Arafat, who listened with great sympathy and persuaded them to sit tight a little longer, but divulged nothing.

Rabin and his intelligence analysts had always assumed that the locals were more pragmatic and moderate than Tunis because they were the ones who had to live under occupation and were most directly accountable to residents. But he could see that a curious reversal was taking place. With the negotiations stalled and with their own credibility ebbing, the locals were becoming more hard-line, while Arafat increasingly played the role of moderate. At the table in Washington the Palestinian stance was unyielding, but in the secret talks in Norway the PLO was much more forthcoming. In May the delegates in Washington paralyzed the talks by demanding anew that East Jerusalem be part of the autonomy deal; in Oslo that same month Abu Alaa withdrew East Jerusalem from Arafat's own list of demands.

At the same time Rabin was receiving daily intelligence reports from Tunis about the growing weakness of the organization. Arafat was running out of money, support and rabbits to pull from his peaked keffiyeh. PLO newspapers were folding, universities were closing their doors, welfare payments to the families of martyrs and the wounded were drying up. The entire billion-dollar apparatus was folding around Arafat's shoulders. Rabin could sit back and watch it die. Or he could try to breathe new life into it with an interim agreement and see if he could help produce a moderate Palestinian partner for peace. In the end Rabin faced a painful decision to help his enemy. Tactical opportunist that he was, the old general knew he had no real choice. "I had to make a decision: we go for it, or we don't," Rabin later recalled. "And going for it meant going to the landlord"—Arafat.

Rabin tried the Syrians once more in early August, hoping that the recent exchange of understandings over Israel's bombardment of southern Lebanon might blossom into a broader agreement over peace. But Warren Christopher could not find an opening in Damascus. Rather than initiate a new round of shuttle diplomacy between Rabin and Assad to capitalize on the opening he had achieved in the Lebanon talks, Christopher and his staff broke for vacation. The road to Damascus remained closed. There was only one other place to go.

The first five months of meetings between the Israelis and Abu Alaa had concentrated on practical arrangements for autonomy in Gaza and the West Bank—who would control how much land, when would elections be held, what would be the status of the Jewish settlements, who would police the borders and the roads? Arafat had insisted on an extraterritorial corridor between Gaza and Jericho to tie together the two autonomous zones, while Rabin demanded that the IDF be able to enter the zones without warning.

But periodically the Palestinians raised another issue. They wanted Israel formally to recognize the PLO.

At first the Israelis were not interested. They argued that the agreement they were hammering out in Oslo was too fragile to be burdened with such a weighty historic transformation. Give it some months, they insisted, and if things go well then we can discuss mutual recognition. "Let's not talk about it now," Rabin told Beilin. In the end, however, it was Rabin's own question that led to a reconsideration of the issue. In July he pointed out that the two sides were nearing agreement on a document that said nothing about ending violence. "We're going to sign a Declaration of Principles without binding them to ending terrorism?" he asked Beilin.

The Israeli negotiators went back to Abu Alaa to insist that the Palestinians renounce violence. "For such a step you need the PLO," he told them. "But you don't recognize that the PLO exists. Only if we exist can we end terrorism."

Rabin gave his consent, provided that the PLO agreed to end the intifada and amend its charter to delete those portions calling for the destruction of Israel. None of the Israelis involved quite grasped at the time that mutual recognition, which seemed little more than an afterthought, would prove to be the most sweeping and historic part of the agreement.

After Savir and Singer took over in June, the two sides would need ten more meetings to iron out the details of the declaration. They went through twenty-five drafts of the document. Each side had its imperatives: the Israelis, operating under Rabin's intricate instructions, emphasized stringent security safeguards; the Palestinians, eager to establish their authority, pushed for greater powers over their autonomous areas. The weekend sessions were intense, usually starting late Friday and continuing with few breaks for sleep until early Monday morning. The talks got tougher, with ultimatums, demands and occasional walkouts. In Jerusalem a steering committee consisting of Rabin, Peres, Beilin and Singer reviewed each weekend's session and issued detailed instructions for the next. Peres preferred to deal in concepts and principles, and his eyes tended to glaze over when it came to the gritty work of sentences, subordinate clauses and punctuation. But Rabin focused on every word. "He knows every comma [in the declaration]," said an aide.

In the end there were two sets of documents. The first was the Declaration of Principles, along with annexes and minutes, that gave the Palestinians autonomous control over the entire Gaza Strip and a West Bank enclave in Jericho. This was finalized in an all-night, eight-hour conference call with Norwegian Foreign Minister Johan Jørgen Holst mediating between Peres and Arafat. Peres was in Stockholm on an official trip to Scandinavia. The next day he flew to Oslo where, with a certain amount of clandestine choreography, he and PLO foreign secretary Abu Mazen signed the declaration on August 20.

Embedded in the declaration was a brutally swift time clock. One month after the signing Israel was to transfer authority for education and culture, health, social welfare, direct taxation and tourism to "authorized Palestinians," while a joint Israeli-Palestinian Economic Cooperation Committee was due to begin work on water, electricity, energy, finance, transport and communications, environment, news media, labor relations and overall economic development—in all nearly forty areas that had to be discussed, arranged and transferred. "The negotiators deserve the Nobel Prize for ambiguity," complained Jad Isaac, who as head of the Palestinian technical committees for planning, water, environment and other matters suddenly found himself facing an insane deadline. "My God, they've left it all to us to somehow work it out in a hurry."

Two months later Israeli military withdrawal from Gaza and Jericho was due to begin. The army was to complete the withdrawal by April 1994. Three months later elections would take place for a Palestinian authority to govern the territories and the army would redeploy outside the populated areas of the West Bank. The civil administration would dissolve, marking the formal end of military occupation. Negotiations on the permanent ownership of the territories would begin within seventeen months—by December 1995. Israel would maintain control over Jewish settlements, army bases and the roads connecting them to Israel proper. The boundaries of Jericho and the question of whether the Palestinian authority would extend to the Allenby Bridge between the West Bank and Jordan were matters that were left for the negotiators to deal with later.

Within days word of the declaration began to leak to the press. Israelis were stunned. To many it looked as if Yitzhak Rabin, the leader who had promised during the 1992 election campaign never to negotiate with the PLO, had been hijacked by his party's left wing. Rabin himself hinted that he was dissatisfied with the agreement; it was too vague and too forthcoming, he complained. Nonetheless, he endorsed it with increasing passion and many Israelis followed his lead, setting aside their anxieties to give the agreement a wary welcome. What could be better than getting rid of Gaza? What was the big deal about Jericho? And if the PLO demonstrated it could rule in those places, why not give it jurisdiction over Palestinians in the rest of the West Bank as well? Let the PLO enforce order, not the IDF. Within two weeks nearly 60 percent of the public was registering approval of the accord. Israelis were reacting with the same cautious pragmatism as their leader.

The IDF's official reaction was lukewarm. Both Chief of Staff Ehud

Barak and his deputy, Amnon Shahak, who had been kept in the dark while the negotiations went on, raised questions about how the army could implement withdrawal on such short notice and still maintain control over security, as the agreement stipulated. Terrorism was certain to increase, they warned.

Those on the ground, however, had a more spontaneous and heartfelt response. "I won't miss a thing," a much-relieved Brigadier General Yom Tov Samiah, Israeli commander of Gaza, told the *Washington Post*'s Laura Blumenfeld as they drove down one of the strip's main roads in his battered command car. "Not this house. Not this road. . . . I'm leaving all the stones behind."

It was astonishing how quickly many Israelis came around to the notion of ceding territory and legitimacy to Arafat and the PLO, a man and an organization that for them had epitomized terrorism for so many years. The answer was simple: no one had fallen in love with Arafat; they were simply prepared to make the tradeoff in return for peace.

Mira Avrech, the popular social columnist for *Yediot,* traveled to Tunis a few days after the declaration was signed. She had lunch with Arafat and his wife. Mrs. Arafat explained how her husband liked his eggs cooked and how he darned his own socks. *Yediot* published color pictures of their bedroom and kitchen, just as it had done when Avrech did a similar interview with Anwar and Jihan Sadat in 1977. "You get the sense the blood feud with the Palestinians is over, and the habits of a lifetime, the dehumanization and demonization of both sides are over," said author Zeev Chafets. "When Mira Avrech comes to visit, you're no longer a mass murderer but a political leader. It's a harbinger of spring."

There was another set of documents. These were letters exchanged between Arafat and Rabin extending mutual recognition. It took nearly three weeks to negotiate them after the signing in Oslo. Arafat kept trying to duck the issues of changing the charter and announcing an end to the intifada, but Rabin insisted. The two sides spent one long night arguing over whether the PLO should recognize Israel's "right to live," which was Arafat's language, or its "right to exist," which Israeli negotiators argued was a broader concept. After a flurry of last-minute maneuvering, the two sides announced on Thursday, September 9, that they had reached agreement.

The next morning Rabin sat down at a desk in his office and signed the letter in front of a dozen television cameras. *New York Times* correspondent Clyde Haberman described Rabin as "looking much like a man on a used-car lot who wants to make sure that the contract in front of him is indeed what he and the dealer had negotiated."

· · ·

Throughout the negotiations in Oslo, American diplomats were conspicuously absent. The Norwegians kept them informed of the meetings between Israelis and Palestinians and gave Washington a copy of the draft declaration in March. Beilin even hoped for a time that Washington would agree to sponsor the final agreement by presenting it publicly as an American proposal. But the Americans were not interested. They expressed vague support for the talks, but it was clear to the Norwegians that they did not take the negotiations—or the Norwegians themselves—very seriously.

Ever since the Clinton administration had taken office in January 1993, its role in the peace talks had been ambivalent. In formulating this stance, the administration largely deferred to the ambivalence of American Jewish leaders, who were torn between their loyalty to the new Rabin government and their instinctive sympathy for the old Likud worldview. During fifteen years of Likud dominance many Jewish leaders in the United States had taken on the mind-set and ideology of the Israeli right. They, too, saw Israel as vulnerable and endangered and Palestinians as devious terrorists. They may have been comfortable with Yitzhak Rabin's gritty, hard-bitten persona, but they were not at ease with his policies. They could not grasp why he was making concessions to the Arabs. Was Rabin really prepared to exchange land for peace? Or was he just going through a charade as Yitzhak Shamir had done for so many years? Those on the right who began to suspect that Rabin was serious about territorial compromise—*Commentary* editor Norman Podhoretz, *New York Times* columnist A. M. Rosenthal and a handful of others—publicly distanced themselves from him.

Rabin made matters worse by expending little effort to rally American Jewish support. He expected American Jews to fall in line behind his policies without question or hesitation. And his government lacked the kind of spokesmen who could sell his policies in the United States the way that Benjamin Netanyahu, Dan Meridor, Ehud Olmert and Moshe Arens had sold the Likud's. Professor Itamar Rabinovich, the new ambassador to the United States, was a man of impressive intellect and calm demeanor, but he lacked Netanyahu's charisma and mastery of colloquial English.

Unlike Bush, Bill Clinton had been elected president with massive American Jewish support. He was not prepared to alienate a key domestic constituency. Seeing that American Jews were torn and uncertain over Rabin's policies, administration officials chose to proceed with caution. Martin Indyk, the new national security adviser for Middle Eastern affairs, and Dennis Ross, the main architect of the Madrid conference who was kept on as a special adviser to Warren Christopher, were activists who sought ways to unfreeze the peace process. Christopher maintained a close personal relationship with Rabin, who the administration quickly decided was the best hope for a peace accord that Israelis could live with. But the administration took few initiatives and fewer risks.

In one sense, the inactivity was useful. Arafat came quickly to understand that Bill Clinton, unlike George Bush, would apply no serious pressure on Rabin. Realizing he would get no concessions from Washington, Arafat determined to make his own opportunities in Oslo.

After the Oslo signing, Rabin dispatched Peres to California where Christopher was vacationing. Christopher and Ross seemed surprised by the comprehensiveness of the agreement, but they told Peres he had their full support. Still, for several days American officials said little about the agreement in public and expressed reservations in private. Some were not at all certain whether the document was another wishful concoction from Peres and Beilin or a genuine breakthrough that had Rabin's full support.

Finally it was Clinton himself who broke the ice. He told reporters on August 30—a full ten days after the Oslo signing—that he was "very much encouraged by what has happened there and very hopeful." And he went on to do much more than merely embrace the accord. The administration decided to stage a ceremony on the White House lawn to echo the 1979 signing of the Camp David accords by the leaders of Israel and Egypt. The Americans exhumed the same walnut table that had been the centerpiece of that signing, but they needed new actors to play the roles of Menachem Begin and Anwar Sadat. At first it looked as if they would have to settle for Shimon Peres and Abu Mazen. But Yasser Arafat would not be denied his moment of glory. He needed to demonstrate to Palestinians that he had wrung a powerful concession—American recognition—in return for the Gaza/Jericho accord, so he insisted on being invited. The Clinton administration, determining that an internationally televised ritual would somehow enhance the meaning of the already signed agreement—and perhaps its own tattered reputation for diplomacy—did not resist.

After the letter-signing ceremony in Jerusalem on Friday, Rabin informed Christopher that Peres would represent Israel at the signing in Washington. But early the next morning Christopher called back to tell Rabin that Arafat had decided to personally represent the PLO at the ceremony, so the United States was officially inviting the prime minister as well. As he listened to Christopher, Rabin realized he had little choice but to go. He could not say no to the president of the United States. Besides, like Arafat he hoped that a White House ceremony would add to his credibility with his own people. He told the secretary of state that he, too, would attend.

Eitan Haber warned him that the signing would inevitably mean standing on the same platform with Arafat. "Yitzhak, I want you to understand—you'll be shaking hands with Arafat, maybe he'll try to hug you. You'll have to sit with him in the same room and speak with him." Rabin only shrugged. There was, he felt, no other choice.

That evening in an interview he confessed to Clyde Haberman that he felt butterflies in his stomach when he contemplated standing on the White House lawn alongside Arafat. He recalled having lost half his brigade in the battle for Jerusalem in the 1948 Independence War, and he invoked the memory of the dead as the reason he was willing to take such a distasteful step. "I'm an old guy. I served twenty-seven years in the military. My son served. Now my grandson serves. Let's give a hope that at least my grandson will not need to fight. If there will be a need, I'm sure that a fourth generation also will do it. But I feel a responsibility to give a chance that it will not happen."

A few hours before the ceremony Ahmed Tibi, an adviser to Arafat, appeared at Peres's hotel room with more demands. He warned that Arafat would be on the next plane if they were not met. He wanted to delete a paragraph that referred to a "joint Palestinian-Jordanian team" and to substitute PLO for "the Palestinian team" throughout the document. Peres rejected the first demand and accepted the second, but that was not quite good enough. Arafat was still leaving. "Let me know when you're going, because we will be going, too," Peres told Tibi. The Palestinians backed down, but it was a harbinger of things to come.

Rabin and Peres invited several Israelis whose relatives had been killed in terrorist attacks to attend the signing. A handful agreed, but one notable invitee did not make it to Washington that morning. Her name was Smadar Haran. In 1979 Palestinian terrorists had broken into her home in the seafront town of Nahariya in northern Israel. The raiders had shot her husband and smashed the head of one of her children with a rock. Meanwhile, Smadar Haran hid in the attic with her other daughter. The child had not been able to contain her cries so her mother had put her hands tightly over the child's mouth to muffle them. The child suffocated.

Yitzhak Rabin offered Smadar Haran, who had since remarried and given birth to two more children, a seat on the flight to Washington. She agreed at first to accompany him. But as the hour drew near, she could not bring herself to sit across from the men who had given the orders to her family's killers. She arrived at Ben-Gurion Airport minutes before takeoff, but she could not board the plane.

"I wouldn't be able to bear it," she told Rabin. "I can't shake his hand. But you are my messenger." Then she left the airport and drove to the cemetery, where she laid olive branches on the graves of her husband and her two small daughters.

"I know it is very difficult to make this emotional switch," she told *Maariv*. "I wouldn't preach to anyone. But we have to understand that the sense of revenge, which is very human, won't lead us anywhere. We have to transcend this as a people, not only as victims. We've had enough counting our dead and thinking about the price in blood. Now, just as we are strong in war, we have to be strong in peace. We have to learn to see the Palestinians as our neighbors."

Sometimes it happens that a leader comes to embody the emotions of an entire nation during a moment of trial—such as Roosevelt at the birth of the New Deal in 1933, or Churchill during the Battle of Britain, or De Gaulle during the Algerian crisis. On the White House lawn that dazzlingly sunny Monday morning in September, before a crowd of former presidents, secretaries of state, Arab dignitaries, Jewish American leaders and a worldwide audience of television viewers, Yitzhak Rabin radiated the misgivings, the anguish and the grim determination of the Israeli people.

His face was etched in pain. He stared at his shoes, at his fingernails, at an abstract speck on the horizon, anywhere but to his left, where a beaming Yasser Arafat awaited his eyes. He fidgeted like a man desperate for a cigarette and a scotch—a man who would rather have been anywhere else on the face of the earth.

His speech was brief, no more than six minutes. The words were not especially memorable, but the delivery was unforgettable. In a voice that was weary yet emphatic, he confessed that it was not so easy for him to be there, nor for Jews in Israel and abroad to watch an Israeli prime minister standing on the same platform with the leader of the PLO.

Rabin addressed his own people, but also the Palestinians. For the first time, he seemed to speak to them without paternalism or condescension, without that veiled strain of contempt in his voice. "Let me say to you, the Palestinians, we are destined to live together on the same soil, in the same land. We, the soldiers who have returned from battle stained with blood, we who have seen our relatives and friends killed before our eyes, we who have attended their funerals and cannot look into the eyes of their parents, we who have come from a land where parents bury their children, we who have fought against you, the Palestinians—we say to you today in a loud and clear voice: 'Enough of blood and tears. Enough.' "

He told them Israel sought no revenge, felt no hatred. He asked them "to open a new chapter in dignity, in empathy, as human beings, as free men." And he promised "a new era" in Middle East history.

Next came Arafat. He gave a facile and elegant performance. Smiling, friendly, speaking the words of peace with ease, he lived up to his reputation as the perfect international houseguest—a man happy to say whatever he thinks his hosts wish to hear. Yet surely it pained him as well to stand across from the Israeli leader who, as defense minister, had crushed the intifada and authorized the bombing of Palestinian refugee camps in Lebanon.

After Arafat finished, Peres and Abu Mazen took turns sitting at the walnut table and signing the accord. Then came the moment Rabin most dreaded. Clinton took a grinning Arafat in his left arm and a grimacing Rabin in his right and gracefully pulled them toward each other. Clinton then planted his palm gently on Rabin's back and coaxed him further forward. Arafat's hand sprang out and Rabin, after hesitating slightly, reached forward and met it with his own. The president stepped back slightly, his eyes misty, his arms extended as if embracing both sides. The crowd, which had held its breath, sighed.

Later Rabin confessed: "Of all the hands in the world, it was not the hand that I wanted or dreamed of touching." He looked shaken, but his sardonic sense of humor remained intact. After the handshake, he turned to his old rival Peres and whispered in English, "You are next." And soon Peres, too, was shaking hands with Arafat and Abu Mazen while the cameras clicked and back home 5 million Israelis watched in stunned disbelief.

Among those most caught off-balance by the agreement was Benjamin Netanyahu and his fellow Likudniks. Netanyahu, who looked so comfortable and sounded so smooth when working from a script, seemed lost and flustered when forced to improvise. He could not oppose the concept of Palestinian autonomy—after all, it was Likud that had first proposed it at Camp David and championed it at Madrid. Nor could he oppose the politically popular idea of returning Gaza to Palestinian rule. Instead, Netanyahu sought to concentrate on the mutual recognition agreement with the PLO. Rabin had broken his word, Netanyahu argued. The prime minister had signed a pact with a terrorist organization that was not only murderous and duplicitous but increasingly irrelevant—Arafat could not stop Palestinian violence even if he wanted to. Why revive a corpse that Israel had spent so many years killing off? And how could the government allow the PLO to set up headquarters in Jericho, just ten miles down the road from Jerusalem?

Netanyahu stumbled for the proper historical metaphors. He compared the agreement rather inexactly to famous betrayals such as Munich and the U.S. peace treaty with North Vietnam. The agreement would inevitably lead to a Palestinian state in the West Bank and Gaza, he argued, and put the

Arabs back in control of the strategic highlands Israel had held since the 1967 war. Rabin, the architect of that victory, was now the engineer of its demise. His plan would leave Israel vulnerable and defenseless.

Netanyahu wound up isolating himself. He appeared at a giant rally in Jerusalem against the accord that was mostly populated by right-wing settlers from the West Bank and by *haredi* followers of the Lubavitcher rebbe in New York. The mainstream secular right—security hawks and working-class Sephardim—was conspicuously absent.

The fact was that while they did not trust Arafat, many in Likud were not unhappy with the accord. They had no use for Gaza, little more for the West Bank, and they were prepared to accept the deal with some wariness if it meant more security for them and an end to Palestinian terrorism on the streets of Israel proper. Meir Sheetrit, the Moroccan-born Likud politician who had criticized Likud's ideological purity after the 1992 defeat, warned Netanyahu that the party would be committing "political suicide" if it could not come to terms with the practical longings of its supporters. Likud had to remain a party of the political center, he argued. Netanyahu shrugged; perhaps, he agreed, but the ideological right wing of the party, led by Ariel Sharon, demanded that he adhere to a hard-line stand.

One elderly Likudnik, of course, was desperately opposed to the accord. Yitzhak Shamir had watched all year with mounting horror as the Rabin government inched toward trading territory for peace in the West Bank and Gaza. In May Shamir had called on Israelis to rebel against a government that would rip out parts of Israel "and throw them to those who wish us dead." But the accord was the final straw. Shamir watched Rabin and Arafat on the White House lawn in a state of cold shock. He was devastated to see an Arab leader who had devoted his entire life to Israel's destruction smiling and shaking hands with an Israeli prime minister. Shamir's old rivals, Peres and Rabin, had committed a crime against Israel and against the Jewish people.

Shamir denounced the accord as a betrayal and he promised that any future Likud government would disown it. He even violated one of his own cardinal rules by speaking out against the accord to the Presidents' Conference during a trip to New York. Two of his old lieutenants, Yossi Ben-Aharon and Yoram Ettinger, did the same in Washington, where they lobbied pro-Israel congressmen against the agreement. When left-wing Israelis had engaged in similar lobbying against the Likud government, Shamir and his aides had denounced them as traitors.

The reason for Shamir's fury seemed clear. Although he denied it publicly, he felt a deep sense of responsibility for having initiated the process that led directly to Oslo and the White House lawn. The taboo against sitting with Palestinians had been broken in Madrid. Everyone there had engaged in a charade—the Palestinians had not called themselves PLO representatives and the Israelis had acted as if they were meeting with independents. But the reality was clear. Yitzhak Rabin may have recognized the PLO, but it was Yitzhak Shamir who, however reluctantly and inadvertently, had recognized the Palestinian people. He regretted it, he resisted it and he denied it. But he had done it, and this was the inevitable result.

Shamir was responsible in another way as well. For fifteen years Likud had bottled up Palestinian and Israeli aspirations for a resolution of the conflict, substituting slogans and ideology for practical arrangements. It had insisted on building Jewish settlements at the same time that it had refused to deal with the grievances of the Arab population or even communicate with the West Bank's emerging leadership. Rather than preside over a gradual resolution, it had created the raw materials for an explosion. In the end Shamir's stubborn refusal to compromise built up the pressure that led first to the intifada and then to the handshake. He was in many ways the inadvertent father of the deal. The betrayal was his own.

Shamir was not the only one to react hysterically to the accord. Right-wing American Jewish activists heckled Shimon Peres at the United Nations in September and threw tomatoes at Ambassador Rabinovich at a New York synagogue when he came there to speak about the agreement. Followers of the Lubavitcher Rebbe and American supporters of Tehiya and Tsomet took out newspaper advertisements attacking Rabin for consenting to "the phased destruction of Israel."

But mainstream organizations, heeding polls that showed overwhelming majority support among American Jews for the accord, lined up behind Rabin. The Presidents' Conference, AIPAC and the Anti-Defamation League, organizations that had forged and enforced a consensus behind the Likud's policies for fifteen years, now were prepared to do the same for Labor.

They saw no inconsistency in this sudden turnabout—it was just a question of backing the elected government of Israel, Malcolm Hoenlein and Abe Foxman insisted. But others saw a disturbing moral flexibility from organizations that over the years had demonized Yasser Arafat and the PLO to the point where they had become the modern equivalent of Hitler and the Nazis. Columnist Michael Kinsley in the *New Republic* could not help noting a parallel between some American Jewish leaders and members of the American Communist Party who reversed direction overnight in 1939 to endorse the Hitler-Stalin pact, and then reversed yet again after the German invasion of the Soviet Union in 1941.

When Israelis suddenly reversed direction and recognized the PLO, it looked like enlightened self-interest. When American Jews followed Israel's lead, it looked like hypocrisy.

American Jews were afraid for Israel's future. They could see the risks involved in embracing Arafat. But they were also afraid for themselves. An Israel at peace with its neighbors might no longer need their massive support. The *gevalt* strategy was nearly bankrupt. And without a beleaguered, vulnerable Israel to shore up, what could American Jews rally around? A needy Israel had been one of the pillars of the unique civil religion Jews had built in the United States; the Holocaust was the other. Without them, Jews had to rethink who they were and their relationship to Israel, Washington and one another.

Many of the mainstream Jewish organizations came to face crises around the time of the pact. AIPAC's president, executive director and a vice president were all forced to resign within a year of one another following a series of gaffes. Abe Foxman of the ADL came under fire for allegations that the group had improperly obtained police files on antisemitic organizations. Henry Siegman was forced to resign as executive director of the American Jewish Congress. While none of these changes were directly related to each other or the changes in Israel, all of them suggested the difficulties these groups faced in finding a new role in a changing world.

As Israel neared its historic agreement with the PLO, Arye Deri was moving toward a showdown over the police investigation into his financial dealings as interior minister. The attorney general's office delivered a charge sheet to Deri in June alleging that he had accepted bribes, violated the public trust and committed fraud. It claimed he had taken nearly $400,000 in payoffs over a six-year period for using his influence to help friends and associates. Deri strongly denied all of the charges and said he would step down as minister so that he could spend his time preparing for his day in court. He was even ready to forfeit his immunity as a Knesset member. But he claimed that Rabbi Ovadia Yosef, the spiritual leader of his Shas Party, refused to let him resign. Without Deri at the helm, Yosef contended, Shas would fall apart.

Deep in negotiations with the PLO, Yitzhak Rabin was content to let Deri remain in the cabinet. The last thing Rabin wanted was a cabinet crisis in the middle of a national debate on the peace accord. Besides, he needed Shas's six votes for the agreement to pass the Knesset with a Jewish majority. Without Shas, Rabin might end up winning with a sixty-one to fifty-nine vote in which five of his votes would come from two non-Zionist parties supported largely by Israeli Arabs. The margin was enough to pass the accord, but not enough to give it legitimacy. Rabin still needed Shas. And while Deri never said it explicitly, Rabin understood that if the Shas leader was forced from the cabinet, his party would not support the Oslo agreement. Peace had become a hostage to Israel's poisonous internal politics.

Despite Rabin's support Deri found himself under enormous pressure from two sources. One was Shas's own right-wing constituency, which remained viscerally anti-Arab and suspicious of the agreement. Most had little emotional attachment to the occupied territories—their real concerns were economic prosperity and personal safety—but they were not convinced that the agreement ultimately would serve their interests. Forceful leadership from Yosef, whom they revered, might have convinced them to go along. But despite his dovish views, the rabbi was too mired in Shas's struggle for political survival to devote his attention to the greater issue of Israel's fate.

The other source of pressure was the Israeli legal establishment. For three years it had tolerated the spectacle of a senior cabinet minister retaining his position while under criminal investigation. Now that the charge sheet had been issued, it was fed up. When a reformist maverick filed a petition with the Supreme Court demanding Deri's immediate removal from office, the legal establishment threw its weight behind him.

At the seven-hour hearing Rabin's own lawyer, Attorney General Yosef Harish, refused to defend the government's position. Two of the justices pleaded with Deri to suspend himself or resign. "It is too bad that we have to discuss this at all," Justice Meir Shamgar told Deri's lawyer.

The justices took only a week to render their decision. On September 8, 1993—just two days before Rabin signed the letter recognizing the PLO—the court unanimously ordered the prime minister to fire Deri and fellow Shas minister Raphael Pinhasi, who was also under indictment. Before Rabin could do so, Deri and Pinhasi resigned. Shas formally pulled out of the coalition, although Deri continued quietly to operate the Interior Ministry from his apartment in Harnof. Still, his resignation left Israel for the first time in its forty-five-year history with a government without a religious party.

Journalist Amnon Levy, who had grown close to Deri over the years, pleaded with him in an open letter not to sacrifice the peace process to his legal troubles: "After 45 years of war with the Palestinians, there's a crack, a chance for peace. . . . If you choke that hope in order to save your own skin, they won't forgive you. You'll go down in history as the man who will carry on his conscience the tragedies of war.

"Throughout your brief political life, you never agreed to be just one more *haredi* small-time politician. You always perceived yourself as part of the national leadership. . . . If you topple the peace at the most critical moment because of your criminal case, you're through."

But Deri felt too weakened by his legal problems to take the political risk of defying his own constituents and endorsing the PLO accord. Rabin pleaded personally for Ovadia Yosef's intervention on behalf of the agreement. He even sent Army Chief of Staff Barak to Yosef to explain how the plan would work. But Yosef would not budge. At best, he could offer Shas's abstention in the upcoming Knesset vote.

Faced with a challenge that defined who he was and what kind of party he led, Arye Deri again backed down and retreated, as he had in 1990. He kept his constituency intact, but he failed to lead it in the new direction he himself had always wanted it to go. When the moment of truth arose, Shas could not be counted on. The party was "like a bank that only gives a loan when you don't need it," commented *Yediot*'s Nachum Barnea.

Natan Sharansky spent the first night of Hanukah with Arkady and Irina Tsurkov. Arkady had shared a cell with him in Chistopol prison. Now the couple and their three children lived in the West Bank settlement of Gush Etzion, one of the historic areas that Rabin vowed to retain. Arkady had been unsure about the move to Israel, while Irina had been the confident one. But now, after the PLO accord, she told Sharansky that she felt the same fears she once felt in Russia. Like Gorbachev, Rabin had begun a process that could have unpredictable consequences and bring about the same turmoil and chaos she had hoped she had escaped forever. "If we are going to be so uncertain here," she asked Sharansky, "why have we come?"

Something else bothered Sharansky about the agreement. He heard Rabin talking with a certain measure of satisfaction about the fact that now the PLO, not Israel, would have the task of repressing Palestinians in the territories. Someone else, Rabin told *Yediot*, "will be responsible for the internal problems in Gaza. He will deal with them without the Supreme Court, without Btselem, without some diehard liberals and without all sorts of mothers and fathers." Or as Peres put it in *Haaretz:* "Let the Palestinians kill each other."

As far as Sharansky was concerned, this approach was not only immoral but disastrous. The only hope for the accord was if Palestinians gained a measure of control over their own lives and felt they had something at stake in the newly unoccupied territories. Free elections were vital, he believed, even if not promising. After all, when had there ever been free elections in an Arab country? He heard the talk of some Israeli officials who speculated that the elections would never take place, that instead the PLO must take on Hamas in the streets of Gaza, that a bloodbath in which the PLO emerged victorious would be the best thing. He feared the territories would deteriorate into another Lebanon—blood and chaos on the streets and outside forces, Israel and Syria included, attempting to manipulate and control the situation.

When the vote came in the Knesset on September 23, Arye Deri, engaging in verbal gymnastics, announced his support for an agreement he was about to abstain on. "It is impossible to vote against a chance to reduce the possibility of war," he told the Knesset, and then did not vote.

It did not matter. Benjamin Netanyahu led a spirited opposition to the agreement, but he could not hold all of his own troops. Despite threats of expulsion from the party, three Likudniks joined with the six members from Shas in abstaining: Meir Sheetrit; Ronnie Milo, who had long advocated getting rid of Gaza and who was running for mayor of Tel Aviv, where the agreement was highly popular; and Assad Assad, a member of the Druze community. A handful of others made it known that they, too, had no real problem with the agreement, but were voting against it for the sake of party unity.

While Netanyahu talked about Vietnam and other betrayals, Rabin spoke far more convincingly to the Knesset about practical choices and opportunities. "It would have been possible to act like an ostrich, it would have been possible to lie to ourselves, it would have been possible to hide in the sand," Rabin told the Knesset. ". . . We have decided not to act as such. . . . We cannot choose our neighbors or our enemies, not even the cruelest among them. We only have what there is: the PLO.

"Above all else," he concluded, "I want to tell you: this is the victory of Zionism, which has also won the recognition of its most sworn and bitter enemies."

With the nine abstentions, Rabin won a sixty-one to fifty victory—large enough to claim a popular mandate. The accord had passed its first hurdle. There would be many more.

Listening to the optimistic, inspiring speeches and thrilling to the dazzling picture of long-standing, bitter enemies shaking hands in bright September daylight, one could be excused for believing that the agreement between Israel and the PLO had been born of good will, hope and reconciliation. Instead, it was born of anger and despair—the burning, relentless desire of each side to rid itself of the other. Thus it was not surprising that the reaction of both peoples to the deal was one of grim determination rather than satisfaction or optimism.

"We all understand that we are no longer on the diving board, but in the water," wrote Yair Lapid in *Maariv* on the day of the White House ceremony. "It behooves us to step off to the side, to check again, to stop at the red light, to find a wise man on the mountain who will give us all the right answers. But it is already too late. . . . Even if we have made a mistake, a tragic mistake, more frightening than we can even imagine, it has been done. Even now there is nowhere to retreat to."

For all its complex provisions, the agreement was full of holes. It left largely undefined the details of who would control security and policing in the territories. Who would be responsible for pursuing alleged terrorists from one jurisdiction to another? Which police force would preside when an Israeli car collided with a Palestinian one? What would happen to the 8,000 to 10,000 Palestinians in Israeli prisons? How big would Jericho be—the old Jordanian district of 140 square miles, or the Israeli-ruled 10.4-square-mile zone?

Then there were all the nightmare issues that the agreement confined to the closet: the fate of Arab East Jerusalem and of Jewish settlements in the West Bank; the readjustment of the old 1967 borders to meet Israel's security demands and demographic shifts; and the demand of a right of return for the 3 million Palestinians living abroad. All of these hovered like uninvited ghosts above Bill Clinton's walnut table. But while Israelis and Palestinians had not solved these issues, at least they had finally agreed that the question no longer was who among them would own the whole pie, but how big each one's slice should be.

The Declaration of Principles was a defective, ambiguous document, subject to the whims of deadlines and negotiators, that could easily collapse under the weight of its own contradictions and breakneck timetable. But the accompanying letters of mutual recognition were irreversible. Two peoples who had demonized and dehumanized each other for decades recognized each other's existence and legitimacy in one breathtaking leap. And once across the chasm, there was no going back.

There was a huge imbalance in power between Israel and the Palestinians. Still, each side had something the other needed. Israel offered Palestinians legitimacy as a nation and territory for a homeland; Palestinians, in return, offered Israel the opportunity to eliminate the basic motive behind the entire Arab-Israeli conflict. Once Palestinian aspirations were addressed, the Arab states had no pretext for waging war on Israel. The great alibi of Arab political life—the constant invocation of the Zionist threat—would disappear.

The pact marked the triumph of the Israeli and Palestinian middle classes over their own history. Pressed by pragmatism, hope and a sense of their own exhaustion, each side had decided it no longer wanted to shed its blood in a perpetual conflict. Each willingly sacrificed some of its ideological purity in the hope of a practical solution. Each chose to get on with its national life, to strive to make money and live in comfort. And each pledged to control its own extremists, the self-declared keepers of its destiny and its past.

The agreement was the logical culmination of sweeping events and forces. The crumbling of the Soviet Empire had robbed the PLO of its largest sponsor. The decision to support the losing side in the Gulf War further weakened its power. But ultimately the intifada was the key. After two decades in which the PLO outside Israel had functioned without accountability, Palestinians in the territories presented their bill. They were no longer prepared to be history's doormat. For twenty years they had failed to obtain justice from their enemies; now they demanded it from their own leaders.

The intifada broke the political stalemate within Israel as well. It touched Israelis through the one institution they commonly revered, their citizen army. Because it challenged the army in so many difficult ways, the intifada raised the price of the occupation beyond Israel's willingness to pay. When it came to Palestinians, Israelis remained unsentimental and tough-minded—few hearts bled for their plight. But there developed a strong desire to be rid of them and their problems, to let them sink or swim on their own. There was also, for the first time, a recognition among Israelis that they were no longer dealing with groups of refugees, or with a series of disconnected small towns and villages, but with another people. Through fire and suffering the intifada had made the Palestinians a nation in the eyes of their enemy.

By itself the intifada might merely have flamed out, leaving scar tissue but no permanent damage. But it combined with other ruptures taking place inside Israel—in the formerly socialist economy, in the balance of political power between right and left, in the political maturation of the Sephardim, in the arrival of a half million Soviet Jews, in the traumatic vulnerability demonstrated by the Gulf War. Together, these changes thawed Israel's social and political stalemate and propelled Israelis forward into a new era.

There arose what *Haaretz* columnist Gideon Samet dubbed "the new Israeli majority . . . a quiet, secular—and maybe a little tired—majority, that is mostly busy with its own affairs. Nobody fiercely opposes anything, or lovingly clings to any political symbol. . . . All this majority wants is the assurance that, at long last, it will be able to live in quiet. Nobody would have taken it away from its air conditioners and cable TV. . . . It does not want the mysticism of land or the sanctity of hills and tombs."

Political scientist Yaron Ezrahi saw in this transformation nothing less than the recovery of the Jewish people from the Holocaust. The nation that journeyed to the White House lawn to shake Yasser Arafat's hand was not Yitzhak Shamir's fearful and paranoid Israel, but a proud and self-confident country. The myths that Shamir had lived by and propagated—that Israel dwelled in mortal danger, that it had a historic mission and that this mission demanded great personal sacrifice—were consigned to the graveyard from which they had sprung. Led by the first Israeli-born prime minister, Israelis shed the fears and anxieties of the diaspora for the security of nationhood. "We are confident enough in ourselves, we feel sufficiently at home in this region," said Ezrahi. "We are not haunted or paralyzed by nightmares of the distant past. This is a different mentality."

For years the question of ownership of the occupied West Bank and Gaza Strip had seemed the Great Divide between Israelis as it was between Labor and Likud, an issue as momentous and divisive as slavery had been in the nineteenth-century United States. But six years of intifada, stabbings and closures showed that most Israelis had never been sold on permanent ownership of the territories. They were far more interested in security and prosperity than in land. As long as Likud could make the case that security depended upon ownership, they were willing to go along. But once Rabin argued that the opposite was true—and demonstrated it with the March 1993 closure—they were prepared to listen.

The key, of course, was Rabin. Only he could forge a new consensus around the idea of separation and returning territory for peace. Shamir had the strength to make such an agreement, but lacked the will. Peres had the will, but not the strength. Only Rabin possessed both. He was a man of many weaknesses and infuriating habits, a man mired in past grievances and petty feuds. But he understood, in ways that Shamir never could, that Israel had to resolve its past in order to reach its future.

Rabin was a centrist but he was no moderate. To sell the agreement to Israelis, he took to the offensive against the right-wing settlers who were the most adamant and obstructive opponents of the deal. After they blocked traffic in Jerusalem and fought with police, he called them "crybabies" and "not real Israelis." When confronted with noisy demonstrators outside the doors of his office and his home, he responded with a crude IDF putdown, "They don't move me"—meaning they didn't arouse him sexually. At the same time, however, he hesitated to take steps to defuse the threat the settlers posed to the agreement by disarming them or removing them from the most sensitive of West Bank areas, such as the city of Hebron. The radical fringe of settlers remained free to embark on a campaign of vigilante violence against Arabs in order to undermine the accord.

The prime minister dismissed Netanyahu as a frightened boy whose ideas were unworthy of serious discussion. "I'm embarrassed when I hear leaders in the Likud and extreme right compare our situation today to the period of the Holocaust," Rabin told one audience. "For Jews who have an army like this, how is it possible to talk about a threat to our existence from the Palestinians? What are they blabbering?"

Rabin never had much confidence in the autonomy process with the PLO, even after he signed the documents. He told himself the process was reversible, that it could be tested each step along the way. Yet he knew that history was not reversible. Israel could terminate the agreement, but it could not go back to what had existed the day before the pact was signed. Even if the new turned out to be unworkable, the old was dead. Israelis and Palestinians would have to go someplace new together. He told his people that he still opposed the idea of an independent Palestinian state; he did not say that there would not be one. Everyone understood, if the process unwound to its logical conclusion, what the end result would be.

"After this revolution, if and when it succeeds, we will find ourselves in another world, a world with new definitions, different concepts," Rabin promised Israelis. "Our lives will change, the economy will change, cultural life will change. The whole country will be changed."

For years Likud had warned that losing territory would render Israel smaller, more claustrophobic and more vulnerable. Instead, the prospect of peace seemed to open up the country, making it more expansive and powerful.

Rabin stopped in Morocco on the way back from Washington, then traveled to China and Indonesia. Israeli officials held talks in Tunisia. The Vatican announced it was establishing diplomatic relations. Rabin met secretly with King Hussein, while Peres held talks in New York with the foreign minister of Qatar about a giant natural gas cooperative venture. Turkey sent its foreign minister to Jerusalem for the first time.

The new messianic age was not about God, land and Torah but about money and joint ventures. Arab and Jewish businessmen met quietly in Europe to talk about deals. One Israeli official told David Makovsky that there were ten to twenty large-scale cooperative projects in the works between Arabs and Jews worth $2.5 billion. Koor, the giant conglomerate, set up a project called Peace 2000 with $15 million in investments from Palestinian, Spanish and Moroccan partners. The head of Coca-Cola Israel said he was talking to Palestinians about cooperative projects. There was talk of constructing a highway to Istanbul and a railroad line to Cairo. Feeding on rumors, and rumors about rumors, the Tel Aviv Stock Exchange soared—and later plunged.

There were diplomatic changes as well. Israel and various Arab leaders began discussing tactical alliances. Suddenly Israel was a player rather than just an enemy. Egypt, Jordan, the PLO, Morocco, Tunisia, Saudi Arabia, Kuwait, even Syria—each saw Israel as a potential partner in its ongoing struggles against its neighbors and its fellow Arabs.

One month after the White House signing, representatives of forty-three countries met in Washington to pledge $2 billion to the economic development of Gaza and the West Bank over the next five years. Israel itself offered $75 million. It was the first time in anyone's memory, noted Finance Minister Avraham Shohat, that Israel came to a conference as a donor rather than a recipient.

Most of the projects and the alliances were dreams—some might eventually become real, most probably never would. But what was undeniably real were the changes within Israel itself. Areas that for years had been frozen by the siege began to thaw. The Knesset held its first legislative hearing on gay rights. It passed legislation mandating a recycling program and closing most of Israel's four hundred illegal garbage dumps. Ehud Barak recommended to the cabinet that the three-year compulsory military service for most male soldiers be shortened by four months.

The major political parties, which were organized around the siege and had supplied its high priests for decades, were beginning to shatter. The Likud coalition of right-wing ideologues, populists and economic liberals already was unraveling. Labor, under whose banner of territorial compromise had nestled old-line socialists, reformers and neoconservative free marketeers, also faced upheaval. The smaller parties that had formed around the concept of Greater Israel—some championing it, others opposed—would lose their reason for existence and be forced to find new ones or wither away. Direct election of the prime minister in 1996 would be a further blow to the old politics.

The new Israel would have to deal with issues that had festered for years in the closet of the siege: Was Israel a Jewish state or a state of the Jews? Could it compromise the demands of democracy with those of religion? Could it come to terms with its own Arab citizens and ultra-Orthodox Jews whose relationship with the state had been tenuous and unhappy? What role would Jews in the diaspora play in a new, more powerful, more independent nation?

Some warned that the siege had enforced a tenuous truce among Jews by imbuing them with a common purpose and fear. Once it was lifted, the truce would break down and Jews might soon be at war with other Jews. Perhaps so, but it seemed as if these prophets had mistaken words for bullets. Israeli public discourse was raw, bitter and often vituperative, but seldom violent. There would be much anger, heartache and recrimination among Jews in the emerging Israel—but the notion that a Jew might raise his hand in violence against a fellow Jew still seemed the ultimate taboo. It could not happen here, or so people told themselves.

Two months after the signing on the White House lawn, a familiar face took the oath of office for mayor at Haifa City Hall. Retired general Amram Mitzna wore a white shirt, dark pants and civilian shoes instead of his old olive-green fatigues and black army boots, and his beard was flecked with gray. Nonetheless, he exuded the same sense of purpose that he had displayed during his thirty years as a soldier.

That career had been permanently damaged by his two-and-one-half-year stint as commander of the West Bank during the intifada. When Mitzna returned from Harvard in 1990 after a year's sabbatical, his old sponsor Yitzhak Rabin had arranged for his appointment as chief of military planning. It was a prestigious position, but Mitzna realized he would never rise to be chief of staff. He had developed too many enemies, both in the general staff and the cabinet.

When Mitzna decided to retire from the army in January 1993, Rabin offered him the prospect of becoming director general of the Defense Ministry—the country's highest-ranking defense post for a civilian—once the distinguished David Ivri retired. But Mitzna turned him down.

Instead, he moved back to his boyhood home of Haifa, a seaport city of 251,000, and ran for mayor on the Labor Party ticket. Mitzna was an amateur campaigner; his speaking style was less than polished and his knowledge of the nitty-gritty of local politics rather imprecise. Nonetheless, he worked eighteen hours a day—just like during the intifada—and many of his former aides and officers volunteered their help. With a vast army of campaigners, he easily defeated the city's longtime mayor in the Labor primary, then won nearly 60 percent of the vote in the general election. City hall became his new command post.

It was a much grubbier and tougher post than the Defense Ministry job, but Mitzna had no regrets. As Israel began to make peace arrangements with its neighbors, he believed, security would no longer be the most important issue on the national agenda. "Now it's economic and social questions that are going to decide Israel's future," he said. "This is where we're heading and this is where I want to get involved."

Mitzna knew that everything could still go badly wrong. The Arab states and the Palestinians could fail to rise to the occasion and deliver what Syria's Hafez Assad called "the peace of the brave" that both Arabs and

Jews needed. Israelis could still fall victim to their past and their demons and the contradiction between their growing self-confidence and the deep-seated, institutionalized pessimism that always seemed to surface when the subject was war and peace.

The old Israel—heroic, insular, beleaguered and collectivist, surrounded by implacable enemies in a constant state of siege—would still capture most of the headlines. But the new Israel, on display at the White House ceremony, had come of age. It was still cognizant of its tragic, heroic, bloodstained past, but it was more self-confident, pluralistic, open and bourgeois. Mitzna could measure the change in his own lifetime and with his own choices. The old Israel had needed generals, so he had become one. But the new Israel needed mayors, creative entrepreneurs, modern managers, pragmatic politicians and lots and lots of hungry, demanding consumers. And, of course, to really blossom, it needed peace.

EPILOGUE

O Captain! my Captain! our fearful trip is done.
The ship has weathered every rack, the prize we sought is won.
But O heart! heart! heart!
O the bleeding drops of red.
Where on the deck my captain lies,
Fallen cold and dead.

— WALT WHITMAN

THE Rabin-Arafat treaty signing sent a jolt of electricity through Israeli and Palestinian society. Israel's slowly awakening entrepreneurial economy suddenly came to life. Other countries in the region scrambled to catch up to the peace process or else find some obstacle to retard its progress. Political movements within Israel splintered and regrouped. American Jewish leaders struggled to cope with changes that both thrilled yet deeply troubled them. Radicals on both sides attempted to kill the agreement and reassert their control with bombs and bullets. A country that had undergone rapid political and social change during its first five decades now seemed to shift into an even faster gear. It was messy, it was uncertain, it was frightening and exhilarating all at the same time. Days of hope and days of frustration and horror mingled freely. All the old rules seemed cast aside with a sudden vehemence; new ones took shape only slowly.

Throughout it all, Yitzhak Rabin remained the reluctant peacemaker. Hesitant, uncertain, angry, he expressed constant doubts about Yasser Arafat's abilities and commitment to the accord. He distrusted Shimon Peres, ridiculed Yossi Beilin, and threatened more than once to scuttle the entire deal. Each time Peres would come to him with a bold new scheme for speeding the process with the Palestinians or for reaching out to the Syrians, Rabin would put on the brakes. Peres and the Palestinians are conspiring against me, he would complain to his generals. They're boxing me in, leaving me no room to maneuver. More than once, after touring the site of a

Palestinian suicide bomb, he privately expressed regret over ever having signed the Oslo accord in the first place.

Yet he continued.

Chained together like sullen prisoners, Rabin and Arafat groped for supremacy and compromise over the unresolved details in their joint declaration of principles. They met in Cairo on December 12, 1993, the day before Israeli military withdrawal from Gaza and Jericho had been due to begin. It was not a happy session; Rabin emerged grim-faced and irritated, Arafat ashen and visibly shaken. Arafat called the December 13 date sacred; Rabin indicated that he was in no hurry to initiate withdrawal while important security matters remained unresolved. He told his aides that the Palestinians could "start to sweat." The date for withdrawal came and went; it was the first of many unfulfilled deadlines.

All of the issues that had been glided over in the Oslo negotiations had come back to haunt them—the size of the Jericho autonomous district, control of the bridges from Jordan and Egypt, protection of Jewish settlers and the Israeli army's right to preemptive strikes and hot pursuit in the self-rule zones. Negotiating with his more powerful foe from a position of weakness, Arafat continued to play the feckless bazaar merchant, offering Israel miniscule concessions at inflated prices. One of his favorite ploys was to dispatch aides like Nabil Shaath to negotiate compromises that uncovered Israel's final bottom-line position; Arafat would then renege on the deal and use the Israeli position as his starting point for a new round of demands.

The refugee camps of Gaza hovered uneasily in a twilight zone, not quite occupied yet not autonomous either. On the streets it was business as usual—soldiers shooting at Palestinian stone throwers and Hamas gunmen ambushing soldiers, all as if the ceremony on the White House lawn had never occurred.

The PLO struggled to make the perilous transition from liberation movement to government. Arafat held the reins tight: As of January 1994 he had still not chosen members of the Palestinian Authority that was to rule Gaza and Jericho. He took personal control of the Palestinian Economic Council for Development and Reconstruction, the body that was supposed to channel millions of dollars from the World Bank and Western donors into the territories. And he refused to convene the Palestine National Council, the PLO's parliament-in-exile, for fear it would reject the agreement. The PLO was beginning to look like one old man with a fax and a tattered checkbook.

Rabin, meanwhile, inadvertently did to Arafat what he had previously done to Faisal Husseini—score points with his domestic Israeli con-

stituency by undermining his Palestinian partner. The Israeli prime minister
seemed in no hurry, apparently oblivious to the fact that with each passing
day he was helping erode Arafat's influence and support in the occupied
territories. Weeks passed; more deadlines fell by the wayside.

While the two leaders dithered, others sought to fill the vacuum with violence. Between the September 13 signing and the end of 1993, at least
forty Palestinians were shot dead by Israeli soldiers or Jewish settlers and
twenty Israelis were killed by Palestinian gunmen. Increasingly the violence began to resemble that of Belfast—gunmen on both sides did much
of the killing, sparing each other as if by mutual, unspoken agreement and
concentrating instead on unarmed civilians who were easy prey. Brutal as
they were, however, the killings were only a preamble to the bleak Friday
morning in late February 1994 when a zealot from the Jewish settlement of
Kiryat Arba walked into the Tomb of the Patriarchs in Hebron and opened
fire on Muslim worshippers inside, killing twenty-nine of them before they
overwhelmed and killed him.

Brooklyn-born physician Baruch Goldstein's massacre was an act of religious pornography: a pious man with a machine gun cutting down other
pious men as they knelt in a house of prayer. Israelis were stunned by the
audacious and suicidal grandiosity of the deed; only an American, Israeli
philosopher Avishai Margalit said, could have dreamed up and choreo-
graphed such a terrifyingly obscene act.

The killings had several effects that Goldstein could not have foreseen.
They further weakened the already frail legitimacy of the settler movement
and sharpened the desire of mainstream Israelis to separate themselves and
their country from the craziness of the West Bank and Gaza. For years the
settlers had successfully portrayed themselves to fellow Jews as peace-
loving Zionists carrying out the true vision of Israel's founding fathers.
They had claimed to be morally superior to the supposedly violence-prone
Arabs who lived in their midst. But with one burst from his Galil automatic
rifle, Goldstein unseated his fellow settlers from the high moral ground and
exposed the brutality and arrogance behind their argument.

Goldstein's killings also exposed an anti-Arab cancer eating away at
Israeli society. Many Israelis, rightists and leftists alike, were appalled to
discover the amount of popular support Goldstein's deed commanded,
especially among younger Israelis. At least one classroom held a moment
of silence in his memory. "This murderer lived among us and we gave him
legitimacy to exist and express opinions," Alma Zohar, sixteen, told the
Washington Post's David Hoffman. "This kind of thing has been predictable
for years now."

Some Israelis, Yitzhak Rabin among them, reacted as if they were seeing the cruelty of the occupation for the first time. In his opening address to the Knesset in April 1994, Rabin reviewed the casualties that had occurred since the intifada began in December 1987: 2,156 Palestinians killed either by Israeli soldiers and civilians or by their own people; at least 25,000 wounded, and between 120,000 and 140,000 detained and imprisoned. At the same time, 219 Israeli soldiers and civilians had been killed, Rabin noted, a figure roughly the same as the number of dead his brigade had suffered during the Independence War.

"I want to tell the truth," intoned Rabin, in language he had never before used in public. "For twenty-seven years the Palestinians . . . have risen in the morning and cultivated a burning hatred for us as Israelis and as Jews. Every morning they awake to a difficult life and it is partly our fault. . . . It cannot be denied: The continued rule of a foreign people who does not want us has a price. There is first of all a painful price, the price of constant confrontation between us and them."

After several days of resisting, Rabin succumbed to pressure from Washington and Tunis and ordered a commission of public inquiry into the Hebron massacre. Its hearings, which were broadcast daily on radio and television, revealed much about the iniquities of the occupation to Israelis who had never before concerned themselves about the matter. The Shamgar Commission, headed by the chief justice of Israel's Supreme Court, heard testimony on how the law had disintegrated over the course of nearly three decades in the territories. There was no regular police protection for Palestinians, a dual system of justice that favored Jews and punished Arabs, an ill-trained army operating under inconsistent orders including different rules for opening fire depending upon whether the target was an Arab or a Jew. "Here, to a certain degree, there really is only a semblance of law," testified Inspector General Rafi Peled, Israel's national police chief, at one hearing.

For years human-rights critics and Palestinans themselves had made such claims. What was different this time was that the cream of the Israeli security establishment, including Peled and Army Chief of Staff Ehud Barak, confirmed the accusations.

Palestinians had long seen themselves as the passive victims of the Arab-Israeli conflict, preyed upon by forces outside their control, able to influence events solely by spasms of violence. It was only with the coming of the intifada that they had begun to take control of their own destiny and demand change, not just from Israel but from their own flawed leadership. However, the lack of progress in the peace talks, the continued occupation and then the massacre at Hebron threatened to thrust Palestinians back into their old passive role and to derail the process. Like other Palestinian moderates, Jad Isaac watched from the sidelines with growing trepidation. "I fear a madman from our side will create another tragedy," he said on the day of the massacre. "Emotions are very high. Everyone is talking revenge, and everyone is saying we have nothing more to lose. It's opened the Pandora's box."

It didn't take long for Palestinian militants to fulfill his prophecy. In the northern Israel town of Afula in early April, a suicide car bomber killed seven Israelis and wounded forty-four others outside the bus station. A week later—on Holocaust Memorial Day—another suicide bomber boarded a crowded commuter bus in Hadera during morning rush hour and blew up himself and five passengers, wounding thirty others. Angry crowds gathered to denounce Rabin as a traitor; some even sang "Baruch, King of Israel" to honor Goldstein. At eleven that morning, Israeli rescue workers stood still for a minute of silence as sirens wailed to mark the Holocaust. Then they returned to the bleak task of removing corpses and body parts and hosing black pools of blood from the pavement.

Amazingly, despite all the killings and bad blood, the truce between Israel and the PLO held. The negotiations stalled but did not break down. If anything, the killings produced what all of the reconciliatory rhetoric had not—a sense of urgency.

It all finally came together in early May 1994. Rabin and Arafat met in Cairo, in the presence of Hosni Mubarak, Warren Christopher and Russian Foreign Minister Andrei Kozyrev. Arafat tried one more ploy, threatening to walk out of the signing ceremony when the boundaries on the map of Jericho did not appear to reflect the terms of the deal. He was persuaded to remain. The pact was signed, and within days Israeli forces duly withdrew from Gaza and Jericho and a Palestinian police force, operating under the PLO flag, entered both areas. Palestinians, who for months had seen little or nothing from the pact their leader had signed with Israel, suddenly had reason to celebrate. A few weeks later, Arafat himself returned to Gaza, stepping foot on his native soil for the first time in nearly three decades. It was hardly a triumphant moment, but it was a tangible step nonetheless.

In the fall of 1994 the radicals of Hamas and Islamic Jihad struck anew, kidnapping and murdering a young Israeli corporal, Nahshon Waxman, and dispatching a suicide squad to spray bullets at cafe-goers on the sidewalks of Yoel Salomon Street in West Jerusalem. But their main tactic was the one they had used with such terrifying effect in Afula and Hadera: the suicide bus bomb. The next was a belt of explosives carried aboard a civilian commuter bus by an Arab passenger on Dizengoff Street in the heart of downtown Tel Aviv. It killed twenty-two people and injured forty-eight more, sending the chilling message that the conflict could not be confined to the territories nor to the settlers: all Jews, even those in Israel's most liberal and disengaged city, were fair game. And it undermined Yitzhak Rabin's most basic promise to his people—that the peace agreement and separation from the territories would enhance their personal security.

Three months later, two suicide bombers at the Beit Lid junction near Hadera killed twenty-one Israelis at a bus stop where soldiers congregated for rides. In July another bomber blew up a bus in Ramat Gan, killing six and wounding twenty-eight. And in August yet another bomb exploded in a bus during morning rush hour in Jerusalem, killing five and wounding more than one hundred. All told, eight suicide bombings left nearly one hundred people dead in Israel over the eighteen-month period following the Rabin-Arafat signing. The attacks became a national ritual—after each one, radio stations would broadcast somber ballads, interspersed with live reports from the scene. Ultra-Orthodox workers, who believed every piece of Jewish flesh was sacred, would comb the wreckage for body parts. Settlers and other rightists would stage enraged demonstrations and pelt hapless government officials with eggs and epithets. It got so bad that Rabin stopped visiting the sites. The following morning, Israel's two major tabloids, *Yediot* and *Maariv,* locked in an escalating circulation war, would run page after page of hysterical headlines and grisly photographs.

Rabin responded with grim determination. He authorized the Shin Bet security police to use tougher interrogation techniques, citing with approval the claim of the Shin Bet chief who told reporters that his men had failed to preempt the Jerusalem bus bomb because they were not allowed to use "extreme forms of interrogation." One Palestinian detainee died from severe "shaking." It didn't matter to many Israelis. "If Shin Bet investigators were allowed to operate as necessary, the attack on Bus No. 26 in Jerusalem would likely have been avoided," Rabin told the Knesset after the August attack. But he refused to call off, or even postpone, negotiations with the PLO.

The response within the Palestinian community was more ambiguous. At first, many Palestinians—angered by the fact that the Oslo accord had not delivered its promise of economic improvement and an end to the humiliation of occupation—applauded the bombers. But as time went on, the moderate majority began to reassert itself. After each bombing, Rabin sealed off Gaza and the West Bank, denying access to work to the 30,000 or so Palestinians still employed in Israel. Gazans not only needed the money, they also longed for tranquility after years of unrest and deprivation. By the fall of 1995 Palestinian polls suggested that support for Hamas and its radical partner, Islamic Jihad, had fallen to below 25 percent in the territories. What was most interesting was that support in Gaza—the purported hotbed of fundamentalism but also the first area to gain autonomy—was lower than in the West Bank.

In Gaza there was much talk about Palestinian democracy, but the reality was that Arafat and his self-appointed cronies moved swiftly to establish control over their new fiefdom. With Gaza's economy in tatters, Arafat's Palestinian Authority was one of the few sources of employment: it supported 22,000 civil servants and 28,500 security personnel. Those whom the authority couldn't buy it dealt with in other ways. Hundreds were detained, including local leaders of Hamas, and two people died in their cells after interrogation. This harsh approach was encouraged by Israeli security officials, who secretly cooperated with Arafat's police in an attempt to crack down on Hamas bombers. Gaza journalist Taher Shriteh, who was frequently detained at Israeli security police headquarters during the taut days of the intifada, found himself just as frequent a guest in that same building under Arafat's rule.

In the West Bank, the Israelis allowed the Palestinian Preventive Security Service, which was supposed to be confined to Jericho, to roam freely through the territory and even East Jerusalem. The service, run by Colonel Jibril Rajoub, one of Arafat's most powerful lieutenants, basically operated like a private army. Its men didn't wear uniforms and made it known they could be employed to intervene in private disputes and personal vendettas. Barton Gellman of the *Washington Post* described how members of the service helped a prominent Christian family in Ramallah who didn't like their daughter's Muslim suitor. They abducted the young man to Jericho and beat him intermittently for several days until he agreed to give up his pursuit of the girl.

After the Israeli human rights group Btselem issued a report accusing the service of "gross human rights violations," Rajoub targeted the organization's chief Palestinian field worker, Bassam Eid, for assassination. There was no little irony in this, for Eid had previously been arrested several times by the Israeli army. It was not hard to see why many Palestinians believed they had not gained freedom following the agreement with Israel but had simply traded an Israeli occupation regime for a Palestinian one.

Arafat's wife, Suha Tawil, passed her own judgement on her husband's new regime by refusing to give birth to their first child in the Gaza Strip. Instead, she returned to her mother's home in Paris for the delivery. Still, Gaza slowly but painfully began to revive. The new Palestinian housing ministry built 4,000 new apartments during its first year in business, while the education ministry added 250 classrooms. Large parts of Shifa Hospital in Gaza City were renovated, as was the hospital in Jericho. A modicum of nightlife returned to Gaza. Restaurants, bars, hotels, even cinema houses sprang up in Gaza City and new high rises pierced the skyline. The grip of fundamentalist preachers who had sought to Islamicize the strip during the intifada was loosened.

For all his blunders, Arafat remained the only leader Palestinians felt comfortable with. His popularity ratings remained steady even when life in Gaza was at its lowest. People did not seem to blame him. And even Rabin began to trust him after his security forces cracked down hard on Hamas. Rabin began to see him as an errant relative, unreliable but irreplaceable. The Israeli prime minister came to realize what Gaza's Palestinian residents instinctively grasped: although he was no bargain, Yasser Arafat was all they had.

Bibi Netanyahu continued to suffer from a split political personality: radical hawk and capitalist apostle. He opposed Rabin's peace moves and hinted broadly that he would try to renege on the spirit, if not the letter, of any agreement with Arafat over the West Bank. Indeed, his rhetoric and ideology were almost identical to Yitzhak Shamir's, only smoother. Netanyahu had certain attributes that Shamir had lacked—most particularly a high level of popular support from grassroots Likudniks. But he was young and inexperienced, and at times he looked like he was flailing. In 1995, for example, he inadvertently saved Rabin's government from a needless confrontation with Arafat and the Arab world. Under pressure from its own right wing, the government proposed the annexation of 140 acres of land belonging to Arabs in East Jerusalem. The Knesset's small Arab parties opposed the move and Netanyahu tried to bring down the government by joining them in a vote of no confidence. This gave Rabin and Peres the opportunity to give up the annexation plan and blame Netanyahu for the decision, making him look weak and unprincipled.

Netanyahu's standing in the polls tended to fluctuate according to incidences of terrorism. After each bus bombing, his ratings would soar, then settle back down to Rabin's level within a few weeks. This led observers such as Avishai Margalit to predict that the outcome of the 1996 election would depend largely on whether or not Hamas staged successful terrorist attacks close to the time of the elections. If the extremists indeed wanted to blow up the peace process—and believed they had enough support within the Palestinian community to do so with impunity—they would almost certainly intensify their attacks. "What Bibi thinks about Hamas will not affect his own chances in the upcoming elections," wrote Margalit. "What will matter is what Hamas thinks about Bibi."

Stimulated by the peace process and the opening of once-forbidden markets like India and China, Israel's economy bloomed and its economic culture completed the leap from socialistic and inward-looking to entrepreneurial and international. High-tech firms—many of them the talented offspring of the old state-funded military-industrial complex—carved out niches in telecommunications, semiconductors, digital printing, software and pharmaceuticals. Foreign investors, who had stayed away from Israel during its first forty-five years due to fears of state bureaucrats and wars, began pouring their money into Israeli companies, and nearly seventy Israeli firms joined the New York Stock Exchange. The computer giant Intel announced plans to build a $1.6 million factory to make computer chips. Israel became the only Western-oriented economy outside of Hong Kong and Singapore to have grown an average of at least 6 percent during the past five years, while unemployment fell to under 7 percent from its 1992 high of 11 percent. Meanwhile, the state sector shrank, especially the once-dominant armaments industry. Israel for the first time bought the major portion of its weaponry and defense technology from the United States. State security, or *bitahon*, was no longer an excuse for inefficiency.

Critics bemoaned the increasing Americanization not only of Israel's economy, but of its governing institutions, culture and social attitudes. Daniel Elazar, director of the Jerusalem Center for Public Affairs, deplored the "new privatism that does not encourage great public purposes or individual sacrifice for public tasks," and detected a new fissure between those Israelis interested in creating a rich Jewish life and those more concerned with the pursuit of "hedonistic individualism."

Ezer Weizman, who succeeded Chaim Herzog in the ceremonial post of president, complained after four young people were killed in a riot at a rock concert in the Negev Desert city of Arad that "the nation is infected with Americanization. [We have] to understand what is Israeli culture, Israeli tradition and Jewish tradition. We have to be careful of McDonald's, Michael Jackson and Madonna. It is part of what happened in Arad."

What Weizman and the traditionalists feared most was the way the new attitudes infected the army. While some young men still competed for slots in elite units in the same way that high-school graduates in the United States compete for admission to Ivy League colleges, many others were simply not interested. Draft evasion was fast becoming a popular pastime. When pop star Aviv Geffen bragged at concerts about his psychiatric discharge, thousands cheered. In the army itself, discipline was hard to enforce. Soldiers serving in southern Lebanon often took time out from patrols to call their parents and girlfriends on their cellular phones. When Hizbollah gunmen killed nine Israeli soldiers in a week in southern Lebanon in October 1995, the government hesitated to retaliate in part because it didn't want to disrupt the fall tourist season in northern Israel. And while the 1982 invasion of Lebanon was dubbed "Operation Peace for Galilee," the 1995 response was dubbed "Operation Peace for Hotel Rooms." It was part of the growing schizophrenia between serving in the army, the last great Zionist institution, and participating in an increasingly bourgeois, consumer-oriented society, between the army camp and the shopping mall.

The peace process also opened new fissures among American Jews. While polls showed that a substantial majority favored the process, a passionate minority that was predominantly Orthodox and pro-Likud was deeply opposed, and its ranks grew as the suicide bombings fueled anguish and doubts about the agreement. The same people who had once demanded solidarity with Shamir's government and condemned dissenters as traitors now sought to undermine Rabin's policies in every way possible. They received strong encouragement from Netanyahu and a small group of organizers, led by Shamir's former aide Yossi Ben-Aharon and former ambassador to the United States Zalman Shoval. The American group Friends of Likud in New York faxed copies of the periodic *Jerusalem Insider* to 5,000 influential Americans on Capitol Hill and elsewhere. Netanyahu and his aides lobbied openly against U.S. aid to Arafat's Palestinian Authority, opposed the stationing of U.S. peacekeepers in the Golan Heights as part of an Israeli-Syrian deal and pressed for legislation requiring the Clinton administration to relocate the U.S. embassy from Tel Aviv to Jerusalem. Other opponents of the government targeted Israel Bonds, urging synagogues to cancel their annual Yom Kippur bond drives and instead donate at least some of the money to the rival One Israel Fund's Yesha Heartland Campaign to raise funds for Jewish settlements in the West Bank.

The most aggressive American opponent of the process was Morton Klein of the Zionist Organization of America. A former government economist from Philadelphia, Klein breathed new fire into the moribund, conservative group, defying the American Israel Public Affairs Committee's longstanding monopoly on lobbying for Israel by personally campaigning against the PLO on Capitol Hill. AIPAC officials complained to the Conference of Presidents of Major American Jewish Organizations, but it refused to take action against Klein, formulating instead a set of guidelines for future lobbying. Nevertheless Klein made clear he had no intention of honoring any rules that would limit his freedom of movement on issues he cared about. Why, he asked, when both Israeli and American Jews were deeply divided on the peace process, should Jews speak with only one voice on Capitol Hill? It was a fair question—and one, of course, that Jews on the left had asked ten years earlier.

The tepid response from the presidents' conference to Klein's activities was an indication of the ambivalence of many American Jewish leaders toward the peace process. Although Rabin repeatedly exhorted and cajoled them to do more, they were not prepared to risk their reputations by working for a process in which they had such little faith. Ironically, one of the few leaders who took a strong stand was one of those with the most reservations. Abe Foxman of the Anti-Defamation League quit the Orthodox synagogue in Tenafly, New Jersey, where he had worshipped for twenty years, after the rabbi wrote articles and letters accusing Rabin of leading the Jewish people on another Holocaust-style "death march." In an essay explaining his resignation, Foxman said the rabbi was entitled to his views, but deplored his "hate-filled rhetoric" and intolerance. And Foxman regretted the loss of "diversity, tolerance and civility" in his congregation.

Having shattered the longstanding prohibition on dealing with the PLO by brokering the Israeli-Palestinian accord, Yossi Beilin turned his sights on yet another sacred cow. In January 1994 he told a meeting of Jewish donors from the diaspora that Israel no longer needed their charity. Our standard of living is higher than in some European countries and we have one of the world's strongest growth rates, he told the angry delegates, some of whom tried to shout him down. "You want me to be the beggar and say we need money for the poor people?" he retorted. "Israel is a rich country, I'm sorry to tell you."

The remarks caused a stir. Rabin, who still bore a grudge against Beilin for past indiscretions, called the new statement "completely moronic." But Beilin wasn't just baiting his enemies. He was making a declaration of independence. The new Israel didn't need other people's money or charity or pity. It could stand on its own two feet.

Even while he delivered Israel to its future, Rabin remained firmly rooted in the old mindset that saw security issues as paramount and everything else as a distant second. Although he had been elected prime minister because of his stance on economic issues, Rabin saw them largely as a distraction. He was willing to give ground on them in order to avoid fracturing his fragile governing coalition and jeopardizing the only thing that really mattered to him—the peace process.

Thus it was that when Health Minister Haim Ramon's elaborate plan to reform Israel's bloated and bankrupt health care system was challenged by the old-line socialists of the Histadrut labor federation, Rabin first sought unsuccessfully to find a compromise and then backed away from his commitment to Ramon. The reform plan foundered and the proud, mercurial Ramon, Arye Deri's old political ally, resigned in fury from the cabinet. He mounted a political challenge within the Labor Party to the renomination of Haim Haberfeld, the Histadrut's leader. When Haberfeld easily vanquished Ramon's handpicked candidate, Ramon retaliated by forging a maverick alliance with the Shas and Meretz parties and running himself against Haberfeld as an independent.

It was a daring move: Ramon at forty-four had been one of Labor's favored sons to succeed Rabin as prime minister, and now he and two of his allies were drummed out of the movement for violating party discipline. He had chosen to gamble on an incongruous political marriage of the disparate elements of post-Zionist Israel.

Ramon campaigned passionately against the gray men of the Histadrut, their affection for red tape and corruption. He promised to repair the federation's ailing health and pension funds, but on a deeper level he was the candidate of enlightened self-interest running against the collectivism and egalitarianism of the old Israel. Eschewing party organization and traditional campaign techniques, he relied instead upon the media to deliver his message to the federation's 1.6 million members. And on election day in May 1994 he won a stunning victory: he and his ticket took nearly 50 percent of the vote, crushing Haberfeld and the Labor ticket, as well as the Likud, which finished a distant third. Labor lost control of an institution the party had dominated since the Histadrut's inception seventy-four years earlier.

It was a triumph as well for Ramon's old friend, Arye Deri. Deri managed to rally not only Shas's supporters but also many other Sephardim to support Ramon, despite the fact that the former health minister was far more dovish than they. Still facing his court date on corruption charges, Deri was wounded but far from politically dead. And Ramon's triumph reestablished Deri as Israel's most important power broker.

A few months later, Avraham Burg, the iconoclastic Laborite whose outspoken views had so alienated Yitzhak Rabin that the prime minister had denied him a cabinet post, won the chairmanship of the Jewish Agency, a position left vacant after party veteran Simcha Dinitz was forced to resign while facing corruption charges. Like Ramon, Burg outmaneuvered a party apparatchik to win the post by appealing to the anger and disaffection of those whom the agency was supposed to serve but who had felt shut out for decades. In this case, it was American Jewish donors who were the most alienated constituency. With their support he won an easy victory and, like Ramon, began the hard task of dismantling key parts of the bloated bureaucracy he was elected to reform.

Rabin quickly sought to bring Ramon and his supporters back to Labor and made his peace with Burg. But these victories foreshadowed the larger political transformation to come and demonstrated beyond all doubt that Israel was in the midst of political revolution. The same forces that had demanded resolution of the conflict with the Arabs were now demanding domestic reform as well. Israelis were no longer prepared to wait to have the country they wanted.

The self-rule that took effect in Gaza and Jericho in May 1994 was supposed to trigger a five-year interim period during which Israeli troops would withdraw from the West Bank, Palestinians would elect an autonomous governing council and an executive leader, and the two sides would begin talks on a permanent settlement. But negotiations on the West Bank withdrawal quickly fell behind, hung up largely over the thorny issue of security for Jewish settlers. The talks, conducted by more than two hundred negotiators in technical committees at the Hilton Hotel in the Egyptian-controlled Red Sea enclave of Taba, dragged on through the summer of 1995. Then with Rosh Hashona just around the corner, negotiators finished up in a sudden rush. They beat the Jewish New Year by two and a half hours.

After weeks of forced intimacy, negotiators on both sides were elated. At the end they welcomed the new year with apples and honey, and Arafat offered holiday greetings to Israelis at the press conference. His smiles and enthusiastic words belied the fact that he had staged a last-minute tantrum on the final night, walking out of a meeting with Peres shouting, "We are not slaves!" Emergency calls from Hosni Mubarak in Cairo and U.S. special envoy to the Middle East Dennis Ross from his home in Bethesda, Maryland, had coaxed Arafat back.

The two sides produced a 400-page document, including 350 pages of annexes—one U.S. official said it exceeded the bulk of the last U.S.-Soviet arms-control treaty. The pact, dubbed Oslo Two, did not stipulate the relocation of a single Jewish settler, but it mandated Israeli withdrawal from the major Arab population centers of Jenin, Nablus, Kalkilya, Tulkarm, Ramallah, Bethlehem and part of Hebron, as well as from 450 smaller villages and towns. It also provided for a massive transfer of authority from the Israeli military administration to an eighty-two–member Palestinian council, with elections to be held twenty-two days after troops withdrew from the cities, and for the release of all Palestinian women prisoners and many men. In return, Arafat promised that within two years the PLO would expunge from its covenant all articles calling for Israel's destruction.

As Bart Gellman pointed out, the future of the West Bank had always been a question of which side would end as the islands and which side as the sea. Settlers had long sought to abolish the old Green Line—and along with it any notion of the West Bank as a separate political entity. They wanted an ocean of settlements with small islands of Palestinian urban population centers, cut off from each other, floating separately within that ocean. But the agreement made the Palestinians the ocean and the settlers the small islands, with narrow, tenuous ribbons of highway linking them with the mainland of Israel proper. Oslo One had legitimized the idea of Palestinians as a people; Oslo Two legitimized the idea of a united West Bank and Gaza Strip as their homeland. It said specifically that "the two sides view the West Bank and the Gaza Strip as a single territorial unit"—a claim the settlers would never accept.

The settlers were correct in arguing that the new pact laid the groundwork for a sovereign Palestinian state. Within six months of the signing, Palestinians would have a chief executive, legislative body, police force—and a small piece of territory to go with them. The Palestinian government would have the power to determine land use, levy taxes, regulate commerce and broadcasting, issue passports, maintain foreign currency reserves and enter into limited international agreements. It was statehood in all but name.

After the deal was struck, an unidentified Clinton administration official boasted to the *New York Times,* "We've been indispensable," but the U.S. role again seemed minor. While Dennis Ross was a helpful sounding board, he did his work over the phone from seven time zones away during the last two weeks of the talks. Still, the Americans were eager to host yet another signing ceremony and both the Israelis and Palestinians had reasons to comply: Rabin wanted to pay back Bill Clinton for his moral support, while Arafat sought to convince potential aid donors that he and his movement were worthy of their largesse.

Held in a stuffy and confined East Room under hot television lights, the second signing was like a summer rerun: all the suspense and exhilaration were drained. More than two hundred guests sweltered while in Clinton's private dining room Rabin and Arafat spent ten minutes clearing up another last-minute glitch over the language of redeployment of Israeli troops in Hebron. Warren Christopher fell asleep during the speeches. Arafat made his predictable plea for more aid, telling the audience, "Our participation in the great peace process means that we are betting everything on the future."

But once again it was Rabin who best captured the mood, comparing the ennui and hardheaded realism of the new signing with the electricity and optimism of the ceremony two years earlier. "Perhaps this picture has already become routine," he conceded. "The handshakes no longer set your pulse racing. Your loving hearts no longer pound with emotion, as they did then. We have begun to get used to each other. We are like old acquaintances. . . . Today we are more sober. We are gladdened by the potential for reconciliation, but we are also wary of the dangers that lurk on every side."

Those dangers were no longer just confined to the conflict between Arab and Jew. The violence was turning inward. Palestinians had fought with each other since the early days of the intifada when purported collaborators with the Israelis had been marked for death. But now Israelis were turning on each other as well. The rhetoric on both sides became more heated and vituperative. It was only words, some said, not to be taken too seriously. For a Jew to raise his hand against another Jew was the ultimate taboo in a state created expressly as a sanctuary for the Jewish people. And yet the radicals on the far right, abetted by the angry pronouncements of Likud leaders and other politicians and rabbis, were laying the rhetorical groundwork for fratricide.

Even before the Oslo Two agreement, radical settlers and their sympathizers in the Likud had sought to demonize the Labor-led government and undermine its legitimacy. They had always considered Peres a hopeless leftist, but now they focused on Rabin. He was the one who had truly sold them out, the one whose support for the peace accord had been critical to its acceptance by the Israeli mainstream. And he was the one who had always been the most contemptuous of the settlers, the one who had called the Gush Emunim movement "a cancer" and warned that its fanaticism and intolerance could deeply damage Israeli democracy. They saw him as the ultimate pragmatist, the anti-visionary—and the biggest threat to their dream.

The far right saw the peace deal as a direct challenge to the survival of the nation. Any surrender of Jewish land was a violation of God's will and therefore heresy and treason. By this reasoning, Rabin endangered Jewish lives and was responsible for Jewish deaths. His face became a symbol of hate. In posters he was depicted in an Arab headdress or wearing a Nazi armband. One poster superimposed a target over his face. A death certificate in his name was circulated in the settlements with "suicide" listed as the cause of death. He was accused of "crimes against the Jewish people," the same charge made against the Nazis. Rabin was leading Israel to another Holocaust, some said, and must be stopped. There were reports that right-wing rabbis had issued a self-defense edict against Rabin, branding him a *rodef:* a "pursuer" of Jewish lives. Halachic code says it is permissible to kill such a man in order to save the lives of his potential victims.

Each Friday afternoon at the end of the work week when Rabin returned to his apartment building in Tel Aviv, demonstrators held back by police barricades would yell epithets and abuse from across the street at him and his wife Leah. On Friday, November 3, 1995, she would later recall, one protester called out, "Do you remember Mussolini and his mistress? That's what we are going to do to you! . . . We will kill you both!"

Netanyahu denounced the most venomous of the personal attacks on Rabin as "absolutely repugnant and unacceptable," but he played to the feelings behind them. While some Likud leaders like Dan Meridor and Benny Begin kept their rhetoric within bounds, Netanyahu and some of his colleagues embarked on a campaign to delegitimize Rabin and the Labor government. Ariel Sharon warned that the Oslo agreements would lead to the gas chambers and Rafael Eitan of the rightist Tsomet party compared the pact with Arafat to capitulation to Hitler. He repeatedly called Rabin a "quisling." Netanyahu did not endorse such language, but he compared Labor party activities to "the methods of Ceausescu."

After each bus bomb Netanyahu would tour the carnage, and after the Dizengoff Street blast he told a reporter that Rabin was "personally responsible" for the deaths because the government had turned over control of Gaza to Arafat. Never mind that Netanyahu himself had long favored withdrawal from Gaza and that it later turned out the bomber came not from Gaza but from the West Bank city of Kalkilya, still occupied by the Israeli army. He told Rabin in the Knesset, "You, Mr. Prime Minister, are going to go down in history as the prime minister who established an army of Palestinian terrorists."

When the Likud no longer seemed capable of attracting large mainstream crowds to its anti-government rallies, Netanyahu solicited support from the far right by attending its rallies and supporting protests that blocked traffic and disrupted normal life. At a rally in September 1995, he accused Rabin's government of "dragging the nation to the brink of an awful abyss. . . . No Jew hitherto ever longed to give up slices of the homeland." The next month he spoke at a rally in Jerusalem's Zion Square where demonstrators displayed a large effigy of Rabin dressed in an SS uniform. Netanyahu later claimed he hadn't seen the effigy.

When he addressed Westerners, Netanyahu adopted the same pose Shamir had once displayed: that of the hard-bargainer, holding out for the best deal before compromising on land with the Arabs. But the truth was something else. Like Shamir, Netanyahu was firmly opposed to territorial compromise in the West Bank. This opposition was rooted not only in Netanyahu's hard-line security views, but in a more fundamental attachment to the land. As he told the rally in Zion Square: "You say the Bible is not a property deed. But I say the opposite—the Bible is our mandate, the Bible is our deed." His dispute with Labor wasn't merely over the extent of how much land to give back, but over the fundamental nature of the state. When Rabin relied on the five votes of the leftist Israeli Arab parties to win a razor-thin 61-to-59 majority for Oslo Two, Netanyahu charged that Rabin had failed to win a "Jewish majority"—as if the votes of Israel's Arab citizens were somehow invalid. Ultimately, when the Western veneer was scraped off his rhetoric, Netanyahu was an ethnic leader, appealing on an atavistic level to his tribesmen.

Soon after the Zion Square rally, Netanyahu asked for a personal meeting with Rabin in order to cool the heated political climate. But Rabin refused. During the Knesset debate in October over Oslo Two, he accused Netanyahu of "inflaming the atmosphere under the guise of preventing a rift among the people. . . . I recommend that we stop this hypocrisy."

Rabin remained unbending. He had been a reluctant peacemaker, portraying himself as dragged into the Oslo agreements by the hyperenthusiastic Peres. But now he saw himself locked in mortal combat with the right, waging a war for Israel's fate. As settler protests grew more and more disruptive, under Rabin's authority the police adopted harsher tactics, turning their nightsticks, tear gas and water hoses on protesters who were often women and children, using the same ruthless methods they had once reserved for Palestinians. The demonstrators were "crybabies" and "foreign elements," proclaimed Rabin, and they could spin uselessly in place "like propellers" for all he cared. He was, he declared, the prime minister of the 97 percent of Israelis who lived within the old Green Line of Israel proper. The rest, he implied, were on their own.

Rabin fired back rhetorically at Netanyahu as well. Each time Arab extremists struck, he noted, the Likud leader sought to gain political advantage. "Bibi Netanyahu is a Hamas collaborator," he told one interviewer. "Hamas and the Likud have the same political goal." On the trip to Washington in September 1995 when he signed Oslo Two with Arafat, Rabin lambasted American Jewish leaders for their timidity. They needed to get off the fence and make a clear expression of their support for the peace process, he told them. At the same time, he indicated he was moving toward abandoning some of the West Bank settlements. He told the editors of *Time* magazine in New York during a stopover that he was tired of maintaining three battalions of soldiers in Hebron to protect 450 settlers from their Arab neighbors. "I don't feel the justification for that," said Rabin. "If you ask whether the Israelis believe that the settlements in the densely populated (Arab) area have any security value, the majority will say no." As for his wafer-thin parliamentary majority, Rabin was unfazed. "As long as I have a majority of one, I will continue," he told the *Time* editors.

As Oslo Two moved through the Knesset, Jewish radicals became more desperate and more enraged. One spotted Environment Minister Yossi Sarid's car on the Tel Aviv–Jerusalem highway and ran him off the road. A few weeks later, demonstrators attacked the car of Housing Minister Binyamin Ben-Eliezer as he arrived at the Knesset to cast his vote in favor of Oslo Two. They damaged the car and nearly upended it. Another angry mob outside the Knesset tore the hood ornament off Rabin's official Cadillac. "Just like we got the ornament, we can also get Rabin," one of them told Israel Television.

One of the settler movement's most fervent supporters was twenty-five-year-old Yigal Amir, a student of law, computer science and theology at Bar Ilan University outside Tel Aviv. Amir had grown up not in some wild West Bank settlement but in the Israeli heartland, in the coastal city of Herziliya north of Tel Aviv. He was one of eight children and his parents were Sephardi immigrants from Yemen; his father was a Torah scroll calligrapher and kosher butcher, his mother ran a nursery in the back of their modest white stucco house on Borochov Street.

Like Arye Deri, Amir was a bright student who impressed his teachers as he made his way through the elite Ashkenazi religious academies: the New Colony high school in Tel Aviv, the Kerem D'Yavneh yeshiva and the Institute for Advanced Torah Studies at Bar Ilan. At the yeshiva Amir learned the aggressively nationalistic Judaism of the religious Zionist movement and upon graduating he entered the Israeli Defense Forces' elite Golani brigade, where many religious Zionists served. Still, even among this tough crowd he stood out as fanatically religious and brutal with the Palestinians. One of his fellow soldiers recalled how Amir treated Palestinians during a routine search in the Jabaliya refugee camp in Gaza. "He hit them in the mouth, shoved them around and destroyed their property," the soldier told *Maariv*. "He enjoyed taunting them, just for the fun of it." He also expressed admiration for Baruch Goldstein, and saw Goldstein's massacre of Arab worshippers as a righteous act.

This was the behavior Yitzhak Rabin had most feared, the kind of brutality that had led him to conclude that policing the territories was scarring the morale and the morals of his cherished army. And Yigal Amir's pious equation of God and land and politics was an ideology that Rabin most deeply detested.

Amir participated in many emotional demonstrations against the peace process and helped launch the wildcat West Bank settlement of Maale Yisrael in June 1995 as a protest against Rabin's withdrawal plans. He and his older brother Hagai and a handful of friends also planned acts of violence against Palestinians in hopes of undermining the peace process. They kept a cache of grenades, detonators and plastic explosives in the attic and backyard of his home in Herziliya. They called themselves *Eyal*—the Hebrew acronym for Jewish Fighting Organization—and had hoped to model themselves after Yitzhak Shamir's Lehi, the small Jewish resistance movement that had fought British rule in the 1940s. But Amir chose a target for himself that even Shamir would never have countenanced: Yitzhak Rabin. For nearly a year Amir stalked the prime minister, looking for a momentary opening.

In January 1995 he had taken a gun to Yad Vashem, the Holocaust memorial in Jerusalem, on the day Rabin was supposed to make an appearance to mark the fiftieth anniversary of the liberation of Auschwitz. But the ceremony was cancelled after the terrorist attack of the bus stop in Beit Lid killed twenty soldiers. In July Amir rushed to the scene of another suicide bus attack in Ramat Gan in expectation that Rabin would go there, but security men held back the frenzied crowd far from the site. In September he attended the dedication of a new highway interchange outside Herziliya, but again he couldn't get close enough to the prime minister. Instead he screamed slogans against the abandonment of the settlers and was hauled off kicking and struggling by police. Next he began to organize a plan to pick off Rabin with a high-powered rifle at the prime minister's Tel Aviv home. But early in November he saw another possibility. Tens of thousands of Israeli peace supporters planned to gather at Kings of Israel Square in downtown Tel Aviv for a Saturday-night rally. It was the left's attempt to take back the initiative. Rabin and Peres were special guests. Amir saw an opportunity to kill them both. He waited until sunset to avoid desecrating the Jewish Sabbath, then took a bus to Tel Aviv.

The security forces were on alert for an assassination attempt that night and fanned out among the vast crowd. But in the aftermath of the recent assassination by an Israeli hit squad of an Islamic Jihad leader in Malta, their focus was on preventing a Palestinian suicide car bomber, not a Jewish gunman. Rabin himself refused to wear a bulletproof vest. Amir was dressed in a blue T-shirt, black jeans and a black skullcap, a 9-mm Beretta pistol concealed in a clip-on holster under the shirt. He found it easy elude security and mingle among the drivers who were passing the time smoking cigarettes in an open area behind the stage while waiting to ferry home government officials. There Yigal Amir waited too.

The crowd had gathered under the slogan, "Peace yes, violence no." Rabin gave a brief, confident speech. "I was a military man for twenty-seven years," he told them. "I fought as long as there was no chance for peace. I believe now there is a chance for peace, a great chance, and we must take advantage of it."

Singer Miri Aloni led the crowd in "The Song of Peace" and cajoled Peres and Rabin to join in. They linked arms and swayed on stage. Peres joked, "We know how to make peace. We don't know how to sing." Rabin made an off-key stab at the words, then neatly folded the lyric sheet in quarters and placed it in the breast pocket of his dark blue suitcoat.

Peres left the stage first and emerged down the back stairway. Amir held his fire, waiting instead for Rabin. Within a minute, the prime minister followed. Amir rushed forward, pulled the Beretta from under his shirt, shoved the barrel into Rabin's back and opened fire, pumping two rounds into the prime minister a third into the arm of a bodyguard. As he shot, Amir shouted to the stunned security guards who had allowed him to slip through their perimeter, "It's nothing! Blanks! Blanks!"

Rabin fell forward to the curb, then managed to pull himself up and climb into the back seat of his car. "Drive! Drive!" the wounded bodyguard screamed at Menachem Damati, the driver. Damati rushed to nearby Ichilov hospital, just five minutes away. When he asked, "Where does it hurt?" Rabin replied, "In the back. . . . It hurts, but it's not so bad." Then Rabin's head slumped. In the chaos, no one had thought to phone ahead to the hospital. By the time they wheeled Rabin into the emergency room, he had no heartbeat.

The days that followed were a fevered kaleidoscope of images and sounds: the sirens at 2 P.M. on the day of Rabin's funeral wailing for two minutes as the entire country stood at attention; the gathering of dignitaries from eighty countries at the ceremony, including the leaders of Egypt and Jordan, stepping foot officially for the first time on Israeli soil; the grief-stricken granddaughter who spoke with simple eloquence; the bloodstained lyric sheet that Eitan Haber pulled from his coat pocket to show the stunned mourners; the horrified parents of the assassin renouncing their son and begging forgiveness from the widow; the arrogant killer, still clad in the clothes he wore on the night of the murder, declaring his joy in court and claiming God as his accomplice. "It was my duty, my calling," said Yigal Amir. "A Jew who turns over his land and people to enemies—Halachic law allows him to be killed."

Afterward there was a national reckoning. Police cracked down hard on the extreme right, arresting Amir's alleged collaborators and searching for those who might have expressed support for the assassination in words or deeds. But the bigger debate was over the connection between the killer and the mainstream right. Netanyahu blamed "wild weeds on the very fringe of our side of the spectrum" for producing people like Amir and denied any responsibility. To blame the Likud for Amir's heinous deed was like blaming Republicans for the assassination of John F. Kennedy—"guilt by association." And Netanyahu called for a period of national healing and reconciliation and promised not to oppose the formation of a new Labor-led government under Shimon Peres.

But Amir was no Lee Harvey Oswald. His ideology was shared by Netanyahu and the Likud leadership. They could disown his deed, but not his argument. Many on the right instinctively acknowledged their own responsibility. Bumper stickers and posters denouncing Rabin as a traitor or merely expressing opposition to the process came down overnight.

Leah Rabin, who had lost her husband of forty-seven years, was determined to emphasize the political meaning of this most political of murders. When hundreds of mourners held a candlelight vigil outside her apartment building, she came down to thank them but quietly rebuked them for coming too late to help her husband. "It's a pity that you all weren't here when there were demonstrators on the other side of the street here calling him a traitor and murderer," she told them. "It's too bad you didn't come then."

She had even harsher words for Netanyahu and the Likud in a barrage of interviews she gave during the first week of mourning. "Surely I blame them," she said. "If you ever heard their speeches, you would understand what I mean. They were very very violent in their expressions. 'We are selling the country down the drain, there will be no Israel after this peace agreement.' I mean, this was wild."

She said she had wanted to avoid shaking hands with Netanyahu at her husband's funeral but had chosen to avoid a scene. But she added, "He knew, and we both understood that we would have both loved to avoid shaking each other's hand." Noting the Nazi effigy of her husband, she said of Netanyahu: "Now he can say from here to eternity that he didn't support it. But he was there, and he didn't try to stop it."

At a meeting in Jerusalem four nights after the assassination, right-wingers and rabbis from the settlement movement gathered to discuss their own culpability. There was anger and some remorse. Yoel Bin-Nun of Ofra, who had challenged settler leaders after the 1992 election, spoke bitterly of rabbis who had guided young Jews toward intolerance and hatred. "We are guilty of bringing up an entire generation to think primitively, according to slogans and cliches," said Rabbi Yehuda Amital, one of the moderate religious figures. "We have to stop using Jewish law in political matters; we have to stop delegitimizing the democratically elected government and demonizing it as treasonous."

Yigal Amir's deed was an act of patricide. Rabin was one of the last Zionist patriarchs, a direct heir of David Ben-Gurion and a remnant from the days when political giants ruled the land of Israel. His presence on the Israeli scene had been a constant for the entire forty-seven-year history of the state. He had guided its army, served as its emissary to its one sure ally in Washington, then twice led its government. He was never well loved, but he was trusted. His gruff judgement, his crude language, his stubborn logic—all were valued by Israelis who had grown up under his watchful eye. Many were surprised by how deeply affected they were by his death. Part of it, of course, was the circumstances: A Jewish leader assassinated by another Jew because he had sought peace. But part of it was the man himself. Rabin had been their anchor, a solid reality amid the sometimes terrifying chaos of Israel's national existence. And now the anchor was gone.

Only one patriarch was left. Shimon Peres, now seventy-two years old, the former Ben-Gurion hatchetman turned visionary, returned to the prime minister's chair from which he had ruled so effectively for two years in the mid-1980s but which had eluded him ever since. He made clear he did not intend to function as a caretaker; there was much unfinished business. Within weeks Israeli forces completed their withdrawal from the major Arab population centers in the West Bank and Palestinians took part in territory-wide local elections. The occupation ended with stunning swiftness, almost as if an afterthought, completing Rabin's legacy. Peres would also begin the "final phase" talks, in which all of the nightmare, time-bomb issues that the two sides had put off—the fate of Jerusalem, Jewish settlements and Palestinian refugees, and the question of Palestinian statehood—would have to be negotiated. And there was Hafez Assad of Syria, waiting inscrutably in his Damascus palace.

For three years, Peres and Rabin had functioned as a brilliant team. They were poetry and prose, the lofty dreamer and the hard-headed military man. Now the dreamer was all alone. He had many advisers and friends, but he ruled from a solitary chamber deep within himself. He was less confrontational than Rabin. He immediately appointed Rabbi Amital to his new cabinet as a gesture of reconciliation to the religious right. It was a simple case of divide and conquer. Peres saw two forces in the opposition, one motivated by religion, the other by nationalism. He sought to co-opt the former in order to undermine the latter.

An election would be coming soon, but Peres professed not to really care. He saw himself as the last Zionist, the man entrusted by fate to write the final chapter to the past. In truth, the past was already finished, even if the future remained uncertain. Even Netanyahu and the Likud conceded there was no going back to the days before the Oslo accord. Despite a renewed wave of Palestinian suicide bombings that killed several dozen Israelis, the argument in the 1996 election was over who could strike the best bargain with the Arabs rather than whether to negotiate at all. Israel had shed too much of its own blood and its own skin ever to return to what it had been. Shimon Peres and his heirs would see to that.

Rabin's assassination had underscored a new reality: the conflict in the Middle East was no longer between Arabs and Jews, but rather between moderates and extremists on both sides, between those who believed that the two peoples could reach a peaceful accommodation that would allow each to live side by side and those who demanded that the blood feud be honored and sustained with yet more corpses. In that sense Yigal Amir's Beretta spoke not only for the radical fringe of the Jewish settler movement, but for Islamic extremists as well. Like Baruch Goldstein's massacre in Hebron and like the suicide bus bombs of Hamas and Islamic Jihad, Amir's deed was the ultimate expression of contempt for the peace process.

Three days after her husband was buried, Leah Rabin received an unusual visitor at her apartment. Yasser Arafat had been told not to attend the funeral. Security would be difficult and besides, too many Israelis might take offense. Instead, he asked to come to Tel Aviv. It was the first time he had stepped foot in modern Israel's most magnificent urban achievement, but his visit was not overtly political. There was no entourage, no array of reporters and photographers. It was a simple personal gesture, so purely human that even the Israeli opposition could not condemn it. Yasser Arafat had come to pay his respects.

He flew in by helicopter from Gaza City. A military escort brought him to the building, past the pile of flowers and melted candle wax on the sidewalk outside the lobby. When he entered the eighth-floor apartment, he greeted the entire family—the widow, the son and daughter, the three grandchildren. When he met Noah, the granddaughter who had spoken at the funeral, he smiled sadly and said "This one, she made me cry." Then he removed his kaffiyeh and sat on the sofa in the living room.

He stayed for ninety minutes, chatting pleasantly with the widow of his longtime enemy, drinking coffee and gently teasing the grandchildren. "We lost a great man, who made the peace of the brave with us," he told Leah Rabin. "He was our partner." The children asked Arafat if he himself ever feared being assassinated. He only smiled. But when he rose to leave, he kissed each of them on the forehead. "You are my family now," he told them. And then the leader of the Palestine Liberation Organization bid farewell to the family of the late prime minister of Israel, and returned home.

Notes on Sources

Most of this book is the result of my own original reporting and interviews over the past decade. Some of the writing has appeared in various forms in the *Washington Post*.

Most of the interviews were conducted on the record, but some were on "background"—I could use the material, but could not attribute it directly to the subject of the interview. This was especially true with Israeli politicians, who are no more inclined than their American counterparts to be portrayed disclosing sensitive information about themselves and their colleagues. Everything that appears in direct quotations was verified by one or more of the participants. When I couldn't rely on interviews for that kind of specificity, I simply described what someone said without quoting them directly. Several active Israeli politicians and military figures who agreed to be interviewed insisted on total anonymity. Their accounts are especially crucial to the chapters of this book that deal with the 1990 breakup of the national unity government, the Gulf War and the confrontation between Israel and the Bush administration. But as any journalist should, I have treated their versions of events with a greater degree of skepticism than I have those from sources who were willing to be interviewed on the record.

During a decade of visits and four years of living in Israel, I interviewed or attended briefings with hundreds of people. What follows is a short and incomplete list of those who were most important in shaping my understanding of the events in this book:

Morris B. Abram, Yosef Achimeir, Mohammed Abu Aker, Joseph Alpher, Yoki Amir, Moshe Amirav, Ghassan Andoni, Kemal Abu Aras, Moshe Arens, Kemal Abu Arer, Yedidya Atlas, Shlomo Avineri, Amal Awad, Akram Baker, Azzam Bani Shemseh, Ehud Barak, Hillel Bardin, Elan Baruch, David Bedein, Yitzhar Be'er, Yossi Beilin, Yossi Ben-Aharon, Oded Ben-Ami, Yaron Ben-Ami, Eliahu Ben-Elissar, Meron Benvenisti, Dov Berkovits, Stephanie Black, Hijazi Burbar, Avraham Burg, Naomi Chazan, David Clayman, Wat Cluverius, Steven M. Cohen, Meir Dagan, Leonard Davis, Arye Deri, Thomas A. Dine, Mattiyahu Drobles, Uri Dromi,

Rolando Eisen, Warren Eisenberg, Daniel J. Elazar, Yisrael Eldad, Saeb Erakat, Oded Eran, Yoram Ettinger, Moshe Even-Chen, Yaron Ezrahi, Leonard Fein, Abraham H. Foxman, David and Toba Frankel, Yaacov Frenkel, Menachem Friedman, David Froelich, Reuven Gal, Eliezer Gerabin, Ehud Gol, Zeev Golan, Dore P. Gold, Uri Gordon, Haim Goren, Leonid Gorovets, Judith Green, Carolyn Greene, Richard Haass, Eitan Haber, Elyakim Haetzni, Loie Haniani, Neville Harris, David Hartman, Susan Hattis-Roelof, Arthur Hertzberg, Malcolm Hoenlein, Rafi Horowitz, Samir Huleileh, Faisal Husseini, Martin Indyk, Jad Isaac, David Ivri, Bassam Jarrar, Elihu Katz, Eliezer Kein, Leonid Kelbert, Teddy Kollek, Jonathan Kuttab, Zvi Lanir, Shlomo Lecker, Yehiel Leiter, Guy Levi, Chana Levinson, Samuel Lewis, Alon Liel, Gilead Limor, Edward Luttwak, Hawad Mabhouh, Fyodor Makarov, Avishai Margalit, Yisrael Medad, Yehuda Meir, Efraim Melamed, Yair Mendels, Dan Meridor, Salai Meridor, Natan Meron, Yusef Milhem, Yishai Minicheem, Amram Mitzna, Zalman and Tanya Mogilnitsky, Mahmoud Muhaisen, Arye Naor, Danny Naveh, Benjamin Netanyahu, Nimrod Novik, Sari Nusseibeh, Ehud Olmert, Yosef Olmert, Michael Oren, Avi Pazner, Tamar Peleg, Yisrael Peleg, Shimon Peres, Thomas Pickering, Menachem Porush, Yitzhak Rabin, Alvin Rabushka, Haim Ramon, Omer Rasner, Avraham Ravitz, Uri Regev, Seymour Reich, Elias Rishmawi, Mona Rishmawi, Shlomo Riskin, Yadin Roman, David Rosen, Menachem Z. Rosensaft, Dennis Ross, Danny Rothschild, Yom Tov Rubin, Amnon Rubinstein, Elyakim Rubinstein, Buki and Etti Sagi, Eli Sagi, Edward Said, Jamal Salameh, Danny Sanderson, Uri Savir, Alan Schneider, Nachman Shai, Yair Shamir, Yitzhak Shamir, Natan Sharansky, Ariel Sharon, Dan Shomron, Zalman Shoval, Eli Shperling, Yuri Shtern, Yishai Shuster, Henry Siegman, Haim Silberstein, Hanna Siniora, Hanoch Smith, Rivka Sofer, Howard Squadron, Amnon Strashnow, Amnon Toledano, David Tsemach, Mina Tsemach, Leah Tsemel, Hanna Tsemer, Harry Wall, Emma and Boris Weinberg, Dov Weisglas, Philip Wilcox, Molly Williamson, Gad Yaacobi, Ehud Yaari, Ruth Yaron, Ahmed Yassein, Ornan Yekutieli, David Yerushalmi, Hanoch Yerushalmi, David Yosef, Samer Zaket, Said Zeedani, Yisrael Zeev, Hannah Zohar, Dedi Zucker, Efraim Zuroff.

Two reference books have been of critical use: *Israel Yearbook & Almanac* (Jerusalem IBRT Translation/Documentation Ltd.) 1992 & 1993 editions; and *Political Dictionary of the State of Israel,* edited by Susan Hattis Rolef (Jerusalem: Jerusalem Publishing House, 1993). I have frequently relied on Israel's most distinguished daily newspaper, *Haaretz,* and its best-selling one, *Yediot Ahronot.* I have also relied on the sole English-language daily, the *Jerusalem Post* (abbreviated below as *JP*) although the quality and breadth of its reporting has sadly fallen in recent years, and on the *Jerusalem Report (JR),* a semiweekly magazine that has quickly become an essential tool to understanding modern Israel.

Other books: Amos Elon (*The Israelis: Founders and Sons* and *Jerusalem: City of Mirrors*), David Grossman (*The Yellow Wind* and *Sleeping on a Wire*), Amos Oz (*In the Land of Israel* and *The Slopes of Lebanon*) and Tom Segev (*1949: The First Israelis* and *The Seventh Million*) have each written essential works on Israeli society. David Shipler's *Arab and Jew* (New York: Times Books, 1986) and Thomas L.

Friedman's *From Beirut to Jerusalem* (New York: Farrar Straus & Giroux, 1989) are primers on Israeli and Palestinian attitudes toward each other and themselves; Conor Cruise O'Brien's *The Siege* (London: Weidenfield & Nicolson, 1986) is the best recent popular history of Zionism, even though I disagree with his realpolitik conclusion; Zeev Chafets's *Heroes and Hustlers, Hard Hats and Holy Men* (New York: William Morrow, 1986) offers the best popular guide to Israeli society; Zeev Schiff and Ehud Yaari's *Intifada* (New York: Simon & Schuster, 1991) is required reading on the Palestinian uprising. Avishai Margalit's articles in *The New York Review of Books (NYRB)* are also essential. I drew upon them all frequently.

Other source abbreviations:

GPO = Government Press Office
ITV = Archives of Israel Television
LAT = Los Angeles Times
NYT = New York Times
WP = Washington Post

The following notes describe basic sources and material not self-evident from the text itself:

Epigraphs

"Resisting fate is not enough": David Ben-Gurion, "The Imperatives of the Jewish Revolution," in *The Zionist Idea,* edited by Arthur Hertzberg (New York: Atheneum, 1976), p. 609. "Once I sat on the steps": Yehuda Amichai, *Poems of Jerusalem* (Tel Aviv: Schocken Publishing House Ltd., 1987), p. 177.

Chapter 1: The Guardian

Yitzhak Shamir is one of the most elusive figures in Israeli history, a mystery to his closest advisers and aides and perhaps to himself as well. I have interviewed him a half dozen times and each session was a test of will in which I struggled to extract some small personal insight from a warm, often charming but sealed-off human being. Interviews with Yosef Achimeir, Nachum Barnea, Yosef Ben-Aharon, Charles Enderlin, David Makovsky, Avishai Margalit and Avi Pazner helped enormously. The only full-length biography of Shamir is in French: Enderlin's *Shamir* (Paris: Olivier Orban, 1991). The best articles are Margalit's "The Violent Life of Yitzhak Shamir," *NYRB*, May 14, 1992, and Makovsky's work in the *JP*. Although they are often as opaque as the man himself, Shamir's recently published memoirs, *Yitzhak Shamir: Summing Up* (London: Weidenfeld and Nicolson, 1994), were also helpful.

For the most prescient journalistic analysis of Israel's socioeconomic changes, see Jackson Diehl, "Israeli Quest for 'Normalcy' Reshaping Society," *WP,* June 8, 1992. Sharon's Lebanon anecdote: Ariel Sharon, *Warrior* (London: Macdonald & Co. Ltd., 1989), p. 511. A small trove of details on Shamir's daily routine: Lailan Young, "A Day in the Life of Yitzhak Shamir," (London) *Sunday Times Magazine,* September 22, 1991. "When one of them does": Shamir interview with Menachem Shalev, *JP,* May 9, 1989.

Irgun and Lehi attacks: Yaacov Eliav, *Wanted* (New York: Shengold Publishers, 1984). "A tiny group of strange men" and Stern poem: J. Bowyer Bell, *Terror Out of Zion* (New York: St. Martin's Press, 1977), pp. 85–86. "A man who goes forth": Gerold Frank, *The Deed* (New York: Simon & Schuster, 1963), p. 35. Shamir's Mossad career: Ian Black and Benny Morris, *Israel's Secret Wars* (New York: Grove Weidenfeld, 1991), pp. 195–97. For Shamir's role in Sabra and Shatila see "Testimony of Foreign Minister Yitzhak Shamir Before the Commission of Inquiry into Events at the Beirut Refugee Camps, 24.11.82," GPO: Jerusalem, November 24, 1982. "For me it's not burning": interview with Howard Goller and David Makovsky, November 3, 1992.

Chapter 2: Jad Isaac's Shed

I first met Jad Isaac in May 1988 when he was a subversive gardener struggling to stay one step ahead of the authorities and amazed at the intifada happening all around him. I have spent hours at his home, interviewed him and his wife, Ghada, more than a dozen times, read his prison diary, which he wrote in English in pencil, and his other notes and articles. Meron Benvenisti, Daoud Kuttab, Samir Huleileh, Sari Nusseibeh and Elias Rishmawi also helped me understand the meaning and power of the intifada.

Epigraph is from author's interview with Benvenisti.

For Rabin's account of the Lydda evacuation, see Shipler, pp. 33–35. "You may not be interested in war": quoted in Michael Walzer, *Just and Unjust Wars* (New York: Basic Books, 1977). Mohammed Abu Aker's story was first recounted by Ori Nir, "Local Hero," *Haaretz,* October 7, 1988.

Chapter 3: Buried Alive in the West Bank

I first encountered Amram Mitzna outside Dehaishe in May 1987, just after he'd taken over as OC/Central Command and confronted Jewish settlers who had raided the refugee camp in retaliation for stone throwing. I followed him closely until we both left Israel in the summer of 1989, and interviewed him four more times for this book during the hectic year he left the army and ran for mayor of Haifa. He has never been less than candid and helpful, yet has always reserved an inner core that seemed off-limits to my probing.

Yoki Amir, Ehud Barak, Reuven Gal, Raanan Gissin, Yehuda Meir, Ofra Preuss, Yitzhak Rabin, Omer Rasner, Yadin Roman, Zeev Schiff, Amnon Strashnow, Amnon Toledano and Hanoch Yerushalmi also helped my understanding of the IDF and its response to the intifada.

"Okay so we hurt them . . .": from the documentary film *Testimonies* (1993) written and directed by Ido Sela. "If anyone wishes": *Davar* interview with Shomron, March 18, 1988.

Chapter 4: Souls on Fire

I got to the outskirts of Beita on the day Tirza Porat and the two Palestinians were killed, circumvented an army blockade to enter the village a few days later, interviewed many of the principals and attended the April 10, 1988, press conference at which the Elon Moreh youths told their tale. I covered the Yisrael Zeev case at the time of the shooting at Shiloh and finally interviewed Zeev in April 1993. And I interviewed the principals and wrote about the story of the two hearts in January 1989 in what remains for me the saddest story to arise from the intifada. Amal Awad, Azzam Bani Shemseh, Dov Berkovits, Judith Green, Elyakim Haetzni and Dedi Zucker were also key interviewees for this chapter.

"The local equivalent of Injun country": and "Nobody with any common sense": *JP,* April 15, 1988.

Mitzna at the Alfei Menashe meeting: ITV, February 9, 1989. "I took her out in the street": ITV, Dec. 1, 1989. Black Panthers barbershop killing: *JP,* December 3, 1989. Yasser Abu Samahadna photo: *JP,* December 4, 1992. "The beast that devours": *Al Fajr*, June 5, 1991.

Chapter 5: The Breakup

Here the attribution gets murky because most of the politicians involved are still active and many insisted on anonymity. Israeli political journalists Nachum Barnea, Akiva Eldar, David Makovsky and Menachem Shalev were of tremendous help. The epigraph is from author's interview with Shamir, November 3, 1992.

Shamir in Nablus: ITV, January 16, 1989. For details of Yitzhak Rabin's life and career, see Robert Slater, *Rabin of Israel* (New York: St. Martin's Press, 1993), and Yitzhak Rabin, *The Rabin Memoirs* (Boston: Little, Brown & Company, 1979). Although couched in the usual boilerplate, the memoirs are more honest than most and particularly scathing about Peres. But they reveal more about the author than the intended victim: Rabin seems to have believed he could destroy Peres's standing within the party with these revelations. Instead he merely wounded his rival— and himself as well. See also Avishai Margalit, "The General's Main Chance," *NYRB,* June 11, 1992.

"He sat in that chair right there": Thomas L. Friedman and Maureen Dowd, "The Fabulous Bush & Baker Boys," *NYT Magazine,* May 6, 1990. "We'll see": *JP,* March 8, 1990. "He spoke to me with great respect": ITV, March 18, 1990.

For the best account of Schach's speech and secular reaction, see David Landau, *Piety and Power* (London: Secker & Warburg, 1993), pp. xvii–xviii, and pp. 114–18. "Even if he lets me rape his wife": *JP,* October 18, 1990. "I would say about Shimon": *JP,* July 6, 1990.

Chapter 6: Manchild in the Promised Land

Writing about Arye Deri posed a special challenge because he comes from a much different world than the Israel I know best and usually write about. But Deri and some of his aides and friends were willing to talk to me, and I received invaluable help from a handful of Israeli journalists who have closely followed Deri's remarkable career. David Landau's book (see above) provides essential background on Ovadia Yosef, as do Peter Hirschberg's *JR* articles.

"We must melt down": Lawrence Meyer, *Israel Now* (New York: Delacorte Press, 1982), p. 161. For more on El Hamaayan, see Yossi Bar-Muha, "Like a Fountainhead," *Haaretz,* June 11, 1993.

"I was born to be an *askan*": Deri made these remarks to an Israeli journalist who insisted upon anonymity.

The Gilat-Kempner articles, headlined "Minister Arye Deri's Reign of Money and Fear," began in *Yediot* on June 1, 1990, and ran for three successive Fridays. Deri filed a libel suit disputing the articles, but the suit was dismissed without prejudice after Deri's lawyers told the court he had been unable to prepare for trial because of the police investigation.

See also Summary of Comptrollers Report, "Support by Local Councils for Institutions," July 23, 1991. "I didn't invent it": *JP,* July 24, 1991. For September 1990 predawn raids, see *Maariv,* September 10, 1990. Aides' arrests: *JP,* May 10, 1991. Wolf's arrest: *JP,* September 17, 1991. Tally of Shas officials under investigation: *Haaretz,* February 8, 1993. Deri's resignation letter: Peter Hirschberg, "Arye Deri Hits Back," *JR,* February 20, 1992.

Chapter 7: The Desert Generation

I have interviewed Natan Sharansky some ten times since his arrival in Israel in 1986 and watched him evolve from Zionist icon to flawed but determined political leader. Sergei Makarov's *Israel Russian News Digest,* published on a shoestring and in constant danger of disappearing, is an excellent compendium of anecdotes and attitudes from the Russian language press. Sergei also helped guide me to sources in the Russian community and served as translator. A more scholarly overview is Stewart Reiser, "Soviet Jewish Immigration to Israel," published by the Wilstein Institute of Jewish Policy Studies, Spring 1992. Other guides included Zeev Chafets, Uri Gordon, Leonid Gorovets, Efraim Melamed, the late Louis Rapoport, Yuri Shtern, Emma and Boris Weinberg and Ari Weiss.

The epigraph is one of the passages Natan Sharansky read on the plane taking him to freedom in 1986. This and other pieces of his life as a prisoner in the Gulag are from his autobiography, *Fear No Evil* (New York: Random House, 1988). The airport scene is from Jackson Diehl's occasional series in *WP* in 1990 on the Pelvitzsky family, and Edward Norden, "The Ingathering," *Commentary,* April 1991. "They act like they own the place": *Hadashot,* July 26, 1991. "Now is a time of national mourning": Margalit, "The Great White Hope," *NYRB,* June 27, 1991.

Many of the anecdotes come from the colorful Russian press. "He was over 50": *Vremya,* April 23, 1992. For the plight of Soviet workers in Tel Aviv, see Nili Mendler, "Marek may have a roof over his head, but he's right up against my dressing table," *Haaretz,* May 10, 1991. Police data on Russian mafia: *Vremya,* September 21, 1992, and *Kaleidoscope,* August 14, 1992. "White meat": *Novosti Nedeli,* April 3, 1992. Ella's story of dishwashing and sex: *Yerushalayim,* December 4, 1992. "That place on earth": *Piatnitsa Weekly,* April 10, 1992. "They smell bad": *Novosti Nedeli,* July 7, 1992.

For a withering analysis of how Israel's anemic economy harmed the *aliya,* see Joel Brinkley, "Israeli Economy Is Keeping Many Jews in USSR," *NYT,* May 5, 1991. The best postmortem on Sharon's housing boom is Tom Sawicki, "The $5 Billion Folly," *JR,* January 14, 1993. "Where are those ideological flags?" from Amit Dovkin, "Rabin Is Making a Terrible Mistake," *Tzomet Hasharon,* May 28, 1993. Employment statistics from JDC/Brookdale Institute, "Study of Immigrants 25–64 from the Former FSU," May 6, 1993.

Chapter 8: The Sealed Room

I wasn't in Israel during the Gulf War, but it was relatively easy to reconstruct events and emotions because everyone there has searing memories. Joseph Alpher, Moshe Arens, Yossi Ben-Aharon, Zeev Chafets, Hirsh Goodman, Richard Haass, David Ivri, Dan Meridor, Avi Pazner, Robert Rosenberg, Zeev Schiff, Nachman Shai and Yitzhak Shamir were especially helpful. Ruth Resnick, Rivka Sofer and Buki and Etti Sagi were interviewed by Eeta Prince-Gibson.

For written sources, the *Jerusalem Report* from the weeks of the war offered many small nuggets, especially Yossi Klein Halevi, "The Longest Week," January 31, 1991, and "Learning to Live With It, Somehow," February 7, 1991. So did the *IDF Daily Report.* The Jaffee Center's *War in the Gulf: Implications for Israel,* edited by Joseph Alpher (Jerusalem: Jerusalem Post Press, 1992), is a trove of excellent analysis, as is Zeev Schiff's essay "Israel After the War," in *Foreign Affairs,*

Summer 1991. Amos Elon, "Report from Jerusalem," in *The New Yorker,* April 1, 1991, is a fine journalistic summary.

Eli Shperling took me on a guided tour of Ramat Gan, which two years after still showed its war scars. The narration of Yarin Kimor's ITV documentary, "Between Scud and Patriot: Routine Emergency," is aimed too blatantly at the viscera of non-Israeli Jews, but there are many vivid moments, including the Doron Nesher monologue. Alex Fishman, defense correspondent for the late *Hadashot,* offered his own intriguing analysis in "We Didn't Know What to Do," *Hadashot,* January 15, 1993.

For Shamir's role and thinking, see David Makovsky's account in *U.S. News & World Report, Triumph Without Victory* (New York: Times Books, 1992), and Rick Atkinson, *Crusade* (Boston: Houghton Mifflin, 1993). Makovsky also allowed me access to his detailed notes and interviews for the book. "Saddam Hussein has fired a shot": quoted in *WP,* October 18, 1990. Dan Shomron's comments are from his "Personal Report on the Gulf War," *Yediot,* September 8, 1991. "Don't tell me what the public wants": Makovsky. "Nothing has changed": Doron Brosh, "My Grandfather," *Maariv,* January 20, 1991. Broken clock analogy: Doron Rosenbloom, "Shamir's Adventures and Successes," *Haaretz,* November 13, 1992.

Chapter 9: "We Are One"

I reported from Israel on the aftermath of the Pollard affair and the Who Is a Jew crisis, interviewed the principals and observed the political fallout. The most helpful sources included Morris B. Abram, Yossi Ben-Aharon, Shlomo Avineri, Avraham Burg, Zeev Chafets, David Clayman, Steven M. Cohen, Leonard Davis, Thomas A. Dine, Abraham H. Foxman, Carolyn Greene, Arthur Hertzberg, Malcolm Hoenlein, Robert J. Lifton, Ehud Olmert, Michael Oren, Seymour Reich, Menachem Rosensaft, Alan Schneider and Harry Wall.

Epigraph is from Amichai, *Poems of Jerusalem.*

Descriptions of the Ramat Gan scene are from Charles Hoffman, "A somber warning," *New York Jewish Week,* February 1, 1991; and Joel Sprayregen, "53 intense hours," *JUF News,* Chicago, n.d. "Your heart is torn": Michal Kapra, "Jewish Solidarity for 48 Hours," *Maariv,* January 29, 1991.

Steve Cohen has done the most thorough surveying of American Jews about Israel in recent years. I've drawn from his unpublished paper, "Did American Jews Really Grow More Distant from Israel (1983–1991)—A Reconsideration," as well as "Israel-Diaspora Relations: A Survey of American Jewish Leaders" (Tel Aviv: Israel-Diaspora Institute, December 1989). Passages from Matti Golan, *With Friends Like You* (New York: The Free Press, Macmillan Publishing, 1992), pp. 12, 37, 40–41, 51, 123, 177–78, are used with permission. "Falling over each other": Shlomo Avineri, "Letter to an American Friend," *JP,* March 10, 1987. "If there is any collective neurosis": Abraham Foxman, *JP,* March 17, 1987.

For an example of the *gevalt* strategy, see AIPAC, "Discussion Points on the Arab-Israeli Military Balance." It lumps together military spending and numbers of troops, combat aircraft and tanks for seven Arab states, including Egypt, Saudi Arabia and Kuwait, and compares them to Israel. It also offers some astounding assessments of Arab military prowess, for example, calling the Jordanian army "one of the Arab world's most modern and qualitatively superior ground forces." One Israeli general, speaking privately, called the paper "a joke."

"A sea of posters": *Summing Up,* p. 175.

For Israel's favorable terms for foreign aid, see Edward T. Pound, "Politics & Policy: A Close Look at U.S. Aid to Israel Reveals Deals That Push Cost Above Publicly Quoted Figures," *Wall Street Journal,* September 19, 1991.

Chapter 10: The Fatal Embrace

My guides to the sea change in Palestinian-Israeli relations included Ghassan Andoni, Janet Aviad, Hillel Bardin, Saeb Erakat, Samir Huleileh, Faisal Husseini, Jad Isaac, Daoud Kuttab, Sari Nusseibeh, Danny Rothschild, Danny Rubinstein, Taher Shriteh and Levi Weiman-Kelman. Linda Gradstein interviewed Jonathan Kuttab.

Epigraph is quoted by Bernard Crick, "The High Price of Peace," in *The Elusive Search for Peace,* edited by Hermann Giliomee and Jannie Gagiano (Oxford: Oxford University Press, 1990), p. 264.

Foreign ministry brochure: Zeev Chafets, "Memories of coexistence," *JR,* December 20, 1990. For an excellent account of how the Baka violence reverberated, see Douglas Struck, "Cycle of vengeance holds peace at bay," *Baltimore Sun,* April 7, 1991. "Here Arabs are not employed": *Haaretz,* November 26, 1990. "The thought of Palestinian workers with sharp implements": Chafets, "My New Kitchen," *JR.*

"Almost every Palestinian has a personal grudge" and other dialogue quotations are from an undated transcript supplied by the Rapprochement Center, Beit Sahur, and used with permission. Sarid's two seminal articles ran in *Haaretz,* August 18, 1990, and January 31, 1991.

The best portrait of Faisal Husseini is by Daniel Williams in the *LAT Magazine,* May 31, 1992. "We are facing a stage": *WP,* October 24, 1991. Husseini's role in first Baker talks: *WP,* June 16, 1991.

Account of the killing of four Israeli women: *Yediot,* March 11, 1991. James Ron supplied a transcript of his interview with the Israeli prison guard, used with permission of Human Rights Watch. Taher Shriteh's hearing: *NYT,* February 19, 1991. See also *Middle East Watch,* "Reuters' Gaza Correspondent Enters Fifth Week in Investigative Detention," February 27, 1991. "I understand your reaction": Meron Benvenisti, *Conflicts and Contradictions* (New York: Villard Books, 1986), pp. 112–13.

Chapter 11: Farewell to the Kibbutz

I met Haim and Ayala Goren during my first visit to Israel in 1970 and we have remained close friends. Bank of Israel Governor Yaacov Frenkel, Zeev Golan, Edward P. Luttwak, Yair Mendels, Alvin Rabushka, Eli Sagi, Yair Shamir and David Yerushalmi were also helpful.

Link magazine, an English-language semimonthly, is an important window into the new Israeli business world. This chapter was especially influenced by *Link*'s special anniversary issue in April 1993. See also Bernard Avishai, "Making the Desert Bloom," *NYT,* September 29, 1993; "At Ease in Zion," *The Economist* Survey of Israel, January 22, 1994; and numbers on import/exports and direct investment from Central Bureau of Statistics, *Statistical Abstract of Israel 1992,* No. 43, Jerusalem.

"The kibbutznik by nature": Gertrude Samuels, *The Secret of Gonen* (New York: Avon Books, 1969), p. 99. "One farm-produce exporter": *Israel Yearbook & Almanac,* Vol. 47, 1–2. For details of Histadrut economic dominance, see Meyer, *Israel Now,* pp. 96–119.

Alvin Rabushka issues a caustic annual "scorecard" on the economy that Israeli economists love to hate, published by the Institute for Advanced Strategic and Political Studies in Jerusalem.

Eventually McDonald's got its french fries. Rather than accept low-quality Israeli fries, the company's Israeli investors imported seedlings, persuaded growers to plant and harvest the crop and built their own processing plant to turn the potatoes into frozen fries. Soon Tapud's bankers called in their loans and the local factory was on its way to bankruptcy. The big boys won, after all.

Chapter 12: "It Will Not Be a Problem"

I made three reporting trips to Jerusalem in 1991 but mostly watched the Shamir-Bush confrontation from a safe distance in London. Many Israeli officials and American Jewish representatives helped me piece together the train wreck, but the best sources were the reporters who covered Baker, Shamir and Bush daily: Jackson Diehl and David Hoffman of *WP,* Thomas L. Friedman and Clyde Haberman of *NYT,* Daniel Williams of *LAT,* David Makovsky of *JP,* and Akiva Eldar and Ori Nir of *Haaretz.*

Epigraph: George F. Kennan, *American Diplomacy 1900–1950* (Chicago: University of Chicago Press, 1951), p. 50.

"Tell me how this hurts you": David Hoffman, "Baker's Touch Eased the Way to Peace Talks," *WP,* October 27, 1991.

Throughout the settlements controversy, the administration was influenced by

Diehl's articles detailing the expanding settlements program. See *WP:* February 14, April 5 and 24, May 14, October 16, 1991, and January 9 and 29, 1992.

The best postmortems of the events leading up to the September 12 showdown are: Winston Pickett, " 'One Lonely Guy' Revisited," *Long Island Jewish World,* September 11–17, 1992; and Makovsky and Allison Kaplan, "What went wrong with the U.S.–aliya loan guarantees," *JP,* March 20, 1992.

Howard Squadron was so alarmed by Meridor's accusation that the Bush administration was seeking to force Israel back to its 1967 borders and cripple its nuclear capability that he wrote a letter to Meridor, April 3, 1992, outlining Meridor's statements and his own refutations. Meridor since has denied his remarks were as vehement as Foxman and Squadron recall.

Chapter 13: "Israel Is Waiting for Rabin"

I returned to Jerusalem soon after the Israeli election in 1992 to begin research for this book. Among those who helped me recount Yitzhak Rabin's comeback and first months in office: Shlomo Avineri, Oded Ben-Ami, Avraham Burg, Arye Deri, Uri Dromi, Yaron Ezrahi, Eitan Haber, Elihu Katz, Channa Levinsohn, Dan Meridor, Benjamin Netanyahu, Ehud Olmert, Haim Ramon, Yitzhak Shamir, Natan Sharansky, Hanoch Smith and Mina Tsemach.

Epigraph: quoted in Nadine Gordimer, *The Essential Gesture* (New York: Alfred A. Knopf, 1988), p. 263.

"The Likud took your money": *JR,* June 18, 1992.

The Btselem Information Sheet, "The Killing of Palestinian Children and the Open-Fire Regulations," Jerusalem, June 1993, caused a huge uproar in Israel. Many Israelis could not accept the remotest possibility that the IDF was killing children it didn't have to kill. They fixed the blame on the kids themselves, their parents, the PLO and even Btselem. For allegations against undercover units, see *Middle East Watch,* "A License to Kill," July 1993.

David Hoffman wrote the best assessment of the closure of the territories: "Israel Cutoff Puts Palestinians in Uneasy Rehearsal of Autonomy," *WP,* April 25, 1993, while best overall analysis of Rabin's first year was Makovsky, "Me, Myself and I," *JP,* July 2, 1993.

Chapter 14: "Enough"

My interviews with Yossi Beilin, Oded Ben-Ami, Uri Dromi, Eitan Haber and Uri Savir helped me understand the Oslo connection from the Israeli side, as did reports in *Yediot, Maariv* and *Haaretz* and detailed accounts from David Hoffman and Laura Blumenfeld in *WP* and Clyde Haberman in *NYT* in September 1993. See also Amos Elon, "The Peacemakers," *The New Yorker,* December 20, 1993. For the Norwegian and Palestinian sides, I relied upon Jane Corbin's *Gaza First* (London: Bloomsbury, 1994), a reliable if somewhat hagiographic account, as well as detailed reporting by David Makovsky for the Washington Institute for Near East Policy, presented in his January 27, 1994, lecture at the institute.

Epilogue

"Start to sweat": Israel Radio, January 2, 1994.

"I want to tell the truth": Rabin speech to Knesset, GPO Press Bulletin, April 18, 1994. "Only a semblance of law": *NYT,* April 3, 1994. Accounts of abuses by Palestinian police in Jericho: *WP,* August 28, 1995.

Economic progress in Gaza: *Time,* July 31, 1995.

Netanyahu's rhetoric and dilemmas are best described by Avishai Margalit in "The Terror Master," *NYRB,* October 5, 1995.

Israel's economic boom: *Business Week,* August 21, 1995. Remarks of Elazar and Weizman denouncing Americanization: *Moment,* October 1995. "Operation Peace for Hotel Rooms": Tom Friedman, *NYT,* October 29, 1995. Beilin's remarks on charity: *WP,* February 20, 1994.

Gellman's excellent analysis of the meaning of Oslo Two: *WP,* September 27, 1995. "We've been indispensable": *NYT,* September 25, 1995.

Gellman reviewed some of Netanyahu's more inflammatory remarks in *WP,* November 8, 1995. "Dragging the nation to the brink": *NYT,* November 10, 1995. Rabin interview with *Time* editors: *Time,* November 13, 1995.

Of the various profiles of Yigal Amir, the best is by Barton Gellman and Laura Blumenfeld, "Israel's Mainstream Brings Forth a Killer," *WP,* November 12, 1995. The eyewitness account of the assassination is from Menachem Damati's interview with Channel 2, November 7, 1995.

Arafat's visit with Leah Rabin: Blumenfeld, "A Long Bad Dream," *WP,* November 21, 1995.

Glossary

Common Hebrew and Arabic words and phrases used in this book:

AGUDAT YISRAEL "Association of Israel," Ashkenazi-dominated ultra-Orthodox political party

ALIYA ascent, or immigration to Israel

ALLAH AKHBAR "God Is Great," Muslim religious expression

ASHKENAZI Jew of European origin

BETAR Zionist youth movement affiliated with Zeev Jabotinsky's Revisionist movement

BITAHON security

BTSELEM Israeli human rights organization

DAHAF Tel Aviv–based market research firm

DEGEL HATORAH "Torah Flag," ultra-Orthodox political party allied with Rabbi Eliezer Schach

D'FUKIM downtrodden Sephardi Jews

FATAH Yasser Arafat's mainstream PLO movement

GUSH EMUNIM "Bloc of the Faithful," right-wing settler movement

HAARETZ Israel's most respected daily newspaper

HADASHOT lively Israeli tabloid; folded in 1993

HAGANAH "Defense," preindependence Jewish self-defense movement and forerunner of the Israeli army

HALACHA Jewish religious law

EL HAMAAYAN "To the Source," Shas's religious child care organization

HAMAS "zeal"; the Arabic acronym for "Islamic Resistance Movement"

HAREDIM "those who tremble before God," ultra-Orthodox Jews

HISTADRUT "General Federation of Workers in the Land of Israel," founded in 1920

INTIFADA "shaking off" in Arabic; the Palestinian uprising

KEFFIYEH Arab scarf used as a headdress

KETZIOT "dried figs" in Hebrew; Israeli nickname for Negev Desert prison

KIBBUTZIM formerly agrarian collectives

KIPPA Jewish skullcap

KIRYA defense headquarters in Tel Aviv

KUPAT HOLIM nationwide health maintenance organization run by Histadrut

LEHI "Fighters for Israel's Freedom," Shamir's underground movement

LIKUD "Union," the main right-wing political bloc

MAARIV prominent Hebrew tabloid

MABAT nightly Israel Television newscast

MERETZ combined left-wing list formed for 1992 election

MOLEDET "Homeland," Rehavam Zeevi's ultrarightist party

MOSHAVIM formerly agrarian cooperatives

MUKHTAR Arab village leader

OLIM new immigrants to Israel

RATZ "Civil Rights Movement," left-wing political party

RISHON LE ZION "The First in Zion," honorific of chief Sephardi rabbi

SAYERET MATKAL "unit of the general staff," a special operations army unit

SEPHARDIM Eastern Jews, many of whom lived in Arab countries

SHABAB "guys" in Arabic, the young warriors of the intifada

SHAS "Sephardi Torah Guardians, " Arye Deri's religious party

SHIKKUNIM drab, boxlike apartments

SHIN BET Israel's internal security police

TEHIYA "Hope," ultrarightist political party associated with Jewish settlers

TSOMET "Crossroads," Rafael Eitan's rightist party

WADI "dried riverbed" or "valley" in Arabic

YEDIOT AHRONOT Israel's best-selling daily newspaper

YISHUV Jewish community in prestate Palestine

Acknowledgments

This book is the product of a twenty-four-year relationship with Israel that dates back to 1970, when my future wife and I spent the summer at Kibbutz Gonen, our first introduction to this improbable country and its indefatigable people. The book began to take shape during my three years as the *Washington Post*'s Jerusalem correspondent between 1986 and 1989; it became a concrete proposal in 1992 after I made five more trips to Jerusalem for the *Post*; and it was researched in Jerusalem between August 1992 and July 1993 and finished in Washington, D.C., in April 1994.

Some debts I can never repay. Haim and Ayala Goren were the first Israelis I ever met and they remain the most important ones in my life. I owe them and the other people who appear in this book my deepest thanks for the time they gave me and for their constant willingness to serve as both teachers and subjects for an all-too-eager if clumsy student. Shlomo Avineri, Yossi Ben-Aharon, Meron Benvenisti, David Clayman, Ehud Gol, Hirsh Goodman, David Hartman, Jad Isaac, Daoud Kuttab, Avishai Margalit, Dan Meridor, Amram Mitzna, Sari Nusseibeh, Ehud Olmert, Avi Pazner, Ofra Preuss, Natan Sharansky, Harry Wall and Dedi Zucker were all especially generous over the years with their time and cooperation, for which I am grateful. And I must single out Taher Shriteh, my colleague and friend, who has been my faithful guide to the troubled intricacies of Gaza ever since we first met outside Shifa Hospital on a nasty day in December 1987.

My colleagues in the Israeli press have earned a reputation for being resourceful, persistent, well informed and cantankerous. What is less known is that underneath their hard-bitten exteriors they are also extremely generous. David Makovsky of the *Jerusalem Post* and *U.S. News & World Report*, who is the world's foremost journalistic authority on Yitzhak Shamir, gave me the full benefit of his insights into the Shamir years and shared much of his reporting. Nachum Barnea of *Yediot Ahronot* shared both his vast knowledge and his dry wit. My good friend Linda Gradstein of National Public Radio supplied me with an astute second set of journalistic eyes and ears. Zeev Chafets, novelist, columnist for the *Jerusalem Report* and all-around literary subversive, kept steering me back to the Israeli mainstream and to the joys of Tel Aviv.

I must acknowledge a special debt of gratitude to my successors at the *Washington Post*'s Jerusalem bureau. Jackson Diehl wrote some of the most perceptive articles of any journalist to pass through Israel, while David Hoffman was unstintingly generous with his time and intelligence, his valuable insights and his remarkable computer expertise. There are times when I have shamelessly ransacked the storehouse of knowledge they both left behind.

Eeta Prince-Gibson, my one-woman research staff in Jerusalem, did a very skillful job of translation and research and shared as well her own intimate knowledge and experiences as an Israeli. Micha Odenheimer guided me through the world of the ultra-Orthodox *haredim,* while Jim Ron helped me better understand the motives and morals of the Israel Defense Force. Sergei Makarov served ably and with great enthusiasm as my Russian guide and translator. The late Louis Rapoport was both an invaluable interpreter of Israeli society and a dear friend. I am grateful to these other journalists, Israeli, Palestinian and American, for their generous help: Akiva Eldar, Amos Elon,Charles Enderlin, Dan Fisher, Peter Hirschberg, Pinchas Inbarri, Isabel Kershner, David Landau, Jim Lederman, Amnon Levy, Ori Nir, Amir Oren, Arye O'Sullivan, Michael Parks, Robert Rosenberg, Danny Rubinstein, Zeev Schiff, Michal Sela, Menachem Shalev, Bob Simon, Robert Slater, Douglas Struck and Daniel Williams. I must also acknowledge the help I received from my colleagues and friendly competitors at the *New York Times* Jerusalem bureau: Joel Brinkley, Sabra Chartrand, Thomas L. Friedman, Joel Greenberg, Clyde Haberman and Edie Sabbagh.

Friends who contributed to this book, each in his or her own special way, include: Lucia Annunciata, Lisa Beyer, David and Rachel Biale, Cliff Churgin, Nabil Feidy, Candice Fisher, Bill and Ellen Gertzog, Ben and Sarah Glazer, Allan and Suzy Levine, Steve Mufson, Myra Noveck, Sylvia Rapoport, Allister and Sue Sparks, Carol Spencer, Levi and Paula Weiman-Kelman, and Ari and Shira Weiss. Parts of the manuscript were read by Nachum Barnea, David Biale, Steve Coll, Jackson Diehl, Clyde Haberman, David Hoffman, David Makovsky and Jim Ron, all of whom contributed to its improvement. I am of course solely responsible for its judgments and its errors.

At the *Washington Post,* Donald Graham, Leonard Downie, Robert Kaiser, David Ignatius and Tom Wilkinson lent moral support, enthusiasm and encouragement to this project and granted me an eighteen-month leave of absence as well as a generous sabbatical. Karen DeYoung and Fred Barbash were supportive and patient in easing my return. My special thanks go to Jim Hoagland for breaking with tradition to send me to Jerusalem in 1986 as correspondent for the *Post,* and to Michael Getler for his unique blend of journalistic excellence, personal warmth and good common sense. I also thank Raphael Sagalyn, my literary agent, who did an excellent job in helping this book on its journey from vague longing to final product; and Alice E. Mayhew and Eric Steel, my editors at Simon & Schuster, who applied a firm hand and rigorous vision in helping shape a long manuscript into a finished narrative. Thanks, too, to Lydia Buechler and her fine team of copy editors.

Institutions to which I owe gratitude include:
Israel's Government Press Office, including the personable Uri Dromi and his able predecessor, Yosef Olmert; David Kreizelman, Linda Rivkind, Etty Bar, Daniel Seaman and the incomparable Rivka Zippur; the Israel Defense Force, and most especially Maj. Natan Rotenberg and Col. Ranaan Gissin; the Al Haq and Btselem human rights organizations; Nina Keren-David and her friendly crew at the *Jerusalem Post* Archive; Linda Lipschitz and Abigail Wisse at the *Jerusalem Report*; and the Palestinian Center for Rapprochement Between People in Beit Sahur. When I returned to the United States, Robert Satloff granted me access to the library of the Washington Institute for Near East Studies; and Kathy Foley, Melody Blake, Pam Smith and William Hifner aided me at the *Washington Post.*

I thank my parents, Herbert and Betty Frankel, and my mother-in-law, Betsy H. Yeager, for their forbearance and moral support; my children, Abra, Margo and Paul Frankel, for their resilience, patience, good humor, high spirits and unquenchable sense of adventure; and my wife, Betsyellen Yeager, for all of the above. This book is hers at least as much as it is mine.

Jerusalem, 1992–93
Washington, D.C., August 1994

Index

Abu Jalala, Mohammed Mustafa, 255–57

Agudat Yisrael, 132, 135–36, 137, 146, 148, 149, 153, 155, 294

Al Haq, 64, 247

Alaa, Abu, 349, 352–55

Aldubi, Romam, 95–96, 97–98, 99, 100

Aliya. See Russian immigrants

Aloni, Shulamit, 331–32, 336

American Israel Public Affairs Committee (AIPAC): Baker speech to, 124–25; crises in, 363; and Oslo Agreement, 362; and peace process, 124–25, 362; and Rabin/Rabin government, 332–33; and Shamir, 230, 333; and U.S.–Israeli relations, 124–25, 215, 222–23, 224, 286, 298, 300–306, 313; and Who Is a Jew question, 220–21.

American Jewish community: antagonisms between Israelis and, 214–15, 216–22; and Bush administration, 226, 302–4, 313, 332; and Clinton administration, 356; and diaspora concept, 217–19; divisiveness among, 230, 362; embarrassments for, 214, 219, 220–22, 232; and future of Israel, 19, 363; Golan's book about, 216–17; and Gulf War, 188–89, 192, 207, 212–14, 215–16, 291; and intifada, 113, 221, 223, 224, 225, 229, 232; Israel as organizing principle of, 218; and Israeli internal affairs, 217, 222, 224–25; and Israel's image, 214, 215, 217, 222–23, 228–29, 363; and Jewish dissent, 225–27, 229–33; and Labor party, 221, 224–25; and Likud party, 220–22, 223–25, 229, 312, 333; and media, 113, 232; and peace process, 227–29, 312, 356, 362; and Peres, 362; and Peres's international peace conference, 225, 230; and PLO, 222, 312, 362–63; and Pollard affair, 219, 225, 232; and private funding for Israel, 312, 341, 363; and Rabin/Rabin government, 224, 332–33, 356, 362; and

settlement program, 225, 232, 307, 312; and solidarity with Israel, 227–28; and Temple Mount killings, 232; and territorial cession, 222, 312; as tourists, 188–89, 212–14; and Who Is a Jew question, 220–22, 225; and Zionism, 218. *See also* American Jewish community—and Shamir; American Jewish community—and U.S.–Israeli relations; *specific person or organization*

American Jewish community—and Shamir: and basic principles of Jewish lobby, 222–23; and criticisms of Israeli policies, 229–33, 306–7, 312; and funding for Likud, 224–25, 312; and Gulf War, 189; and intifada, 223, 228; and Jewish dissent, 225–27; and Jewish solidarity, 227–29; and peace process, 227–28, 312; and Peres's peace conference, 225; and Pollard affair, 219; and Shamir's advisors, 126; and Shamir's personality, 222; as Shamir's supporters, 286; and territorial cession, 312; and U.S.–Israeli relations, 222–24, 286, 288, 299, 300–304, 305–7, 311–12, 313; and Who Is a Jew question, 220, 221

American Jewish community—and U.S.–Israeli relations: and aid for Israel, 215, 218, 220–21, 231, 285, 286, 297, 299, 300–304, 305–7, 311–12, 333; and American Jews–Israeli relations, 333–34; and basic principles of Jewish lobby, 222–23; and Bush–Shamir relationship, 288, 299, 300–304, 311–12; and Bush's reelection campaign, 332–33; and congress, 286, 288, 300–303, 305, 307, 333; and criticisms of Israeli policies, 230–31, 312; and Golan book, 216; and National Leadership Action Day, 303–4; and Rabin government, 332–33; and territorial cession, 312; and U.S.–PLO dialogue, 226

Gulf War: and American Jewish community, 188–89, 192, 207, 212–14, 215–16, 291; and change in Israeli society, 368; and gas masks/sealed rooms, 12, 190–91, 195, 196, 199, 202, 203, 205, 208–9, 211, 213; and IDF, 189–91, 196, 207, 247–48; and intelligence information, 187, 206–7; and Israeli alienation, 188, 189–91, 196, 211; Israeli preparation for, 190–93; and Israeli psyche, 201–2, 208–9; Israeli restraint during, 12, 186–87, 189–91, 197–98, 199–200, 207, 208; and Israeli retaliation policy, 12, 188, 196–98, 208; and Israel's image as defenseless, 206; and Jordan, 197, 198, 199; and media, 192, 195, 202–3; as Middle East turning point, 288–89; missile attacks on Israel during, 193–96, 198–99, 200–201, 206, 212–14; as new kind of warfare, 211; and occupied territories, 186, 204, 247–48; and Palestinians/PLO, 188, 234–35, 236–37, 243–53, 262–63, 368; and peace movement/process, 210–11, 244–46, 262–63, 290, 322; and Rabin, 203; and Shamir/Shamir government, 186, 187, 188, 189–91, 197–98, 199–200, 202, 207, 208, 209–10; and Syria, 199, 208; winners and losers in, 208–11, 235, 290. *See also* United States–Israeli relations: and Gulf War

Gush Emunim movement, 93, 105, 118, 146, 327

Hamas: and elections in occupied territories, 379–80; emergence of, 47, 235; and expulsion strategy, 336–39, 351; and IDF beatings/brutalization, 257–62; membership of, 253–55; and a Palestinian police force, 379; and peace process, 365–66, 374, 375; and PLO, 235, 253–55, 365–66; violence of, 255–57, 333, 334, 339. *See also* Islamic fundamentalists

Haredim, 143–44, 153, 156, 220, 326, 328, 361

Hawwash, Mohammed Nasir, 109–11

Heart transplant case, 109–11

Hebron, 13, 327, 369, 375–78

Heroes: and Gulf War, 196, 206; of Israel, 23; and kibbutzim, 268; Mitzna on, 72; of Palestinians, 39–40, 48, 57–59; and Russian immigrants, 168–69; of Shamir, 28

Herut party, 34, 121

Hezbollah, 332, 340

Hirschfeld, Yair, 347–50

Histadrut (General Federation of Workers in the Land of Israel), 69, 268, 269, 270, 282, 284, 331, 341, 384

Hoenlein, Malcolm, 226, 230, 299, 300, 301–2, 304, 362

Hoffman, Rami, 96, 99, 100–101

Hoffman, David, 376

Holocaust, 205, 217, 302, 309, 369, 370, 378

Housing Ministry, 181, 317. *See also* Settlement program

Human rights, 60, 170–71, 224, 257, 377

Hussein (king of Jordan), 37–38, 197, 198, 249, 267, 346, 370

Husseini, Faisal, 119, 235, 248, 250–51, 252, 253, 290, 334, 336, 350, 351–52

IDF (Israeli Defense Forces): and Ashkenazim, 69; beatings/brutality by, 75–87, 88–89, 236–37, 257–58; and beginning of intifada, 42–44, 48, 49, 52, 54–55; and civil defense, 190–91; and civilian population, 62–66, 74, 75–87, 333, 335; compulsory service in, 24, 68–69, 294, 371; and economic issues, 285; generals/officers of, 68, 70, 113, 189–90; and Hamas, 334, 336–38; hierarchies/generals in, 69, 79, 189–90; impact of intifada on, 57, 65–66, 79–80, 84–87, 368; and implementation of Oslo Agreement, 374–75; influence of, 113; intelligence capabilities of, 190–91; internal dissension in, 79–80, 88–89; and "intifada generation," 86–87; and Israel's image, 76; and Jewish settlers/settlements, 41, 87, 90, 96–100, 104–7; legal actions against, 81–83, 88–89; and media, 259; morale of, 76, 78–80, 81, 84–87, 108, 112–13, 118, 196; as an occupation force, 70, 84; origins of, 68, 69; and Oslo Agreement, 354–55; and Palestinian heroes, 48, 57–59, 110; and Palestinian youth, 39, 42, 44, 47–48, 49, 75–84, 92; and peace movement, 241–42, 243; and politics, 87–90, 99–100; and Rabin/Rabin government, 76–77, 78, 82, 84, 116, 118; and religious parties, 294; reputation/image of, 68, 69–70, 80, 81–82, 84, 88–89, 100; and "rules of the game," 92; and sealing off occupied territories, 339–40; and Sephardim, 69; and Shamir, 112–13, 189; undercover squads of, 108, 334–35, 378; as unprepared/ill-equipped, 44–45, 48, 68, 70, 73–74, 75, 76, 78, 83; and Wazir assassination, 17–18; weapons of,

Schneerson, Menachem Mendel, 148, 153, 220, 224–25, 361, 362
Scitex, 275–77, 383
Security issues: and change in Israeli society, 369; and economic issues, 24, 285, 342; and election of 1992, 323; as legacy of Six-Day War, 33; and Likud party, 341; and peace process, 351, 353, 361, 367, 374; and Rabin/Rabin government, 332, 338, 340, 384; and sealing off occupied territories, 340; and Shamir, 27
Sephardi Torah Guardians. *See* Shas
Sephardim: and Ashkenazi Jews, 143–44, 147–48, 156; and Bat Yam, 142; and birth of Israel, 142; and change in Israeli society, 368; and class issues, 268; culture of, 142–43; and election of 1992, 315–16, 317, 318, 319, 326, 327; and IDF, 69; and Labor party, 142, 320; and Likud party, 121, 146, 316, 317, 319; and local movements, 146–47; poverty of, 142–43; and Rabin/Rabin government, 320; and Ramon, 384; and religious laws, 147; and religious parties, 146; and Russian immigrants, 164, 165; and Zionism, 142. *See also* Shas (Sephardi Torah Guardians); *specific person*
Settlement program: and American Jewish community, 307, 312; and corruption, 317; and economic issues, 274; and election of 1992, 322, 327; and media, 295; and peace process, 292, 293, 297, 309, 362; and Rabin/Rabin government, 332; and Russian immigrants, 130, 139, 164, 176–77, 178–79, 294–95, 298; and Shamir/Shamir government, 39, 164, 176–77, 178–79, 180, 293, 294–301, 306, 308, 312, 314, 322, 362; and U.S.–Israeli relations, 124–25, 129, 130, 139, 177, 180, 289, 294–304, 305, 306, 311–14, 332; weakening of, 376. *See also* Jewish settlers/settlements; *specific person*
Shabab (the "guys"), 48, 49, 55
Shai, Nachman, 195–96, 201, 203
Shamir government: collapse of, 131–32, 155; coup against the, 132–39, 140, 178, 319; divisiveness within, 293, 294; problems facing, 139; as right-wing, 138–39; and "stinking maneuver", 154–57. *See also specific person or topic*
"Shamir Plan," 14, 119–20, 123, 124, 125, 128, 230
Shamir, Yair, 31, 275–76, 383

Shamir, Yitzhak: achievements of, 329–30; advisors to, 34, 126–28, 132–38, 294, 299–301, 316; as an anachronism, 26, 369, 381; arrest/imprisonment of, 31; as custodian, 26; downfall of, 14, 139, 310–11, 313–14, 328–29; early career of, 29–32, 34; family of, 16, 27–28, 31; as foreign minister, 34–35; goals of, 39; heroes of, 28; as a leader, 28–29, 31–32, 37, 139, 209–10, 328–29; personality/style of, 26–27, 28, 34, 38–39, 121, 127, 134, 139, 209, 222, 287, 294, 305, 329, 381, 382; physical appearance of, 26; pressures on, 113–14, 129–30, 177; as prime minister, 37; on principles, 112; religion of, 220; reputation/image of, 26, 28–29, 31, 126, 128, 130–31, 209–10, 315–16, 317–18; risks of, 16; as a terrorist, 29–32. *See also* Shamir government; "Shamir Plan"; *specific person or topic*
Sharansky, Natan: and adjustment to Israel, 169–70; and elections, 326, 382; and electoral process, 171; as a fund raiser, 171–72, 180; health of, 16, 169; as human rights leader, 170–71; and Labor party, 382; and Oslo Agreement, 365–66; and Palestinian problem, 170–71; physical characteristics of, 169; and political parties, 181–82; reputation/image of, 169, 170, 172, 180–81; and Russian immigrants, 171–72, 178, 180–82, 382; as a Russian prisoner, 16, 169, 170, 172; scars of, 16; and settlement program, 178, 180; and Shamir/Shamir government, 176–77, 178, 180–81; and Zionism, 169, 172, 182
Sharon, Ariel: as agriculture minister, 93; and American Jewish community, 224, 227; and Begin, 296; and Beita incident, 99; and elections, 122, 318–19, 326; and Gaza Strip, 46; as a general, 46; and Gulf War, 199–200; as housing minister, 294–96, 317; and intifada, 88, 99, 113; and Jewish dissent, 225, 227; and Lebanon War (1982), 35, 72, 177, 296; and Likud party, 318–19, 361, 382; and media, 295; and Mitzna, 72, 73, 88, 99; and Modai, 178, 179; and peace process, 122, 125–26, 129, 361; personality/style of, 296; as a politician, 122; resignations of, 122; as right wing, 177–78; and Russian immigrants, 177–79, 326; and settlement program, 93, 177–79, 294–96, 297, 298; and Shamir/Shamir government, 36, 122,